R

ZAGAT
7th Edition

America's Top Golf Courses

GOLF EDITORS
Joseph Passov with Tom Bedell, Brandon Tucker
and Ken Van Vechten
STAFF EDITOR
Yoji Yamaguchi

Published and distributed by
Zagat Survey, LLC
76 Ninth Avenue
New York, NY 10011
T: 212.977.6000
E: golf@zagat.com
www.zagat.com

ACKNOWLEDGMENTS

We thank Lynn Bedell, Teresa Gallavan and
Betsy Passov, as well as the following members
of our staff: Caitlin Miehl (editor), Brian Albert,
Sean Beachell, Maryanne Bertollo, Kathryn
Carroll, Reni Chin, Larry Cohn, Nicole Diaz,
Kara Freewind, Jeff Freier, Alison Gainor,
Matthew Hamm, Marc Henson, Ryutaro
Ishikane, Natalie Lebert, Mike Liao, Vivian Ma,
Polina Paley, Albry Smither, Stefanie Tuder,
Sharon Yates, Anna Zappia and Kyle Zolner.

The reviews in this guide are based on public
opinion surveys. The ratings reflect the average
scores given by the survey participants who
voted on each establishment. The text is based
on quotes from, or paraphrasings of, the
surveyors' comments. Phone numbers,
addresses and other factual data were correct
to the best of our knowledge when published
in this guide.

Contents

Ratings & Symbols

Zagat Top Spot	Name	Symbols		Zagat Ratings				
				COURSE	FACIL.	SERVICE	VALUE	COST

Area, Contact, Yardage, USGA Rating, Slope

Z Tim & Nina's 村   ▽ 17 | 19 | 15 | 18 | $95

New York | 76 Ninth Ave. | 212-977-6000 | 800-333-3421 | www.zagat.com | 6100/5000; 65.7/63.4; 119/105

Review, surveyor comments in quotes

"It ain't Pebble Beach", but play is still "kinda rocky" at this "rodent-infested" urban course where the "concrete fairways" fill with "hackers" "ducking errant balls" and "aging caddies" "getting older and older" with each of the "very slow rounds"; since "its best hole is the 19th", golfers who gush over "gorgeous links" aren't referring to the "weedy greens" so much as the "killer hot dogs" from the "infrequent snack carts"; P.S. at $95 a round, the neighbors call this course "el cheapo."

Ratings

Course, Facilities, Service and **Value** are rated on a 30-point scale. Properties listed without ratings are **newcomers** or survey **write-ins**.

0	– 9	poor to fair
10	– 15	fair to good
16	– 19	good to very good
20	– 25	very good to excellent
26	– 30	extraordinary to perfection
	▽	low response | less reliable

Cost

Cost is the price per non-member or non-guest to play 18 holes on a weekend in high season (excluding the extra cost of a cart), i.e. the highest possible price of play.

Symbols

Z	highest ratings, popularity and importance
村	caddies/forecaddies
🛒	carts only
⚬⚊	resort guests only
⏲	restricted tee times (call ahead for public hours)

Top Lists and Indexes

Properties throughout Top Lists and Indexes are followed by nearest major city/area. The alphabetical index at the back of the book lists their page numbers.

About This Survey

This Seventh Edition of our **America's Top Golf Courses Survey** is an update reflecting significant developments since our last Survey was published. It covers 1,164 top courses in the U.S., including the Virgin Islands and Puerto Rico, with coverage of 36 recent additions. We've also indicated new addresses, phone numbers and other major changes. Besides ratings and reviews of the best public, semi-private and resort layouts, we have included listings of urban driving ranges and 99 leading private courses in case you have friends who are members. Like all our guides, this one is based on input from avid consumers – 6,054 all told. Our editors have synopsized this feedback, including representative comments (in quotation marks within each review).

Z **ABOUT ZAGAT:** In 1979, we started asking friends to rate and review restaurants purely for fun. The term "user-generated content" had yet to be coined. That hobby grew into Zagat Survey; 33 years later, we have over 375,000 surveyors and cover airlines, bars, dining, fast food, entertaining, golf, hotels, movies, music, resorts, shopping, spas, theater and tourist attractions in over 100 countries. Along the way, we evolved from being a print publisher to a digital content provider, e.g. **zagat.com** and Zagat mobile apps (for Android, iPad, iPhone, BlackBerry, Windows Phone 7 and Palm webOS). We also produce marketing tools for a wide range of blue-chip corporate clients. And you can find us on Google+ and just about any other social media network.

UNDERLYING PREMISES: Three simple ideas underlie our ratings and reviews. First, we believe that the collective opinions of large numbers of consumers are more accurate than those of any single person. Second, course quality is only part of the equation when choosing where to tee off, thus we ask our surveyors to rate courses, facilities, service and value separately. Third, since people need reliable information in an easy-to-digest format, we strive to be concise and we offer our content on every platform – print, online and mobile. Our Top Ratings lists (pages 9–19) and indexes (starting on page 249) are also designed to help you quickly choose the place that's best for you, whether you're a scratch golfer or a high-handicapper.

THANKS: We're grateful to our local editors, Joseph Passov, author of *The Unofficial Guide to Golf Vacations in the Eastern U.S.*; Tom Bedell, golf writer for American Airlines' *Celebrated Living* magazine; Brandon Tucker, senior writer for the TravelGolf Network; and Ken Van Vechten, author of *Golf Las Vegas – The Ultimate Guide*.

JOIN IN: To improve our guides, we solicit your comments – positive or negative; it's vital that we hear your opinions. Just contact us at **nina-tim@zagat.com.** We also invite you to join our surveys at **zagat.com.** Do so and you'll receive a choice of rewards in exchange.

New York, NY
April 25, 2012

Nina and Tim

Nina and Tim Zagat

What's New

Like every other sector of the economy, golf took its lumps from the recent recession, with course openings tumbling to historic lows. According to industry reports, only 19 18-hole courses debuted in 2011, down from 46 in 2010. Still, there are plenty of green shoots on the fairways.

UNLOCKED GATES: The sour economy has actually been a boon to some public players, as a handful of private clubs have opened their doors to non-members in order to make ends meet. Notable among them are Arizona's **Quintero,** New Jersey's **Ballamor,** North Carolina's **Dormie Club** and Utah's **Victory Ranch.**

OH MY KAUAI: While many major resort destinations stopped spending during the downturn, Hawaii's Garden Isle is a glorious exception. Within the past two years, **Poipu Bay,** the former home of the PGA's Grand Slam of Golf, reopened with new Paspalum greens; **Kauai Lagoons** debuted its three new Jack Nicklaus holes and reintroduced its fabled back nine after a four-year closure; and at **Princeville,** the **Prince** and sibling **Makai** are back after Robert Trent Jones II makeovers.

IN MY TRIBE: Most of the new courses coming online are Native American projects, many connected with casinos, but with no accompanying residential real estate (read: courses with nary a condo in sight). Freed from many zoning, water and residential restrictions, these new tracks meld to the land like their early-20th-century predecessors. Kansas' **Firekeeper,** Washington's **Salish Cliffs,** New York's **Seneca Hickory Stick** and North Carolina's **Sequoyah National** each exemplify the tribal tradition of minimal disturbance.

RETRO-GRADE: Similarly, famous classic courses are going retro. Restorations are booming, such as at North Carolina's acclaimed **Pinehurst No. 2,** where architects Bill Coore and Ben Crenshaw reestablished the sandy scrub look of the 1940s created by original architect Donald Ross. In California, **Pasatiempo** now sports restored Alister MacKenzie bunkers and strategies, courtesy of Tom Doak, while Puerto Rico's **Dorado Beach (East)** looks young again thanks to Robert Trent Jones II, who spruced up his father's masterwork.

BANDON BANDWAGON: Developer Mike Keiser shows no signs of slowing expansion at Oregon's **Bandon Dunes,** one of the Survey's highest-rated destination. **Old Macdonald,** a Tom Doak/Jim Urbina–designed seaside tribute to pioneering American architect C.B. Macdonald, debuted in 2010, while **Bandon Preserve,** a dramatic 13-hole par-3 course along the Pacific created by Bill Coore and Ben Crenshaw, is slated to open in 2012.

Phoenix, AZ
April 25, 2012

Joseph Passov

Golf Travel Tips

LEAVE YOUR STICKS AT HOME: Consider using rental sets when traveling. Rental quality has improved recently, and "borrowed-club syndrome" suggests you'll play better with someone else's sticks. Plus, you'll avoid some heavy lifting. If you must bring your clubs, don't trust the airlines – instead, consider a club-shipping service.

GET THE BEST RATES: Check into discounts via corporate affiliations, affinity groups, senior citizenship and frequent-flier clubs. Skip the toll-free number and call resorts directly to ask about package upgrades, extra room nights and reduced replay fees. When a rate is quoted, always ask: "Is this the lowest price you have?"

RESEARCH ONLINE: Most courses have websites providing descriptions, photos and course maps, as well as online-only bargains. We've provided these website addresses throughout this guide.

GO AGAINST THE SLOPE: If you go to Palm Springs or Scottsdale on a winter weekend, you'll pay top dollar, wait to play or face other booking restrictions. You'll get better value and easier access during shoulder seasons and weekdays, especially at some of the less well-known destinations listed herein.

KNOW YOUR ARCHITECT: Since 71% of surveyors say that the course architect influences their decision on where to play, it's helpful to know which design styles suit your game. For example, Pete Dye uses waste and pot bunkers and hazards shored by railroad ties. Wide fairways and natural shaping are Tom Fazio trademarks. Flanking fairway bunkers and large, elevated, well-protected greens characterize Robert Trent Jones Sr. layouts. Jack Nicklaus delivers downhill drives and demanding approaches, while Arnold Palmer favors doglegging, risk/reward par 5s. For a full list of courses created by these and other celebrity designers, see page 252 of the indexes.

DON'T COUNT ON A CAREER ROUND: You shouldn't expect to score well your first time on any course. GPS, yardage books and pin position sheets can only do so much. Consider planning two rounds at a track, or if you're with a group, try a scramble format or a betting game that keeps everyone interested.

FLASH SOME GREEN: Sometimes, to be treated like a king you need to show the money. Golf isn't a high-paying industry unless your name is Tiger or Jack, so a few bucks' tip can often make a difference in how you're treated (TIP = To Improve Performance).

TAP-INS – A FEW FINAL THOUGHTS: Don't forget the rain gear and pack an extra pair of golf shoes if you're playing more than three rounds. A good travel planner can also make your life easier, as will calling the course a few days in advance to double-check your tee time, make sure the greens aren't being aerated that day and so on. Lastly, enjoy yourself no matter how you play. After all, it sure beats working!

Key Newcomers

Our editors' picks since the last edition. See full list at p. 250.

Bandon Dunes Golf Resort, Old Macdonald | *Coos Bay, OR*

CommonGround | *Denver, CO*

Doral, Jim McLean | *Miami, FL*

Dormie Club | *Pinehurst, NC*

French Lick, Pete Dye | *French Lick, IN*

Harbor Shores | *Kalamazoo, MI*

Prairie Club, Dunes | *Valentine, NE*

TPC San Antonio, AT&T Canyons | *San Antonio, TX*

TPC San Antonio, AT&T Oaks | *San Antonio, TX*

Victory Ranch | *Salt Lake City, UT*

Waldorf Astoria Golf Club | *Orlando, FL*

Wine Valley | *Walla Walla, WA*

New course openings will dwindle to a precious few in the coming year, but golfers can still expect fresh offerings from several high-profile architects. In December 2012, Florida welcomes **Streamsong,** a 36-hole resort in remote southwestern Polk County, some 75 minutes east from the Tampa Airport and 90 minutes from Orlando's. The draw is side-by-side courses, one by Tom Doak, the other by Bill Coore/Ben Crenshaw, unfolding among massive dunes hewn from a former phosphate mine. Donald Trump is more active than ever, enlisting architect Gil Hanse to redesign Florida's legendary **Doral TPC Blue Monster** in 2013, even as work continues on the Trump-managed **Ferry Point** course in the Bronx, now slated to open in spring 2014. In November 2012, **Max A. Mandel Municipal** in Laredo, Texas, is scheduled to debut a Robert Trent Jones II original design, while on the redesign front, look for Florida's **Pompano Beach Pines** course to reopen in late fall 2012, following a Greg Norman makeover.

Most Popular

1. Pebble Beach | *Monterey Peninsula, CA*
2. Bethpage, Black | *Long Island, NY*
3. Spyglass Hill | *Monterey Peninsula, CA*
4. Whistling Straits, Straits | *Kohler, WI*
5. Bandon Dunes, Pacific Dunes | *Coos Bay, OR*
6. Kiawah Island, Ocean | *Charleston, SC*
7. Bandon Dunes, Bandon Dunes Course | *Coos Bay, OR*
8. Pinehurst, No. 2 | *Pinehurst, NC*
9. Kapalua, Plantation | *Maui, HI*
10. TPC Sawgrass, PLAYERS Stadium | *Jacksonville, FL*
11. Torrey Pines, South | *San Diego, CA*
12. Doral, TPC Blue Monster | *Miami, FL*
13. Caledonia Golf & Fish | *Pawleys Island, SC*
14. Pasatiempo | *Santa Cruz, CA*
15. Spanish Bay | *Monterey Peninsula, CA*
16. Bethpage, Red | *Long Island, NY*
17. Blackwolf Run, River | *Kohler, WI*
18. Half Moon Bay, Ocean | *San Francisco Bay Area, CA*
19. Aviara | *San Diego, CA*
20. Princeville, Prince | *Kauai, HI*
21. Troon North, Monument | *Scottsdale, AZ*
22. Montauk Downs | *Long Island, NY*
23. Arcadia Bluffs | *Traverse City, MI*
24. Crystal Springs, Ballyowen | *NYC Metro, NJ*
25. Challenge at Manele | *Lanai, HI*
26. Poipu Bay | *Kauai, HI*
27. Torrey Pines, North | *San Diego, CA*
28. Arnold Palmer's Bay Hill | *Orlando, FL*
29. Harding Park | *San Francisco Bay Area, CA*
30. Grayhawk, Raptor | *Scottsdale, AZ*
31. Whistling Straits, Irish* | *Kohler, WI*
32. Poppy Hills | *Monterey Peninsula, CA*
33. Kapalua, Bay | *Maui, HI*
34. Sea Pines, Harbour Town | *Hilton Head, SC*
35. Wolf Creek | *Las Vegas, NV*
36. Experience at Koele | *Lanai, HI*
37. Bulle Rock | *Baltimore, MD*
38. Bethpage, Blue | *Long Island, NY*
39. We-Ko-Pa, Saguaro | *Scottsdale, AZ*
40. Bandon Dunes, Bandon Trails | *Coos Bay, OR*

* Indicates a tie with course above

Top Ratings

Excludes places with low votes

TOP-RATED COURSES

30| Bethpage, Black | *Long Island, NY*

29| Arcadia Bluffs | *Traverse City, MI*
Bandon Dunes, Pacific Dunes | *Coos Bay, OR*
TPC Sawgrass, PLAYERS Stadium | *Jacksonville, FL*
Whistling Straits, Straits | *Kohler, WI*
Kiawah Island, Ocean | *Charleston, SC*
Bandon Dunes, Bandon Dunes Course | *Coos Bay, OR*
Spyglass Hill | *Monterey Peninsula, CA*
Pebble Beach | *Monterey Peninsula, CA*
Paa-Ko Ridge | *Albuquerque, NM*
Grand View Lodge, Deacon's Lodge | *Brainerd, MN*
Dancing Rabbit, Azaleas | *Jackson, MS*
WeaverRidge* | *Peoria, IL*
St. Ives Resort, Tullymore | *Grand Rapids, MI*
Sea Island, Seaside | *Low Country, GA*
Longaberger | *Columbus, OH*
Kapalua, Plantation | *Maui, HI*
Red Sky, Fazio | *Vail, CO*
Pinehurst, No. 2 | *Pinehurst, NC*

28| Homestead, Cascades | *Roanoke, VA*
Bay Harbor | *Petoskey, MI*
Branson Creek | *Springfield, MO*
Red Sky, Norman | *Vail, CO*
World Woods, Pine Barrens | *Tampa, FL*
We-Ko-Pa, Cholla | *Scottsdale, AZ*
Challenge at Manele | *Lanai, HI*
Circling Raven | *Coeur d'Alene, ID*
Bulle Rock | *Baltimore, MD*
Golden Horseshoe, Gold | *Williamsburg, VA*
Chambers Bay | *Tacoma, WA*
Sea Pines, Harbour Town | *Hilton Head, SC*
Blackwolf Run, River | *Kohler, WI*
TPC Deere Run | *Moline, IL*
Purgatory | *Indianapolis, IN*
Redstone, Tournament* | *Houston, TX*
Caledonia Golf & Fish | *Pawleys Island, SC*
Princeville, Prince | *Kauai, HI*
Gold Mountain, Olympic | *Bremerton, WA*
Wolf Creek* | *Las Vegas, NV*
Pasatiempo | *Santa Cruz, CA*
Eagle Ridge, General | *Galena, IL*
Capitol Hill, Judge | *Montgomery, AL*
Gold Canyon, Dinosaur Mountain* | *Phoenix, AZ*
Turning Stone, Atunyote | *Finger Lakes, NY*
Camp Creek | *Panhandle, FL*
We-Ko-Pa, Saguaro* | *Scottsdale, AZ*
Raven at Three Peaks | *Vail, CO*
Tribute | *Dallas, TX*
Cascata | *Las Vegas, NV*
Troon North, Monument | *Scottsdale, AZ*

TOP COURSES BY REGION

ARIZONA
28 We-Ko-Pa, Cholla | *Scottsdale*
    Gold Canyon, Dinosaur Mountain | *Phoenix*
    We-Ko-Pa, Saguaro | *Scottsdale*
    Troon North, Monument | *Scottsdale*
27 Troon North, Pinnacle | *Scottsdale*
26 Grayhawk, Raptor | *Scottsdale*
    Ventana Canyon, Mountain | *Tucson*
    Boulders, North | *Phoenix*
    Grayhawk, Talon | *Scottsdale*
    Boulders, South | *Phoenix*

CALIFORNIA
29 Spyglass Hill | *Monterey Peninsula*
    Pebble Beach | *Monterey Peninsula*
28 Pasatiempo | *Santa Cruz*
    Torrey Pines, South | *San Diego*
    La Purisima | *Santa Barbara*
27 Old Greenwood | *Lake Tahoe*
    Whitehawk Ranch | *Lake Tahoe*
    Desert Willow, Firecliff | *Palm Springs*
    Pelican Hill, Ocean South | *Orange County*
    CordeValle | *San Francisco Bay Area*

CAROLINAS (NC, SC)
29 Kiawah Island, Ocean | *Charleston, SC*
    Pinehurst, No. 2 | *Pinehurst, NC*
28 Sea Pines, Harbour Town | *Hilton Head, SC*
    Caledonia Golf & Fish | *Pawleys Island, SC*
    Ocean Ridge, Leopard's Chase | *Myrtle Beach Area, NC*
27 Ocean Ridge, Tiger's Eye | *Myrtle Beach Area, NC*
    Pinehurst, No. 8 | *Pinehurst, NC*
    Pine Needles | *Pinehurst, NC*
    Pinehurst, No. 4 | *Pinehurst, NC*
    Linville | *Asheville, NC*

FLORIDA
29 TPC Sawgrass, PLAYERS Stadium | *Jacksonville*
28 World Woods, Pine Barrens | *Tampa*
    Camp Creek | *Panhandle*
27 Arnold Palmer's Bay Hill | *Orlando*
    Hammock Beach, Ocean | *Daytona Beach*
    Kelly Plantation | *Panhandle*
    Innisbrook Resort, Copperhead | *Tampa*
    Doral, TPC Blue Monster | *Miami*
    Hammock Beach, Conservatory | *Daytona Beach*
26 Orange County National, Panther Lake | *Orlando*

HAWAII
29 Kapalua, Plantation | *Maui*
28 Challenge at Manele | *Lanai*
    Princeville, Prince | *Kauai*
27 Poipu Bay | *Kauai*
    Experience at Koele | *Lanai*
26 Mauna Lani, North | *Big Island*

Turtle Bay, Arnold Palmer | *Oahu*
Mauna Lani, South | *Big Island*
Wailea, Gold | *Maui*
Wailea, Emerald | *Maui*

MID-ATLANTIC (DC, DE, MD, PA, VA, WV)

28 Homestead, Cascades | *Roanoke, VA*
Bulle Rock | *Baltimore, MD*
Golden Horseshoe, Gold | *Williamsburg, VA*
Links at Lighthouse Sound | *Ocean City, MD*
27 Golf Course at Glen Mills | *Philadelphia, PA*
Olde Stonewall | *Pittsburgh, PA*
Nemacolin Woodlands, Mystic Rock | *Pittsburgh, PA*
Penn National, Founders | *Gettysburg, PA*
26 Whiskey Creek | *Frederick, MD*
Kingsmill, River | *Williamsburg, VA*

MIDWEST (IA, IL, IN, KS, MI, MN, MO, ND, NE, OH, SD, WI)

29 Arcadia Bluffs | *Traverse City, MI*
Whistling Straits, Straits | *Kohler, WI*
Grand View Lodge, Deacon's Lodge | *Brainerd, MN*
WeaverRidge | *Peoria, IL*
St. Ives, Tullymore | *Grand Rapids, MI*
Longaberger | *Columbus, OH*
28 Bay Harbor | *Petoskey, MI*
Branson Creek | *Springfield, MO*
Blackwolf Run, River | *Kohler, WI*
TPC Deere Run | *Moline, IL*

NEW ENGLAND (MA, ME, NH, RI, VT)

27 Taconic | *Berkshires, MA*
Belgrade Lakes | *Central ME*
Pinehills, Jones | *Boston, MA*
Newport National, Orchard | *Southern RI*
Pinehills, Nicklaus | *Boston, MA*
26 Crumpin-Fox | *Berkshires, MA*
Sugarloaf | *Central ME*
Farm Neck | *Martha's Vineyard, MA*
Green Mountain National | *Southern VT*
Red Tail | *Worcester, MA*

NEW YORK & ENVIRONS (CT, NJ, NY)

30 Bethpage, Black | *Long Island, NY*
28 Turning Stone, Atunyote | *Finger Lakes, NY*
Lake of Isles, North | *New London, CT*
27 Leatherstocking | *Albany, NY*
Hominy Hill | *Freehold, NJ*
26 Crystal Springs, Ballyowen | *NYC Metro, NJ*
Saratoga National | *Albany, NY*
Bethpage, Red | *Long Island, NY*
Wintonbury Hills | *Hartford, CT*
Montauk Downs | *Long Island, NY*

PACIFIC NORTHWEST (OR, WA)

29 Bandon Dunes, Pacific Dunes | *Coos Bay, OR*
Bandon Dunes, Bandon Dunes Course | *Coos Bay, OR*
28 Chambers Bay | *Tacoma, WA*

Gold Mountain, Olympic | *Bremerton, WA*
Sunriver, Crosswater | *Bend, OR*
27 Pumpkin Ridge, Ghost Creek | *Portland, OR*
26 Desert Canyon | *Wenatchee, WA*
Bandon Dunes, Bandon Trails | *Coos Bay, OR*
Bandon Crossings | *Coos Bay, OR*
25 Trophy Lake | *Bremerton, WA*

ROCKY MOUNTAINS (CO, ID, MT, NV, UT, WY)

29 Red Sky, Fazio | *Vail, CO*
28 Red Sky, Norman | *Vail, CO*
Circling Raven | *Coeur d'Alene, ID*
Wolf Creek | *Las Vegas, NV*
Raven at Three Peaks | *Vail, CO*
Cascata | *Las Vegas, NV*
27 Shadow Creek | *Las Vegas, NV*
Las Vegas Paiute, Sun Mountain | *Las Vegas, NV*
Las Vegas Paiute, Wolf | *Las Vegas, NV*
Las Vegas Paiute, Snow Mountain | *Las Vegas, NV*

SOUTH CENTRAL/SOUTHWEST
(AR, LA, MS, NM, OK)

29 Paa-Ko Ridge | *Albuquerque, NM*
Dancing Rabbit, Azaleas | *Jackson, MS*
27 UNM Championship | *Albuquerque, NM*
26 Black Mesa | *Albuquerque, NM*
25 Bluffs | *Baton Rouge, LA*
Grand Biloxi, Grand Bear | *Gulfport, MS*
Twin Warriors | *Albuquerque, NM*
23 Oaks | *Gulfport, MS*
TPC Louisiana | *New Orleans, LA*
22 Carter Plantation | *Baton Rouge, LA*

SOUTHEAST (AL, GA, KY, TN)

29 Sea Island, Seaside | *Low Country, GA*
28 Capitol Hill, Judge | *Montgomery, AL*
Ross Bridge | *Birmingham, AL*
27 Reynolds Plantation, Great Waters | *Lake Oconee, GA*
Cambrian Ridge | *Montgomery, AL*
Reynolds Plantation, Oconee | *Lake Oconee, GA*
Cuscowilla | *Lake Oconee, GA*
26 Grand National, Lake | *Auburn, AL*
Grand National, Links | *Auburn, AL*
Sea Island, Retreat | *Low Country, GA*

TEXAS

28 Redstone, Tournament | *Houston*
Tribute | *Dallas*
Horseshoe Bay, Ram Rock | *Austin*
27 Barton Creek, Fazio Canyons | *Austin*
Barton Creek, Fazio Foothills | *Austin*
Texas Star | *Dallas*
26 Wolfdancer | *Austin*
Augusta Pines | *Houston*
La Cantera, Palmer | *San Antonio*
Cypresswood, Tradition | *Houston*

TOP COURSES BY SPECIAL FEATURE

In some categories, clubs with more than one course are listed once, with their highest Course rating.

BUDGET ($50 AND UNDER)

27 Annbriar | *St. Louis Area, IL*
Tanglewood Park, Championship | *Winston-Salem, NC*
Willingers* | *Minneapolis, MN*
25 Wild Horse | *North Platte, NE*
Riverdale, Dunes | *Denver, CO*
24 Quail Hollow | *Boise, ID*
Aldeen | *Chicago, IL*
23 Alvamar Public | *Kansas City, KS*

BUNKERING

30 Bethpage, Black | *Long Island, NY*
29 Bandon Dunes, Pacific Dunes | *Coos Bay, OR*
TPC Sawgrass, PLAYERS Stadium | *Jacksonville, FL*
Kiawah Island, Ocean | *Charleston, SC*
Harvester | *Des Moines, IA*
Bandon Dunes, Bandon Dunes Course | *Coos Bay, OR*
Sea Island, Seaside | *Low Country, GA*
28 Red Sky, Norman | *Vail, CO*

CONDITIONING

30 Bethpage, Black | *Long Island, NY*
29 Bandon Dunes, Pacific Dunes | *Coos Bay, OR*
TPC Sawgrass, PLAYERS Stadium | *Jacksonville, FL*
Whistling Straits, Straits | *Kohler, WI*
Kiawah Island, Ocean | *Charleston, SC*
Bandon Dunes, Bandon Dunes Course | *Coos Bay, OR*
Spyglass Hill | *Monterey Peninsula, CA*
Sea Island, Seaside | *Low Country, GA*

ENVIRONMENTALLY FRIENDLY

30 Bethpage | *Long Island, NY*
29 TPC Sawgrass | *Jacksonville, FL*
Kiawah Island | *Charleston, SC*
Spyglass Hill | *Monterey Peninsula, CA*
Pebble Beach | *Monterey Peninsula, CA*
Bay Creek | *Virginia Beach, VA*
Longaberger | *Columbus, OH*
Kapalua | *Maui, HI*

EXCEPTIONAL CLUBHOUSE

29 Arcadia Bluffs | *Traverse City, MI*
TPC Sawgrass | *Jacksonville, FL*
Kiawah Island | *Charleston, SC*
Harvester | *Des Moines, IA*
Pebble Beach | *Monterey Peninsula, CA*
Elk Ridge | *Gaylord, MI*
Sea Island | *Low Country, GA*
Red Sky | *Vail, CO*

EXPENSE ACCOUNT ($250 AND OVER)

29 Bandon Dunes, Pacific Dunes | *Coos Bay, OR*
TPC Sawgrass, PLAYERS Stadium | *Jacksonville, FL*

Vote at zagat.com

Whistling Straits, Straits | *Kohler, WI*
Kiawah Island, Ocean | *Charleston, SC*
Bandon Dunes, Bandon Dunes Course | *Coos Bay, OR*
Spyglass Hill | *Monterey Peninsula, CA*
Pebble Beach | *Monterey Peninsula, CA*
Sea Island, Seaside | *Low Country, GA*

FINE FOOD TOO

29 Bandon Dunes | *Coos Bay, OR*
TPC Sawgrass | *Jacksonville, FL*
Whistling Straits | *Kohler, WI*
Kiawah Island | *Charleston, SC*
Harvester | *Des Moines, IA*
Pebble Beach | *Monterey Peninsula, CA*
Sea Island | *Low Country, GA*
28 Homestead | *Roanoke, VA*

INSTRUCTION

29 TPC Sawgrass | *Jacksonville, FL*
Kiawah Island | *Charleston, SC*
Spyglass Hill | *Monterey Peninsula, CA*
Pebble Beach | *Monterey Peninsula, CA*
28 Gold Canyon | *Phoenix, AZ*
Troon North | *Scottsdale, AZ*
Sunriver | *Bend, OR*
27 Arnold Palmer's Bay Hill | *Orlando, FL*

19TH HOLES

29 TPC Sawgrass | *Jacksonville, FL*
Whistling Straits | *Kohler, WI*
Kiawah Island | *Charleston, SC*
Pebble Beach | *Monterey Peninsula, CA*
28 Homestead | *Roanoke, VA*
Golden Horseshoe | *Williamsburg, VA*
Cascata | *Las Vegas, NV*
Troon North | *Scottsdale, AZ*

OUTSTANDING ACCOMMODATIONS

29 Whistling Straits | *Kohler, WI*
Kiawah Island | *Charleston, SC*
Pebble Beach | *Monterey Peninsula, CA*
Sea Island | *Low Country, GA*
Red Sky | *Vail, CO*
28 Homestead | *Roanoke, VA*
Bay Harbor | *Petoskey, MI*
Challenge at Manele | *Lanai, HI*

PRACTICE FACILITIES

29 TPC Sawgrass | *Jacksonville, FL*
Whistling Straits | *Kohler, WI*
Kiawah Island | *Charleston, SC*
Sea Island | *Low Country, GA*
Longaberger | *Columbus, OH*
Kapalua | *Maui, HI*
Pinehurst Resort | *Pinehurst, NC*
28 Homestead | *Roanoke, VA*

PRO SHOPS

29] Bandon Dunes | *Coos Bay, OR*
    TPC Sawgrass | *Jacksonville, FL*
    Whistling Straits | *Kohler, WI*
    Kiawah Island | *Charleston, SC*
    Spyglass Hill | *Monterey Peninsula, CA*
    Pebble Beach | *Monterey Peninsula, CA*
    Sea Island | *Low Country, GA*
    Longaberger | *Columbus, OH*
    Red Sky | *Vail, CO*

SCENIC

29] Arcadia Bluffs | *Traverse City, MI*
    Bandon Dunes, Pacific Dunes | *Coos Bay, OR*
    TPC Sawgrass, PLAYERS Stadium | *Jacksonville, FL*
    Whistling Straits, Straits | *Kohler, WI*
    Kiawah Island, Ocean | *Charleston, SC*
    Bandon Dunes, Bandon Dunes Course | *Coos Bay, OR*
    Spyglass Hill | *Monterey Peninsula, CA*
    Pebble Beach | *Monterey Peninsula, CA*

STORIED

30] Bethpage, Black | *Long Island, NY*
29] TPC Sawgrass, PLAYERS Stadium | *Jacksonville, FL*
    Kiawah Island, Ocean | *Charleston, SC*
    Spyglass Hill | *Monterey Peninsula, CA*
    Pebble Beach | *Monterey Peninsula, CA*
    Sea Island, Seaside | *Low Country, GA*
    Kapalua, Plantation | *Maui, HI*
    Pinehurst Resort, No. 2 | *Pinehurst, NC*

WOMEN-FRIENDLY

29] Pebble Beach | *Monterey Peninsula, CA*
    Bay Creek, Arnold Palmer | *Virginia Beach, VA*
    Sea Island, Seaside | *Low Country, GA*
    Longaberger | *Columbus, OH*
28] Challenge at Manele | *Lanai, HI*
    Bulle Rock | *Baltimore, MD*
27] Hammock Beach, Ocean | *Daytona Beach, FL*
    Treetops, Rick Smither Signature | *Gaylord, MI*

TOP-RATED FACILITIES

Facilities include clubhouses, pro shops, practice areas, restaurants and, at resorts, lodging and other amenities. Clubs with more than one course are listed once, with their highest Facilities rating.

29
Cascata | *Las Vegas, NV*
Sea Island | *Low Country, GA*
Whistling Straits | *Kohler, WI*

28
TPC Sawgrass | *Jacksonville, FL*
Ross Bridge | *Birmingham, AL*
Bay Harbor | *Petoskey, MI*
Pinehurst | *Pinehurst, NC*
Greenbrier | *White Sulphur Springs, WV*
Hualalai | *Big Island, HI*
Broadmoor | *Colorado Springs, CO*
Four Seasons at Las Colinas | *Dallas, TX*
CordeValle | *San Francisco Bay Area, CA*
Longaberger | *Columbus, Ohio*
Pebble Beach | *Monterey Peninsula, CA*
Blackwolf Run | *Kohler, WI*
Challenge at Manele | *Lanai, HI*

27
Pinehills | *Boston, MA*
La Cantera | *San Antonio, TX*
Capitol Hill | *Montgomery, AL*
Redstone* | *Houston, TX*
Forest Dunes | *Gaylord, MI*
Boulders | *Phoenix, AZ*
Kiawah Island | *Charleston, SC*
Pelican Hill | *Orange County, CA*
Red Sky | *Vail, CO*
Nemacolin Woodlands | *Pittsburgh, PA*
Aviara | *San Diego, CA*
Tiburón | *Naples, FL*
Turning Stone | *Finger Lakes, NY*
Kapalua | *Maui, HI*
Bandon Dunes | *Coos Bay, OR*
Turnberry Isle Resort | *Miami, FL*
Spanish Bay | *Monterey Peninsula, CA*
Phoenician | *Scottsdale, AZ*
Arcadia Bluffs | *Traverse City, MI*
Grand Cypress | *Orlando, FL*
Troon North | *Scottsdale, AZ*
Reynolds Plantation | *Lake Oconee, GA*
TPC Deere Run* | *Moline, IL*
Princeville | *Kauai, HI*
Ritz-Carlton Orlando | *Orlando, FL*
Cordillera | *Vail, CO*
Grayhawk | *Scottsdale, AZ*

26
Barton Creek | *Austin, TX*
Treetops* | *Gaylord, MI*
Wailea Golf Club | *Maui, HI*
Poipu Bay | *Kauai, HI*
Shadow Creek | *Las Vegas, NV*
Sunriver | *Bend, OR*
Desert Willow | *Palm Springs, CA*

TOP-RATED SERVICE

Clubs with more than one course are listed once, with their highest Service rating.

29)
Sea Island | *Low Country, GA*
Cascata | *Las Vegas, NV*

28)
Whistling Straits | *Kohler, WI*
Greenbrier | *White Sulphur Springs, WV*
Longaberger | *Columbus, OH*
Pinehurst | *Pinehurst, NC*
Broadmoor | *Colorado Springs, CO*

27)
Blackwolf Run | *Kohler, WI*
Bandon Dunes | *Coos Bay, OR*
St. Ives Resort | *Grand Rapids, MI*
Red Sky | *Vail, CO*
Shadow Creek | *Las Vegas, NV*
Hualalai | *Big Island, HI*
Challenge at Manele | *Lanai, HI*
Boulders | *Phoenix, AZ*
TPC Sawgrass | *Jacksonville, FL*
Four Seasons at Las Colinas | *Dallas, TX*
Keswick Club | *Charlottesville, VA*
Capitol Hill | *Montgomery, AL*
Circling Raven* | *Coeur d'Alene, ID*
CordeValle | *San Francisco Bay Area, CA*
Camp Creek | *Panhandle, FL*
Grand View Lodge | *Brainerd, MN*

26)
Spanish Bay | *Monterey Peninsula, CA*
Golden Horseshoe | *Williamsburg, VA*
Pelican Hill | *Orange County, CA*
Wynn | *Las Vegas, NV*
Pebble Beach | *Monterey Peninsula, CA*
Kiawah Island | *Charleston, SC*
Bay Harbor | *Petoskey, MI*
Grand National | *Auburn, AL*
Homestead* | *Roanoke, VA*
Pinehills* | *Boston, MA*
Aviara | *San Diego, CA*
Ross Bridge | *Birmingham, AL*
Caledonia Golf & Fish | *Pawleys Island, SC*
Poipu Bay | *Kauai, HI*
Experience at Koele | *Lanai, HI*
Tiburón | *Naples, FL*
Ponte Vedra Beach Inn | *Jacksonville, FL*
Arcadia Bluffs | *Traverse City, MI*
LPGA International | *Daytona Beach, FL*
Olde Stonewall* | *Pittsburgh, PA*
Arnold Palmer's Bay Hill | *Orlando, FL*
Ocean Ridge | *Myrtle Beach Area, NC*
La Cantera | *San Antonio, TX*
Coeur d'Alene | *Coeur d'Alene, ID*
Cordillera* | *Vail, CO*
Kapalua | *Maui, HI*
Grayhawk | *Scottsdale, AZ*

29 Cambrian Ridge | *Montgomery, AL*
28 Capitol Hill, Judge | *Montgomery, AL*
Grand National, Links | *Auburn, AL*
Bethpage, Black | *Long Island, NY*
Bethpage, Red | *Long Island, NY*
Gold Mountain, Olympic | *Bremerton, WA*
27 Willingers | *Minneapolis, MN*
Grand National, Lake | *Auburn, AL*
Capitol Hill, Senator | *Montgomery, AL*
Pacific Grove Municipal | *Monterey Peninsula, CA*
Capitol Hill, Legislator | *Montgomery, AL*
Circling Raven* | *Coeur d'Alene, ID*
TPC Deere Run* | *Moline, IL*
26 World Woods, Pine Barrens | *Tampa, FL*
Black Mesa | *Albuquerque, NM*
PGA Golf Club, Wanamaker | *Port St. Lucie, FL*
University Ridge | *Madison, WI*
Oxmoor Valley, Ridge | *Birmingham, AL*
Bandon Dunes, Pacific Dunes | *Coos Bay, OR*
Bandon Crossings | *Coos Bay, OR*
Penn National, Founders* | *Gettysburg, PA*
Treetops, Tom Fazio Premier | *Gaylord, MI*
Victoria Hills | *Daytona Beach, FL*
St. Ives Resort, Tullymore | *Grand Rapids, MI*
Annbriar | *St. Louis Area, IL*
Riverdale, Dunes* | *Denver, CO*
Flanders Valley, White/Blue | *NYC Metro, NJ*
Paa-Ko Ridge | *Albuquerque, NM*
Oxmoor Valley, Valley | *Birmingham, AL*
Legacy | *Pinehurst, NC*
UNM Championship* | *Albuquerque, NM*
Bandon Dunes, Bandon Dunes Course | *Coos Bay, OR*
25 ThunderHawk | *Chicago, IL*
La Purisima | *Santa Barbara, CA*
Fox Hollow at Lakewood | *Denver, CO*
Trophy Lake* | *Bremerton, WA*
Tobacco Road | *Pinehurst, NC*
Montauk Downs | *Long Island, NY*
Texas Star | *Dallas, TX*
World Woods, Rolling Oaks | *Tampa, FL*
Dancing Rabbit, Azaleas | *Jackson, MS*
Grand View Lodge, Deacon's Lodge* | *Brainerd, MN*
We-Ko-Pa, Cholla* | *Scottsdale, AZ*
Bandon Dunes, Bandon Trails | *Coos Bay, OR*
We-Ko-Pa, Saguaro | *Scottsdale, AZ*
Rustic Canyon | *Los Angeles, CA*
Orange County National, Panther Lake | *Orlando, FL*
Camp Creek | *Panhandle, FL*
Flanders Valley, Red/Gold | *NYC Metro, NJ*
Branson Creek | *Springfield, MO*

COURSE
DIRECTORY

	COURSE	FACIL.	SERVICE	VALUE	COST

Alabama

TOP COURSES IN STATE

28 Capitol Hill, Judge | *Montgomery*
   Ross Bridge | *Birmingham*
27 Cambrian Ridge | *Montgomery*
26 Grand National, Lake | *Auburn*
   Grand National, Links | *Auburn*

Auburn

☒ Grand National, Lake | 26 | 25 | 26 | 27 | $64 |

Opelika | 3000 Robert Trent Jones Trail | 334-749-9042 |
800-949-4444 | www.rtjgolf.com |
7149/4910; 74.3/68.7; 136/117

"Another great value on the RTJ Trail", this "awesome course" convenient to Auburn U. is "long, scenic and challenging", boasting 12 holes that hug the shore and offer "beautiful views of Saugahatchee Lake"; although it can be "brutally tough if you're in the rough", it promises "perfect public golf" thanks to a "beautiful facility" and "wonderful hospitality."

☒ Grand National, Links | 26 | 26 | 26 | 28 | $64 |

Opelika | 3000 Robert Trent Jones Trail | 334-749-9042 | 800-949-4444 |
www.rtjgolf.com | 7311/4843; 75.1/69.6; 135/113

Some consider this "well-maintained" layout "the best course on the whole RTJ Trail", and it's part of a facility that's "one of the best values in the country", thanks to "excellent hospitality" combined with "great greens fees"; wayward wallopers warn of "thick rough", but it remains a "beautiful" choice that's "worth a trip by itself" or if you're "playing the entire trail."

Birmingham

FarmLinks at Pursell Farms | - | - | - | - | $125 |

Sylacauga | 2200 FarmLinks Blvd. | 877-292-3276 | www.farmlinks.org |
7444/5250; 75.5/69.7; 140/124

The doves, quail, turkeys and ducks on the 3,500-acre property may be the only birdies you'll ever see on this rugged, hilly 1999 Hurdzan-Fry design in the foothills of the Appalachians, 40 miles southeast of Birmingham; a wide variety of grasses is used on what is called the world's only agronomic research and demonstration course, boasting handsome pine- and oak-framed fairways and an unforgettable par-3 5th, which plunges 17 stories tee to green.

Limestone Springs | ▽ 28 | 23 | 24 | 28 | $99 |

Oneonta | 3000 Colonial Dr. | 205-274-4653 | www.limestonesprings.com |
6987/5042; 74.2/69.6; 139/128

Located 30 minutes north of Birmingham, this "don't-miss" design is a "remote" "gem" featuring "memorable holes in a fabulous ridge-and-valley setting" that are "challenging without being penal"; "the many pines and white-sand bunkers give it a 'working-man's Augusta' feel", while "nice touches", like "free chilled apples", add to the experience.

Oxmoor Valley, Ridge
23 | 23 | 24 | 26 | $64

Birmingham | 100 Sunbelt Pkwy. | 205-942-1177 | 800-949-4444 | www.rtjgolf.com | 7055/4974; 73.3/68.9; 129/119

Devotees declare they'd "pay three times the price for a course like this" "rolling, well-maintained" RTJ Trail track that offers a "variety of holes" featuring "difficult approach shots" and a staff that's "so-o nice"; a few grouse about "tricky" greens and "exaggerated ups and downs", but most consider it a "good value" that's "close to Birmingham, even if it's in the countryside."

Oxmoor Valley, Valley
23 | 26 | 26 | 26 | $64

Birmingham | 100 Sunbelt Pkwy. | 205-942-1177 | 800-949-4444 | www.rtjgolf.com | 7167/4924; 74.6/62.7; 130/98

This "entertaining", "straightforward" spread may be "a bit more ordinary than the Ridge", but it's still a "nice companion course" insist admirers of Oxmoor Valley's longer, "easier" layout; a few critics complain that it's "too crowded", but it's kept "in excellent shape" and the greens are always "up to par."

☑ Ross Bridge 🏞
28 | 28 | 26 | 22 | $136

Birmingham | 4000 Grand Ave. | 205-949-3085 | www.rtjgolf.com | 8191/5312; 78.5/70.2; 135/123

"From the 1st hole stunner" to the "bagpiper that plays at sunset", this "phenomenal", "expensive" course is perhaps the "best of the RTJ Trail" options – as long as you "play the right tees" (if not "you'll hate yourself afterwards"); the "outstanding" facilities include "fabulous" GPS-equipped carts, a "great clubhouse" and a "spectacular on-site hotel", making it a "wonderful stay-and-play" in the Birmingham area.

Silver Lakes
▽ 26 | 25 | 27 | 28 | $65

Glencoe | 1 Sunbelt Pkwy. | 256-892-3268 | www.rtjgolf.com
Backbreaker/Heartbreaker | 7674/4922; 77.7/68.8; 151/124
Heartbreaker/Mindbreaker | 7407/4865; 76.6/68.3; 148/122
Mindbreaker/Backbreaker | 7425/4686; 76.1/67.5; 155/118

"Club selection is key" on this "visually striking" RTJ Trail course 90 minutes northeast of Birmingham, where "each nine is harder than the last"; "steep drop-offs after the tee boxes" make the course "difficult to walk", and some report "too many elevated greens", but most embrace the "friendly" staff, "really good layout" and "low greens fees."

Huntsville

Hampton Cove, Highlands
- | - | - | - | $64

Owens Cross Roads | 450 Old Hwy. 431 | 256-551-1818 | 800-949-4444 | www.rtjgolf.com | 7438/4951; 75.7/68.3; 136/113

The farthest reaches of northeastern Alabama is where you'll find this links-style layout dotted with Japanese black pines, crepe myrtles, creeks and gaping bunkers; you "can't beat the value" of playing it as "part of the RTJ Trail" or in combination with its sister River course.

Hampton Cove, River
- | - | - | - | $64

Owens Cross Roads | 450 Old Hwy. 431 | 256-551-1818 | 800-949-4444 | www.rtjgolf.com | 7668/5278; 77.8/70.4; 136/119

Built on such low-lying land that they couldn't dig bunkers, this layout features "almost unapproachable" elevated greens, along with oak forests, dozens of water hazards and "long, long par 4s" – which "make up for no sand"; the result is a test that provides "outstanding value, especially when played in conjunction with the other RTJ Trail courses."

Shoals, Fighting Joe

▽ 27 | 25 | 26 | 27 | $64

Muscle Shoals | 990 Sunbelt Pkwy. | 256-446-5111 | www.rtjgolf.com | 8092/4978; 78.7/69.0; 138/122

Located 90 miles west of Huntsville, this "excellent RTJ Trail challenge" is "well maintained in a beautiful setting on bluffs above the Tennessee River"; while it's "long" (more than 8,000 yards), it's not just the length that can wreck your scorecard – you'll need to "keep your drives out of the marshes and lakes to have a chance at par."

Mobile

Craft Farms, Cotton Creek 🏞

▽ 22 | 21 | 20 | 19 | $89

Gulf Shores | 3840 Cotton Creek Blvd. | 251-968-7500 | 800-327-2657 | www.craftfarms.com | 7127/5160; 72.3/70.0; 133/118

"You can almost smell the Gulf" as you traverse this "well-maintained" Arnold Palmer design that dishes up "great Southern hospitality" on the Alabama coast, along with ample, contoured fairways that provide a "good test of directional control"; a few cynics sniff it's "too bland", but no one complains about the "friendly staff or "don't-miss" breakfast buffets.

Kiva Dunes

25 | 23 | 23 | 21 | $93

Gulf Shores | 815 Plantation Dr. | 251-540-7000 | 888-833-5482 | www.kivadunes.com | 7092/5006; 73.9/68.5; 132/115

Architect Jerry Pate "knocked it out of the park" with this "stunning", "classy links-style" layout between Mobile Bay and the Gulf featuring "diverse holes" with "beautiful views"; while critics warn that it's "remote" and "very natural", with "lots of gnats" and winds that "really pick up in the afternoon", most tout it as "this is one we'll return to."

Peninsula Golf & Racquet 🏞

25 | 25 | 25 | 22 | $90

Gulf Shores | 20 Peninsula Blvd. | 251-968-8009 | www.peninsulagolfclub.com
Cypress/Lakes | 7055/4978; 72.4/69.6; 124/121
Lakes/Marsh | 7026/5072; 72.6/70.1; 125/120
Marsh/Cypress | 7179/5080; 73.2/68.7; 121/115

"Taking advantage of a beautiful setting" on Mobile Bay, this "fair and challenging" 27-holer is perhaps the "nicest course on Alabama's Gulf Coast" thanks to amenities that include "iced apples at the first tees" and attendants handing out "chilled, scented towels"; "keep your driver in the bag", due to "narrow fairways" and a "dense, deep rough", but all agree it's "a must-visit if you're in lower Alabama."

Rock Creek 🏞

23 | 21 | 24 | 21 | $59

Fairhope | 140 Clubhouse Dr. | 251-928-4223 | www.rockcreekgolf.com | 6920/5831; 72.9/68.1; 128/117

"Demanding" yet "playable", this "great course" in Fairhope near Mobile Bay may have "plenty of challenges" in the form of hills and other "trouble", but "generous fairways" make it suitable for all levels of play; meandering through pine and hardwood forests, it offers scenic views, another reason supporters consider it "a must" when in southern Alabama.

TimberCreek

▽ 23 | 23 | 25 | 23 | $61

Daphne | 9650 Timbercreek Blvd. | 251-621-9900 | 877-621-9900 |
www.golftimbercreek.com
Dogwood/Magnolia | 7062/4885; 73.6/66.7; 130/114
Magnolia/Pines | 7090/4990; 73.6/68.4; 125/113
Pines/Dogwood | 6928/4911; 72.5/67.5; 122/110

There's "something for every golfer" at this 27-hole layout that's "hillier than it looks", with wetland preserves and bountiful wildlife accentuating the woodlands terrain; with "three great nines", "excellent service" and "fair prices", it's "fun to play."

Montgomery

⊠ Cambrian Ridge

27 | 24 | 25 | 29 | $68

Greenville | 101 Sunbelt Pkwy. | 334-382-9787 | www.rtjgolf.com
Canyon/Sherling | 7427/4857; 75.3/68.0; 142/130
Loblolly/Canyon | 7297/4772; 75.2/67.7; 129/126
Sherling/Loblolly | 7232/4785; 74.5/66.9; 128/119

Combine a "challenging layout" that's rich in "excellent elevation changes" with a "view that can't be beat", and the result is a "course worth playing", and one of "the best on the RTJ Trail"; "wonderful hospitality" is another plus, and while it's a 40-mile drive from Montgomery, some suggest its "in-the-middle-of-nowhere" location "makes it even better."

⊠ Capitol Hill, Judge

28 | 26 | 26 | 28 | $74

Prattville | 2600 Constitution Ave. | 334-285-1114 | 800-949-4444 |
www.rtjgolf.com | 7813/4951; 78.5/64.7; 147/115

One of "the best opening holes in public golf" (the first tee sits 200 feet above the fairway) sets the tone for this "scenic stop on the RTJ Trail", a "challenging", "well-kept" layout that "wows" with "one forced carry after another" – be sure to "bring your A+ game or a lot of golf balls"; the verdict is in – it's a "must-play" for its "excellent value and great hospitality."

⊠ Capitol Hill, Legislator

23 | 26 | 27 | 27 | $64

Prattville | 2600 Constitution Ave. | 334-285-1114 |
800-949-4444 | www.rtjgolf.com |
7477/5253; 76.9/66.1; 149/117

The most traditional of the Capitol Hill courses boasts a "totally distinct" routing through tall, Carolinas-style pines with several river holes, but while it's a "favorite" for some, a few say it's "nothing compared to the Judge or Senator"; still, it's a "fun" option among the RTJ Trail tracks, with a staff that "sets the example for what service and support should be."

⊠ Capitol Hill, Senator

24 | 27 | 27 | 27 | $64

Prattville | 2600 Constitution Ave. | 334-285-1114 |
800-949-4444 | www.rtjgolf.com |
7724/5155; 77.7/64.7; 133/110

This dune-clad links layout on the RTJ Trail offers across-the-pond looks and "American playability", with "interesting holes" that demand "a more positioned game"; although a few find it "too artificial", the "great conditions", "outstanding service and facilities" and "reasonable prices" make it work for most.

	COURSE	FACIL.	SERVICE	VALUE	COST

Alaska

Anchorage

Anchorage Golf Course ▽ 20 | 14 | 16 | 17 | $62

Anchorage | 3651 O'Malley Rd. | 907-522-3363 |
www.anchoragegolfcourse.com | 6628/4843; 72.1/68.2; 130/119

A "good time" can be had at this forested course that peers over the Anchorage Bowl area and features frequent moose, bear and fox sightings, plus panoramic views of Mt. McKinley, the Chugach mountains and Cook Inlet; the midsummer 10 PM tee times are another enticement.

Eagleglen ⊘ ▽ 22 | 20 | 20 | 20 | $45

Anchorage | 4414 First St. | 907-552-3821 | www.elmendorfservices.com |
6689/5443; 71.6/70.9; 126/123

Elmendorf Air Force Base in Anchorage is home to this densely wooded RTJ Jr. design that features the swift Ship Creek zigzagging through four of the final five holes; though some quip the "cruise [to Alaska] was more adventurous" than the round, most enjoy teeing off under the midnight sun, as well as the wildlife sightings.

Arizona

TOP COURSES IN STATE

28 We-Ko-Pa, Cholla | *Scottsdale*
    Gold Canyon, Dinosaur Mountain | *Phoenix*
    We-Ko-Pa, Saguaro | *Scottsdale*
    Troon North, Monument | *Scottsdale*
27 Troon North, Pinnacle | *Scottsdale*
26 Grayhawk, Raptor | *Scottsdale*
    Ventana Canyon, Mountain | *Tucson*
    Boulders, North | *Phoenix*
    Grayhawk, Talon | *Scottsdale*
    Boulders, South | *Phoenix*

Bullhead City

Laughlin Ranch ⊠ - | - | - | - | $127

Bullhead City | 1360 William Hardy Dr. | 928-754-1243 | 866-866-5729 |
www.laughlinranch.com | 7155/4985; 73.4/68.1; 142/117

Fans say this "challenging but fair layout" in Bullhead City is perhaps "the nicest course in the area"; "overlooking the Colorado River", it offers "some great holes" with elevation changes and undulating greens, but while nearby casinos make it an all-season destination, insiders caution "beware of the summer heat" and remember to "hydrate yourself."

Phoenix

Arizona Biltmore, Adobe ⊠ 19 | 23 | 24 | 17 | $185

Phoenix | 2400 E. Missouri Ave. | 602-955-9655 | www.arizonabiltmore.com |
6430/5417; 70.3/70.7; 123/120

Part of a "wonderful desert oasis" in Phoenix, this Arizona Biltmore track is a "playable", "parklike layout" featuring "wide, flat, tree-lined fairways" along with "scenic views" of Piestewa (Squaw) Peak and "fabulous mansions"; it's a "classic resort course", which for some means "pedestrian" and "overpriced", but most consider it a "comfortable walk" in a "first-class" facility with "excellence service."

Arizona Biltmore, Links 🏌

| 21 | 23 | 23 | 19 | $185 |

Phoenix | 2400 E. Missouri Ave. | 602-955-9655 | www.arizonabiltmore.com | 6300/4747; 69.5/66.8; 125/110

Considered the "better of the two courses" at the Biltmore, this "short, tight" Phoenix layout offers "more challenge and more elevation changes" as it "winds through large estate homes"; while critics insist "the best part of the course is staying at the hotel", it does boast "helpful" service, "great conditions" and a "fabulous setting", especially the 15th and its "superb views of the mountains."

ASU Karsten

| 20 | 20 | 21 | 23 | $130 |

Tempe | 1125 E. Rio Salado Pkwy. | 480-921-8070 | www.asukarsten.com | 7002/4765; 73.8/62.7; 131/103

Admirers say the "home course of the ASU Sun Devils" is the "best bang for the buck in this premium golfing area", offering a "bear" of a Pete Dye design featuring "lots of moguls" and "sculpted mounds" on its "variety of holes"; it's "not the prettiest, with visible power lines", but it gets high marks for its "easy access" and "excellent short-game practice facility."

⧉ Boulders, North

| 26 | 27 | 27 | 21 | $220 |

Carefree | 34831 N. Tom Darlington Dr. | 480-488-9028 | www.thebouldersclub.com | 6811/4900; 72.6/68.4; 137/114

You'll "feel like you're in the *Flintstones* movie" at this "awesome" Carefree course boasting "beautiful rock formations", "breathtaking vistas" and "plenty of wildlife"; it's especially "fabulous in springtime, when everything's in bloom", but remember – "if you miss the fairway by much, you're off in the cacti with the rattlers"; P.S. it's "expensive", but "summer rates rock, just like the boulders."

⧉ Boulders, South

| 26 | 27 | 27 | 22 | $220 |

Carefree | 34831 N. Tom Darlington Dr. | 480-488-9028 | www.thebouldersclub.com | 6726/4684; 71.9/68.4; 140/118

Located in the "highlands overlooking Scottsdale", this "aptly named" course – "it rocks!" – plays through a "dramatic" desert landscape of "massive boulders" and "beautiful scenery", with an "intelligent design" that's "challenging" "but fair"; it's "expensive", but most agree it's a "classy" experience enhanced by "tremendous practice facilities" and "courteous" service that's "scripted as well as a Broadway play."

Dove Valley Ranch

| 17 | 16 | 16 | 18 | $110 |

Cave Creek | 33750 N. Dove Lakes Dr. | 480-488-0009 | www.dovevalleyranch.com | 7011/5337; 72.7/70.8; 131/120

"You can actually pull your driver out of your bag" at this RTJ Jr. design north of Phoenix that may have "a challenging back nine" but is "more forgiving than most Arizona desert courses"; "incredible views of the valley" add to the "good value", and if some find it merely "average", others appreciate the "wide fairways" – "you don't want to wander in the brush among the snakes."

☒ Gold Canyon, Dinosaur Mountain ⛳

28 | 19 | 21 | 23 | $189

Gold Canyon | 6100 S. Kings Ranch Rd. | 480-982-9449 | 800-827-5281 | www.gcgr.com | 6653/4833; 71.3/67.0; 143/117

"Dramatic elevation changes", "phenomenal views" and "wildlife on the course" make this "true mountain golf" experience from architect Ken Kavanaugh "a must-play if you're in the Phoenix area"; though some gripe that "the drive is too long" (it's 40 minutes east of Scottsdale), others insist this "truly pretty" desert design is "worth the trip."

Gold Canyon, Sidewinder ⛳

21 | 22 | 21 | 23 | $99

Gold Canyon | 6100 S. Kings Ranch Rd. | 480-982-9449 | 800-827-5281 | www.gcgr.com | 6509/4426; 71.6/65.8; 132/112

Perhaps "not as scenic" as its sibling, this "traditional desert layout" is still an "attractive" option, with a "nice backdrop" and "strategically placed hazards" that "require shot placement"; a few feel the track is "not all that exciting", but for wallet-watchers the "price is right" – and it's a "great value in the off-season."

Golf Club of Estrella ⛳

24 | 22 | 22 | 22 | $139

Goodyear | 11800 S. Golf Club Dr. | 623-386-2600 | www.estrellagolf.com | 7139/5124; 73.0/68.5; 137/116

Situated in the Sierra Estrella foothills west of Phoenix, this "immaculate" "hidden gem" may be "a bit out of the way" but it comes "highly recommended" by golfers who appreciate its "fabulous" desert design (a "challenge for all handicaps"); "excellent conditions" and "beautiful" mountain views enhance the experience, as do "reasonable rates", which make this Troon-managed "value" "well worth the drive."

Las Sendas ⛳

24 | 20 | 21 | 21 | $149

Mesa | 7555 E. Eagle Crest Dr. | 480-396-4000 | www.lassendas.com | 6914/5100; 73.1/70.5; 144/126

"Playing up and down Las Sendas Mountain" with "views of the Phoenix area", this RTJ Jr. "gem" near Mesa offers "a lot of target golf for a straight hitter" along with "ridiculously fast greens" that make it "a challenge for the low-handicapper" and "vacation player" alike; some suggest there are "too many houses" around, but most prefer to focus on the "beautiful scenery" and say the "awesome staff" is another reason they "would like to play it again."

Longbow

19 | 16 | 20 | 21 | $155

Mesa | 5601 E. Longbow Pkwy. | 480-807-5400 | www.longbowgolf.com | 7003/5202; 72.2/70.2; 129/124

The "best value in the Phoenix area" according to admirers, this "user-friendly" Ken Kavanaugh desert design in Mesa offers "some good risk/reward holes" on a "relatively flat" layout that can be "challenging from the back tees"; it's an ideal choice "if you're looking for a quick round" "on your way to Sky Harbor Airport."

Lookout Mountain ⛳

22 | 21 | 22 | 21 | $149

Phoenix | 11111 N. Seventh St. | 602-866-6356 | 800-947-9784 | www.tapatiocliffshilton.com | 6535/4557; 71.2/65.3; 135/113

Part of the Pointe Hilton Tapatio Cliffs Resort, this "short, tight" yet "very forgiving" desert design dishes out "interesting water hazards" and "lots of elevation drops", and ladies laud it as an "ex-

cellent women's course with generous tee box distance breaks";
"outstanding" service and "spectacular views" of Lookout Mountain
seal the deal.

Los Caballeros

| - | - | - | - | $90 |

Wickenburg | 1551 S. Vulture Mine Rd. | 928-684-2704 |
www.loscaballerosgolf.com | 7014/5511; 73.0/70.6; 135/125

"It's well worth the trip to Wickenburg" to play this "wonderful,
challenging course" at a "first-rate resort" that serves up "some excellent par 4s"; yes, it's in the middle of "virtually nowhere", an hour's
drive from Phoenix, but the "air is clear and clean" and the layout
is "never crowded."

Marriott's Wildfire, Faldo Championship ⛳

| 24 | 25 | 24 | 21 | $199 |

Phoenix | 5350 E. Marriott Dr. | 480-473-0205 | 888-705-7775 |
www.wildfiregolf.com | 6846/5245; 71.6/69.6; 127/120

Though "you could land a 747" on the "wide fairways" of this "challenging, unusual design", it can be a challenge to "stay out of the sand"
that's "everywhere"; it offers "great facilities" and "impeccable service" in a "beautiful" setting next to Arizona's largest resort, but the
sun gets "as hot as blazes" – so book "early AM tee times" or watch
"your golf clubs melt."

Marriott's Wildfire, Palmer Signature ⛳

| 23 | 25 | 24 | 18 | $199 |

Phoenix | 5350 E. Marriott Dr. | 480-473-0205 | 888-705-7775 |
www.wildfiregolf.com | 7145/4915; 73.3/67.2; 135/112

"Perfect for the resort player in all of us", this "typical Arnold Palmer"
track in Phoenix is "different than its Faldo sibling but still requires precise shot-making" on a "pretty", "traditional" layout that's a "nice
change of pace from the desert courses"; some find it "a bit pricey",
but a "spectacular driving range" is another reason it's "worth playing"
whether "you're in the area" or "staying at the hotel."

Ocotillo ⛳

| 22 | 22 | 22 | 21 | $175 |

Chandler | 3751 S. Clubhouse Dr. | 480-917-6660 | 888-624-8899 |
www.ocotillogolf.com
Gold/Blue | 7016/5128; 72.2/69.6; 133/124
Gold/White | 6804/5124; 71.5/69.3; 128/118
White/Blue | 6782/5134; 72.2/70.2; 133/117

"Somehow, this Florida course got lost in Arizona" assert admirers of
this "plush" 27-holer "in the middle of the desert" near Chandler that's
drenched with "water everywhere"; it's "well kept" and "beautiful, no
matter which of the nines you play", and "wonderful facilities", a
"great clubhouse" and amenities such as "iced towels" on hot days
add to the "outstanding value."

Papago Municipal

| 20 | 12 | 13 | 22 | $57 |

Phoenix | 5595 E. Moreland St. | 602-275-8428 | www.papagogolfcourse.net |
7333/5404; 75.0/70.5; 130/121

Supporters say this "classic" "gem in the rough" "may be the best municipal course in America for the money" thanks to an "old-style layout" that's "a fair test of your game" even as it offers "scenic views" of
the Papago Buttes; it underwent a $5.8 million overhaul in 2008.

Quintero Golf & Country Club, Founders 🏌

| – | – | – | – | $190 |

Peoria | 16752 W. Carefree Hwy. | 928-501-1500 | www.quinterogolf.com | 7208/5984; 74.9/69.2; 147/128

A once private layout that went public in 2011, this 2000 Rees Jones creation on the farthest edge of northwest Phoenix unfolds over a complex canvas of dense desert shrubbery and vertigo-inducing elevation changes; while it's a long drive from the major resort areas, the remarkable mountain vistas, superb conditioning and memorable holes such as the downhill par 3 6th and the uphill par 4 15th make it worth the journey.

Raven at Verrado 🛋

| 24 | 25 | 26 | 23 | $149 |

Buckeye | 4242 N. Golf Dr. | 623-388-3000 | www.ravenatverrado.com | 7258/5402; 73.8/65.3; 132/111

For "first-class golf at a reasonable price (by Phoenix standards)", head to this "well-conditioned course" that "plays through a housing development", with desert-edged nines to ensure that "anything off the fairways is an unplayable lie"; it offers even "better service and amenities" as well as views of the White Tank Mountains, so many agree it's "worth" the 30-mile drive from the city.

Raven Golf Club 🛋

| 23 | 22 | 24 | 22 | $89 |

Phoenix | 3636 E. Baseline Rd. | 602-243-3636 | www.ravenphx.com | 7078/5759; 73.9/72.9; 133/124

"You might think you're in the pines of New Jersey" on this "parkland-style course in the middle of the desert", where "wide", tree-lined fairways and "large, undulating greens" add up to "a fun challenge for all skill levels"; the course is kept in "pristine condition", but what really makes it a "value" is the "friendly, helpful" service and a "beautiful" setting "only minutes from the airport."

Southern Dunes Golf Club

| – | – | – | – | $119 |

Maricopa | 48456 W. Hwy. 238 | 480-367-8949 | www.golfsoutherndunes.com | 7517/5036; 76.2/71.7; 141/124

Built as a private men's club in 2002, this tournament-worthy tribal course located an hour from Scottsdale now thrives as a public-welcome amenity to the nearby Harrah's Ak-Chin Resort; architects Lee Schmidt and Brian Curley (with Fred Couples consulting) engineered a pristine, yet brawny layout sprinkled with broad, fescue-framed fairways, sprawling, strategically placed bunkers, artfully contoured greens and stirring mountain backdrops.

Superstition Mountain, Prospector ⏱

| – | – | – | – | $150 |

Superstition Mtn. | 8000 E. Club Village Dr. | 480-983-3200 | 877-983-3200 | www.superstitionmountain.com | 7225/5223; 73.4/70.2; 135/121

A highly regarded stop on the LPGA Tour in the aughts, this former private club an hour east of Phoenix is acclaimed for the gimmick-free design by Jack Nicklaus and son Gary, featuring skating rink–quick greens, a risk/reward par-5 18th with a lake bordering the fairway landing area to the green and a Tour-worthy practice range, which stares straight at the Superstition Mountains; it's slated to revert back from public to members-only in 2014.

Whirlwind, Cattail
▽ 24 | 24 | 24 | 22 | $165

Chandler | 5692 W. North Loop Rd. | 520-796-1840 |
www.whirlwindgolf.com | 7334/5383; 73.4/70.8; 132/123
At this "aptly named" Gary Panks design, there's "always a nice 'breeze'" to make it a "real challenge for a resort course", while the "wide-open fairways" also "make it a good choice for the higher handicapper"; it's "worth the dough" thanks to "good maintenance", "excellent service" and a location "near the Phoenix Airport" with panoramic desert and mountain views.

Whirlwind, Devil's Claw
▽ 23 | 24 | 25 | 23 | $165

Chandler | 5692 W. North Loop Rd. | 520-796-1840 |
www.whirlwindgolf.com | 7029/5540; 72.6/71.4; 129/124
For "true desert/target-style" golf "at a reasonable price", head to the Sheraton Wild Horse Pass Resort near Phoenix to play this "fun, but not overly difficult" Gary Panks layout; some suggest it's "not as good as the Cattail", its younger sibling, but it's nevertheless a "very nice course" in "great condition", with "excellent facilities" and scenic mountain views.

Wigwam, Gold
21 | 21 | 20 | 20 | $160

Litchfield Park | 300 E. Wigwam Blvd. | 623-935-9414 | 800-909-4224 |
www.wigwamresort.com | 7430/5885; 74.5/72.3; 135/119
Designed by RTJ Sr., this "nice old track with lots of trees" west of Phoenix is "still a good test" despite being "fairly flat and open, so you can stay out of trouble"; putters reserve particular praise for the "underrated" Wigwam resort ("like stepping back into the '30s") and its staff, but the presence of this recently renovated course is certainly a "plus."

San Carlos

Apache Stronghold ⌂
- | - | - | - | $35

San Carlos | Hwy. 70 (5 mi. east of Hwy. 77) | 928-475-7800 | 800-272-2438 |
www.apachegoldcasinoresort.com | 7519/5535; 74.5/70.9; 146/123
Located "in the middle of nowhere" 90 miles east of Phoenix, this "minimalist" Tom Doak design "plays through, up and around a variety of canyons" on the San Carlos Apache Reservation; its 3,200-ft. elevation means "your ball goes a long way", and the scenic mountain-desert setting (complete with nearby casino) makes it "a deal for the money."

Scottsdale

Camelback, Indian Bend ⌂
19 | 22 | 22 | 20 | $99

Scottsdale | 7847 N. Mockingbird Ln. | 480-596-7050 |
www.camelbackinn.com | 7014/5808; 72.6/71.5; 122/118
This "frisky" Scottsdale spread makes it "hard to believe you're in the desert" thanks to its tree-framed fairways, and offers "little trouble" on a layout that's quite "playable"; while the course strikes some as "not particularly remarkable", it does come complete with a hotel, a "wonderful pro shop" and "beautiful" mountain views.

Camelback, Padre ⌂
22 | 23 | 24 | 21 | $139

Scottsdale | 7847 N. Mockingbird Ln. | 480-596-7050 |
www.camelbackinn.com | 6903/5132; 72.3/67.1; 131/119
"A nice change from the typical desert track", this "well-kept" Arthur Hills design is a "scenic, tree-filled course" that's "playable" but with

just enough challenge so that "you'll be praying to your padre" at times; "high mountain vistas" "add to the experience" but some sniff they're "not enough to justify the equally high greens fees."

Eagle Mountain 🏕
25 | 21 | 23 | 22 | $195

Fountain Hills | 14915 E. Eagle Mountain Pkwy. | 480-816-1234 | 866-863-1234 | www.eaglemtn.com | 6800/5065; 71.2/66.5; 136/121

"Ride the side of the mountain" at this "gorgeous layout in the hills above Scottsdale", with "more ups and downs than a roller coaster" that make it "challenging" but still "fun for almost any level" of player; the many elevation changes can be "tough on the legs", but "incredibly awesome views", "nice facilities" and a "friendly, efficient staff" make it a "must-play when in Arizona" for many.

Gainey Ranch 🏕 ⛳
20 | 23 | 23 | 20 | $169

Scottsdale | 7600 E. Gainey Club Dr. | 480-951-0022 | www.gaineyranchcc.com
Arroyo/Dunes | 6662/5515; 70.8/69.7; 130/120
Arroyo/Lakes | 6800/5312; 71.9/70.2; 128/125
Dunes/Lakes | 6614/4993; 71.0/68.5; 125/122

"Enjoyable for vacationers of all handicaps", this trio of "playable" nines will make you "feel like a hero" as you "make lots of pars and some birdies" on layouts with "wide fairways, light rough" and "nice water features"; a few say it's "nothing special", but as part of the Hyatt Regency Scottsdale Resort, it's a "good choice for couples", providing "just enough challenge and just enough service" for "just enough money."

🎲 Grayhawk, Raptor
26 | 27 | 26 | 21 | $230

Scottsdale | 8620 E. Thompson Peak Pkwy. | 480-502-1800 | 800-472-9429 | www.grayhawkgolf.com | 7135/5309; 74.5/71.2; 143/124

It "doesn't get much better than this" Tom Fazio–designed "shot-makers' course" in Scottsdale (a PGA Tour host from 2007–2009) boasting "dramatic holes" with "lots of natural desert areas" and "tee boxes like velvet"; while a few find it "pricey", most agree the "phenomenal facilities" ("fantastic 19th hole") and "expert" service make it the "equivalent of a private club in every way."

Grayhawk, Talon
26 | 26 | 25 | 21 | $230

Scottsdale | 8620 E. Thompson Peak Pkwy. | 480-502-1800 | 800-472-9429 | www.grayhawkgolf.com | 6973/5143; 73.3/70.1; 146/126

A "memorable" David Graham/Gary Panks design featuring "tight fairways" and "insanely fast greens" helps to make this "tough course" a "must-play" in the Scottsdale area; a "value multiplay package with the Raptor" takes the edge off "expensive" greens fees, and the "first-class pro shop", "super practice area" and "even better service" are all reasons to "spend the bucks and enjoy the ride"; P.S. sliders and drinks at Phil's Grill "after the round are a must."

Kierland
22 | 25 | 24 | 19 | $210

Scottsdale | 15636 N. Clubgate Dr. | 480-922-9283 | www.kierlandgolf.com
Acacia/Ironwood | 6974/4985; 72.8/67.8; 127/118
Acacia/Mesquite | 6913/4898; 72.5/67.7; 127/116
Ironwood/Mesquite | 7017/5017; 73.1/68.1; 127/114

Offering "something different for Scottsdale", this "challenging but not-too-difficult" Scott Miller design is a "sea of green with lots of rolling fairways", and while the three nines feature "plenty of sand", they're "wide-open" and "forgiving"; "tied to the Westin Kierland Resort", it's a "great facility" that's sure to "boost your ego" – but not your temperature, thanks to air-conditioned golf carts that are a "plus" in the summer.

Legend Trail
24 | 21 | 22 | 22 | $195

Scottsdale | 9462 Legendary Ln. | 480-488-7434 | www.legendtrailgc.com | 6845/4910; 72.3/68.2; 138/115

"Everything you want in desert target golf", this "underrated" Rees Jones design is a "nice layout at the foot of the McDowell Mountains", offering "scenic" "views of the valley" as it "winds its way through [housing] development"; it's a "solid" option that's a "favorite" of many, including "rock star Alice Cooper, who's a regular."

McDowell Mountain Golf Club (fka Sanctuary at Westworld)
21 | 19 | 22 | 22 | $145

Scottsdale | 10690 E. Sheena Dr. | 480-502-8200 | www.mcdowellmountaingc.com | 7072/4880; 73.3/68.1; 137/109

"Desert vistas abound" at this this "tight", "target-style" desert layout (fka Sanctuary at Westworld) near Scottsdale, which reopened in October 2011 with enhanced length, courtesy of new owner Phil Mickelson and original architect Randy Heckenkemper; though it's "difficult to find" and you may be "playing under power lines", it's "very playable and affordable", with "lovely views of the McDowell Mountains" and "friendly" service adding value.

Phoenician, The 🏯
23 | 27 | 26 | 20 | $195

Scottsdale | 6000 E. Camelback Rd. | 480-423-2449 | 800-888-8234 | www.thephoenician.com
Canyon/Desert | 6310/5024; 70.3/69.7; 130/113
Desert/Oasis | 6068/4777; 70.0/68.7; 130/107
Oasis/Canyon | 6258/4871; 69.0/67.4; 131/111

"Set amongst the pomp and splendor of The Phoenician", one of Arizona's top resorts, this "immaculate" 27-holer consists of three "relatively short" nines that are draped across "beautiful terrain" with "dramatic elevation changes" and mountain, desert and city views; it's "fun and challenging without being torturous" and boasts "fine service", but be sure to "bring your credit cards *and* your friends' credit cards."

SunRidge Canyon 🏯
24 | 21 | 23 | 22 | $170

Fountain Hills | 13100 N. Sunridge Dr. | 480-837-5100 | 800-562-5178 | www.sunridgegolf.com | 6823/5193; 72.6/70.1; 142/128

You "better have your A-game ready" for this "hilly", "challenging" layout "located in a valley of the McDowell Mountains", featuring "nosebleed elevation changes" and a "tough but beautiful 18th"; while this Keith Foster design is "not recommended for rookie players", it's a "favorite" of many for its "great service", "wonderful practice facil-ity" and "spectacular views."

Talking Stick, North
22 | 22 | 21 | 20 | $175

Scottsdale | 9998 E. Indian Bend Rd. | 480-860-2221 | www.talkingstickgolfclub.com | 7133/5532; 72.7/70.2; 125/116

A links-style layout that's "unusual for the desert", this "wide-open", "walker-friendly" design from Bill Coore and Ben Crenshaw is a "thinking man's course" featuring lots of "good bunkering" and "elevated greens";

while some find "nothing exciting" here, it's situated on a Native American reservation near Scottsdale, a "tranquil, scenic" setting with "no homes viewable" and "wild horses on the adjacent property."

Talking Stick, South
23 | 22 | 23 | 23 | $175

Scottsdale | 9998 E. Indian Bend Rd. | 480-860-2221 | www.talkingstickgolfclub.com | 6833/5331; 72.1/69.1; 127/117

For "a little relief from all the mountain courses out here", look no further than this "minimalist" Coore/Crenshaw layout done up "parkland-style", with "wide fairways, superb greens and water features"; it's "one of the better values in the land of overpriced golf" thanks to "excellent conditioning" and a staff that "knows what it's doing."

TPC Scottsdale, Champions ⚲
24 | 23 | 24 | 23 | $139

Scottsdale | 17020 N. Hayden Rd. | 480-585-4334 | 888-400-4001 | www.tpc.com | 7115/5342; 73.7/69.8; 140/120

"Now a much closer match to the famous Stadium course", this layout is "something special", a "challenging oasis" where you can "play among the cacti and tumbleweeds" at a "fair price for a TPC" track; forecaddies are a "great addition to the experience", making it one of the "best bargains" around and a "must-play on any trip to Scottsdale."

TPC Scottsdale, Stadium ⚲
24 | 25 | 23 | 19 | $299

Scottsdale | 17020 N. Hayden Rd. | 480-585-4334 | 888-400-4001 | www.tpc.com | 7216/5455; 74.6/72.9; 138/130

"Where the pros play", this "demanding" yet "fair" Weiskopf/Morrish design (host of the Phoenix Open) offers "beautiful mountain views", "plenty of risk/reward" and "great finishing holes" like the 18th; it may be "pricey in season", but the "good practice facilities" and "highly trained staff" are two more reasons to "find a client in Scottsdale and use your expense account."

☒ Troon North, Monument ⏲
28 | 27 | 25 | 21 | $340

Scottsdale | 10320 E. Dynamite Blvd. | 480-585-5300 | www.troonnorthgolf.com | 7070/5099; 72.9/68.5; 147/121

"The epitome of desert golf", this "gorgeous" Weiskopf/Morrish design "cut through the rocks" near Scottsdale is an "outstanding" layout that'll "wear you out" with "demanding tee shots" and "forced carries" yet remains "playable" and "fair"; it's an "expense-account" option that "can play slow", but the "awe-inspiring views", "great grass driving range" and "wonderful service" help make it "worth the money."

Troon North, Pinnacle ⏲
27 | 27 | 25 | 21 | $340

Scottsdale | 10320 E. Dynamite Blvd. | 480-585-5300 | www.troonnorthgolf.com | 7025/4883; 73.0/67.7; 149/115

Located at the base of Pinnacle Peak, this "Scottsdale favorite" is a "stunning" "classic desert course", with "manicured fairways" that offer "spacious views of the valley"; while the "price is high", the "fabulous amenities" and "superior service" make it a "real treat" for most.

☒ We-Ko-Pa, Cholla
28 | 25 | 25 | 25 | $185

Fort McDowell | 18200 E. Toh Vee Circle | 480-836-9000 | 866-660-7700 | www.wekopa.com | 7225/5289; 73.0/69.9; 136/126

"Desert golf just doesn't get any better" than this "gorgeous layout" loaded with "lots of split fairways" that are kept in "perfect condition", plus "incredible views" of "cacti with golf balls lodged in them" and the majestic mountain it's named after; "unmarred by housing or development", it offers "plenty of wildlife viewing" to go with its "upscale pro shop" and facilities and "outstanding service."

⚡ We-Ko-Pa, Saguaro

28 | 25 | 25 | 25 | $185

Fort McDowell | 18200 E. Toh Vee Circle | 480-836-9000 | 866-660-7700 | www.wekopa.com | 6966/5061; 72.4/68.4; 138/112

"Take your camera" to this "secluded" "desert golf paradise" where the "excellent", "walkable" Coore/Crenshaw design boasts "challenging but playable holes" that are framed with "more saguaros than at a national park"; the "forgiving fairways" have "not a condo in sight", while "spectacular conditioning" and "great facilities" enhance its "value", and if you play it "with the Cholla, you have the best one-two punch around."

Sedona

Sedona Golf Resort

24 | 22 | 22 | 22 | $89

Sedona | 35 Ridge Trail Dr. | 928-284-9355 | 877-733-9885 | www.sedonagolfresort.com | 6646/5075; 70.6/69.6; 128/128

The "views of the red rocks are so amazing, you may forget to keep score" as you play this "stunning" Gary Panks design with "surprising elevation changes" (and, a few say, "too many houses" around the fairways); a "helpful staff" and "great selection in the pro shop" add to its appeal, but to some it's "worth a day trip to Sedona" just to "see the sun going down while the rocks turn orange and red."

Tucson

Arizona National 🏠

25 | 21 | 21 | 21 | $110

Tucson | 9777 E. Sabino Greens Dr. | 520-749-3636 | www.arizonanationalgolfclub.com | 6785/4469; 72.5/66.5; 143/112

"Sweeping vistas and a forest of giant saguaros" distinguish this "desert favorite" in the foothills of the Santa Catalina Mountains offering a "difficult", "well-designed" RTJ Jr. layout featuring "lots of variety" and "challenging greens"; it "gets a lot of play" and the "facilities need updating", but it's "well maintained" as the U. of Arizona's home field.

El Conquistador, Conquistador 🏠

21 | 22 | 21 | 19 | $79

Tucson | 10555 N. La Cañada Dr. | 520-544-5000 | www.hiltonelconquistador.com | 6755/4804; 72.6/68.2; 129/123

Crafted three decades ago by Jeff Hardin and Greg Nash in the desert north of Downtown Tucson, this "hilly" layout offers "gorgeous" Santa Catalina Mountain vistas to complement the Hilton resort's "laid-back feel"; while naysayers suggest it "needs some improvements", it's a "nice" option overall, especially when you factor in the "fun" nine-hole executive track "for less serious golfers."

La Paloma 🏠 ⛳

25 | 25 | 24 | 21 | $205

Tucson | 3660 E. Sunrise Dr. | 520-299-1500 | 800-222-1249 | www.lapalomacc.com
Canyon/Hill | 6997/5057; 72.7/66.2; 146/125
Hill/Ridge | 7017/4878; 72.0/65.9; 145/127
Ridge/Canyon | 7088/5075; 72.9/66.9; 151/129

A "tough" "target-golf" track crafted by Jack Nicklaus in 1984, this semi-private 27-holer nestled "in the Santa Catalina foothills" above

Tucson offers a "variety of holes" on each of the different nines; "the desert always makes each shot a challenge", but the course is "fair from any set of tees", and "all-around great service" and "beautiful resort" grounds are reasons many "would return in a second."

Omni Tucson National, Catalina 🏌 | 25 | 23 | 23 | 22 | $188 |

Tucson | 2727 W. Club Dr. | 520-297-2271 | www.tucsonnational.com | 7262/5414; 75.4/66.3; 136/120

"They don't make them like this anymore in Arizona" note those nostalgic for "long", "traditional" "Eastern-style" tracks like this "classic" course that's distinguished by its use of "grass everywhere, i.e. no island fairways with waste areas"; the longtime home of the PGA Tour's Tucson Open, it has a "pedigree of golf history", making it a "must" for "passionate golfers."

Omni Tucson National, Sonoran 🏌 | ▽ 22 | 23 | 23 | 20 | $188 |

Tucson | 2727 W. Club Dr. | 520-297-2271 | www.tucsonnational.com | 6552/4579; 71.0/62.0; 131/108

The Catalina's "newer sibling" is a "shorter but challenging desert golf course" crafted by former Ryder Cup captain Tom Lehman that includes natural washes and strategy-laced tee shots; it's nestled in the foothills of the Santa Catalina Mountains with panoramic views, and while many warm to the impressive collection of par 3s (notably Nos. 3 and 10), the "good tee time values" also entice.

Ritz-Carlton, Dove Mountain | - | - | - | - | $225 |

Marana | 6501 Boulder Bridge Pass | 520-572-3500 | www.ritzcarlton.com/dovemountain
Saguaro/Tortolita | 7849/5238; 77.1/71.6; 147/132
Tortolita/Wild Burro | 7852/5234; 77.2/70.2; 145/126
Wild Burro/Saguaro | 7791/5250; 76.7/71.0; 147/125

The home of the PGA Tour's WGC-Accenture Match Play Championship hosts the world's top players every February on its Jack Nicklaus design consisting of 27 holes – with nine more planned – in the high desert north of Tucson; the three layouts ribbon through thick desert flora, with wide fairways serving as green islands amid the sand and cacti.

Starr Pass 🏌 | 23 | 24 | 22 | 21 | $190 |

Tucson | 3645 W. Starr Pass Blvd. | 520-670-0400 | 800-503-2898 | www.jwmarriottstarrpass.com
Coyote/Rattler | 7002/5262; 73.0/67.5; 138/123
Coyote/Roadrunner | 6753/4963; 71.6/67.2; 143/118
Rattler/Roadrunner | 6731/5039; 71.7/66.2; 142/116

"A good test for the better-than-average" player (Phil Mickelson captured three PGA Tour titles here), this "challenging" 27-hole design from Bob Cupp and Arnold Palmer "requires accurate shot-making" on three "fantastic" nines featuring "lots of forced carries and blind shots"; connected to the JW Marriott Starr Pass, it boasts "outstanding desert vistas" that make it both "tough and beautiful."

Ventana Canyon, Canyon 🏌 | 25 | 25 | 24 | 21 | $159 |

Tucson | 6200 N. Club House Ln. | 520-577-1400 | 800-828-5701 | www.thelodgeatventanacanyon.com |
6836/4939; 71.9/71.1; 139/121

Considered "a must-play in the Tucson area", this "amazing" desert design from Tom Fazio is defined by "tough bunkers", "lightning-fast greens" and "fabulous scenery", all of which come together at the "three fun canyon holes"; some find it "a little expensive", but since it's adjacent to a "first-rate resort", it's "well cared for" and offers "fabulous service" and "good practice facilities."

Ventana Canyon, Mountain 🏌

| 26 | 24 | 24 | 22 | $159 |

Tucson | 6200 N. Club House Ln. | 520-577-1400 | 800-828-5701 | www.thelodgeatventanacanyon.com | 6898/4695; 73.2/68.2; 145/125

Arguably the "best course in Tucson", this "beautiful" Tom Fazio-designed "Santa Catalina Mountain track" features "fast" greens, "gorgeous vistas" and a "wonderful par-3 3rd" that goes "mesa to mesa" "over a deep canyon"; it's "well maintained" despite "heavy play", with "excellent" service and accommodations, but while it's "heaven for the good golfer", others should "bring lots of balls" and "beware the cacti", where "rattlesnakes hide."

Vistoso

| 25 | 22 | 23 | 24 | $130 |

Tucson | 955 W. Vistoso Highlands Dr. | 520-797-7900 | 877-548-1110 | www.vistosogolf.com | 6954/5095; 72.1/70.1; 143/121

"What a find!" gush golfers about this "beautifully kept" Tom Weiskopf design that offers scenic "views up into the mountain foothills" north of Tucson, and while it's "challenging enough" that you'd "better be accurate", it's a "more forgiving version of desert golf"; a staff that's one of the "friendliest anywhere" and "cheap" fees help make it a "local favorite" of many.

Arkansas

Fayetteville

Stonebridge Meadows

| - | - | - | - | $55 |

Fayetteville | 3495 E. Goff Farm Rd. | 479-571-3673 | 866-589-7753 | www.stonebridgemeadows.com | 7150/5215; 75.1/71.6; 133/135

Located on the Natural State Golf Trail near the U. of Arkansas, this "interesting" Randy Heckenkemper design is a "remarkable bargain compared to high-priced markets"; while a few conclude it's "nothing to get excited about", the roomy fairways and forested terrain and a pair of go-for-broke, watery par 5s on the back nine help make it an "excellent value for the money."

Hot Springs

Glenwood

| - | - | - | - | $43 |

Glenwood | 584 Hwy. 70 E. | 870-356-4422 | 800-833-3110 | www.glenwoodcountryclub.com | 6561/5086; 71.7/64.1; 126/114

"Great scenery in a great location" is how some describe this "challenging, rewarding" layout located 30 minutes southwest of Hot Springs that's draped over rolling terrain and surrounded by dense hardwood and pine forests; it now features bentgrass greens and Bermuda fairways after a 2010 renovation, and those who enjoy difficult, memorable holes will appreciate the watery, 178-yard, par-3 5th, which features a peninsula green well guarded by rocks.

	COURSE	FACIL.	SERVICE	VALUE	COST

Hot Springs Country Club, Arlington   - | - | - | - | $121

Hot Springs | 101 Country Club Dr. | 501-624-2661 | www.hotspringscc.com | 6690/5549; 73.9/74.2; 127/127

"The best-kept secret in Hot Springs" is this "beautiful course" tucked into the Ouachita foothills, a layout that's "fun to play" and "plenty challenging" thanks to narrow, hilly fairways and undulating greens kept "in excellent condition"; though it's located in a "small town", most agree it's "anything but small-town quality"; new bentgrass greens slated to open in 2012 should enhance playability.

California

TOP COURSES IN STATE

Lake Tahoe

Coyote Moon   26 | 21 | 22 | 19 | $149

Truckee | 10685 Northwoods Blvd. | 530-587-0886 | www.coyotemoongolf.com | 7177/5022; 74.4/68.4; 136/127

"It feels like you're playing in the wilderness – and you are!" – at this "stunning" "hidden gem" near Tahoe that's "carved out of the trees and rocks" "with no houses around"; it's "a roller coaster" with "no driving range", but most are over the moon about the "great service", "outstanding conditioning" and overall "value" – "verdant vistas plus fresh mountain air equals near perfection for the price."

Golf Club at Gray's Crossing, Gray's Crossing   - | - | - | - | $185

Truckee | 11406 Henness Rd. | 530-550-5800 | www.oldgreenwoodgolf.com | 7466/5030; 37.5/32.0; 147/112

At 6,500 feet, this once-private 2007 Peter Jacobsen/Jim Hardy design (an Audubon International Gold Signature Sanctuary) 45 minutes west of Reno provides countless occasions to crush longest-ever drives amid jaw-dropping vistas of Mt. Rose, but stray shots will plunge into the towering pines, wetlands and wildflowers that frame the fairways; still, let 'er rip at the par-4 6th, which plummets nearly 100 feet to the green.

Old Greenwood   27 | 25 | 25 | 20 | $185

Truckee | 12915 Fairway Dr. | 530-550-7010 | 800-754-3070 | www.oldgreenwood.com | 7518/5419; 75.2/69.8; 140/133

The "beautiful" "vistas sometimes get in the way of a great shot" at this "superb" "mountain course that plays like a traditional risk/reward" layout thanks to a "challenging Jack Nicklaus design" featuring "tough greens"; it's "not the cheapest course in the Tahoe area, but it's one of the best", with "great conditioning", "top-class service" and "tremendous practice facilities."

Schaffer's Mill Club

-	-	-	-	$160

Truckee | 9045 Heartwood Dr. | 530-582-6964 | www.schaffersmill.com | 7010/6535; 72.9/67.6; 139/126

Formerly the private Timilick Tahoe, this John Harbottle/Johnny Miller design now permits public players on its two distinctive nines – the front (Meadow), which rolls through spruce, firs and Ponderosa pines, and the back (Mountain), which soars via 400 feet of elevation change on a hillside, with 360-degree views of the Martis Valley, Lookout Mountain and Northstar Ski Resort before concluding with two watery gems; a new clubhouse is slated for 2013.

Whitehawk Ranch

27	23	25	22	$125

Clio | 768 Whitehawk Dr. | 530-836-0394 | 800-332-4295 | www.golfwhitehawk.com | 6983/4816; 72.6/62.9; 133/105

"One of the best layouts in the Sierras", this "challenging" course north of Truckee is routed "through tall pines and meandering streams", with "plenty of bunkers and water" and mountain views to "thrill you"; it's kept "in excellent shape", and comes complete with an "enormous driving range" and a "clubhouse deck for watching the sunset after your round."

Los Angeles

Angeles National 🏌

23	11	18	17	$188

Sunland | 9401 Foothill Blvd. | 818-951-8771 | www.angelesnational.com | 7141/4899; 74.7/68.9; 143/116

For "Arizona-style desert golf in LA", head to this "interesting" Steve Nicklaus design that boasts "well-manicured fairways" and "some great par 3s", but sits at the base of the Angeles National Forest, which means "rattlesnake country" and "lots of environmentally protected areas" – "hit 'em straight or hit 'em again"; a "top-notch" all-grass practice area helps to compensate for "abrupt" service, while the post-Survey addition of a Spanish Mission–style clubhouse may outdate the Facilities score.

Industry Hills, Eisenhower 🏌

23	19	18	21	$105

City of Industry | 1 Industry Hills Pkwy. | 626-810-4653 | 800-542-4557 | www.ihgolfclub.com | 7211/5662; 75.1/73.9; 142/139

A "lushly landscaped escape from LA's urban sprawl", this "hilly" "gem" just 25 miles east of the city is blessed with "wonderful topography" and "interesting elevation changes", but you'd better "bring your best shots" because this "brute" is a "stern", yet "moderately priced" test; regulars recommend playing "during the winter months, when the smog is less."

Industry Hills, Zaharias 🏌

22	21	19	20	$100

City of Industry | 1 Industry Hills Pkwy. | 626-810-4653 | 800-542-4557 | www.ihgolfclub.com | 6826/5333; 73.9/73.3; 135/129

Although "not as long" as its counterpart, Eisenhower, this "short", "solid test" is "kinder and better company"; the "narrow" design is a "tough little number", with "lots of variety" and "fun elevation changes", so "bring lots of balls if you're not a single-digit kind" of player; P.S. don't miss the "incredible views."

Lost Canyons, Shadow

| 24 | 24 | 21 | 21 | $69 |

Simi Valley | 3301 Lost Canyon Dr. | 805-522-4653 | 866-384-5678 | www.lostcanyons.com | 7005/4795; 75.0/69.1; 149/125
"It's tough to beat the 'wow' factor" of this "immaculate" "target golf" collaboration between Pete Dye and Fred Couples that offers "memorable holes" as it "winds between the mountains and valleys" northwest of LA; although "it's not known as 'Lost Ball Canyons' for nothing", "wonderful service" and a "well-stocked pro shop" help make it a "nice getaway."

Lost Canyons, Sky

| 24 | 23 | 21 | 20 | $99 |

Simi Valley | 3301 Lost Canyon Dr. | 805-522-4653 | 866-384-5678 | www.lostcanyons.com | 7285/4885; 75.6/70.0; 147/120
"It feels like you're in another world" ("like playing on the moon") at this "silent, secluded" Simi Valley course boasting a "narrow, target-based" track that features "lots of Pete Dye tricks" and "considerable" carries; the "rolling terrain" and "wind tunnel" conditions can make it seem "too hard for mortals", but thanks to the "amazing views" and "excellent facilities", some say it's their "favorite place to lose a lot of balls."

Los Verdes

| 20 | 13 | 13 | 22 | $35 |

Rancho Palos Verdes | 7000 W. Los Verdes Dr. | 310-377-7370 | www.americangolf.com | 6617/5772; 71.7/67.7; 121/113
A "beautiful oceanside course" near Los Angeles, this "poor man's Trump National" is perhaps "the prettiest muni in America", although some lament it's "sadly also [one of] the slowest", "even on good days"; while it's "difficult to get a tee time" and the "clubhouse is classic '70s", you "can't beat" the "awesome ocean views at municipal prices."

Moorpark

| 24 | 24 | 21 | 20 | $125 |

Moorpark | 11800 Championship Dr. | 805-532-2834 | www.moorparkgolf.com
Canyon Crest/Creekside | 6939/4867; 73.0/68.7; 134/119
Canyon Crest/Ridgeline | 6902/4839; 73.1/68.2; 133/116
Creekside/Ridgeline | 6977/4722; 73.7/67.8; 137/118
With "at least 20 memorable holes", this "lush" spread only 45 miles from LA is "one of the must-play courses in SoCal", boasting three "hilly", "challenging" nines with greens that are "true and quick", plus "wonderful facilities" and "great service"; the "Creekside/Ridgeline combo is relentless" ("especially on windy days"), so "it's nice to have Canyon Crest in the mix for a bit of light relief."

Ojai Valley Inn & Spa

| 23 | 25 | 25 | 20 | $180 |

Ojai | 905 Country Club Rd. | 805-646-2420 | 800-422-6524 | www.ojairesort.com | 6292/5211; 71.0/70.8; 132/128
A "wonderful little course at a fabulous resort and spa" in Ojai, this "classic, old-time" track is a "hidden jewel in the Topa Topa Mountains", offering "breathtaking" ups and downs and "elevated greens" plus oak trees, arroyos and "short but wicked rough"; a "great staff", "exquisite setting" and "first-rate spa" are further reasons many declare it "a must-play for everyone."

Palos Verdes Golf Club 🏐 ⏲

| 22 | 18 | 19 | 20 | $235 |

Palos Verdes Estates | 3301 Via Campesina | 310-375-2533 |
www.pvgc.com | 6313/4696; 71.3/69.4; 130/124
Nestled in Palos Verdes Estates, in a "gorgeous setting" next to the
Pacific Ocean, this "classic course" dishes out "heavy kikuyu" grass,
"smallish greens and eucalyptus-lined fairways" on a layout that's
"not long, but plays long because of hills and no roll"; some warn "it's
not cheap or easy to get on", but it's "not to be overlooked"; open to
the public on weekdays only.

Rancho Park

| 19 | 9 | 11 | 22 | $39 |

Los Angeles | 10460 W. Pico Blvd. | 310-838-7373 | www.rpgc.org |
6630/6021; 71.6/68.7; 126/118
"Conveniently situated behind the Fox Studios lot", this "historic"
muni in the "heart of West LA" features a "traditional, well-treed"
"park atmosphere" featuring "moderate hills and many doglegs"; despite "bare-bones" facilities, most consider it a "great value" and
"worth your time."

Robinson Ranch, Mountain

| 23 | 23 | 24 | 21 | $117 |

Santa Clarita | 27734 Sand Canyon Rd. | 661-252-7666 |
www.robinsonranchgolf.com | 6508/5076; 72.3/69.5; 137/121
"Spectacular views of the surrounding mountains" and perhaps the
"best-kept greens in SoCal" add up to "bliss in the Santa Clarita Valley"
at this "wonderful", "quiet" "target course in the desert" that's "narrower and steeper than its Valley counterpart", with "aged oaks" and
"some treacherous terrain"; a "first-class clubhouse", "friendly staff"
and "great practice range" also help make it a "special place."

Robinson Ranch, Valley

| 24 | 22 | 22 | 21 | $117 |

Santa Clarita | 27734 Sand Canyon Rd. | 661-252-7666 |
www.robinsonranchgolf.com | 6903/5408; 74.4/72.2; 149/126
Although it's a "long drive from Los Angeles", this "beautifully
groomed" Santa Clarita course is "worth the trek" for an "enjoyable"
layout that's especially "challenging from the blue or black tees", with
"lots of hills" and "slick but true greens" that can be "sneaky"; it can
get "tough when the wind blows", but "nice" mountain vistas and
"first-class" facilities help make it a "memorable" experience.

Rustic Canyon

| 23 | 15 | 19 | 25 | $63 |

Moorpark | 15100 Happy Camp Canyon Rd. | 805-530-0221 |
www.rusticcanyongolfcourse.com | 6988/5275; 73.3/69.4; 128/113
It's "worth the trip" to Moorpark to play the "best golf value in the Los
Angeles area", this "visually compelling", "difficult links-style course"
that requires "lots of strategy", so "bring your bump-and-run game"
and your putter to tackle "some of the largest, most challenging
greens" around; while some snort the "facilities are blah", no worries –
the "masterful layout" has "character up the wazoo."

Trump National Golf Club 🏐

| 21 | 25 | 23 | 15 | $375 |

Rancho Palos Verdes | 1 Ocean Trails Dr. | 310-265-5000 |
www.trumpnational.com | 7242/4538; 75.0/68.6; 146/124
"Trump even outdid Trump" with this "upscale", "world-class facility"
in Rancho Palos Verdes, where "drop-dead views of Catalina Island
and the Pacific" dazzle duffers, and an "amazing clubhouse" and a

"first-rate staff" add to the allure; "you'll need to bring some coin" and "lots of balls" to tackle the "tougher-than-heck", "immaculately conditioned" layout that some say has "more gimmicks than Epcot Center."

Monterey Peninsula

Bayonet Black Horse, Bayonet

| 25 | 16 | 18 | 23 | $145 |

Seaside | 1 McClure Way | 831-899-7271 | www.bayonetblackhorse.com | 7104/5229; 74.8/70.2; 141/123

"This is why military officers used to reenlist" quip admirers of this "brutal" "old-style" "former army base course" at Fort Ord that "demands a straight ball off the tee" if you don't want to be "confined to the brig in the trees"; it's one of "the best values in the Monterey area", but before you "feel like a general", be forewarned that the afternoon wind and fog can "make it play extra long."

Bayonet Black Horse, Blackhorse

| 24 | 16 | 16 | 21 | $145 |

Seaside | 1 McClure Way | 831-899-7271 | www.bayonetblackhorse.com | 7024/5084; 73.7/69.4; 141/118

"A former army course" at Fort Ord, this "underrated sister of the Bayonet" offers "challenging holes" that "require thoughtful attack" but are "a lot of fun to play"; although the "facilities are ex-military" in quality, the "lovely fairways" are "beautifully manicured" and "set amid the pines, with knockout views of Monterey Bay", making it "a better deal than anything inside 17-Mile Drive."

Carmel Valley Ranch ⦿ ⊙

| 21 | 23 | 22 | 19 | $195 |

Carmel | 1 Old Ranch Rd. | 831-626-2510 | www.cvrgolf.com | 6117/4433; 70.1/66.2; 131/114

"Set in the mountains" at the Carmel Valley Ranch resort, this "lush, beautiful" layout is a "tale of two nines" – the "crazy but fun" Pete Dye design has a "flat" front that's "walkable", while the "terrific back nine" succeeds with its "many elevation changes"; it seems "a little tricked up" to some, but most regard it as a "serene" "escape from the coastal fog", with "very good facilities and service."

☑ Pacific Grove Municipal

| 21 | 13 | 16 | 27 | $48 |

Pacific Grove | 77 Asilomar Ave. | 831-648-5777 | www.ci.pg.ca.us/golf | 5727/5305; 67.5/70.2; 118/116

"A mere seagull's flight from one of the best courses in the world", this "poor man's Pebble Beach" is the "best value in the state" thanks to a layout that's "not glamorous or pristine" but pairs its "tame inner nine" with a "spectacular back bordering the Pacific Ocean"; it's "a gem of an old muni" that's "just plain fun to play" as it "delivers the beauty of the Monterey Coast."

☑ Pebble Beach 村 ⊙

| 29 | 28 | 26 | 18 | $495 |

Pebble Beach | 1700 17-Mile Dr. | 831-624-3811 | 800-654-9300 | www.pebblebeach.com | 7040/5249; 75.5/71.8; 146/129

"Heaven can't be more beautiful" than this "majestic" "golf mecca" "nestled along the Monterey coastline", so take a "walk on hallowed ground" and experience the "nostalgia and jaw-dropping scenery"; although a few find it "crowded" ("the first hole is like Times Square") and suggest the "pricing has gotten out of hand", most insist this "legendary" layout is "worth every penny."

▣ Poppy Hills 🏌

25 | 21 | 22 | 23 | $218

Pebble Beach | 3200 Lopez Rd. | 831-625-2035 | www.poppyhillsgolf.com | 6863/5410; 74.3/71.4; 144/129

"Control your tee shots or pay dearly" at this "deceptively tricky", "world-class" RTJ Jr. design that's "not super long" but features "tight", "hilly, tree-lined" fairways routed through "groves of cypress" and Monterey pine; kept in "impeccable shape" and boasting "beautiful vistas", it's "a joy to walk", and an "unbelievable value for NCGA members."

Quail Lodge ⏲

20 | 24 | 23 | 20 | $150

Carmel | 8000 Valley Greens Dr. | 831-620-8808 | 888-828-8787 | www.quaillodge.com | 6449/5478; 71.4/72.4; 129/127

"Put this on your list to play" advise admirers of this "flat", "forgiving" layout that "isn't on the ocean" but is a "value compared to its neighbors" in the "beautiful Carmel Valley"; though it "lacks excitement" for some, "convenient" facilities, a "great staff" and an "outstanding restaurant" make it a "perfect escape" for a "romantic golf getaway."

San Juan Oaks

23 | 21 | 20 | 22 | $80

Hollister | 3825 Union Rd. | 831-636-6113 | 800-453-8337 | www.sanjuanoaks.com | 7133/4770; 74.6/68.1; 140/120

"Removed from civilization" in an "open, rural setting" south of San Jose, this "well-kept", "awesome layout" is "challenging for any level", with a "welcoming front nine" and a "humbling back nine" that "goes up into the hills"; the "fairways and greens are like walking on carpet", and when you factor in the "large banquet facility" and "nice driving range", most agree it's "worth the drive."

▣ Spanish Bay 🏌

26 | 27 | 26 | 20 | $260

Pebble Beach | 2700 17-Mile Dr. | 831-647-7500 | 800-654-9300 | www.pebblebeach.com | 6821/5332; 74.2/72.1; 142/129

This "mind-bending course" offers "everything you hope for in coastal golf" – "dynamic ocean scenery", "sand dunes, fescue, wind" and perhaps "the best greens on the Monterey Peninsula" – on a "brutal" "shot-makers design" from RTJ Jr.; it "competes with its legendary neighbors" "but won't bankrupt you", a plus when it's time for that post-round cocktail "by the outdoor fire pits" while listening to the "bagpiper at sunset."

▣ Spyglass Hill 🏌

29 | 23 | 25 | 22 | $330

Pebble Beach | Spyglass Hill Rd. | 831-625-8563 | 800-654-9300 | www.pebblebeach.com | 6960/5381; 75.5/72.9; 147/133

A "true national treasure", this "unforgettable experience" begins with "breathtaking views of the Pacific", then heads "off to another world" of "tall, towering pines" where "deer and wildlife abound"; "long, uphill, into-the-wind par 4s", "punishing greens" and "afternoon fog" make this "brawny" RTJ Sr. design perhaps the "most expensive torture chamber in America" – but most agree it's "well worth the price."

Orange County

Arroyo Trabuco

21 | 20 | 19 | 21 | $101

Mission Viejo | 26772 Avery Pkwy. | 949-305-5100 | www.arroyotrabuco.com | 7011/5045; 73.7/69.8; 134/121

An "attempt at Scottish links" "carved into the heart of the O.C.", this "unique layout" is loaded with "unspoiled canyon views" ("no houses"), "memorable par-3s" and "many arroyos to play over – or into"; iron experts advise the "tightly mown fairways can cause head-aches", but "friendly service", a "nice clubhouse" and "top-shelf food" provide some relief.

Black Gold
20 | 19 | 20 | 18 | $115

Yorba Linda | 1 Black Gold Dr. | 714-961-0060 | www.blackgoldgolf.com | 6756/4937; 73.1/69.3; 133/124

"Built on a former oil field" "in the hills of Yorba Linda", this "cool, unique" Arthur Hills design is "a great course for billy goats and straight shooters" with its "mountainous terrain" and "tight, challeng-ing back nine"; "it's beginning to be crowded by housing develop-ment", but the "helpful staff", "nice clubhouse and facilities" and "outstanding views from up top" make it a "hidden treasure."

Monarch Beach
21 | 22 | 23 | 17 | $195

Dana Point | 50 N. Monarch Beach Resort | 949-240-8247 | www.monarchbeachgolf.com | 6601/5050; 72.8/70.4; 138/125

"Forget about concentrating on your game" at this "beautiful" RTJ Jr. de-sign next to the St. Regis Resort that's "sprawled out along the ocean cliffs", boasting "three holes by the water" that alone "are worth the price of the loop"; besides its "incredible location", it boasts an "engag-ing staff" and an "unbeatable 19th hole", though some grouse about "limited warm-up facilities" that "don't match the upscale fees."

Oak Creek
23 | 22 | 23 | 19 | $165

Irvine | 1 Golf Club Dr. | 949-653-7300 | www.oakcreekgolfclub.com | 6850/4989; 72.7/69.0; 132/120

"With a nice mix of holes and no visible homes", this "challenging" yet "user-friendly" Tom Fazio design is a "beautiful" Orange County option that's "sure to impress your client" (which works out well, since it's "def-initely an expense-account track"); "fantastic service", a "superb driving range" and a "restaurant overlooking the course" make it easy to ignore its only glitch, the "occasional blast of the Amtrak train whistle."

⊠ Pelican Hill, Ocean North ⌘
27 | 26 | 25 | 19 | $270

Newport Coast | 22800 S. Pelican Hill Rd. | 949-467-6800 | www.pelicanhill.com | 6945/4951; 73.3/69.4; 133/124

"Golf the Newport Coast in style" at this "awesome" Tom Fazio cre-ation that "rivals its sister for design and layout" as it skirts "the bluffs overlooking the Pacific"; it "doesn't offer stunning ocean views as of-ten" as the South course, and "slow play" and "steep prices" irk some, but a "beautiful" clubhouse and a staff that "treats you like royalty" help make it a "premier golfing experience"; the adjacent Resort at Pelican Hill, which opened in 2009, is already a celebrity magnet.

⊠ Pelican Hill, Ocean South ⌘
27 | 27 | 26 | 20 | $270

Newport Coast | 22800 S. Pelican Hill Rd. | 949-467-6800 | www.pelicanhill.com | 6580/4723; 72.1/68.2; 133/119

Boasting a "plush clubhouse and practice facility", this "spectacular" Tom Fazio design is a "treat", offering up a "tough challenge for all lev-els" and "gorgeous views"; it's a "high-rent round" ("bring your cam-era and wallet"), but "you should play it at least once in your lifetime" to experience "exceptional service", "superb facilities" and a layout kept in "perfect condition."

	COURSE	FACIL.	SERVICE	VALUE	COST

Strawberry Farms

19 | **18** | **17** | **16** | **$160**

Irvine | 11 Strawberry Farms Rd. | 949-551-1811 |
www.strawberryfarmsgolf.com | 6700/4832; 72.7/68.7; 136/114

"A challenging course and an excellent strawberry breakfast – how can you go wrong?" at this "jewel" "tucked away in the mountains of Orange County", where a "tight front nine" is paired with a "more scenic" back, which "snakes through a wildlife preserve" and "around a reservoir"; some suggest the layout "does not live up to its price tag", but "modern carts with GPS" help make it "worth the money."

Talega 🏞

22 | **18** | **19** | **20** | **$100**

San Clemente | 990 Avenida Talega | 949-369-6226 |
www.talegagolfclub.com | 6951/5245; 73.8/65.2; 136/110

"Cut out of arroyos" "in the foothills above San Clemente", this "visually appealing" layout runs along a "wildlife preserve", so "you'll never find houses butting up against half of the course"; it boasts "deep gorges and water", along with a "long and tough back nine", and though a few knock the "poor facilities", for most it remains a "good local option."

Tijeras Creek

21 | **18** | **20** | **20** | **$120**

Rancho Santa Margarita | 29082 Tijeras Creek | 949-589-9793 |
www.tijerascreek.com | 6918/5130; 73.2/70.9; 135/129

"Two distinct nines" make up this "fun", if slightly "schizophrenic", course featuring a "flatter, easier" front routed through a "residential" setting and a "hilly, more challenging" back nestled amid "natural areas"; although a few fret about the "variable conditions", most applaud the "great layout", "friendly service" and "fair prices."

Palm Springs

Classic Club 🏌

25 | **24** | **23** | **21** | **$129**

Palm Desert | 75-200 Classic Club Blvd. | 760-601-3600 |
www.classicclubgolf.com | 7322/5300; 75.8/73.2; 144/132

This "well-conditioned", Arnold Palmer–designed "gem" is a "beautiful" "test of golf" that "finishes with a gambler's par-5 with a green fronted by a pond"; it comes complete with a "nice clubhouse" and "restaurant presenting the finest offerings in the area", so be sure to "play it whenever you can"; P.S. "prepare for a windy round."

Desert Dunes

19 | **16** | **19** | **19** | **$99**

Desert Hot Springs | 19300 Palm Dr. | 760-251-5367 |
www.desertdunesgolf.com | 6876/5359; 73.8/70.7; 142/116

"For a links experience with incredibly stiff" breezes, head to this "fairly priced" RTJ Jr. design that's "on the windy side of the freeway" in Desert Hot Springs; a smattering of trees and artful bunkering enhance the experience, and while a few wonder "if there's a flat spot anywhere on the course, including the tee boxes", others enjoy the "great views toward Palm Springs."

Desert Falls

21 | **20** | **20** | **21** | **$119**

Palm Desert | 1111 Desert Falls Pkwy. | 760-340-4653 |
www.desert-falls.com | 7084/5273; 74.0/71.3; 133/124

A "beautiful, well-kept course" in the Coachella Valley, this "playable" layout offers "some challenging holes (particularly the 18th)" with "lots of water" and "large hybrid" Bermuda greens; a few desert-dwellers dismiss it as "pretty flat" and "surrounded by condos", but a "big club-house", "above-average food" and "hospitable" service compensate.

Desert Willow, Firecliff ⛳   27 | 26 | 23 | 24 | $185

Palm Desert | 38995 Desert Willow Dr. | 760-346-7060 | 800-320-3323 | www.desertwillow.com | 7056/5079; 73.6/69.0; 138/120

One of the "best in the Palm Springs area at any price", this "truly memorable" public track "looks and plays like a private course", where "you feel like you're at one with the desert" even as you grapple with "enough water to keep it interesting"; it's "not for the faint of heart or those allergic to sand", but those who appreciate a "beautiful", "well-maintained" layout "without a lot of elevation changes" call it a "must-play if you visit the Coachella Valley."

Desert Willow, Mountain View ⛳   26 | 25 | 24 | 23 | $185

Palm Desert | 38995 Desert Willow Dr. | 760-346-7060 | 800-320-3323 | www.desertwillow.com | 6913/5040; 73.4/68.9; 130/116

This "fantastic course with fabulous views" in Palm Desert offers "plenty of challenge everywhere" ("beware of cacti hazards") on a "pretty", "female-friendly" layout that's kept in "beautiful condition"; although a few feel its "partner course is better", it "exceeds expectations" with "excellent" facilities and service – "from club drop-off to the 19th hole."

Escena   - | - | - | - | $109

Palm Springs | 1100 Clubhouse View Dr. | 760-778-2737 | www.escenagolf.com | 7173/5503; 74.2/71.2; 130/126

Built in 2005 and reopened in 2009 following a lengthy closure and own-ership change, this Nicklaus Design effort in Palm Springs proper bene-fits from a striking 6,000-sq.-ft. mid-century modern clubhouse that recalls the region's Rat Pack glory days; wide fairways, subtly contoured greens, bunkers that a rusty 18-handicapper can escape from and just enough water trouble to keep the good player on his toes are set against a backdrop of mature palms and San Jacinto Mountain panoramas.

Golf Club at La Quinta   22 | 22 | 22 | 22 | $109
(fka Trilogy at La Quinta) ⛳

La Quinta | 60151 Trilogy Pkwy. | 760-771-0707 | www.thegolfclubatlaquinta.com | 7174/4998; 74.3/68.5; 130/116

A "beautiful, rolling" Gary Panks design that's "maturing nicely", this "forgiving" "former home of the Skins Game" features "wide-open fairways" and "huge greens" that are "always in great condition"; it's "playable for golfers of all levels", and while a few deem it "average" ("many holes seem the same"), the "nice grass range and practice fa-cilities" help make it worth a trip to the Coachella Valley.

Indian Wells Golf Resort, Celebrity   23 | 23 | 23 | 21 | $175

Indian Wells | 44-500 Indian Wells Ln. | 760-346-4653 | www.indianwellsgolfresort.com | 7050/5316; 74.2/71.7; 138/128

Site of several recent Skins Games, this city-owned course in the Coachella Valley boasts a "unique" layout loaded with so "many beau-tiful flower gardens" that some dub it "Augusta National West"; "nar-row holes and lots of rough" mean "you'll really need to hit straight", but its "exceptional service" and "wonderful" mountain views make it "perhaps the best value in the desert."

	COURSE	FACIL.	SERVICE	VALUE	COST

Indian Wells Golf Resort, Players   23 | 22 | 23 | 21 | $175

Indian Wells | 44-500 Indian Wells Ln. | 760-346-4653 |
www.indianwellsgolfresort.com | 7376/5108; 75.3/71.3; 139/122
Thanks to an "excellent redesign" in 2007, this "old classic" near Palm
Springs "shines like a starlet", with "yawning bunkers, tight fairways,
greenside water hazards" and "challenging carries"; "nice views" and
a "well-maintained" layout are two more reasons this "beautiful resort
course" offers "value galore."

La Quinta, Dunes 🏨   21 | 24 | 23 | 19 | $159

La Quinta | 50-200 Avenida Vista Bonita | 760-564-7610 |
www.laquintaresort.com | 6712/4877; 72.4/68.7; 134/123
The "milder-mannered of the two La Quinta courses", this resort
"classic" from Pete Dye is a "wide-open desert track with expansive
fairways", "lots of dunes and mountainous terrain" and "four nice finishing holes", including the signature par-4 17th; detractors declare it
"not as interesting as the Mountain", but it offers slightly "more affordable greens fees", "first-class" amenities and a staff that "treats
you very well."

La Quinta, Mountain 🏨 ⏱   26 | 25 | 23 | 21 | $195

La Quinta | 50-200 Avenida Vista Bonita | 760-564-7610 |
www.laquintaresort.com | 6732/4875; 72.9/68.7; 135/123
"Nestled up against the gorgeous Santa Rosa Mountains", this "stunning" Pete Dye design features "lots of water" and "elevation changes"
on a "serious target golf" layout that's "half on the flatlands and half
winding through the mountains"; a few find it "expensive", but many
say the "friendly, helpful staff", "great facilities" and "incredible setting" make it "a bargain even at the high price."

Marriott Desert Springs, Palm 🏨   22 | 24 | 23 | 20 | $160

Palm Desert | 74855 Country Club Dr. | 760-341-2211 | 800-331-3112 |
www.desertspringsresort.com | 6761/5492; 72.1/71.9; 130/125
"Waterfalls, flowers and exotic birds" as well as "exceptional vistas of
the surrounding mountains" highlight this resort course that was redesigned by Ted Robinson Jr. in 2011; ideal for "a getaway with your
spouse", it's part of a "beautiful hotel" with "nice facilities" and a
"friendly staff", all of which make for an "enjoyable" "warm-up in the
Palm Desert area."

Marriott Desert Springs, Valley 🏨   21 | 25 | 23 | 19 | $160

Palm Desert | 74855 Country Club Dr. | 760-341-2211 | 800-331-3112 |
www.desertspringsresort.com | 6627/5262; 71.5/70.2; 127/118
This "short but well-maintained" "twin of the Palm course" is "just as
beautiful" as its sister, with "picturesque holes" that architect Ted
Robinson seems to have "designed so that the view from the tee takes
your breath away with lush landscaping and mountains" in the distance; a few critics complain it's "nothing special", but it's a "user-
friendly" layout with a "great staff" and "wonderful resort" setting.

Marriott Shadow Ridge   26 | 26 | 25 | 22 | $125

Palm Desert | 9002 Shadow Ridge Rd. | 760-674-2700 |
www.golfshadowridge.com | 7006/5158; 73.9/68.7; 134/118
Architect "Nick Faldo did a masterful job of re-creating the dunesland
look and feel of Australia" on this "beautiful", "playable" layout featur-

ing "lots of water" and "deep fairway bunkers" (though "afternoon winds" can "make it difficult"); add "great mountain vistas", "knowledgeable service" and "amazing facilities" (including "a nice 19th hole, grass range and teaching program"), and it's no wonder fans call it a "piece of paradise in Palm Desert."

PGA West, Jack Nicklaus Tournament 🔊

24 | 25 | 24 | 22 | $195

La Quinta | 56-150 PGA Blvd. | 760-564-7170 | 800-742-9378 | www.pgawest.com | 7204/5023; 75.3/69.4; 143/124

The "desert sky and striking mountains" near La Quinta set the stage for this "PGA West sleeper course", a "deceptively hard" track with all "the typical Nicklaus design hallmarks": "length, multi-tiered greens and generous waste areas" that make the terrain a veritable "moonscape"; "hit it straight", for "bouncing drives off roofs can come at a price", but most deem this "enjoyable" "Q-School host" a "wonderful challenge."

PGA West, Stadium 🔊

26 | 25 | 23 | 21 | $225

La Quinta | 56-150 PGA Blvd. | 760-564-7170 | 800-742-9378 | www.pgawest.com | 7300/5092; 76.1/70.2; 150/124

"Get ready for a ride" on this "butt-kicker of a course" that's "like a funhouse" – "nothing is what it seems and you leave feeling dizzy" – thanks to a "tough" design that's "devious Pete Dye at his best"; despite "lightning-fast greens" and "traps you could lose your car in" (including "the infamous bunker with stairs"), it's an "absolute blast" that's "worth every dime" of the "beaucoup bucks" you'll pay.

SilverRock Resort, Arnold Palmer Classic

26 | 18 | 22 | 21 | $165

La Quinta | 79-179 Ahmanson Ln. | 760-777-8884 | 888-600-7272 | www.silverrock.org | 7578/4884; 76.3/68.4; 139/118

"Bring your A-game or plenty of golf balls" to this "way long, way tough" Arnold Palmer design, a "beautiful new muni" in La Quinta featuring "lots of sandy waste areas", "well-protected greens" and the "occasional bighorn sheep"; it's a "serene" "treat" with "dramatic mountain views", while a new hacienda-style clubhouse may outdate the Facilities score.

Westin Mission Hills, Gary Player

22 | 20 | 22 | 20 | $145

Rancho Mirage | 70705 Ramon Rd. | 760-770-9496 | www.westinmissionhillsgolf.com | 7062/4907; 73.4/68.0; 131/118

One of two "lovely" layouts at the Westin Mission Hills, this "user-friendly" track proves that "Gary Player knows how to design a course"; while it can be "impossible if the wind is howling", women are sure to "love the shorter ladies' tees" and everyone will appreciate the "excellent views" and "value" "stay-and-play packages."

Westin Mission Hills, Pete Dye

23 | 22 | 22 | 20 | $145

Rancho Mirage | 71501 Dinah Shore Dr. | 760-328-3198 | www.westinmissionhillsgolf.com | 6706/4841; 72.2/67.6; 131/117

A combination of "beautiful par 3s", "tough greens" and "mounding that sends shots toward the fairways" means you should "be prepared to laugh or cry" while playing this "fantastic" Pete Dye layout in Rancho Mirage that's "not as difficult as nearby PGA West, but more enjoyable for mere mortals"; although a few feel it's "a bit contrived", it's "playable for all" and part of an "excellent hotel."

Sacramento

DarkHorse
23 | 13 | 19 | 20 | $69

Auburn | 24150 DarkHorse Dr. | 530-269-7900 | www.darkhorsegolf.com | 7096/4978; 75.0/68.3; 139/122

Wandering "majestically through 7,000-plus yards of Auburn pines", "oaks and rolling hills", this "truly great" Keith Foster design "blends in wonderfully with the surrounding landscape", offering "lots of ups and downs", rock outcroppings and yawning, handcrafted bunkers; although a few critics claim it's "overrated", most maintain "the course speaks for itself" and is a "bang for the buck."

Diablo Grande, Legends West
∇ 27 | 19 | 18 | 25 | $69

Patterson | 9521 Morton Davis Dr. | 209-892-4653 | www.diablogrande.com | 7112/4905; 75.1/69.3; 139/123

"Well worth the drive" 90 miles south of Sacramento, this lightly trafficked Jack Nicklaus/Gene Sarazen design is considered one of the "best in the Central Valley" thanks to a layout with "greens, fairways and tees in good shape" as well as "beautiful views of the hills" and vineyards; a few fret about the "poor facilities" and "heat in summer", but most conclude that "it's worth finding this off-the-beaten-path gem."

Diablo Grande, Ranch
∇ 22 | 19 | 19 | 21 | $69

Patterson | 9521 Morton Davis Dr. | 209-892-4653 | www.diablogrande.com | 7243/5291; 75.4/70.8; 138/118

An "impressive but long" and "narrow" layout by Denis Griffiths, this track is the lengthier sibling of Legends West; expect a swift pace and views of the ancient oaks, creeks and grapevines that border the course (the 650-yard, par-5 12th offers greenside views of Mikes Peak).

San Bernardino

Oak Quarry 🏯
25 | 18 | 20 | 22 | $95

Riverside | 7151 Sierra Ave. | 951-685-1440 | www.oakquarry.com | 7002/5408; 73.9/71.9; 137/121

"Threaded through an old mineral quarry", this "architectural marvel" is "well worth the drive" to Riverside with a layout featuring "huge elevation changes" and a "dramatic" routing "through scraped canyons"; it's "fun for all levels", and though the "mediocre facilities" and "mandatory carts" irk some critics, the signature par-3 14th is so "magnificent", it's "worth the greens fees just to play that hole."

Oak Valley 🏯
21 | 17 | 17 | 20 | $69

Beaumont | 1888 Golf Club Dr. | 951-769-7200 | www.oakvalleygolf.com | 7003/5349; 74.0/71.9; 138/128

"Meandering through low rolling hills" near San Bernardino, this "wonderful" Schmidt/Curley design is a "deal if you don't want to drive all the way out to Palm Springs", offering "some arroyos to carry" along with "receptive greens and an occasional water hole"; most consider it a track "you'll want to return to", especially high-handicappers who'll "have some fun because it does not intimidate."

	COURSE	FACIL.	SERVICE	VALUE	COST

Tukwet Canyon, Champions
(fka East Valley, Champions) 村 🏌

23 | 23 | 22 | 23 | $64

Beaumont | 36211 Champions Dr. | 951-845-0014 | 877-742-2500 |
www.eastvalleygolfclub.com | 7377/5274; 76.1/72.4; 139/128
One of "the best-kept secrets" in the San Bernardino area, this "real links
course" crafted by Lee Schmidt and Brian Curley is a "true test of your
game" with large, sculpted bunkers, "slick greens" and "lots of wind";
while some feel it "was better before they built homes" all around, it still
offers "beautiful scenery" and "top-notch service at a muni price."

Tukwet Canyon, Legends
(fka East Valley, Legends) 村 🏌

24 | 21 | 21 | 24 | $64

Beaumont | 36211 Champions Dr. | 951-845-0014 | 877-742-2500 |
www.eastvalleygolfclub.com | 7442/5169; 75.9/70.9; 141/130
Home to the PGA of Southern California, this breeze-fueled
Schmidt/Curley design is routed over rolling, woodland terrain, with
strategy-infused holes featuring bold bunkering and undulating greens;
scenic mountain views help make it just "as fun as its sister course."

San Diego

❷ Aviara 🏌

26 | 27 | 26 | 20 | $235

Carlsbad | 7447 Batiquitos Dr. | 760-603-6900 | www.parkaviara.hyatt.com |
7007/5007; 75.0/69.3; 144/127
"Picturesque holes" with plenty of "blooming flowers" and a "lush,
tropical feel" make this "challenging" Carlsbad course seem like a "botanical garden where golf is allowed"; designed by Arnold Palmer, the
"superbly groomed" spread sports "elevated tees, water and undulating greens", and though it's "a bit expensive", "spectacular amenities"
and "top-notch" service ensure you "get your money's worth."

Barona Creek

25 | 21 | 21 | 22 | $160

Lakeside | 1932 Wildcat Canyon Rd. | 619-387-7018 | 888-722-7662 |
www.barona.com | 7088/5296; 74.5/70.6; 140/126
"One of the best in the San Diego area", this Barona Reservation course
is "a bit remote", but it's a "challenging test" with "generous fairways",
"lightning-fast, undulating greens" and "over 100 bunkers"; there's also
a "great little casino" next door – although some warn the "biggest
gamble might be [driving on] the twisting Wildcat Canyon Road."

CrossCreek

20 | 16 | 19 | 21 | $89

Temecula | 43860 Glenn Meadows Rd. | 951-506-3402 |
www.crosscreekgolfclub.com | 6853/4706; 73.2/67.4; 140/118
Winding through groves of oak and sycamore near the "Temecula wine
country" ("where your cell phone doesn't work"), this "unique", "uncrowded" Arthur Hills design is a "tranquil" track "with no houses lining
the fairways"; though a few feel it could "be so much better", "fair
prices" and a "very good finishing hole" make it a "great value" to many.

Golf Club at Rancho California
(fka SCGA Golf Course)

19 | 16 | 17 | 19 | $58

Murrieta | 39500 Robert Trent Jones Pkwy. | 951-677-7446 | 800-752-9724 |
www.thegolfclubatranchocalifornia.com | 7036/5354; 74.7/66.5; 136/115
Formerly the home of the Southern California Golf Association, this
"classic RTJ Sr. target" design an hour southeast of LA dishes out ele-

COURSE
FACIL.
SERVICE
VALUE
COST

CALIFORNIA

vated tees and greens, plus bold bunkering and a "nice practice area"; while some suggest the layout is "not in great shape" and "pace of play" is a concern, most consider it a "very enjoyable track"; plans for new, more challenging back tees are in the works.

Grand Golf Club 🔁 ᴏ━ | 24 | 25 | 25 | 19 | $250 |

San Diego | 5300 Grand Del Mar Way | 858-314-1930 | www.thegranddelmar.com | 7160/4895; 74.8/69.2; 139/117
For "a memorable day" of golf near San Diego, check out this Tom Fazio design that's "great in every way", with a layout that plunges through coastal canyons just east of the Pacific; it's the centerpiece of the Grand Del Mar resort, and while some guests find it "ridiculously expensive", most say they would "play there again" thanks to the presence of an "excellent staff" and a "waterfall on the 18th."

Journey at Pechanga 🔁 | - | - | - | - | $200 |

Temecula | 45000 Pechanga Pkwy. | 951-770-4653 | 866-991-7277 | www.journeyatpechanga.com | 7219/4852; 74.8/64.3; 142/116
Nestled amid the rocky hills of Southern California's wine country in the upscale Pechanga Resort & Casino, this Arthur Hills/Steve Forrest design features roller coaster–like climbs and plunges on holes such as the 488-yard, par-4 6th; an oak in the middle of the 7th fairway and slot machines next door add to the excitement.

La Costa, Champions 🏌 🔁 | 20 | 24 | 22 | 17 | $240 |

Carlsbad | 2100 Costa Del Mar Rd. | 760-438-9111 | 800-854-5000 | www.lacosta.com | 7172/4356; 75.1/66.3; 140/120
A "reminder of days gone by", this "classic old course" appeals to many with its "pedigree" (it played host to the PGA Tour for nearly 40 years) and "beautiful" resort setting; a 2011 makeover by Pascuzzo & Pate (which may not be reflected in the Course score) may quell complaints about the "uninspiring" track, and while a few feel the club is asking "too much money", others say the "wonderful experience" is "pricey, but worth it."

La Costa, South 🏌 🔁 | 20 | 23 | 22 | 17 | $185 |

Carlsbad | 2100 Costa Del Mar Rd. | 760-438-9111 | 800-854-5000 | www.lacosta.com | 7077/5612; 74.6/74.4; 136/136
Tiger Woods, Jack Nicklaus and Phil Mickelson have all conquered the "considerable challenge" of this strategically bunkered, circa-1964 layout that once hosted the Accenture Match Play Championship; the "killer rough" and "mature trees and plantings make it both tough and beautiful", but while some "love the course and facilities", others suggest it's "below par" for a track "of this reputation and price point."

Maderas | 26 | 21 | 22 | 20 | $210 |

Poway | 17750 Old Coach Rd. | 858-451-8100 | www.maderasgolf.com | 7167/4967; 75.4/69.8; 144/127
Offering one of the "best combinations of beauty, conditioning and layout in Southern California", this "hilly", "phenomenally challenging" course near San Diego "will have you laughing and crying"; although a few fret about occasional "slow play", it's a "top-flight" "canyon course" with "feathery fairways" and "immaculate greens", and a "wonderful clubhouse" and "excellent service" make it a "hidden gem."

	COURSE	FACIL.	SERVICE	VALUE	COST

Mt. Woodson ⛳

| 22 | 15 | 18 | 23 | $78 |

Ramona | 16422 N. Woodson Dr. | 760-788-3555 | www.mtwoodsongc.com | 5764/4229; 69.0/65.0; 133/116

"Keep your driver in the bag" at this "narrow" but "stunning" "little course" that's "shoehorned" into the "oak forests" "atop a mountain" near San Diego; it features "lots of elevation changes" and other "fun-filled challenges", and although it's "very short" with "no driving range" and "limited" facilities, most say it's "worth the hike" to "enjoy the beauty", and a "great value" overall.

Pala Mesa

| 18 | 16 | 19 | 18 | $69 |

Fallbrook | 2001 Old Hwy. 395 | 760-728-5881 | 800-722-4700 | www.palamesa.com | 6502/5096; 71.9/64.3; 128/108

Aficionados advise "either go out early or swing easy", because "afternoon winds can play havoc with your shot-making" on this "tight", "interesting layout" that twists through a canyon just north of San Diego; the "flat front nine and hilly back" come at you "with a pack of challenging holes" that feature "little water but plenty of trees" and "native plants"; it's situated at a "great resort" that also boasts a "nice bar and restaurant."

Rancho Bernardo Inn

| 19 | 23 | 24 | 19 | $135 |

San Diego | 17550 Bernardo Oaks Dr. | 858-675-8500 | www.jcgolf.com | 6631/4949; 72.3/68.5; 133/119

"Always fun and pleasant to play", this "nicely kept, old-style course" in San Diego is "friendly for golf with your spouse" thanks to a "short", "easy" layout topped with a "beautiful finishing hole"; the resort is "fabulous", so be sure to "grab a bite at the 19th hole" – although "sipping a cool one on the patio while totaling your score is even better."

Redhawk ⛳

| 20 | 19 | 19 | 21 | $90 |

Temecula | 45100 Redhawk Pkwy. | 951-302-3850 | 800-451-4295 | www.redhawkgolfcourse.com | 7110/5405; 75.4/72.4; 145/126

"Be prepared to be challenged" by this Temecula "gem" that can be "difficult" "for all capabilities" with its multi-tiered greens and a routing "dictated by maximizing housing", so "bring a lot of balls" and "hit them straight"; some suggest it's "nothing spectacular", but for most, the "inexpensive" fees and "beautiful layout" in the foothills of the Palomar Mountains make it "worth the drive out to the wine country."

Steele Canyon ⛳

| 23 | 19 | 20 | 21 | $139 |

Jamul | 3199 Stonefield Dr. | 619-441-6900 | www.steelecanyon.com
Canyon/Meadow | 6741/4655; 73.1/67.0; 139/116
Meadow/Ranch | 6808/4790; 73.4/67.5; 141/119
Ranch/Canyon | 6741/4655; 73.1/67.0; 139/116

"Tucked in the hills east of San Diego", this "scenic" "golf course done right" features "undulating greens, strategic bunkering and some long holes" on a "great combination of nines" designed by Gary Player; though some find the track "tired" and the facilities "just ok", others insist that as long as you make "the Canyon part of your round", it's "an oasis in the desert" that's "well worth the price."

COURSE FACIL. SERVICE VALUE COST

Temecula Creek Inn
18 | 21 | 20 | 20 | $95

Temecula | 44501 Rainbow Canyon Rd. | 951-694-1000 | 877-517-1823 |
www.temeculacreekinn.com
Creek/Oaks | 6784/5712; 72.3/72.8; 127/118
Stonehouse/Creek | 6605/5686; 71.6/72.8; 130/120
Stonehouse/Oaks | 6693/5658; 72.3/73.1; 129/123

Nestled in the heart of Southern California wine country, this "lovely countryside" 27-holer is "fun and fair from the forward tees yet still challenging from the rear", making it a "good couples course"; the three nine-hole options are "long and wild" – particularly the Ted Robinson–designed Stonehouse – and while a few feel it's just "ok for the money", the "pretty setting" and adjacent inn add to its appeal.

☑ Torrey Pines, North
26 | 20 | 20 | 23 | $125

La Jolla | 11480 N. Torrey Pines Rd. | 858-452-3226 | 800-985-4653 |
www.torreypinesgolfcourse.com | 6644/5437; 72.3/75.3; 128/131

Although it's a "more enjoyable" and "gentler companion to the ogre on South", "just try to tame" this "municipal jewel of La Jolla", home of the PGA Tour's Farmers Insurance Open; expect some of the "toughest roughs you ever saw" on "gorgeous" holes with "sweeping views" "overlooking the Pacific", and although a few fret that "conditions aren't great due to constant play", you can expect "perfect weather all the time."

☑ Torrey Pines, South
28 | 19 | 19 | 23 | $229

La Jolla | 11480 N. Torrey Pines Rd. | 858-452-3226 |
800-985-4653 | www.torreypinesgolfcourse.com |
7680/5542; 78.1/73.5; 143/128

A "true tournament course with magnificent views of the Pacific" and the site of Tiger Woods' "epic 2008 U.S. Open victory", this "magical" "seaside monster" may be the "best value in the country" if you're a San Diego resident, with a "brutal rough" and "par 4s [that] feel like par 6s"; while out-of-towners find it "overpriced" for the "spartan" muni facilities, others exhort "you have to play it once, so pony up."

San Francisco Bay Area

Bridges, The
19 | 21 | 20 | 17 | $85

San Ramon | 9000 S. Gale Ridge Rd. | 925-735-4253 |
www.thebridgesgolf.com | 6861/5153; 74.5/71.8; 147/130

"Bring your A-game and some spare ammo" to "one of the hardest tracks around", this Johnny Miller–designed "canyon course" that can be "unforgiving" with its "many forced carries", "blind tee shots", "small landing zones" and "sidehill lie after sidehill lie"; critics call it "gimmicky", but it can be "rewarding if your game is on", offering "unique holes that wrap around the San Ramon hills", with "amazing gorges" and "beautiful views."

Callippe Preserve
21 | 16 | 18 | 21 | $79

Pleasanton | 8500 Clubhouse Dr. | 925-426-6666 | www.playcallippe.com |
6748/4788; 73.0/68.9; 133/118

A terrific "bang for your buck in the East Bay", this "creative and challenging" "thinking man's" muni offers a "wide variety of holes" that are "heavy on bunkers", including a relatively "benign" front and a back nine that serves as "a wake-up call" with its "change of elevation";

	COURSE	FACIL.	SERVICE	VALUE	COST

though some wish the staff could "speed up the pace", most consider it a "fun, playable" option that's "well worth your time."

Cinnabar Hills
25 | 24 | 22 | 21 | $105

San Jose | 23600 McKean Rd. | 408-323-5200 |
www.cinnabarhills.com
Canyon/Mountain | 6641/4859; 72.3/68.1; 135/118
Lake/Canyon | 6688/4959; 72.7/68.4; 138/121
Mountain/Lake | 6853/5010; 73.2/68.1; 140/120

"One of California's best-kept secrets", this "hidden gem in the foothills of San Jose" offers "plenty of variety" on its three "well-maintained" nines, which demand "long carries over barrancas" "often from high tee positions", a task made particularly "tough" on the "narrow", "quirky" Canyon course; while it offers "gorgeous views", some say the "thing to see is the clubhouse with its 'museum' of golf history", and there's a "nice restaurant to boot."

☑ CordeValle 対 ⊿ ᴏ~
27 | 28 | 27 | 19 | $395

San Martin | 1 CordeValle Dr. | 408-695-4500 | 877-255-2626 |
www.cordevalle.com | 7169/5385; 75.3/72.1; 144/130

An RTJ Jr. "stunner" that's one of "the best courses in the South Bay", and host of the PGA Tour's Frys.com Open since 2010, this "awesome course" with "lots of fairway bunkering" "starts gently, then builds in difficulty" as it "winds through oak-studded foothills" in a "spectacular setting - no homes"; it's "pricey", but with a "first-class spa" and "impeccable service", "it feels like a private club."

☑ Half Moon Bay, Ocean
25 | 24 | 23 | 20 | $205

Half Moon Bay | 2 Miramontes Point Rd. | 650-726-4438 |
www.halfmoonbaygolf.com | 6649/4872; 72.5/69.0; 128/119

"A piece of heaven" "right next to the fantastic Ritz-Carlton", this Arthur Hills-designed "American-style links course" leaves swingers "speechless" thanks to three "incredibly scenic" finishing holes that play on a cliff "along the Pacific"; the front nine is "a little bowling alley-esque" and "fog can dampen the mood", but it is a "tremendous value compared to Pebble Beach."

Half Moon Bay, Old Course ⊿
23 | 23 | 23 | 19 | $205

Half Moon Bay | 2 Miramontes Point Rd. | 650-726-4438 |
www.halfmoonbaygolf.com | 7001/5279; 75.3/72.1; 135/120

"There's only one hole on the ocean" at this "beautiful", "well-maintained" course that otherwise plays "among pine tree-lined fairways", but that "spectacular" final hole that "runs along the ocean cliffs" is "worth the greens fee by itself"; for some, it's "diminished by homes that are too close", but it's nonetheless a "good test when the wind is up" or "the fog is rolling in."

Poppy Ridge
23 | 22 | 22 | 24 | $112

Livermore | 4280 Greenville Rd. | 925-447-6779 |
www.poppyridgegolf.com
Chardonnay/Merlot | 7106/5212; 75.0/70.4; 138/120
Merlot/Zinfandel | 7128/5265; 75.0/70.4; 138/120
Zinfandel/Chardonnay | 7048/5267; 75.0/70.4; 138/120

"Wind farms surround this course for a reason", so avoid the "afternoon gusts" when playing this "beautiful" Rees Jones design near Livermore offering a "perfect blend of challenge and reward" "with views of the hills and vineyards", "without the crush of homes"; it's "hilly" and "can be hot in summer", but with "state-of-the-art facilities" and an "excellent staff", you just "can't beat the price."

Presidio

20 | 15 | 16 | 19 | $145

San Francisco | 300 Finley Rd. | 415-561-4653 | www.presidiogolf.com | 6414/5596; 72.3/69.6; 136/128

Located "in the heart of San Francisco", this "old army base" track is a "tight", "hilly", "beautiful" layout routed among Monterey Pines and eucalyptus trees, with "no water" hazards in sight; "painfully slow rounds" and "military"-grade facilities bother some, but those who value its "historic" heritage suggest golfers "check it out"; P.S. "bundle up" for the "British Open conditions" – "chilly", "windy" and "foggy."

Roddy Ranch

21 | 12 | 15 | 20 | $70

Antioch | 1 Tour Way | 925-978-4653 | www.roddyranch.com | 7024/5390; 74.5/71.7; 142/120

A "decent layout in the middle of nowhere" near Antioch, this "rustic, challenging" option is "fun for all" with its "interesting mix of holes" and "firm", "lightning-fast greens"; although a few feel it's "plain-Jane", most "love" this "not-too-crowded" course, saying the "only drawback" is the "long drive" from San Francisco.

Sonoma Golf Club ⌀

24 | 23 | 22 | 19 | $185

Sonoma | 17700 Arnold Dr. | 707-996-0300 | www.sonomagolfclub.com | 7103/6138; 74.6/75.0; 137/132

"Golf and wine – a perfect combination" toast reviewers who've uncorked this "beautifully refurbished" "classic 1920s design", a "regular" stop on the Champions Tour that sports "lots of doglegs but no water" in a "parkland setting with hills and vineyards" all around; since playing "requires a stay at the Fairmont", it can get "expensive", but the "lightning-fast greens" and "absolutely stunning new clubhouse" are two more reasons it's a Sonoma "gem."

StoneTree

20 | 20 | 20 | 15 | $120

Novato | 9 Stone Tree Ln. | 415-209-6090 | www.stonetreegolf.com | 6782/5083; 73.1/65.2; 138/115

It's "like you're playing two courses in one day" at this "windy" "classic" "on the way to Napa Valley" that pairs a "flat but interesting front" with a "narrow, difficult back" routed over "picturesque hills"; "undulating greens" help to make it "tough", and while some suggest it "needs a driving range" and fewer "blind shots", most recommend it "if you want to get out of the city."

◪ TPC Harding Park

24 | 16 | 16 | 21 | $170

San Francisco | 99 Harding Rd. | 415-661-1865 | www.harding-park.com | 6845/5875; 72.8/70.4; 126/116

A "sweet, old-school, tree-lined track" that's "steeped in tradition", this "beauty" of a muni "in the middle of San Francisco", which hosted the PGA Tour's President's Cup in 2009, is highlighted by a "picturesque back" with an "exceptional finishing hole"; though a few gripe about the "mediocre service" and "cold SF fog", most just "bring a sweater" and enjoy "one of the best values in California golf (even better if you're a resident)."

	COURSE	FACIL.	SERVICE	VALUE	COST

Wente Vineyards

| 24 | 24 | 24 | 21 | $125 |

Livermore | 5050 Arroyo Rd. | 925-456-2478 | 800-999-2885 |
www.wentegolf.com | 7181/4866; 75.8/69.4; 145/122

"Like a fine wine, this Greg Norman course gets better with age" thanks to a "challenging layout" that ambles "through vineyards" east of San Francisco, with "crazy elevation changes" and wind that "gets going in the afternoon" (it's "easy to see" why it hosted Nationwide Tour events in the past); expect "super service" and "immaculate" conditions, and be sure to "save time to sip a bit of the local product."

San Luis Obispo

Hunter Ranch

| 23 | 18 | 20 | 22 | $100 |

Paso Robles | 4041 Hwy. 46 E. | 805-237-7444 | www.hunterranchgolf.com | 6741/5639; 72.7/72.0; 138/128

"People drive to the middle of nowhere" to play this oak-studded "thinking man's" layout in the Santa Lucia foothills that sports undulating greens, "well-placed water and sand traps" and "amazing views of the surrounding vineyards"; although a few say they "wouldn't rush back", citing "average facilities", for most it's "worth a special trip", especially if you "leave time to sample the hundreds of wineries in the 'new Napa.'"

Monarch Dunes

| ▽ 26 | 23 | 24 | 26 | $95 |

Nipomo | 1606 Trilogy Pkwy. | 805-343-9459 | www.monarchdunes.com | 6810/4702; 73.0/68.5; 137/126

Those in the know rave about this "hidden gem" that's "a bit out of the way" about 30 minutes south of San Luis Obispo, a "fun, clever" layout where "no two holes are remotely similar", with coastal dunes, eucalyptus trees and "really hard, really fast greens"; factor in the "nice clubhouse" and "scenic" setting, and you see why many consider it "a definite must-play."

Santa Barbara

Alisal Guest Ranch, River

| 21 | 20 | 20 | 20 | $88 |

Solvang | 150 Alisal Rd. | 805-688-6042 | www.rivercourse.com | 6830/5710; 72.7/73.8; 125/128

A "rarely overcrowded" "respite from the valley's spectacular wine-tasting", this "lovely, old-fashioned" resort course near Solvang is "forgiving, but not a pushover", offering "interesting holes" threaded among "the oaks and a meandering creek"; a few feel there are "better choices in the area", but others insist it's "worth the drive" to play a "simple layout in good condition" nestled in a "beautiful setting" along the Santa Ynez River.

Glen Annie

| 19 | 20 | 20 | 20 | $85 |

Santa Barbara | 405 Glen Annie Rd. | 805-968-6400 | www.glenanniegolf.com | 6417/5005; 71.3/69.4; 130/123

"Even the practice range has a unique setting" at this "hilly", "challenging course" where the "many memorable holes" feature "lots of elevation changes" and "pretty" "views down to Santa Barbara and the Pacific"; "beautifully kept" grounds and reasonable prices combine to make it the place to go "if you're in the area and need a relaxed round of golf."

	COURSE	FACIL.	SERVICE	VALUE	COST

La Purisima
28 | 18 | 20 | 25 | $64

Lompoc | 3455 Hwy. 246 E. | 805-735-8395 | www.lapurisimagolf.com | 7105/5763; 75.6/75.6; 143/135

The "stunning contrast between the gorgeous green fairways and the dry straw grass of the hills" distinguishes this "rustic" and "very special" spread that "can't be beat for the pure golf experience"; located 45 minutes north of Santa Barbara, the "tight and twisty" track can be "a real test", especially when the "afternoon winds" "howl", leading some to conclude the club "could charge three times the price if it weren't so far away."

Rancho San Marcos
24 | 17 | 22 | 20 | $120

Santa Barbara | 4600 Hwy. 154 | 805-683-6334 | 877-766-1804 | www.rsm1804.com | 6939/5386; 73.9/71.4; 137/128

"Simply the best-kept secret in the West", this "difficult" "beauty" designed by RTJ Jr. is in a "terrific environment" along the Santa Ynez River (think "elevation changes" and scenic mountain views); a few fret about holes that are "too tricked-up" and "spendy" prices, but the "outstanding staff" and "don't-miss 19th hole" are two more reasons "it's worth the trip if you're in the Santa Barbara area."

Sandpiper
24 | 18 | 19 | 19 | $159

Goleta | 7925 Hollister Ave. | 805-968-1541 | www.sandpipergolf.com | 7068/5701; 74.9/68.4; 136/132

Offering "breathtaking" cliff-top views of the Pacific, this "links-style seaside course" is a "memorable golf experience" featuring "some uniquely challenging holes"; a few say the "greens fees are too high", citing "spotty" conditioning and "facilities that leave a lot to be desired", but for others it remains an "enjoyable" "reason to attend meetings" "close to beautiful Santa Barbara."

Santa Cruz

⌷ Pasatiempo ⚑ ⊙
28 | 21 | 23 | 23 | $220

Santa Cruz | 18 Clubhouse Rd. | 831-459-9155 | www.pasatiempo.com | 6500/5685; 72.4/69.6; 143/133

"If you can't get onto Cypress Point", "do not miss" the chance to play this "rare" "Alister Mackenzie design that's open to the public", a "masterpiece" nestled "in the hills above Santa Cruz", which was "refurbished to perfection" by Tom Doak; it's "short" yet "incredibly tough", featuring "super-fast" greens "with huge breaks", and while some find the driving range "cramped", for most it epitomizes "golf the way it was meant to be played."

Santa Rosa

Links at Bodega Harbour
24 | 18 | 20 | 21 | $90

Bodega Bay | 21301 Heron Dr. | 707-875-3538 | www.bodegaharbourgolf.com | 6275/4751; 71.5/68.6; 122/118

"Bring a sweater", "your hiking boots" "and your A-game" to this "must-play on the bluffs above Bodega Bay", where "lots of elevation changes" make it "challenging but fun to play", as long as the "fog and wind aren't prohibitive"; some gripe the "tight" track is "surrounded by too many houses" and "could use a driving range", but for most the "beautiful seaside" location 90 minutes north of San Francisco "makes it worth the trip."

Stockton

Saddle Creek

| 26 | 23 | 21 | 20 | $105 |

Copperopolis | 1001 Saddle Creek Dr. | 209-785-3700 | 888-852-5787 | www.saddlecreekgolf.com | 6826/4486; 72.9/66.7; 136/122

"Drive to the middle of nowhere, turn left and you'll find" this "hidden gem in the foothills of the Sierra Nevadas", a "wonderful layout" featuring "no parallel fairways", "gorgeous elevated tee shots", sprawling bunkers and "beautiful views", including "the majesty of Yosemite on a clear day"; the "only downside" is the "two-plus hours" trek from San Francisco, so many say it's "worth the splurge" "to do a stay-and-play and visit the wine country too."

Stevinson Ranch

| 24 | 18 | 21 | 21 | $95 |

Stevinson | 2700 N. Van Clief Rd. | 209-668-8200 | 877-752-9276 | www.stevinsonranch.com | 7180/5461; 75.2/72.4; 143/126

"If you don't get lost and miss your tee time, this is a great track" say fans of this "challenging yet fair" "oasis in the Central Valley" that offers large, quick greens and "warm, laid-back service"; though some lament that it's located "in the middle of nowhere", "stay-and-play packages" provide an "opportunity to party with pals."

Colorado

TOP COURSES IN STATE

29 Red Sky, Fazio | *Vail*
28 Red Sky, Norman | *Vail*
   Raven at Three Peaks | *Vail*
27 Breckenridge | *Vail*
   Broadmoor, West | *Colorado Springs*

Boulder

Indian Peaks

▽ | 19 | 16 | 17 | 25 | $47 |

Lafayette | 2300 Indian Peaks Trail | 303-666-4706 | www.indianpeaksgolf.com | 7083/5420; 72.4/70.8; 131/123

Just 10 minutes from Boulder, this mostly open municipal designed by Hale Irwin is a "nice course" that meanders through a housing development, with "challenges" that include plenty of bunkers and water on a handful of holes; "generally in very good condition", the layout delivers "a fair value for the quality" thanks in part to the "great practice facility" and scenic views of the Rocky Mountains.

Mariana Butte

▽ | 18 | 14 | 20 | 22 | $58 |

Loveland | 701 Clubhouse Dr. | 970-667-8308 | www.golfloveland.com | 6724/5918; 71.3/67.1; 129/112

Located on heaving terrain just south of Fort Collins, this "beautiful" but relatively short layout provides a "fun" golfing experience, with an "especially enjoyable back nine" and several holes that skirt the Big

	COURSE	FACIL.	SERVICE	VALUE	COST

Thompson River; the aesthetic appeal is "somewhat lessened by houses on the course", but most still deem it well "worth the drive for the views" of the Rockies.

Colorado Springs

✦ Broadmoor, East 🏌 ⛳

| 27 | 27 | 27 | 22 | $240 |

Colorado Springs | 1 Lake Ave. | 719-577-5790 | www.broadmoor.com | 7355/5738; 74.0/72.8; 135/144

A "world-class destination" in Colorado Springs, this "historic" Donald Ross/RTJ Sr. layout has hosted a "myriad of championships", including the 2008 U.S. Senior Open; once you've taken "a round or two to master" the "difficult greens" (note: they "break away from the Will Rogers monument"), finish up with a "drink on the patio overlooking the 18th green."

✦ Broadmoor, Mountain 🏌 ⛳

| 25 | 26 | 26 | 21 | $205 |

Colorado Springs | 1 Lake Ave. | 719-577-5790 | www.broadmoor.com | 7637/4928; 75.7/67.7; 149/124

"Take your camera – it's perhaps more important than your clubs" – when you tackle this "exquisitely maintained" "mountain gem" that "meanders up and down the dizzying elevations" with a layout that was redone by Nicklaus Design in 2006 to feature "tough fairways" and "cruel greens"; "fantastic vistas overlooking Colorado Springs", "tremendous facilities" and "attentive" service lead many to conclude that it's "pricey, but you get what you pay for."

✦ Broadmoor, West 🏌 ⛳

| 27 | 28 | 28 | 24 | $205 |

Colorado Springs | 1 Lake Ave. | 719-577-5790 | www.broadmoor.com | 7016/5162; 70.7/70.5; 130/131

"It's a pleasure to play" this "classic" Donald Ross/RTJ Sr. design where "immaculate", "tree-lined fairways, lots of doglegs and contoured greens" combined with "spectacular views" and "abundant wildlife" make for a "top-notch" experience; part of an "excellent resort facility", it's a "breathtaking" "test of golf" that has "all the grandeur it deserves."

Cougar Canyon Golf Links

| - | - | - | - | $60 |

Trinidad | 3700 E. Main St. | 877-547-7455 | www.cougarcanyonliving.com | 7669/5327; 76.2/65.9; 143/102

Located in the old mining town of Trinidad, halfway between Albuquerque and Denver, this playable, if trouble-laden, 2007 residential layout by Chris Cochran of Nicklaus Design offers a rugged, high-desert experience, cocooned by volcanic, basalt-capped mesas and the Sangre de Christo Mountains; deep black sand bunkers and the 6,000-foot elevation are among the attractions, but unforgettable is the 163-yard, par-3 16th with its isolated green perched atop a mesa.

Four Mile Ranch

| - | - | - | - | $54 |

Canon City | 3501 Telegraph Trail | 719-275-5400 | www.fourmileranch.com | 7053/5373; 71.6/64.6; 126/101

Located some 35 miles southwest of Colorado Springs, this 2008 Jim Engh design relies not on the architect's signature muscle bunkers, but instead striking, dunelike landforms he calls 'hogbacks'; approach shots and drives play over and around these white shale

| | COURSE | FACIL. | SERVICE | VALUE | COST |

rock ridges, resulting in a lot of variety – but also many blind and semi-blind shots.

Walking Stick
▽ 22 | 18 | 16 | 20 | $44

Pueblo | 4301 Walking Stick Blvd. | 719-584-3400 | 7147/5181; 72.0/68.5; 134/119
An "interesting links design" from Arthur Hills and Keith Foster, this "beautiful" muni 45 minutes south of Colorado Springs serves up "many challenging holes" along with "nice practice facilities"; a few fret about the "dusty", "high-desert" conditions and claim the "service could use improvement", but others point out the course "has been a U.S. Open Qualifying site several times."

Denver

Arrowhead 🏞
23 | 19 | 20 | 20 | $120

Littleton | 10850 W. Sundown Trail | 303-973-9614 | www.arrowheadcolorado.com | 6636/5338; 71.7/65.9; 137/119
Thanks to the "spectacular red rocks", "you'll feel like you're golfing on Mars" at this "visual experience" that also includes "views of the Denver skyline" and of plentiful "deer, foxes and hawks"; while the scenery can be "distracting, leave it to RTJ Jr. to bring you back" to earth with a "tough but fair" design featuring "fast greens", "elevation changes" and a signature par-3 13th where you tee off between two "crazy, slanted formations."

Buffalo Run
20 | 19 | 18 | 22 | $44

Commerce City | 15700 E. 112th Ave. | 303-289-1500 | www.buffalorungolfcourse.com | 7411/5227; 74.5/68.6; 129/117
"One of the better midpriced golf courses in the Denver area", this "links-style" muni designed by Keith Foster is always in "good shape" and "fair for all abilities", featuring "lots of deep rough" and "strong prairie winds"; it's "close to the airport", but check your itinerary because "play can drag" – though most agree it's still "worth playing."

NEW CommonGround Golf Course 🚶
- | - | - | - | $52

Aurora | 10300 E. Golfers Way | 303-340-1520 | www.commongroundgc.com | 7500/5543; 72.9/65.1; 129/108
Architect Tom Doak rendered an extreme makeover of the old Mira Vista Golf Course, 15 minutes southwest of Downtown Denver, yanking out trees, restoring dense native grasses, adding strategically placed bunkers and crafting massive, fast and topsy-turvy greens; two water holes, vistas of the Rockies and the Denver skyline and three tough par-3s on the back nine are strong suits, but the affordability and walkability may be its biggest appeal.

Fossil Trace
25 | 21 | 20 | 22 | $79

Golden | 3050 Illinois St. | 303-277-8750 | www.fossiltrace.com | 6831/4681; 72.5/66.4; 139/119
"An easy drive from Denver", this "well-conditioned" Jim Engh-designed muni is a "unique experience" with "unusual hole layouts" that "take advantage of the landscape", such as the signature 12th with "fossil rock formations" in the fairway; some find it "gimmicky" and play often slows to a "dinosaur's pace" on weekends, but most consider it "thoroughly enjoyable" and "reasonably priced."

	COURSE	FACIL.	SERVICE	VALUE	COST

Fox Hollow at Lakewood
26 | 22 | 20 | 25 | $55

Lakewood | 13410 Morrison Rd. | 303-986-7888 |
www.lakewoodgolf.org
Canyon/Meadow | 6808/4473; 71.6/65.1; 135/111
Links/Canyon | 7030/4802; 73.0/66.1; 137/114
Meadow/Links | 6888/4835; 71.8/66.0; 132/115

Located in a "splendid setting at the base of the Rockies", this "tough" yet "playable" Lakewood layout offers "a little of everything" on three "well-kept" nines that "keep things interesting" with their "distinct personalities" and "memorable holes"; errant hitters are advised to bring "extra balls for the 'natural' areas", but they should have no problem affording another sleeve given the course's "tremendous value."

Green Valley Ranch
∇ 19 | 18 | 17 | 18 | $62

Denver | 4900 Himalaya Rd. | 303-371-3131 | www.gvrgolf.com |
7042/4935; 73.4/63.7; 135/104

Situated in a breeze-fueled prairie landscape, this frequent home of the Colorado Open is a "nice Perry Dye track" that's "interesting for the average player" with its "variety of holes" and "easy-to-get-to" location near Denver's airport; it's "usually in good shape", and there's also a grass driving range and golf academy to help you get the best "bang for your buck."

Legacy Ridge
∇ 23 | 21 | 19 | 23 | $62

Westminster | 10801 Legacy Ridge Pkwy. | 303-438-8997 |
www.golfwestminster.com | 7157/5315; 73.1/71.4; 138/139

Set on the edge of a wildlife sanctuary northwest of Denver, this "nicely maintained" municipal designed by Arthur Hills strikes some as "almost too tough to play", with plenty of bunkers and lakes plus "native grass areas" that are "so high during the summer you might lose your ball *and* your golfing partner"; still, the "decent facilities" and "affordable" greens fees help make it a "great value."

Murphy Creek
∇ 21 | 19 | 17 | 22 | $46

Aurora | 1700 S. Old Tom Morris Rd. | 303-361-7300 | www.golfaurora.com |
7548/5335; 75.5/69.8; 139/128

Though it's "in the plains region", "you can see the mountains in the distance" at this "fabulous" if "no-frills" public "links layout" from architect Ken Kavanaugh that's "more convenient to Denver than you'd think from a map"; some grouse about the "houses on top of the holes" on the back nine, but the risk/reward front dotted with stylish bunkers and old farm equipment is "serene", and you "can't beat the price."

Pole Creek
∇ 25 | 17 | 18 | 24 | $99

Winter Park | 5827 County Rd. 51 | 970-887-9195 | 800-511-5076 |
www.polecreekgolf.com
Meadow/Ranch | 6895/4863; 73.7/69.0; 145/127
Ranch/Ridge | 7065/4985; 73.5/69.2; 139/128
Ridge/Meadow | 6958/4942; 73.6/67.9; 136/132

Located on the southwestern edge of Rocky Mountain National Park, this "awesome mountain course" is "worth the trip" from Denver to sample 27 holes that offer "good variety", with "fun elevation changes", lodgepole pines and the namesake creek all influencing play; some suggest it "isn't always fair", but the "beauty and peacefulness of the area make this an unbelievable golf experience."

	COURSE	FACIL.	SERVICE	VALUE	COST

Red Hawk Ridge
	24	20	23	24	$79

Castle Rock | 2156 Red Hawk Ridge Dr. | 303-663-7150 |
www.redhawkridge.com | 6942/4654; 71.8/66.1; 130/111

"Another interesting Jim Engh course" that "makes you happy you live in Colorado", this "outstanding muni" features "elevated tees" offering "sweeping views of the mountains and plains on the south side of Denver"; it's a "value" that will "challenge" you with "elevation changes" and a pond-guarded closing hole, leading some to dub it a "poor man's" version of the ultraswank private club Castle Pines.

Ridge at Castle Pines North
	25	25	24	21	$145

Castle Rock | 1414 Castle Pines Pkwy. | 303-688-0100 |
www.theridgecpn.com | 7013/5011; 73.0/67.6; 134/123

A "stunning buttelike course with 200-mile views to Pikes Peak", this Tom Weiskopf design is kept in "top condition", with two "awesome" nines featuring "different topography" (hills on the front, woods on the back); the "amazing clubhouse" is another plus, so while it's "expensive" and "out of the way", it's "worth the drive to Castle Rock."

Riverdale, Dunes
	25	18	19	26	$46

Brighton | 13300 Riverdale Rd. | 303-659-6700 | www.riverdalegolf.com |
7067/4884; 73.3/62.7; 134/109

For the "best value in the state", head north of Denver to this Pete and Perry Dye experience in the "prairie lands of the Front Range", where you'll pay a "mere pittance" to tackle a "tough but fair" links-style muni that twists along the South Platte River, with lots of water and railroad ties to make it "harder than it looks"; it's "not fancy", to be sure, but it's "always in fantastic shape."

Saddle Rock
	▽ 22	19	19	24	$49

Aurora | 21705 E. Arapahoe Rd. | 303-699-3939 | www.auroragov.org |
7351/5407; 74.7/71.9; 140/126

"Local knowledge is the key to success" on this "tricky" Dick Phelps design, a "must-play for serious golfers" thanks to the presence of natural wetlands and undulating terrain; this "well-maintained muni" is a "great value in the Denver area", and if you plan ahead, the course's proximity to the airport will allow you to "play and catch a flight on the same day."

Grand Junction

Lakota Canyon Ranch 🏞
	▽ 25	12	17	25	$89

New Castle | 1000 Club House Dr. | 970-984-9700 |
www.lakotacanyonranch.com | 7111/4744; 72.5/65.9; 147/110

"If you're afraid of heights, don't play" this "beautiful, challenging" Jim Engh course that "wows" with a "magnificent front nine" featuring dramatic elevation changes as well as "great views" of the rugged canyons and soaring mountains surrounding New Castle; the fairways and greens are generally well kept, making this "scenic" spread "worth the money."

Redlands Mesa
	26	23	23	24	$89

Grand Junction | 2299 W. Ridge Blvd. | 970-263-9270 |
www.redlandsmesa.com | 7007/4890; 72.1/69.0; 137/115

It's "worth the drive to the Western Slope" to experience one of Colorado's "most beautiful and challenging mountain golf courses", this "fantastic" "test of golf" designed by Jim Engh includes "lots of el-

COURSE · FACIL. · SERVICE · VALUE · COST

evation changes" – there's a 150-ft. drop on the par-3 17th – and "awesome scenery", including red sandstone buttes and bluffs; if some find it "too tricked-up", the "scenic" views and "challenging golf" make it a "must-play" for most.

Vail

Beaver Creek 📧 ⚬⚐ ⏱

23 | 21 | 24 | 20 | $185

Beaver Creek | 103 Offerson Rd. | 970-845-5775 | www.beavercreek.com | 6784/5088; 71.0/69.3; 140/131

"Vail Valley golf at its finest" is what some call this "narrow" RTJ Jr.-designed Beaver Creek course where "stunning views", "running water everywhere and deer to feed at the tee box" "add to the sensory delight"; some suggest there are "too many side-by-side holes for the price", but most find it a "pleasure", although "missing the fairway means your ball rolls down the mountain."

Breckenridge

27 | 23 | 22 | 21 | $114

Breckenridge | 200 Clubhouse Dr. | 970-453-9104 | www.breckenridgegolfclub.com
Bear/Beaver | 7276/5063; 73.9/68.3; 147/133
Beaver/Elk | 7145/4908; 72.9/68.1; 146/133
Elk/Bear | 7257/5045; 74.0/68.4; 145/137

A staggering 9,324 feet above sea level, this "superb" 27-hole municipal has an "excellent routing and hole design" by Jack Nicklaus, making it "the one course you'll want to play when visiting Summit County"; although it's "a bit expensive" "due to the location and short season", it's "a great vacation spot for the family" thanks to "outstanding" scenery, a "cool" climate in the summer and a staff that "treats you like a regular."

Cordillera, Mountain 🏌 📧 ⚬⚐ ⏱

27 | 26 | 26 | 21 | $237

Edwards | 650 Club House Dr. | 970-926-5100 | www.cordillera-vail.com | 7413/6186; 73.6/68.0; 141/130

"One of the prettiest courses you will ever play", this "challenging" Hale Irwin design is "built along the side of Cordillera's rugged mountain terrain", with "tight fairways, small greens" and "serious elevation changes"; although kept "in perfect condition", it's "best to play July through mid-September" because "the grass doesn't have a very long growing season" here – although the "incredible service" and scenery make it an "invigorating" experience "any time."

Cordillera, Summit 🏌 📧 ⚬⚐ ⏱

27 | 27 | 26 | 23 | $237

Edwards | 190 Gore Trail | 970-926-5300 | www.cordillera-vail.com | 7530/5239; 74.4/69.4; 137/129

"Golf at 9,200 feet just doesn't get any better" than this "remarkable" course at the "peak of a mountain", where a "long" links layout "with extensive heather surrounding most of the fairways" and "fast", "undulating greens" "reveals the dark side of Jack Nicklaus as a designer"; on the bright side are "top-notch service" and "breathtaking views."

Cordillera, Valley 🏌 📧 ⚬⚐

24 | 26 | 24 | 22 | $232

Edwards | 101 Legends Dr. | 970-926-5950 | www.cordillera-vail.com | 7005/6033; 73.2/67.2; 138/123

Located "on the floor of the Vail Valley", this "unsung hero of Cordillera" is "the most playable of the three" courses, offering an "interesting layout" from Tom Fazio that "winds through low desert terrain", with "scenic" mountain vistas, and "long par 5s and 3s [to] ensure it's a challenge for all"; the practice facilities are "awesome ", and you can "ski in the morning and play 18 in the afternoon."

Eagle Vail 🏌

| 18 | 16 | 18 | 18 | $98 |

Avon | 459 Eagle Dr. | 970-949-5267 | 800-341-8051 |
www.eaglevailgolfclub.com | 6590/4819; 71.3/68.9; 131/120

"Huge elevation changes", "beautiful views of the Eagle River" and mountain vistas highlight this Vail Valley course, and while it's located on the valley floor it still "plays at an altitude where the ball carries about two clubs farther"; some are cool to "tricked-up" holes and "only fair facilities", but most laud this "beautiful" – and "reasonably priced" – layout, which is undergoing a sustainability project to enhance playabilty.

Keystone Ranch, Ranch

| 25 | 23 | 23 | 21 | $140 |

Keystone | 1239 Keystone Ranch Rd. | 970-496-4250 |
www.keystonegolf.com | 7085/5842; 72.5/69.9; 137/128

One of "two awesome courses" affiliated with the Keystone Lodge, this "classic RTJ Jr. layout" is situated at 9,300 feet "in a spectacular high mountain valley" with "beautiful views" of the Gore Range; a few feel it's "not as exciting as the River course", but it offers "plenty of trouble, with some long carries" over streams, ponds and bunkers; P.S. be sure to try the "outstanding restaurant" too.

Keystone Ranch, River

| 26 | 24 | 23 | 23 | $170 |

Keystone | 155 River Course Rd. | 970-496-4250 | www.keystonegolf.com |
6886/4762; 70.8/65.1; 132/123

"If you think this 'river' course is going to be flat, think again", because this "gorgeous" Hurdzan/Fry–designed "mountain course" includes "great elevation changes", starting with the first tee, which sits 150 feet above the fairway; the "subtle and not-so-subtle challenges" include holes that cross the Snake River and slender fairways, but given the "beautiful views", most consider it a "wonderful place to lose golf balls."

☑ Raven at Three Peaks 🏌 ⏲

| 28 | 23 | 22 | 23 | $149 |

Silverthorne | 2929 N. Golden Eagle Rd. | 970-262-3636 |
www.ravenatthreepeaks.com | 7413/5235; 74.2/65.3; 146/117

"Stunning views", "unbelievable elevation changes" and groves of aspen combine to produce "mountain golf at its best" say fans of this "spectacular" layout in Silverthorne that also features alpine streams, sprawling fingered bunkers and an "eagle's nest off of one of the holes"; the track itself is kept "in great condition", although some "hardly notice, with all of the unforgettable sights."

☑ Red Sky, Fazio 🏌 ⟳

| 29 | 26 | 27 | 23 | $250 |

Wolcott | 376 Red Sky Rd. | 970-754-8425 | 866-873-3759 |
www.redskygolfclub.com | 7113/5265; 72.0/68.2; 135/125

"You will not be disappointed" with the top-rated Course in Colorado, this "spectacular" Tom Fazio design set on a "stunning tract of land" with "lots of elevation changes", "challenging greens", "breathtaking views" and "a friendly staff"; the sagebrush- and aspen-framed fairways are "immaculate", so although it's "very expensive", this "memorable", "must-play in the Beaver Creek area" will provide you with a "true private golf course experience."

	COURSE	FACIL.	SERVICE	VALUE	COST

⛳ Red Sky, Norman 🏌⛳ 28 | 27 | 27 | 24 | $250

Wolcott | 376 Red Sky Rd. | 970-754-8425 | 866-873-3759 |
www.redskygolfclub.com | 7580/5269; 74.2/65.5; 144/124

Part of an "amazing facility that will take your breath away", this "challenging" Greg Norman design is a "great complement to the Fazio course", offering some "unforgettable" "up-and-down" holes with "fantastic views of the mountains" in a "spectacular" resort setting near Beaver Creek; while "challenging", the course "can accommodate all skill levels", and with a "wonderful clubhouse", it's a "real treat."

Sonnenalp ⊕ ▽ 23 | 23 | 22 | 19 | $130

Edwards | 1265 Berry Creek Rd. | 970-477-5370 |
www.sonnenalpgolfclub.com | 7074/5174; 73.8/69.6; 142/131

Situated on "pretty terrain in the heart of the Vail Valley", this "solid" Bob Cupp/Jay Morrish design is "a nice mellow course with a few challenging holes" and a "9,000-ft. elevation" that means "the ball goes a mile" over meadows, streams and sagebrush; it's "a great vantage point for [viewing] the Rockies", and while a few find it "quite pricey", the "fantastic facilities" and "lovely clubhouse" make it "worth playing."

Connecticut

Danbury

Richter Park 25 | 15 | 17 | 22 | $77

Danbury | 100 Aunt Hack Rd. | 203-792-2552 | www.richterpark.com |
6744/5114; 73.6/70.7; 139/124

"Even a crusty Yankee will enjoy" this "big, bold", "shot-makers" municipal that's "built around a reservoir", with "lots of water", "doglegs, elevation changes and an island green or two"; sure, the cost is "steep", it's "hard to get a tee time" for out-of-towners and it "lacks a driving range and smiling faces in the pro shop", but its "fine putting surfaces", "new bunkering" and "nice restaurant add to its appeal."

East Haddam

Fox Hopyard 24 | 23 | 22 | 21 | $104

East Haddam | 1 Hopyard Rd. | 860-434-6644 | 800-943-1903 |
www.golfthefox.com | 6912/5111; 74.1/70.9; 136/127

"One of the prettiest courses in Connecticut", this "challenging", "championship" layout located "off the beaten path" in East Haddam pairs "fabulous New England views" and a "country feel" with "well-laid-out" "risk/reward" holes that'll "take your breath away"; the "private-club ambiance", "attentive staff", "elegant clubhouse" and "nicely stocked pro shop" round out the experience.

Hartford

Gillette Ridge 🏌 20 | 19 | 18 | 17 | $65

Bloomfield | 1360 Hall Blvd. | 860-726-1430 | www.gilletteridgegolf.com |
7191/5582; 74.8/67.2; 135/117

A "nice addition to the Hartford area golf scene", this "solid" Arnold Palmer design "in the middle of an office park complex" is a "challenge from the tips", with "forced carries" and a few "over-demanding holes" that strike some as "not very playable"; although the layout "has improved" since opening in 2004, critics take issue with the "minimal facilities" and relatively "unmotivated staff."

Lyman Orchards, Gary Player 🏌 | 18 | 17 | 19 | 20 | $46 |

Middlefield | 70 Lyman Rd. | 888-995-9626 | www.lymangolf.com | 6725/4900; 72.7/68.3; 133/118

A "summer staple", this "quirky" Gary Player design is a "hilly", "challenging", "target-style course" that requires "many blind shots" and "forced lay-ups", but is "very fair once you learn not to hit the driver every time"; some suggest it's "too tricked-up", but most consider it a "bang for the buck" thanks in part to the "friendly staff" and "incredible" orchard scenery – "you can even pick apples from the trees" as you play.

Lyman Orchards, Robert Trent Jones | 20 | 17 | 19 | 21 | $46 |

Middlefield | 70 Lyman Rd. | 888-995-9626 | www.lymangolf.com | 7011/5812; 73.3/72.0; 132/124

An "old-school RTJ Sr. course" built in 1969, this "picturesque" layout 30 minutes south of Hartford is a "solid, fun and playable" track where you can "grip it and rip it" down "reachable par 5s" featuring "wide fairways", "abundant" water hazards and "treacherous greens"; "it meanders along a river", however, so it can get "soggy on a not-so-great day", although the apple-picking and "farmer's market always makes it a fun trip."

Wintonbury Hills | 26 | 19 | 21 | 21 | $79 |

Bloomfield | 206 Terry Plains Rd. | 860-242-1401 | www.wintonburyhills.com | 6711/5005; 72.3/68.6; 130/111

It's "worth the drive from lower Connecticut" to visit this "upscale" "gem" designed by "master architect" Pete Dye, who – for a fee of only $1 – "gave the town of Bloomfield a marvelous course" that's "playable" "for all levels", with "wide fairways" and "extremely firm greens" that are "always in top-notch shape"; a "friendly, efficient staff" adds to an experience that is "at its most beautiful in the fall."

New Haven

Great River | 25 | 25 | 24 | 19 | $140 |

Milford | 130 Coram Ln. | 203-876-8051 | 877-478-7470 | www.greatrivergolfclub.com | 7060/4997; 75.2/70.4; 150/128

"Worth the drive from Manhattan in I-95 traffic", this "phenomenal" Milford option offers "fabulous views" of the Housatonic River from a back nine that "will bring you to your knees" with "lots of hazards to catch stray balls"; while it's "pricier than most in Connecticut", you can expect a "country-club-for-a-day" experience complete with "top-notch conditions", "superb practice facilities" and an ambiance that exudes "class, from the minute you drop off your bag."

Oxford Greens 🏌 | 22 | 18 | 20 | 19 | $79 |

Oxford | 99 Country Club Dr. | 203-888-1600 | www.oxfordgreens.com | 7186/5188; 74.9/69.9; 134/122

From "soup to nuts", this "beautiful course" northwest of New Haven is "doing it right", offering "isolated" holes with "fairly wide fairways", "no forced carries" and "fast, undulating greens"; although a few fret about "slow play on weekends", "sloped fairways" that "penalize a good tee shot" and houses that are "closing in", most consider it a "great value for the buck" that's run by "nice people."

New London

Lake of Isles, North 🖳

| 28 | 25 | 25 | 18 | $199 |

North Stonington | 1 Clubhouse Dr. | 888-475-3746 | www.lakeofisles.com | 7252/4937; 76.6/68.9; 146/127

"Rees Jones did a masterful job" on Connecticut's top-rated Course, this "brutally long" "target-golf" design that requires "a number of substantial forced carries" as it "winds through a wonderfully preserved area" showcasing "beautiful New England scenery"; Troon Golf management provides "top-shelf service and maintenance", but "perfection does come at a cost", so you may want to head "across the street to Foxwoods" and "double-down that blackjack bet to win enough for the greens fees."

Shennecossett

| 20 | 13 | 17 | 24 | $47 |

Groton | 93 Plant St. | 860-445-0262 | www.shennygolf.com | 6562/5351; 71.7/70.9; 124/123

A "must-play for anyone who loves Donald Ross", "Shenny is a grand old" "traditional" "links-style layout located "right on Long Island Sound" in Groton, with "spectacular views" offering a counterpoint to the "subtle and understated" design with "wide-open fairways" "made challenging by the strategic placement of sand traps"; while some caution "you're not going to find great facilities or service", many "locals and travelers" "simply can't pass up a great bargain."

Stamford

Sterling Farms

| 19 | 16 | 16 | 20 | $50 |

Stamford | 1349 Newfield Ave. | 203-461-9090 | www.sterlingfarmsgc.com | 6509/5539; 71.7/73.3; 129/124

"Get warmed up for the season" at this "above-average" "utility course for all levels", a "well-maintained muni" featuring "open fairways, tight greens" and a "challenging" but "playable" back nine; although it can get "crowded", resulting in "slow play", it's "extremely cheap for residents" of Stamford, and the "covered, heated range", "two restaurants and putting area" add to its "excellent value."

Delaware

Rehoboth Beach

Bayside 🖳

| 26 | 20 | 23 | 21 | $179 |

Selbyville | 31806 Lakeview Dr. | 302-436-3400 | 877-436-9998 | www.livebayside.com | 7545/5165; 76.5/64.9; 139/112

"Jack Nicklaus has designed a masterpiece in Delaware" proclaim proponents of this "pristine" course considered one of "the best in the Ocean City" area thanks to an "awesome", "difficult" layout with "greens that show no mercy" and "excellent conditioning"; it boasts views of Assawoman Bay, and if some find the peak rates "a bit salty", it can still be a "good value in the off-season"; the post-Survey addition of a 7,300-sq.-ft. clubhouse may not be reflected in the Facilities score.

Baywood Greens
26 | 25 | 25 | 24 | $119

Long Neck | 32267 Clubhouse Way | 302-947-9800 | 888-844-2254 | www.baywoodgreens.com | 6983/5136; 73.4/70.9; 135/124
Dubbed the "Augusta of the Mid-Atlantic", this "plush", "impeccable" layout is the "best in the Rehoboth area, bar none", thanks to its "challenging water holes" and "amazing flower arrangements"; a "courteous staff" and a "clubhouse that looks like a European castle" add to the "special" experience, and though it can be "crowded" and "expensive", it's "worth it" to play a track that's "beautiful even in winter."

Bear Trap Dunes
21 | 18 | 19 | 18 | $120

Ocean View | 7 Clubhouse Dr. | 302-537-5600 | 877-232-7872 | www.beartrapdunes.com
Black Bear/Grizzly | 6901/5094; 72.7/69.4; 130/121
Black Bear/Kodiak | 6853/5074; 72.4/69.1; 130/118
Grizzly/Kodiak | 6834/5208; 72.1/69.8; 126/120
"If you're staying near Bethany Beach, there's no need to go anywhere else" aver admirers of this "solid" links-style layout that "allows for a varied experience", with "27 excellent holes" set amid the dunes ("sand and beach grasses are the challenge for errant shots"); "decent" course conditions, a "nice staff and great practice facilities" are all pluses, and while "the golf is relatively easy", it's "not too easy", so "everyone can enjoy the experience."

Wilmington

Back Creek ⚐
▽ 21 | 18 | 19 | 21 | $48

Middletown | 101 Back Creek Dr. | 302-378-6499 | www.backcreekgc.com | 7113/5186; 74.7/65.3; 134/122
Set on farmland once owned by Delaware's first governor, this Middletown option is considered "one of the best in the Wilmington area" thanks to a "thoughtful layout" that offers "wide fairways", "big, undulating greens" and a "variety of shot options"; there's "not much water but enough to get your attention", and while a few feel the "staff sometimes appears to prefer locals", the spread is "always in very good shape."

Florida

TOP COURSES IN STATE

29 | TPC Sawgrass, PLAYERS Stadium | *Jacksonville*
28 | World Woods, Pine Barrens | *Tampa*
     Camp Creek | *Panhandle*
27 | Arnold Palmer's Bay Hill | *Orlando*
     Hammock Beach Resort, Ocean | *Daytona Beach*
     Kelly Plantation | *Panhandle*
     Innisbrook, Copperhead | *Tampa*
     Doral, TPC Blue Monster | *Miami*
     Hammock Beach Resort, Conservatory | *Daytona Beach*
26 | Orange County National, Panther Lake | *Orlando*

Daytona Beach

Hammock Beach Resort, Conservatory ⌘ ⚲

27	24	26	22	$169

Palm Coast | 300 Conservatory Dr. | 386-246-6710 |
www.hammockbeach.com | 7776/5087; 78.2/70.2; 150/123

A "triumph of the bulldozer's art", this "Tom Watson beauty" is in "excellent condition", with "maximum length" plus "plenty of bunkers, elevated greens" and a "cart-path minimal layout that uses waste areas of hard sand"; it's part of an "impressive facility" that includes a clubhouse built in the style of an English conservatory, one more reason fans urge "if you have the chance, go in a heartbeat."

Hammock Beach Resort, Ocean ⌘ ⚲

27	26	26	22	$169

Palm Coast | 105 16th St. | 386-447-4611 | www.hammockbeach.com |
7201/5115; 77.0/71.5; 147/131

"Anyone visiting the St. Augustine area" should try this "breathtaking" Jack Nicklaus design boasting "fantastic ocean views" from a "well-manicured" track that "will punish you", so "bring your A-game" and "avoid it on a real windy day"; the "interesting layout" (the "18th is really something") is "expensive" but it's part of a "first-class resort" that will "treat you special from check-in to check-out."

LPGA International, Champions ⌘

24	24	23	22	$74

Daytona Beach | 1000 Champions Dr. | 386-274-5742 |
www.lpgainternational.com | 7088/5131; 74.8/70.0; 145/123

A "must-play if you're in the Daytona Beach area", this "well-kept" Rees Jones "gem" is "fun" for "all skill levels" – men and women alike; a few say it's "not as exciting" as they expected, with roomy fairways and "a lot of sand" on a layout that's the "polar opposite of its Legends" sibling, but the facilities at the LPGA national headquarters help make it a "great value."

LPGA International, Legends ⌘

25	26	26	24	$74

Daytona Beach | 1000 Champions Dr. | 386-274-5742 |
www.lpgainternational.com | 6984/5155; 74.6/69.9; 148/119

Even though it's located at the LPGA's Daytona Beach headquarters, "men are allowed to play" Arthur Hills' "wonderful" track where "narrow fairways require a high level of skill", and there's just "enough water and sand, but not too much"; some consider it the "better of the two layouts" on-site, but both boast a "friendly" staff and "nice facilities", including the "museum"-like clubhouse, at a "good price."

Victoria Hills

25	20	25	26	$55

Deland | 300 Spalding Way | 386-738-6000 | 866-295-4385 |
www.victoriahillsgolf.com | 7149/4902; 74.2/67.8; 141/116

"It's like Pinehurst in Florida" gush golfers who've tried this "amazing" Ron Garl design, a layout lined in towering pines, with "inspired bunkering" and "quirkily shaped greens as the primary defense"; it's a "real challenge", and while "the addition of housing detracts from the ambiance", the "excellent practice facility" and "friendly" staff help make it "worth the drive" southwest of Daytona Beach.

Ft. Lauderdale

Club at Emerald Hills 🏌

25 | 20 | 20 | 21 | $150

Hollywood | 4100 N. Hills Dr. | 954-961-4000 |
www.theclubatemeraldhills.com | 7368/4939; 76.1/69.2; 145/121

A "hidden gem" five miles south of Ft. Lauderdale, this "impeccably maintained" layout boasts "perfect greens", "plenty of water" and "some exciting elevation" that's "unheard of in South Florida"; though some say the "facilities are out-of-date and the service is ok", admirers insist it "deserves more respect" as a "great track in an area where it's difficult to find standout courses."

Heron Bay 🏌

19 | 21 | 21 | 17 | $99

Coral Springs | 11801 Heron Bay Blvd. | 954-796-2000 | 800-511-6616 |
www.heronbaygolfclub.net | 7268/4961; 74.9/68.7; 133/113

Although it's "not part of the TPC family anymore", this "fun" "test of skills" designed by Mark McCumber offers "its fair share of challenging holes"; still, a few find it "uninspiring" – "just sand and wind" (watch out for "free dermabrasion when the wind blows") on a "flat" layout – but it's kept "in good condition" and is a "value for a former PGA Tour course."

Ft. Myers

Old Corkscrew 🏌

25 | 22 | 23 | 20 | $169

Estero | 17320 Corkscrew Rd. | 239-949-4700 | www.oldcorkscrew.com |
7393/5161; 77.6/69.7; 153/123

"Probably the best course in the Ft. Myers region", this "tough but pretty" Jack Nicklaus Signature is "carved out of the Everglades", with "no houses" in sight; while those "not used to waste bunkers" cry "yikes", most agree it "will be spectacular when it matures" and is already a "scenic" destination – "so many birds to view" – and thus "definitely worth the drive."

Jacksonville

Amelia Island Plantation, Long Point 🏌 ⛳

24 | 24 | 22 | 19 | $150

Amelia Island | 6800 First Coast Hwy. | 904-277-5907 | 888-261-6161 |
www.aipfl.com | 6567/4863; 72.2/69.0; 136/121

"Clearly the best of the bunch" at Amelia Island Plantation, this "brilliant", "well-maintained" Tom Fazio design is a "challenging" "shotmakers course" that dishes out "some beautiful ocean holes" as well as "inland waterway vistas"; a few say it's "a bit overpriced", but it offers a "nice mixture of holes" along with "outstanding facilities and service" at a luxurious seaside resort (which is currently undergoing an $85 million renovation).

Amelia Island Plantation, Oak Marsh 🏌 ⛳

23 | 24 | 24 | 21 | $150

Amelia Island | 6800 First Coast Hwy. | 904-277-5907 | 888-261-6161 |
www.aipfl.com | 6580/4983; 72.2/70.7; 136/124

Offering "interesting links-style" holes with "tricky greens" and "tremendous views" of moss-draped oaks and Intracoastal wetlands, this "mature" early Pete Dye design is "another great course" at the "family-friendly" Amelia Island Plantation resort; "if you can overlook" the "large number of homes" on-site, you'll discover a "solid" spread kept in "great shape" by a "fantastic", "professional" staff, all of which adds up to an "enjoyable experience."

Amelia Island Plantation, Ocean Links 🏊 ⚓

23 | 23 | 24 | 21 | $150

Amelia Island | 6800 First Coast Hwy. | 904-277-5907 | 888-261-6161 | www.aipfl.com | 6108/4341; 69.3/66.4; 128/115

With a "scenic back nine" set "right next to the ocean", this "exciting" Pete Dye/Bobby Weed design sports "some of the most picturesque golf holes in Florida" on a layout that's "not particularly long but is narrow enough to challenge the better player" – that is, when "you're not staring at the view"; "having to play through homes" on the resort property makes the rest of the course seem "pedestrian", but still, it remains an "exceptional experience."

Ponte Vedra Beach Inn, Ocean ⚓

22 | 25 | 26 | 21 | $240

Ponte Vedra Beach | 200 Ponte Vedra Blvd. | 904-285-1111 | 800-234-7842 | www.pvresorts.com | 6817/4967; 73.3/69.5; 138/117

"One of the finest old courses in northern Florida", this "beautiful" 1920s-era track is "short" but sports some "great par 3s", including "the original island hole" (the 9th) that's "only yards from the Atlantic"; renovated by Bobby Weed in 1998, it can be a "real challenge" thanks to "tight Bermuda grass lies", "turtleback greens" and "coastal winds", and while a few find it "expensive", you can always combine it with a stay at the "lodge on the ocean."

🏆 TPC Sawgrass, Dye's Valley 🏌 ⏱

25 | 28 | 26 | 22 | $195

Ponte Vedra Beach | 110 Championship Way | 904-273-3235 | 888-421-8555 | www.tpcsawgrass.com | 6864/5126; 74.1/65.0; 137/115

It's "well worth the effort" to seek out this "hidden gem" in north Florida that serves as a "wonderful warm-up to the Stadium course" with its "good shot values, water-lined fairways and small greens"; it's "without the flash and history" of "its more famous brother", but many suggest this Pete Dye creation "does not get its just due", citing the "great family tee concept", "top-of-the-line service" and "phenomenal clubhouse."

🏆 TPC Sawgrass, PLAYERS Stadium 🏌 ⚓

29 | 28 | 27 | 23 | $395

Ponte Vedra Beach | 110 Championship Way | 904-273-3235 | 888-421-8555 | www.tpcsawgrass.com | 7215/5019; 76.5/72.1; 155/135

"Bring your A+ game" to Ponte Vedra Beach and "play where the big boys play" at Florida's top-rated Course, this "awesomely hard" Pete Dye design that's "one of the finest traditional golf clubs in the U.S." – and "just as brutal as on TV"; the "famous island green on the 17th" is "worth the visit alone", but you'll also "treasure the memory" of the "meticulous" conditions, the "warm, unpretentious staff" and the "mind-blowing" "Taj Mahal of clubhouses."

	COURSE	FACIL.	SERVICE	VALUE	COST

World Golf Village, King & Bear ⏱

| 24 | 25 | 24 | 21 | $129 |

St. Augustine | 1 King & Bear Dr. | 904-940-6200 | www.golfwgv.com | 7279/5119; 74.1/69.1; 138/124

An "incredible" "Nicklaus/Palmer co-design", this "excellent" example of "cooperation between two of golf's greats" is "always in perfect shape", and regulars insist "you can tell which holes were designed by Jack and which by Arnie – nine high power fades and nine hard hooks"; a "pleasant staff" and "terrific facilities" (including a "tour of the Hall of Fame") complete the picture.

World Golf Village, Slammer & Squire ⏱

| 24 | 26 | 25 | 21 | $99 |

St. Augustine | 2 World Golf Pl. | 904-940-6100 | www.golfwgv.com | 6939/4996; 72.7/68.0; 127/115

Set at the "awesome World Golf Village", this Bobby Weed design features "wide-open fairways" and "some great holes where you can get home in two as well as drive the green"; all in all, it's a "solid", "enjoyable course" that's "worth playing" thanks to "nice conditions" and "great facilities" that include the "excellent Golf Hall of Fame nearby" to "unwind at after a draining round."

Miami

Biltmore

| 20 | 22 | 21 | 19 | $209 |

Coral Gables | 1210 Anastasia Ave. | 305-460-5364 | www.biltmorehotel.com | 6742/6303; 72.1/70.2; 126/124

"The Biltmore Hotel is a beautiful backdrop" for "one of the hidden gems of South Florida", this "authentically restored 1926 Donald Ross course" that's "markedly better since the redo" in 2007, particularly when it comes to the "excellent conditions" and "much improved pro shop"; it's "not too challenging" but is "enjoyable" enough that you'll "want to play more than once" – even if the "greens fees are a bit much" for a muni.

Crandon 🏞

| 23 | 18 | 18 | 22 | $180 |

Key Biscayne | 6700 Crandon Blvd. | 305-361-9120 | www.crandongolfclub.com | 7301/5423; 76.2/71.8; 145/130

A "unique course" that "juts out into Biscayne Bay" just 25 minutes from South Beach, this "splendid walk in an unspoiled park" – i.e. "through a mangrove" forest – boasts "breathtaking views of Miami's skyline"; "tropical fauna, iguanas and birds roam" the "tough, slightly mounded, water-laden layout", and while the muni facilities are "nothing special", it's a "good dollar value" overall, so just do "*après*-golf at the beach."

Doral, Gold 🏌

| 21 | 24 | 23 | 19 | $175 |

Miami | 4400 NW 87th Ave. | 305-592-2030 | 800-713-6725 | www.doralresort.com | 6639/5159; 72.2/69.8; 135/117

"A break after playing the 'Monster'", this "terrific test" is perhaps the "most enjoyable at Doral", with "shorter tees and somewhat tight fairways" that present just "enough hazards to make it challenging for an 11 handicap"; although it's a bit tarnished by "average conditions" and lots of "look-alike houses", it's still a "pleasant" option thanks to "great practice and training facilities" as well as a "staff that does a very nice job."

Doral, Great White 🏌

| 22 | 25 | 23 | 19 | $225 |

Miami | 4400 NW 87th Ave. | 305-592-2030 | 800-713-6725 | www.doralresort.com | 7171/5026; 74.5/67.8; 134/117

"One of Greg Norman's finest achievements", this "desert course in Florida" "looks more like Arizona than Miami" thanks to "fairways lined with palm trees and edged with crushed coquina shells"; a few find it "gimmicky", but most praise the "excellent par 3s" and "top-class facilities", concluding "if you can't get onto the Blue Monster, this will eat you up just as well."

NEW Doral, Jim McLean 🏌

| - | - | - | - | $325 |

Miami | 4400 N.W. 87th Ave. | 305-592-2000 | www.doralresort.com | 7100/6200; 75.6/69.5; 153/128

Doral's legendary instructor, Jim McLean, overhauled its 30-year-old off-campus Silver course in 2009 and the result is a water-drenched design with a 153 slope that plays even tougher than the resort's fabled TPC Blue Monster course, a PGA Tour site since 1962; a killer trio of narrow, lake-lined par 4s opens the round, but the real fun arrives at the 'Bermuda Triangle' of holes 13-15, where two beefy par 4s bracket the island green par-3 14th.

☒ Doral, TPC Blue Monster 🏌

| 27 | 26 | 23 | 19 | $325 |

Miami | 4400 NW 87th Ave. | 305-592-2030 | 800-713-6725 | www.doralresort.com | 7288/5392; 76.8/71.3; 143/126

"Tee it high and let it fly" but "leave your ego at the door" when playing this "legendary" PGA Tour stop, a "top-tier" track that will leave you "shaking in your soft spikes" with its "firm, fast fairways", "treacherous hazards" and "punishing rough" sure to "eat you alive"; yes, it's "probably too expensive", but it's "worth the price of admission" to tackle "this famous monster of South Florida lore."

Normandy Shores

| - | - | - | - | $120 |

Miami Beach | 2401 Biarritz Dr. | 305-868-6502 | www.normandyshoresgolfclub.com | 6805/5889; 72.5/68.7; 129/119

An $8 million makeover by Arthur Hills completed in 2008 breathed new life into this 68-year-old muni sitting adjacent to Biscayne Bay on man made Normandy Isle; it relies on subtlety to test all skill levels, so look for strategic bunkering and contouring on holes like the 325-yard, par-4 12th, which offers multiple legitimate options for approaching the green.

Turnberry Isle Resort, Miller (fka Fairmont Turnberry) 🏌🏊⛳

| 23 | 27 | 25 | 19 | $225 |

Aventura | 19999 West Country Club Dr. | 305-933-6929 | www.turnberryislemiami.com | 6417/5100; 74.9/62.2; 149/112

Part of a 36-hole "oasis in the heart of North Miami", this "fabulous" Raymond Floyd redesign delivers "difficult", "target"-style golf, so "bring your scuba gear and lots of balls"; "impeccable service", a "beautiful clubhouse" and other high-end amenities add up to a "wonderful" experience, leading some to say the "only negative is the cost", "since you must stay at the hotel and then pay an exorbitant price to play."

	COURSE	FACIL.	SERVICE	VALUE	COST

Turnberry Isle Resort, Soffer (fka Fairmont Turnberry) 🏌 ⌖

| 24 | 26 | 25 | 19 | $250 |

Aventura | 19999 West Country Club Dr. | 305-933-6929 | www.turnberryislemiami.com | 7047/4971; 74.9/70.1; 149/129

"They've put a lot of money into this course and it shows" on Raymond Floyd's "beautiful" resort redo, a former LPGA Tour site that's kept "in spectacular condition", offering a "target golf" experience that requires you to "hit it straight and accurate"; it "feels artificial" to some, but supporters argue it's "one of the nicest in South Florida."

Naples

Lely, Flamingo Island 🏌

| 19 | 20 | 20 | 20 | $169 |

Naples | 8004 Lely Resort Blvd. | 239-793-2600 | www.lely-resort.net | 7171/5377; 75.0/71.4; 136/123

A "fantastic course near the beach" in Naples, this RTJ Sr. design is a "fair test", peppered with pines and sabal palms; a few demur at the "old-style Florida" layout, but the "great practice facility", "friendly staff" and "GPS system in the carts" are why many "would play it anytime."

Lely, Mustang 🏌

| 20 | 22 | 21 | 21 | $169 |

Naples | 8004 Lely Resort Blvd. | 239-793-2600 | www.lely-resort.net | 7217/5377; 73.9/70.6; 135/126

This "playable Lee Trevino design" resembles a "typical Florida course" – a "flat", "well-maintained" layout with "mucho water" and "forgiving fairways" that's "tame, except when the wind blows"; it can get "slow in season", but the "nice" resort accommodations, "full color GPS in the carts" and "yummy lunches in the clubhouse" make it a "good value."

➜ ⓩ Tiburón, Black 🏌 ⏱

| 25 | 27 | 26 | 20 | $190 |

Naples | 2620 Tiburon Dr. | 239-594-2040 | www.tiburongcnaples.com | 7005/4909; 74.2/69.7; 147/119

The "sense of isolation is fantastic" on this "simply gorgeous" Greg Norman layout that "stretches through a nature preserve" near Naples, with "tight driving areas and long forced carries" requiring "control of the ball and your emotions"; it's "maintained to perfection" and has "a superb staff", so while it's "spendy, treat yourself" to a "stay-and-play" at this "magnificent" Ritz-Carlton complex.

➜ ⓩ Tiburón, Gold 🏌 ⏱

| 24 | 27 | 26 | 20 | $190 |

Naples | 2620 Tiburon Dr. | 239-594-2040 | www.tiburongcnaples.com | 7288/5148; 74.7/69.2; 137/113

"Greg Norman did a heck of a job" on this "beautiful, well-maintained" layout (home of the PGA Tour's Franklin Templeton Shootout) that's "either fairway or trouble", with "lots of water magnets" and "tough bunkers"; the setting is "lovely" and "Ritz-Carlton management gets an A+", making it one "worth visiting if you're in the Naples area."

Ocala

El Diablo

| ▽ 23 | 11 | 16 | 25 | $45 |

Citrus Springs | 10405 N. Sherman Dr. | 352-465-0986 | 888-886-1309 | www.eldiablogolf.com | 7045/5654; 75.3/68.7; 147/121

Located 20 minutes southwest of Ocala, this relatively unknown Jim Fazio design doles out "all the golf you'll ever want" with its rolling fairways, dense pines, sloping greens and ample sand and waste areas; although a few feel it "could have been in better shape", it's a "great value" and a "terrific" "challenge for the skilled."

Orlando

☑ Arnold Palmer's Bay Hill 🏌️ ⛳

27	25	26	22	$300

Orlando | 9000 Bay Hill Blvd. | 407-876-2429 | www.bayhill.com | 7267/5235; 75.3/70.8; 140/128

A "must for any serious golfer", "Arnie's 'home' club" (host of the Arnold Palmer Invitational) is replete with "great history" on a "classic", "relatively flat" layout featuring "plush fairways" and "demanding" hazards, especially on the "outstanding last three holes"; you'll need to stay to play, but the "intimate", "country-club" experience includes "invaluable caddies", "excellent facilities", a "helpful staff" and, if you're lucky, a "cheery wave from the man himself."

Baytree National 🏌️

▽ 20	18	20	21	$53

Melbourne | 8207 National Dr. | 321-259-9060 | www.baytreenational.com | 7043/4803; 72.9/67.8; 137/112

Given that South African superstar Gary Player has jetted all over the planet, it's no surprise that he's responsible for this sturdy design in the middle of Florida's Space Coast, a 45-minute drive southeast of Orlando; it's characterized by mounded fairways, expansive greens and unique red-shale waste areas, with a particularly watery par-4 18th.

Black Bear 🏌️

21	18	19	20	$45

Eustis | 24505 Calusa Blvd. | 352-357-4732 | 800-423-2718 | www.blackbeargolfclub.com | 7062/5044; 74.1/69.7; 132/122

"Challenging yet playable", this linksy P.B. Dye design bares its claws with rolling, treeless terrain, topsy-turvy greens and more than 100 bunkers; it's a bit "out of the way", 40 miles northwest of Orlando, and some say the "facilities need work", but touches like the shootout 19th hole for "settling those lingering wagers at the end of a round" lead many to conclude that "a little more time and money" could make it into a "great course."

Celebration Golf Club 🏌️

22	21	23	19	$129

Celebration | 701 Golfpark Dr. | 407-566-4653 | www.celebrationgolf.com | 7040/5249; 74.7/65.7; 150/115

Expect "tons of Robert Trent Jones goodness" at this "beautifully landscaped" layout that was designed by both Senior and Junior "within Disney's planned community of Celebration", "a Rockwell painting of a town" where "everything is seemingly handled with extra TLC"; it "winds relentlessly through houses" and strikes some as "nothing memorable", but it does boast "numerous water holes" and a "friendly staff."

ChampionsGate, International 🏌️

22	25	23	20	$164

Champions Gate | 1400 Masters Blvd. | 407-787-4653 | 888-558-9301 | www.championsgategolf.com | 7363/5618; 76.3/67.6; 143/117

A "links-style course in the middle of Florida may not sound possible, but Greg Norman comes very close" with this "always windy" Omni Resort "must-play" that "gives you the feel of a British Open" track with "no trees" and "so much sand, you'll swear you're playing on the beach"; although a few find it "difficult but uninspiring", the "first-class facilities" and "friendly staff" make it "worth the high price tag."

ChampionsGate, National ♿ | 22 | 25 | 23 | 20 | $164

Champions Gate | 1400 Masters Blvd. | 407-787-4653 | 888-558-9301 | www.championsgategolf.com | 7128/5150; 75.1/65.2; 133/111

Although it's "not nearly as exciting or as challenging as the International", Greg Norman's "pretty" "North American–style course" (lots of trees and lakes) "can be a much more enjoyable option for the average player"; even those "not overly impressed" with the "plain" design have trouble finding fault with a resort setup that includes "impeccable" conditioning, "outstanding" service and "top-notch" facilities such as the "nationally renowned golf school."

Diamondback ♿ | 21 | 17 | 19 | 20 | $79

Haines City | 6501 State Rd. 544 E. | 863-421-0437 | 800-222-5629 | www.diamondbackgc.net | 6893/5061; 73.3/70.3; 138/122

"Wander from the fairway and you will see how this layout got its name" reveal roundsmen who've made the serpentine journey to "off-the-beaten-path" Haines City to play this boldly bunkered "inland Florida course"; the tight, tree-lined track slithers through "great flora and fauna", and while it's "tough to get to" and "short on amenities", it's "great for a gathering" thanks to reasonable rates and a "friendly" staff.

Falcon's Fire ♿ | 22 | 21 | 21 | 20 | $109

Kissimmee | 3200 Seralago Blvd. | 407-239-5445 | 877-878-3473 | www.falconsfire.com | 7006/5388; 73.2/68.5; 135/126

"Bring the big stick" to "one of the longer courses in Mickey Mouse land", this "top-notch" Rees Jones design that will "test" you with "sand, sand, sand and a gator or two" plus "always breezy" conditions, so be sure to keep it straight to "avoid the mounds"; a few feel it's "overpriced considering the lack of scenery", but "good practice facilities" and a "helpful staff" make it "worth the price at least once."

Grand Cypress 👤 ⏱ | 24 | 27 | 25 | 20 | $250

Orlando | 1 N. Jacaranda St. | 407-239-4700 | 800-835-7377 | www.grandcypress.com
East/North | 6985/5047; 74.6/69.9; 138/125
North/South | 7208/5513; 75.9/72.8; 142/130
South/East | 6953/5036; 74.5/69.7; 138/125

An "interesting but tricky" Jack Nicklaus design, this 27-holer in Orlando serves up "lots of water", "punitive rough", "difficult greens" and a "good pace of play", with the "North/South being the marquee" combination; it may "empty your wallet", but the "amazing" conditions, "superb facilities" and "fantastic service" will "leave you with a memory that money can't buy."

Grand Cypress, New 👤 ⏱ | 25 | 27 | 25 | 20 | $175

Orlando | 1 N. Jacaranda St. | 407-239-4700 | 800-835-7377 | www.grandcypress.com | 6720/5242; 71.9/69.2; 121/112

"Can't get to Scotland?" – then head to this "unique Jack Nicklaus tribute to St. Andrews", a "perfectly maintained" "cover band of a course" that's "wide-open but very tricky, with a burn meandering through" plus "deep pot bunkers, double greens and blind tee shots"; some gripe that the "mounds are out of place" and the "price is high", but the "superior facilities and attentive personnel" are two more reasons it's an "absolute must for anyone who loves golf."

Marriott Grande Pines
| 21 | 21 | 23 | 21 | $119 |

Orlando | 6351 International Golf Club Rd. | 407-239-6108 | www.marriottgolf.com | 7012/5418; 74.3/71.6; 140/126

"Pack your Coppertone" because "you'll spend a lot of time in the sand" at this "challenging" Nick Faldo/Steve Smyers redesign that sports "interesting bunkering and quick, undulating greens"; it can be "very hard for the mid-handicapper", but it boasts facilities that are "as nice as any" ("relax after the round" at the adjacent J.W. Marriott), and parents can "play while the kids ride Thunder Mountain."

Mission Inn, El Campeón ⛳
| 23 | 22 | 22 | 20 | $95 |

Howey-in-the-Hills | 10400 County Rd. 48 | 352-324-3101 | 800-874-9053 | www.missioninnresort.com | 7003/4811; 74.2/68.5; 136/123

"A taste of Old Florida" awaits flatlanders who frequent this "fabulous" "getaway" for "relaxing and enjoying the beauty of this hilly area" northwest of Orlando; an "excellent layout" that dates to 1917, it offers "narrow, challenging", "well-maintained" holes "with lots of elevation", and many who visit also appreciate the "old hacienda-style resort" with its "wonderful facilities", which include a "great restaurant."

Mission Inn, Las Colinas ⛳
| ▽ 19 | 21 | 19 | 19 | $85 |

Howey-in-the-Hills | 10400 County Rd. 48 | 352-324-3101 | 800-874-9053 | www.missioninnresort.com | 7217/4931; 75.5/68.8; 139/120

Make it your mission to try this "interesting" Gary Koch design that's tucked away in a "remote, hilly" area 40 miles from Orlando yet manages to be a much "more Florida-style course" than El Campeón; a few feel it's "not as good" as its sibling, but others find the open, tree-lined layout "very enjoyable", and it boasts the same resort amenities and handsome Mediterranean-style clubhouse that make this facility a "must-play."

Orange County National, Crooked Cat ⛳
| 26 | 24 | 24 | 25 | $119 |

Winter Garden | 16301 Phil Ritson Way | 407-656-2626 | 888-727-3672 | www.ocngolf.com | 7493/5112; 76.0/69.6; 139/120

Regular host of the PGA Tour's Q-School finals, this "super course" has "blind shots, mild mounding and some water hazards" but remains "playable from the middle tees for weekend golfers", with "just the right amount of challenge"; add an "immense practice range", "great clubhouse" and "excellent service" and you have an "amazing value" – and perhaps "one of the best golf havens in the world."

Orange County National, Panther Lake ⛳
| 26 | 24 | 24 | 25 | $134 |

Winter Garden | 16301 Phil Ritson Way | 407-656-2626 | 888-727-3672 | www.ocngolf.com | 7350/5319; 76.0/70.8; 139/123

Considering its "fabulous maintenance, design and value", "it's no wonder this place hosts the PGA Tour's Qualifying School", providing a "substantial challenge from the back tees"; factor in a "staff that couldn't be nicer" and "a top-notch practice facility", and most consider the "twin sisters of Orange County by far the best bang for the buck" around; installation of new ultra-dwarf Bermuda greens in 2011 may outdate the Course score.

	COURSE	FACIL.	SERVICE	VALUE	COST

Orange Lake, Legends ⌘

| 22 | 19 | 21 | 21 | $125 |

Kissimmee | 8505 W. Irlo Bronson Memorial Hwy. | 407-239-1050 | 800-887-6522 | www.orangelake.com | 7072/5188; 74.3/69.6; 132/120

Aptly named considering its designer Arnold Palmer, this Kissimmee course features a longer, more open front nine followed by a tighter back amid oaks, pines and water; it's kept "in great shape" and boasts a "great golf school" too, and the many on-site options – the new Reserve track, a nine-hole executive layout and a second nine-holer designed for all ages – make it a "good place for a family golf vacation."

Reunion Resort, Arnold Palmer ⌘ ⌐

| 23 | 24 | 23 | 21 | $155 |

Orlando | 7599 Gathering Dr. | 407-396-3199 | 888-418-9611 | www.reunionresort.com | 6916/4802; 73.4/67.0; 137/113

Perhaps the "most interesting of the Reunion courses", this "wonderful", flower-laden former LPGA Tour site in Orlando was designed by Arnold Palmer to be a "tough but fair" test offering "surprising elevation changes for central Florida" along with "many options for different players"; the "friendly staff" and "excellent facilities" lead most to conclude the "whole resort is top-notch."

Reunion Resort, Jack Nicklaus ⌘ ⌐

| 24 | 23 | 22 | 20 | $155 |

Orlando | 7599 Gathering Dr. | 407-396-3199 | 888-418-9611 | www.reunionresort.com | 7244/5055; 76.7/69.1; 147/124

This "really nice layout" is a "blast to play" thanks to a "typical Jack Nicklaus" design featuring strategically deployed hazards; the "lack of a pro shop is a downer" and some claim it's "not as woman-friendly as the other Reunion" tracks, but most "can't say enough" about the "fantastic facility" and staff that "couldn't be nicer."

Reunion Resort, Tom Watson ⌘ ⌐

| 23 | 26 | 24 | 21 | $155 |

Orlando | 7599 Gathering Dr. | 407-396-3199 | 888-418-9611 | www.reunionresort.com | 7154/5395; 74.7/66.3; 140/114

A "Tom Watson gem", this "truly fulfilling experience" encompasses a "fantastic design" set atop "unusual terrain for Florida", with "varied elevations" and "beautiful landscaping"; "you won't believe how much dirt they moved" to build this "linkslike" layout, which comes complete with the "excellent facilities and service" and "wonderful lodging" you'd expect from an "amazing resort with three big-name courses."

Ritz-Carlton Orlando, Grande Lakes ⌘

| 23 | 27 | 26 | 18 | $195 |

Orlando | 4048 Central Florida Pkwy. | 407-393-4900 | www.grandelakes.com | 7122/5223; 73.9/69.8; 139/115

"When you play on greens that Tiger Woods says are some of the truest he's ever putted, you know you're playing a great course" fawn fans of this "well-manicured" Greg Norman design that may be "flat as a pancake" but makes "good use of water" amid a "beautiful" Orlando landscape; "very high" fees notwithstanding, it has an "excellent caddie program and facilities", and besides, "you can't go wrong with the Ritz."

Southern Dunes ⌘

| 23 | 18 | 21 | 23 | $120 |

Haines City | 2888 Southern Dunes Blvd. | 863-421-4653 | 800-632-6400 | www.southerndunes.com | 7227/4987; 75.5/68.5; 138/118

"Don't forget your sand wedge" because "there are 188 bunkers ready to gobble up your errant shots" at this "unforgettable monster" that

COURSE · FACIL. · SERVICE · VALUE · COST

"looks very tough but plays fair" thanks to a "wonderful layout" from designer Steve Smyers; the presence of "too many houses too tight to the course" "take away much of the pleasure" for some, but the "friendly, helpful" staff adds to a "don't-miss experience" that's "worth the short drive" from Orlando.

Sugarloaf Mountain
`- | - | - | - | $75`

Minneola | 1455 Mountain Club Dr. | 407-544-1104 | www.hamptongolfclubs.com | 7076/5288; 74.1/70.3; 133/123

Master minimalists Bill Coore and Ben Crenshaw draped an old world, lay-of-the-land spread on some of the state's hilliest terrain, 40 minutes west of Orlando, featuring wide fairways, blind tee shots and a healthy mix of very short and very long par 3s and 4s amid oaks, pines, citrus groves, sandy scrub and 250 feet of elevation change; the highlight is the 507-yard, par-4 13th, which descends from the highest point in peninsular Florida.

NEW Waldorf Astoria Golf Club
`- | - | - | - | $200`

Orlando | 14224 Bonnet Creek Resort Ln. | 407-597-3783 | www.waldorfastoriagolfclub.com | 7108/5179; 74.6/65.4; 139/107

The hospitality titan unfurled its first branded golf course in 2009 to unanimous acclaim, thanks to a tranquil, low-profile Rees Jones design etched onto a rare parcel of undisturbed wetlands within Disney's Bonnet Creek; massive bunkers and a lake-filled back nine are among the high points, as are the first-rate conditioning and amenities, together with an enviable location mere steps away from the hotel's front door.

Walt Disney World, Lake Buena Vista ⌂
`22 | 23 | 24 | 21 | $164`

Lake Buena Vista | 2200 Club Lake Dr. | 407-939-4653 | www.disneyworldgolf.com | 6745/5177; 72.3/69.7; 133/119

This "hidden Disney course" is a "surprisingly enjoyable", "immaculately maintained" layout that "runs through two adjacent resorts", featuring "lots of water and sand" as well as views of boats and canals; perhaps "there are better in the area for less money", but the "fantastic service" and the "volcano cake in the restaurant above the pro shop" are two extras that entice players "to go back."

Walt Disney World, Magnolia ⌂
`24 | 24 | 24 | 22 | $164`

Lake Buena Vista | 1950 W. Magnolia Palm Dr. | 407-939-4653 | www.disneyworldgolf.com | 7488/5127; 76.0/69.6; 141/126

"Wonderfully landscaped", this "top-notch" "getaway from the crowds and the kids" is an annual PGA Tour stop that's "difficult from the championship tees" ("gators will surely gobble your ball up if it's close to the hazards") but manages to be "enjoyable" for all; it's "perfectly run" by the Disney crew, so you can expect "unsurpassed service" and an "enforced speed of play."

Walt Disney World, Osprey Ridge ⌂
`25 | 25 | 25 | 21 | $164`

Lake Buena Vista | 3451 Golf View Dr. | 407-939-4653 | www.disneyworldgolf.com | 7039/5283; 73.7/70.2; 127/124

There's "nothing Mickey Mouse" about "Disney's most interesting layout", this Tom Fazio "favorite" featuring "surprising elevation changes" along with "large bunkers", "huge greens" and "great finishing holes"; if it's "a bit pricey for the market", the "private country-club feel", "excellent service" and "lush wilderness" vibe make it a "first-class" experience and a "nice break from Minnie and friends."

Walt Disney World, Palm 🏌 | 24 | 24 | 25 | 22 | $164 |

Lake Buena Vista | 1950 W. Magnolia Palm Dr. | 407-939-4653 | www.disneyworldgolf.com | 6991/5262; 73.7/70.5; 131/126
A "convenient escape" "from the characters and amusement rides", this Joe Lee "classic" with "lots of water" and "lots of history" as a PGA Tour site is "like being in the wild", yet "easy to navigate" once you realize that "course management is important"; it's "well maintained", with "beautiful scenery", and the "wonderful crew" "goes out of its way to make everything perfect."

Palm Beach

Boca Raton Resort, | 20 | 24 | 23 | 17 | $199 |
Resort Course 🏌 ⛳

Boca Raton | 501 E. Camino Real | 561-447-3419 | 800-327-0101 | www.bocaresort.com | 6253/4577; 69.3/65.5; 128/112
A "piece of heaven in Boca", this "short", sporty design offers "beautiful landscaping" and "perfectly manicured" conditions on a layout that's "playable by all"; some find it "a bit pricey for what you get", but others insist it's "worth the cost" for its "lovely" resort location, "attentive staff" and "great amenities" – "don't forget to [hit the] spa after your round."

Breakers, Ocean 🏌 ⛳ | 19 | 25 | 25 | 18 | $195 |

Palm Beach | 1 S. County Rd. | 561-659-8407 | 888-273-2537 | www.thebreakers.com | 6167/5254; 68.1/69.0; 127/119
"Step back in time" and "feel pampered" at this "historic course at a historic hotel", a "flat", "well-kept" "classic" that's "short and very tight", so beware, as "wayward tee shots are in danger of striking Bentleys and Rolls-Royces"; though some note the "plain" Palm Beach layout has only "limited interaction with the adjacent ocean", the "beautiful setting" includes "great flowers and landscaping", and the "conditions and service are second to none."

Breakers, Rees Jones 🏌 ⛳ | 24 | 24 | 25 | 20 | $195 |

Palm Beach | 1550 Flagler Pkwy. | 561-653-6320 | 888-273-2537 | www.thebreakers.com | 7104/5164; 74.9/69.0; 140/125
There may be "water, water everywhere" on this "underrated" Rees Jones track in South Florida, but regulars reveal it's "not intimidating" and is now a "golfer's heaven" thanks to "phenomenal upgrades" over the years; it's "almost at the Everglades" and is "somewhat expensive" to boot, but "if you don't mind the travel time", you can expect a "pretty good test."

Links at Madison Green 🏌 | 21 | 19 | 20 | 23 | $125 |

Royal Palm Beach | 2001 Crestwood Blvd. N. | 561-784-5225 | www.madisongreengolf.com | 7106/4791; 73.6/67.6; 144/114
"Choose your tees wisely", this "tough", "narrow" John Sanford design "will test your management skills" on a layout with "tricky but fair par 4s", a dizzying array of bunkers and water, and "crowned fairways"

that mean "errant shots end up in deep trouble"; still, the "reasonable rates" will "make you forget that you're playing through condos" just west of Palm Beach.

North Palm Beach Country Club, Jack Nicklaus Signature 🏊

| 25 | 19 | 18 | 22 | $109 |

North Palm Beach | 951 Hwy. 1 | 561-691-347 | www.npbcc.org | 7028/5231; 73.8/69.5; 140/127

Jack Nicklaus "achieved the highest degree of excellence in his redesign" of what was once "a very lackluster" North Palm Beach municipal, adding "brutal greens" and "lots of hazards", and now it's a "classic Florida course" where "water abounds" – two holes run along the Intracoastal – and the wind is "always blowing"; a few take issue with "slow play", but most find it "well worth the value."

PGA National, Champion 🏌 ⛳

| 26 | 25 | 22 | 20 | $350 |

West Palm Beach | 1000 Ave. of the Champions | 561-627-1800 | 800-633-9150 | www.pgaresort.com | 7048/5145; 75.2/71.7; 148/136

"Play where they played the 1983 Ryder Cup", this Jack Nicklaus redesign (currently home to the PGA Tour's Honda Classic) that's a "taxing round" thanks to "lots of sand, wind and water" – "you'll see why it eats the pros for lunch", especially on the "famous 'Bear Trap'" (holes 15–17); while a few suggest the "resort itself is kind of tired" for such "pricey" fees (though it's currently under renovation), most insist it has "everything you could want."

PGA National, Haig 🏌 ⛳

| 21 | 24 | 23 | 20 | $250 |

West Palm Beach | 1000 Ave. of the Champions | 561-627-1800 | 800-633-9150 | www.pgaresort.com | 6806/5574; 73.4/72.1; 139/135

Although "not one you will talk about to friends", this "long and lovely" George and Tom Fazio tribute to hall-of-famer Walter Hagen comes "highly recommended" as a "fun", "challenging", well-bunkered design; it's "excellent for ladies", and the "well-manicured" grounds, "first-class practice facility" and "friendly staff" make it an "ok" choice at PGA National – "if you can't get on the Champion or Palmer."

PGA National, Palmer 🏌 ⛳

| 23 | 24 | 23 | 20 | $250 |

West Palm Beach | 1000 Ave. of the Champions | 561-627-1800 | 800-633-9150 | www.pgaresort.com | 7079/4810; 74.6/68.2; 141/116

The PGA National's former General course has been redesigned by the namesake architect, who "did a truly remarkable job", giving the layout "a more traditional links feel" while retaining "water on most holes" and making it "easier for women than before"; although a few are "not sure it's worth the price", fans say it's "more interesting than the Champion and a much better value."

PGA National, Squire 🏌 ⛳

| 21 | 23 | 23 | 20 | $250 |

West Palm Beach | 1000 Ave. of the Champions | 561-627-1800 | 800-633-9150 | www.pgaresort.com | 6465/4975; 71.9/69.1; 138/122

Named after the legendary Gene Sarazen, this George and Tom Fazio creation is relatively short and fairly open, although "narrow fairways" and "plenty of water" make it "work for all levels", so "bring your aim"; it's "typical Florida" – "thousands of homes line the entire course" – but novices note "it's the best at PGA National for newer golfers" and there's even a "helpful staff" that "makes it a point to be friendly."

	COURSE	FACIL.	SERVICE	VALUE	COST

Polo Trace 🏌️⊕
23 | 19 | 20 | 19 | $119

Delray Beach | 13479 Polo Trace Dr. | 561-495-5300 | 866-465-3765 | www.polotracegolf.com | 7035/5099; 74.8/71.6; 139/125

One of the "best public courses within 20 miles of the Palm Beach area", this "fine links" layout is "lovely and difficult", with "lots of undulation in the fairways" and a "diversity of holes" that are "fairly secluded from one another and don't run through a housing complex"; it's kept "in superb condition", and while it's a "little pricey", most say it's "worth a visit", especially "when on an expense account."

Panhandle

⛳ Camp Creek 🏌️
28 | 24 | 27 | 25 | $95

Panama City Beach | 684 Fazio Dr. | 850-231-7600 | www.campcreekgolfclub.com | 7159/5150; 76.0/71.3; 152/129

"Bravo" applaud admirers of the "very best the Panhandle has to offer", this "terrific" Tom Fazio "jewel" where "no two holes are alike" on a layout featuring "ample fairways" and "fast, undulating greens" that are "large but treacherous"; "unspoiled by development" and staffed by a "friendly, helpful" crew, it also now offers daily fee play.

Kelly Plantation 🏌️
27 | 24 | 24 | 20 | $139

Destin | 307 Kelly Plantation Dr. | 850-650-7600 | 800-811-6757 | www.kellyplantationgolf.com | 7099/5138; 74.2/69.6; 144/113

A "wonderful" Fred Couples design on Choctawhatchee Bay, this "challenging" layout features "generous fairways, large, sloping greens and enough trouble for anyone"; yes, it's "expensive for the Destin area", but it's kept in "great shape" and boasts a "helpful staff" and "several beautiful bay holes", leading many to "highly recommend" it as a "country-club experience at a public course."

Regatta Bay 🏌️⊕
∇ 25 | 25 | 24 | 22 | $129

Destin | 465 Regatta Bay Blvd. | 850-337-8080 | 800-648-0123 | www.regattabay.com | 6864/5154; 73.3/70.3; 136/116

"One of the top courses in the Destin area", this "excellent" track offers "lots of water", sprawling bunkers and a "tough" risk/reward par-5 18th; yes, it's "hot", "humid" and "perhaps a little overpriced", but "great facilities", including an "awesome clubhouse and bar", plus an enviable location near three state parks and Lake Regatta make it "well worth" the greens fees for many.

Sandestin, Baytowne
18 | 21 | 22 | 22 | $105

Destin | 9300 Emerald Coast Pkwy. W. | 850-267-8155 | 800-277-0800 | www.sandestin.com | 6804/4770; 73.2/67.7; 138/120

Sandwiched between the Gulf of Mexico and Choctawhatchee Bay, this "short" Tom Jackson design is both "fun and fair", with "well-kept fairways and greens" and a "great junior setup"; some call it the "most pedestrian of the Sandestin" layouts, though, so you may want to "play this one first to sharpen your game for the others."

Sandestin, Burnt Pine 🔒
23 | 21 | 22 | 22 | $155

Destin | 9300 Emerald Coast Pkwy. W. | 850-267-6500 | 800-277-0800 | www.sandestin.com | 7001/5153; 74.7/71.2; 144/122

A "top-notch Florida course", this Rees Jones design is "beautiful, especially the holes that wrap around the bay", with huge greens, tons of sand, tall pine trees and marsh areas that make it "tough, but still a lot of fun"; some say it's the "best at Sandestin", perhaps because it's for members and resort guests only and thus "doesn't get as much play."

Sandestin, Raven

26 | 22 | 25 | 20 | $135

Destin | 9300 Emerald Coast Pkwy. W. | 850-267-8155 |
800-277-0800 | www.sandestin.com |
6931/5060; 73.8/68.4; 137/124

This "outstanding" RTJ Jr. design offers Panhandlers a "real test" complete with "superb greens" and lots of "water and pines" – it's a "great thinker's course, although you usually think the same thought: don't hit it there"; yes, the resort and course may be "a little overpriced", but fans report that "pros loved it" when it used to host a Champions Tour event.

Shark's Tooth ⊶

- | - | - | - | $150

Panama City Beach | 2003 Wild Heron Way | 850-249-3015 |
www.sharkstoothgolfclub.com | 7204/5149; 74.9/69.1; 136/117

You won't have to clear too many lakes, bunkers or wetlands at this Panama City Beach semi-private, where the architect made a point of minimizing forced carries; flawless fairways melt right into the low-profile greens, and while you won't have to face any rough, you'd best hit it straight, for there's dense foliage and water awaiting most hooks or slices.

SouthWood 🗛

- | - | - | - | $75

Tallahassee | 3750 Grove Park Dr. | 850-942-4653 |
www.southwoodgolf.com | 7172/4521; 74.3/66.2; 135/103

This Gene Bates/Fred Couples design offers a "mix of difficult and forgiving holes" featuring "wide", rolling fairways bracketed by Spanish moss-draped oaks and hardwoods as well as large but "well-protected" greens that "can cause problems for errant approach shots"; it's the home facility for Florida State U., so expect school colors on the carts and a "friendly staff."

Port St. Lucie

PGA Golf Club, Dye 🗛 ⏰

25 | 25 | 25 | 24 | $119

Port St. Lucie | 1916 Perfect Dr. | 772-467-1300 | 800-800-4653 |
www.pgavillage.com | 7279/4963; 75.9/64.9; 147/119

Perhaps the "best course at the PGA Village" in Port St. Lucie, this "links-style" layout is "one of the more user-friendly Pete Dye designs", although it sports "humps, carries and sectioned greens" as well as "tall grasses and waste areas" – but "not much water" and "no houses"; a "professional staff" that "treats you like a member for a day" and the "top-notch teaching facility" add to its "tremendous value."

PGA Golf Club, Ryder 🗛 ⏰

25 | 24 | 24 | 25 | $119

Port St. Lucie | 1916 Perfect Dr. | 772-467-1300 | 800-800-4653 |
www.pgavillage.com | 7037/5126; 73.9/64.2; 134/111

"Dollar for dollar, you can't beat the three courses at PGA Village", and the "most playable" of the bunch is this "Carolina-style" track designed by Tom Fazio (and renovated in 2008) featuring "generous landing areas" framed by pines as well as large, undulating greens; it's "professionally run" by a "uniformly superb staff", and some suggest "the practice area is worth the trip alone"; P.S. history buffs should "check out the golf museum."

PGA Golf Club, Wanamaker ⛳☉ | 25 | 25 | 25 | 26 | $119 |

Port St. Lucie | 1916 Perfect Dr. | 772-467-1300 | 800-800-4653 | www.pgavillage.com | 7123/4964; 74.8/64.7; 144/112

A "traditional Florida course", this "excellent Tom Fazio design" is "always in superb condition" as it travels over "varied terrain" with a "mix of short and long holes", including "good risk/reward par 5s" and a finishing hole that brings "pressure to any close match"; it's the "toughest of the three" at PGA Village, but "still fun to play", and with the site's "awesome teaching facility", it can be a "real value" "for a buddy trip"; a 2011 renovation is not reflected in the Course score.

Sarasota

Legacy at Lakewood Ranch ⛳ | 23 | 22 | 21 | 21 | $99 |

Bradenton | 8255 Legacy Blvd. | 941-907-7067 | www.legacygolfclub.com | 7067/4886; 73.8/68.8; 140/115

A "classic" Arnold Palmer design, this "favorite in the Sarasota area" weaves through forest, grasslands and wetlands, yet is sufficiently open so that "certain holes have a nice links feel"; it's "usually crowded" and relatively pricey, but those who "love it" say it's "always in good shape"; P.S. "stay away from the gators!"

Ritz-Carlton Members Club ⛳⛳☉ | 26 | 26 | 25 | 19 | $220 |

Bradenton | 15150 70th Terrace E. | 941-309-2000 | www.ritzcarlton.com | 7414/5175; 75.6/68.3; 133/108

"Service meets style and scenery" at this "breathtaking" Bradenton layout that's "everything you'd expect from a course affiliated with a Ritz-Carlton"; they "moved lots of soil to make a true Tom Fazio" track, one with "no condos or houses in sight" that's "not too difficult for a high-handicapper" while being "challenging enough for most"; it's pricey, but you can expect an "intimate clubhouse offering fine cuisine" and the "best practice facility in the area."

Riverwood ⛳ | - | - | - | - | $107 |

Port Charlotte | 4100 Riverwood Dr. | 941-764-6661 | www.riverwoodgc.com | 7004/4695; 74.8/68.0; 144/114

Perfect for a "warm-up before playing the tougher courses" in the area, this Gene Bates design zigzags through wooded terrain before hopscotching marshes and lakes on the back nine, so "bring lots of balls to feed the gators"; situated in Port Charlotte, a residential community near some of the best boating and fishing around, it reels in its share of golfers in part because the "price is good!"

University Park ⛳☉   ▽ | 20 | 19 | 15 | 18 | $99 |

University Park | 7671 The Park Blvd. | 941-359-9999 | www.universitypark-fl.com
10/19 | 7152/4949; 74.7/68.9; 139/123
1/10 | 7001/4875; 74.2/69.1; 137/125
19/1 | 7247/4862; 75.3/68.2; 132/120

"For a lower-priced round in the Sarasota area", head to this flat but long 27-holer that features pine- and oak-lined fairways, greens that

FLORIDA

COURSE
FACIL.
SERVICE
VALUE
COST

are "in great shape" and an acclaimed set of par 3s, including a picturesque 5th; some suggest it's "nothing spectacular", but it does have an upscale restaurant and golf school.

Tampa

Bloomingdale 🏌

| 19 | 16 | 17 | 21 | $48 |

Valrico | 4113 Great Golfers Pl. | 813-685-4105 | www.bloomingdalegolf.com | 7165/5397; 75/72.3; 136/131

Nestled amid 100-year-old oaks, towering pines, acres of marshland and 14 lakes just east of Tampa, this "well-kept" track features "water and traps where appropriate", "risk/reward par 5s" and "smaller greens [that] make iron play a must"; though it's quite busy, the "big driving range and excellent putting green" make it a "place to practice as well as play" - at a "very good price."

Innisbrook Resort, Copperhead 🏌 ⚓

| 27 | 23 | 24 | 21 | $245 |

Palm Harbor | 36750 Hwy. 19 N. | 727-942-2000 | 800-492-6899 | www.innisbrookgolfresort.com | 7340/5605; 76.8/73.6; 144/130

It's "all the golf course you will ever want" say fans of this "walk in the woods" near Palm Harbor, a "true test" that's something of a "rarity" – a PGA Tour stop that "pros love" and an "amateur can play and enjoy"; the "top-of-the-line" resort setting and "unmatched facilities" help make it a "premier" – and "pricey" – destination, so "save your pennies" or "go between seasons."

Innisbrook Resort, Island 🏌 ⚓

| 23 | 24 | 25 | 22 | $220 |

Palm Harbor | 36750 Hwy. 19 N. | 727-942-2000 | 800-492-6899 | www.innisbrookgolfresort.com | 7310/5515; 76.4/72.9; 143/128

Phil Mickelson captured the 1990 NCAA Championship at this watery, "challenging" resort track that "holds up nicely in its own right" as "a break from the tough, tough Copperhead"; what's more, it rivals its big brother for "great service" and facilities after a 2009 overhaul; P.S. "if an alligator wants your Pro V1, let him have it."

Saddlebrook 🏌 ⊕

| 20 | 22 | 21 | 19 | $145 |

Wesley Chapel | 5700 Saddlebrook Way | 813-907-4566 | 800-729-8383 | www.saddlebrookresort.com | 6564/4941; 72.6/70.6; 133/126

You'll be "pleasantly surprised" by this "well-maintained" resort course located just 30 minutes north of Tampa, where "tough but fair greens" and an "inexpensive golf clinic" are the highlights of a watery, tree-framed Arnold Palmer design; a few find the course "unmemorable", but the upscale facility offers "many amenities for the non-golfer", including tennis clinics and a full-service spa, making it an ideal "place for a company retreat or family gathering."

TPC Tampa Bay 🏌

| 23 | 23 | 22 | 20 | $159 |

Lutz | 5300 W. Lutz Lake Fern Rd. | 813-949-0090 | 866-752-9872 | www.tpctampabay.com | 6898/4990; 73.6/69.7; 135/119

"As close as Tampa gets to a top-tier public course", this "well-designed" layout offers an "exam on the current state of your game", featuring holes ranging from "fair" to "brutal" – in fact, the "only thing scarier than the fast greens are the gators sunning themselves in the sand traps"; still, many brave the "slow pace of play"

	COURSE	FACIL.	SERVICE	VALUE	COST

and somewhat "plain" facilities to "play where the pros play" during the Champions Tour.

☑ World Woods, Pine Barrens

	28	19	21	26	$119

Brooksville | 17590 Ponce de Leon Blvd. | 352-796-5500 | www.worldwoods.com | 7237/4983; 75.3/68.4; 133/114

"Dedicated golfers" declare "it's worth the drive from civilization" to the "boonies" to play this "fabulous" Tom Fazio design, a "cross between Pine Valley and Bethpage" where "everything is beautiful and peaceful, yet feels so classic"; while "mammoth sand traps" ensure "bad shots will be painful", the "pleasure comes from the quality of the course", its "massive practice facilities" and the overall "excellent value."

World Woods, Rolling Oaks

	25	21	21	25	$119

Brooksville | 17590 Ponce de Leon Blvd. | 352-796-5500 | www.worldwoods.com | 7333/5011; 74.8/68.3; 132/116

A "relatively well-kept secret" that's "totally different but nearly as sweet" as its sibling, Pine Barrens, this "perfectly manicured" Tom Fazio–designed creation is a "gorgeous" "tribute to Augusta", with "rolling fairways", "some neat par 3s" and "challenging par 4s and 5s" "nestled in the trees"; the "world class-practice facility" is another plus, so be sure to visit it in "winter for the best conditions" and again in "summer for the best prices."

Georgia

TOP COURSES IN STATE

29 Sea Island, Seaside | *Low Country*
27 Reynolds Plantation, Great Waters | *Lake Oconee*
   Reynolds Plantation, Oconee | *Lake Oconee*
   Cuscowilla | *Lake Oconee*
26 Sea Island, Retreat | *Low Country*

Atlanta

Achasta 斗

	23	20	19	19	$80

Dahlonega | 150 Birch River Dr. | 706-867-7900 | www.achasta.com | 6964/4999; 73.3/68.0; 136/120

Situated on "beautiful property" in the north Georgia mountains an hour from Atlanta, this semi-private course is scenic and challenging – golfers must cross the river seven times, and the 4th green, entire 5th hole and 6th tee sit on an island – yet playable; still, some suggest it "could be better-maintained."

Barnsley Gardens, General 🏞

	26	25	26	21	$100

Adairsville | 597 Barnsley Gardens Rd. | 770-773-7480 | 877-773-2447 | www.barnsleyresort.com | 7189/5428; 74.8/72.6; 142/129

A "scenic" Jim Fazio design located 70 miles north of the Atlanta airport, this "tough but fair" track boasts "immaculate fairways" and "lots of elevation changes" (especially on the "tough, downhill par 3s") as it "winds through the woods" over "rolling terrain"; the surrounding "top-notch resort" exudes an "elite country-club feel", so whether you come "for the day" or spend a weekend, it's a "real treat" that delivers "value" for the money.

	COURSE	FACIL.	SERVICE	VALUE	COST

Bear's Best Atlanta 🏌

24 | 24 | 24 | 20 | $114

Suwanee | 5342 Aldeburgh Dr. | 678-714-2582 | 866-511-2378 | www.bearsbest.com | 7074/5076; 72.5/70.0; 140/127

"You'd be hard-pressed to find another venue that compares in quality" to this collection of "Jack's best" holes, most of which "you've seen or read about" before; whether you find the replica concept "interesting" or "goofy", you'll be playing on one of the "best-manicured courses in the Atlanta area", with "excellent forecaddies" to make the experience "even better."

Brasstown Valley 🏌

▽ 23 | 26 | 27 | 23 | $89

Young Harris | 6321 US 76 | 706-379-4613 | 800-438-3661 | www.brasstownvalley.com | 7047/5028; 73.8/68.3; 136/118

Located in the Blue Ridge Mountains "over two hours from Atlanta", this "beautiful" Denis Griffiths design is "always in good shape" as it meanders through wetlands and a wildlife preserve; although "a little pricey" for some, the "fun", "challenging" course, "great facilities" and "efficient" service are "worth the occasional splurge" for most; P.S. watch out for "conventions of non-golfers" that can "slow" things down.

Château Élan, Château 🏌

22 | 24 | 22 | 21 | $65

Braselton | 6060 Golf Club Dr. | 678-425-0900 | 800-233-9463 | www.chateauelan.com | 7030/5092; 73.9/70.1; 137/120

"Always at its showtime best", this "top-of-the-line" Denis Griffiths design offers "holes for all levels of play" on a "well-maintained" layout that's part of a 3,500-acre winery and inn some 50 miles north of Atlanta, the "type of course you like to play when on vacation" – "forgiving" but a "test if you're reckless"; there's a "wonderful short game practice area" to boot, and the "friendly, knowledgeable staff" reflects the "high-end" setting.

Château Élan, Woodlands 🏌

22 | 22 | 21 | 20 | $65

Braselton | 6060 Golf Club Dr. | 678-425-0900 | 800-233-9463 | www.chateauelan.com | 6735/4850; 73.1/69.2; 135/129

"Conditions are always up to par" at this Atlanta-area layout that promises a "solid day of golfing" on a Denis Griffiths design featuring a "beautiful parkland setting", memorable lake views and holes complicated by "lots of trees" and elevation; considered by some to be the "best of three challenging tracks" on-site (including a private course), it offers a back nine so "tough" you may consider taking advantage of the adjacent vineyard's tasting room afterward.

Cherokee Run 🏌

21 | 18 | 16 | 20 | $47

Conyers | 1595 Centennial Olympic Pkwy. NE | 770-785-7904 | www.cherokeerungolfclub.com | 7016/4948; 75.1/70.6; 143/124

"One of the best courses for the money in the Atlanta area", this Arnold Palmer design pleases players with a "tough", "well-maintained" layout routed over thickly wooded terrain located just 20 miles east of the city; some of the holes are "not fun for the first-timer" – the "signature par-3 3rd with a stacked-stone backstop can be challenging" – but the zoysia fairways and clubhouse amenities (including an upscale golf shop and restaurant) round out the experience.

	COURSE	FACIL.	SERVICE	VALUE	COST

Cobblestone

| | 24 | 18 | 19 | 23 | $65 |

Acworth | 4200 Nance Rd. NW | 770-917-5152 | www.cobblestonegolf.com | 6759/5400; 73.5/72.5; 139/134

Nestled just northwest of Atlanta, this Ken Dye layout is "terrific for a muni" thanks to its combination of "reasonable prices" and "challenging, attractive" design; water is in play on half of the course (including "beautiful holes on Lake Acworth"), and there are also "pot bunkers and narrow fairways" to make it a "real test" "requiring shot-making and strategy"; a post-Survey renovation featuring new Champion Bermuda greens and new bunkers may not be reflected in the Course score.

Frog at The Georgian 🐸

| | 24 | 20 | 22 | 23 | $85 |

Villa Rica | 2699 Georgian Pkwy. | 770-459-4400 | www.golfthefrog.com | 7018/5336; 73.5/70.3; 138/125

It may be "a bit of a trek from Atlanta", but that doesn't deter supporters of this "Tom Fazio masterpiece" (an Audubon Cooperative Sanctuary) featuring "unique holes" with tree-lined fairways "full of bunkers" and "pristine greens"; some find it "easy for the big hitter", but it's a "favorite" "for the mid-handicapper" and a "value for the money", especially when you factor in a "decent clubhouse" and a staff that "aims to please."

Columbus

Callaway Gardens, Lake View 🐸

| | 22 | 21 | 21 | 20 | $80 |

Pine Mountain | Hwy. 27 S. | 706-663-2281 | 800-225-5292 | www.callawaygardens.com | 6031/5285; 68.6/71.1; 123/121

Located just a half hour north of Columbus, this "lovely" 1952 layout (the older of the two courses on-site) offers challenge in the form of nine water holes, copious landscaping and "plenty of trouble lurking around the greens"; it includes a full set of junior tees and cart paths that were installed in 2002, and fans recommend it as a "good starter course if you haven't played in a while."

Callaway Gardens, Mountain View 🐸

| | 24 | 19 | 21 | 21 | $100 |

Pine Mountain | Hwy. 27 S. | 706-663-2281 | 800-225-5292 | www.callawaygardens.com | 7057/4883; 73.7/69.4; 139/120

An "attractive woodland setting" distinguishes this "minor gem" from Dick Wilson that's "tough" enough to have hosted the PGA Tour's Buick Challenge for a dozen years, but is nevertheless "fun" and "forgiving", with "very puttable greens"; post-Survey renovations have upped the ante, adding white-sand bunkers, new cart paths, tee boxes and a spa facility, making it "worth the trip" from Columbus for golfers and family members alike.

Lake Oconee

Cuscowilla 🏌️ ⏰

| | ✗ | 27 | 23 | 24 | 21 | $130 |

Eatonton | 126 Cuscowilla Dr. | 706-484-0050 | 800-458-5351 | www.cuscowilla.com | 6847/5348; 72.3/69.6; 130/123

For a "wonderful experience", head to this Coore/Crenshaw design on the banks of Lake Oconee, where "elevation changes" and "monster putting surfaces" "filled with movement" make it "as hard a course as there is in the state" and probably "not for the average golfer"; the required caddie for guests (not members) "adds unnecessarily to the "price", but you can expect a "resort" setting with "excellent accommodations" and a "top-notch staff."

Harbor Club

▽ 25 | 23 | 23 | 20 | $125

Greensboro | 1 Club Dr. | 706-453-4414 | 800-505-4653 | www.harborclub.com | 7048/5169; 73.7/70.0; 139/120

This Weiskopf/Morrish design on the shores of Lake Oconee may seem like an unsafe harbor to some, but it's a "must-play" for those who are prepared to skirt creeks – including twice on the "breathtaking 18th hole"; the combination of a "first-rate course and accommodations" makes it a "top-notch place to stay-and-play", and many "wouldn't miss this one regardless of cost."

Reynolds Landing ⛳ 🏤

▽ 25 | 23 | 25 | 20 | $225

Greensboro | 100 Linger Longer Rd. | 706-467-1564 | 888-298-3119 | www.reynoldslanding.com | 7048/5258; 74.4/71.0; 138/129

Host of the 2008 PGA Professional National Championship, this classic Bob Cupp design is a "challenging" course offering a variety of holes that wind through scenic naturally wooded areas and "play around the shoreline of Lake Oconee"; a 26,000-sq.-ft. clubhouse boasting a pool, sauna, gym and restaurant – not to mention "one of the best staffs" around – makes for a particularly easy landing at the 19th hole.

Reynolds Plantation, Great Waters ⛳ ⛳

27 | 26 | 26 | 22 | $265

Greensboro | 100 Linger Longer Rd. | 706-485-0235 | 888-298-3119 | www.reynoldsplantation.com | 7073/5107; 73.7/69.6; 134/122

Considered "one of the prettiest courses anywhere", this "Nicklaus masterpiece will challenge all the clubs in your bag" thanks to a "well-thought-out" layout featuring "tricky greens" and a "fabulous" back nine that's "all water holes"; while it may be "suited to better players", it's "one of the best plays" at the "sophisticated" Lake Oconee complex, which also offers three other public courses, "great practice facilities" and a "beautiful setting and views."

Reynolds Plantation, National ⛳ ⛳

25 | 23 | 25 | 20 | $160

Greensboro | 100 Linger Longer Rd. | 706-467-1142 | 888-298-3119 | www.reynoldsplantation.com

Bluff/Cove | 7034/5296; 73.4/71.4; 137/124
Ridge/Bluff | 6955/5316; 73.8/71.5; 137/127
Ridge/Cove | 6987/5526; 73.6/71.3; 138/126

"Three nines with unique challenges to each" comprise this "beautiful" Tom Fazio–designed course that resembles "its namesake in Augusta" thanks to a profusion of pines and dogwoods; the "greens are fast" and the "elevation changes" "demand accuracy" at this "must-play" layout (where only two of the nines are open at a time), and while it "lacks a quality clubhouse", it is affiliated with the nearby Ritz-Carlton, where "amenities abound."

Reynolds Plantation, Oconee ⛳ ⛳

27 | 27 | 26 | 21 | $245

Greensboro | 100 Linger Longer Rd. | 706-467-1200 | 888-298-3119 | www.reynoldsplantation.com | 7029/5198; 73.4/69.8; 136/121

A "man-sized course that lets you use every club in the bag", but still "woman-friendly", this "awesome" Rees Jones design combines a "beautifully maintained" layout with "fantastic views"; it boasts a

TaylorMade Performance Lab (one of two in the U.S.) to get your game in shape, and the adjacent Ritz-Carlton rounds out the "complete package" of "golf, pool, food, drink", making it a "wonderful" "stay-and-play."

✓ **Reynolds Plantation, Plantation** 🏨 ⚷ | 24 | 24 | 24 | 21 | $134 |

Greensboro | 100 Linger Longer Rd. | 706-467-1135 | 888-298-3119 | www.reynoldsplantation.com | 6698/5121; 72.3/69.9; 132/123

Designed by Bob Cupp with an assist from Fuzzy Zoeller and Hubert Green, this "solid place to play at Lake Oconee" is "worth a try", even if some suggest "it hardly compares" to its "over-the-top" brethren; it benefits from the affiliated Ritz-Carlton's "complete resort" amenities ("good restaurants", "nice accommodations"), so "if you have time for a few rounds", many tout the "immaculate" track as a "wonderful" "add-on to the other courses."

Low Country

☑ **Sea Island, Plantation** 🏨 ⚷ | 25 | 28 | 28 | 22 | $210 |

St. Simons Island | 100 Cloister Dr. | 912-638-5118 | 888-732-4752 | www.seaisland.com | 7058/5914; 74.7/70.4; 136/122

This circa-1927 Walter Travis design was reworked by Rees Jones into a "top-of-the-line golfing experience", with "terrific vistas" and a "few holes right on the Atlantic"; it can be "difficult" but "not so forbidding" that mid-level golfers "can't play from the proper tees", and while it's as "expensive" as its siblings, an "excellent staff", a "relaxing" vibe and "outstanding facilities" enhance the value.

☑ **Sea Island, Retreat** 🏨 ⚷ | 26 | 28 | 28 | 23 | $210 |

St. Simons Island | 100 Cloister Dr. | 912-638-5118 | 888-732-4752 | www.seaisland.com | 7106/5082; 73.9/68.9; 135/117

Davis Love III and brother Mark redesigned this "venerable old course" at Sea Island, creating "a beautiful playing experience" that is perhaps "not as interesting as Plantation or Seaside" but is still a "solid test", with "memorable holes" to make it "worthwhile"; in short, it's "just plain fun" to play as "part of a wonderful week of golf" at a "world-class destination" where "you can see the investment in the quality and amenities."

☑ **Sea Island, Seaside** 🏨 ⚷ | 29 | 29 | 29 | 23 | $295 |

St. Simons Island | 100 Cloister Dr. | 912-638-5118 | 888-732-4752 | www.seaisland.com | 7055/5048; 73.8/68.8; 141/120

Georgia's top-rated Course and No. 1 for Service, this "scenic" "old design updated by Tom Fazio" is "first-class", "beginning with the practice facility and ending with the beautiful seaside vistas and man-icured greens"; "as close to an Irish or Scottish concept" as you can get, it's a "super-tough" track – "especially for low-handicappers" – and while it's "expensive", most agree it's "golf as it should be."

Savannah

Club at Savannah Harbor | 22 | 24 | 22 | 19 | $165 |

Savannah | 2 Resort Dr. | 912-201-2240 | www.theclubatsavannahharbor.com | 7288/5261; 75.1/70.8; 137/124

"Set on an island" with "stunning views" of the Savannah River, this Bob Cupp/Sam Snead design hosts a Champions Tour event each

April, making it a "must-see-and-do" to "test your skills" against the pros; "super golf carts with air-conditioning and GPS", "exceptional facilities" (including a "classy clubhouse and pro shop") and a "courteous staff" add to an already "enjoyable day"; P.S. "watch out" for the "three-legged alligator" lurking on the back nine.

Valdosta

Kinderlou Forest | - | - | - | - | $89

Valdosta | 4005 Bear Lake Rd. | 229-219-2300 | www.kinderlou.com | 7787/5328; 76.6/70.0; 144/110

A "must-play in south Georgia", this Davis Love III design may seem like a forest, with the front nine routed over lush, "rolling terrain" and the back nine lined with spruce, but "every blade of grass and grain of sand is in its place" thanks to a "grounds crew that's on the ball"; the practice areas also "show great potential", as does the long layout - at nearly 7,800 yards, it's an "amazing challenge from the back tees."

Hawaii

TOP COURSES IN STATE

29 Kapalua, Plantation | *Maui*
28 Challenge at Manele | *Lanai*
Princeville, Prince | *Kauai*
27 Poipu Bay | *Kauai*
Experience at Koele | *Lanai*

Big Island

Big Island Country Club | 20 | 11 | 18 | 22 | $85

Kailua-Kona | 71-1420 Mamalahoa Hwy. | 808-325-5044 | www.bigislandcountryclub.com | 7116/5145; 75.6/70.5; 142/120

"One of the best-kept secrets on the island", this inland Pete and Perry Dye design is a "narrow, challenging" course with something "for all levels of play", including "risk/reward holes" and a "memorable island green on the 17th"; nestled near Kailua-Kona in a "beautiful" setting with views of Mauna Kea, it's "an excellent value", especially if you use one of the local or online coupons.

Z Hualalai | 26 | 28 | 27 | 19 | $250

Kaupulehu-Kona | 100 Kaupulehu Dr. | 808-325-8480 | www.hualalairesort.com | 7117/5374; 73.7/68.8; 139/129

"Tested by the Champions Tour every January", this "impeccable" Jack Nicklaus design on the Big Island's Kohala Coast is "open and fair for the average player", although insiders caution the lava hazards "will shred the balls"; the service is among the "best anywhere", and staying at the affiliated Four Seasons is like being "in paradise."

Kona Country Club, Mountain | 20 | 17 | 17 | 20 | $105

Kailua-Kona | 78-7000 Alii Dr. | 808-322-2595 | 888-707-4522 | www.konagolf.com | 6509/4886; 72.9/69.0; 135/116

Located six miles from Downtown Kona, this "short" layout is an "improvement" over the older Ocean course "in terms of views", offering "great" seaside vistas along with "tough greens" and dramatic elevation changes that make "level lies rare"; but while supporters say it's a "beautiful" "must-play" near Keauhou Bay, others say it's "no country club" and recommend it only "if you can't get north to *the* courses along the Kohala Coast."

Kona Country Club, Ocean 🏌 | 23 | 19 | 20 | 22 | $115 |

Kailua-Kona | 78-7000 Alii Dr. | 808-322-2595 | 888-707-4522 | www.konagolf.com | 6613/5276; 72.8/71.7; 129/119
Considered "a little better" than its Mountain sibling, this older William F. Bell layout is "one of the most relaxing courses" on the Big Island, with several "stunning" "oceanside holes" – so get ready to be sprayed by waves breaking on the lava rocks; regulars advise "finding a discount" to make it even more "affordable", then using the savings at the Vista Restaurant, where you can get an "excellent breakfast" or lunch.

Mauna Kea, Hapuna 🏌 | 24 | 24 | 23 | 20 | $125 |

Kamuela | 62-100 Kauna'oa Dr. | 808-880-3000 | 888-977-4623 | www.princeresortshawaii.com | 6875/5067; 73.3/64.4; 136/117
A snow-capped volcano "provides a spectacular backdrop" for this "wonderful" Kohala Coast layout that's one of "the best links-style target courses in Hawaii" thanks to an Arnold Palmer/Ed Seay design that "requires a straight ball"; some say the "views were better before the onslaught of new houses", but it's still a "breathtaking" option, with "nice facilities" and a "helpful staff."

Mauna Kea, Mauna Kea Course 🏌 | – | – | – | – | $250 |

Kamuela | 62-100 Mauna Kea Beach Dr. | 808-882-5400 | www.princeresortshawaii.com | 7250/4992; 76.6/66.0; 144/122
This RTJ Sr. design was burnished in 2008 by his son, Rees Jones, who added bunkers to go with the black lava beds and scenic ocean views; the signature 3rd – playing over the Pacific from a cliffside tee to a cliffside green – remains intact, even after the entire course was reseeded with new Bermuda strains and all of the facilities were upgraded.

Mauna Lani, North | 26 | 24 | 24 | 22 | $215 |

Kamuela | 68-1310 Mauna Lani Dr. | 808-885-6655 | www.maunalani.com | 6913/5383; 73.2/70.3; 136/125
A "gorgeous" setting featuring "green fairways between black lava rock" "adds to the experience" at this Big Island "beauty" that's considered "tougher" than its South sibling, especially when "you hit your ball into a lava outcropping – consider it a donation to the golf gods"; though some grouse about "too many houses on the course" and others find it "pricey if you're not a resort guest", most agree it's "not to be missed."

Mauna Lani, South | 26 | 25 | 25 | 21 | $215 |

Kamuela | 68-1310 Mauna Lani Dr. | 808-885-6655 | www.maunalani.com | 6938/5140; 72.8/69.6; 133/117
"Possibly the most beautiful course on the face of the earth", this "amazing" Big Island resort track features "lava outcroppings surrounding the fairways", so "pray to Pele if you're not straight off the tee" and "don't even think about searching for a ball" on the "treacherous" O.B.; insiders advise booking a "twilight time", which

will "get you to the 15th" ("a tee shot over the ocean") "at sunset – it doesn't get better than that."

Waikoloa Beach Resort, Beach   23 | 22 | 22 | 18 | $165

Waikoloa | 1020 Keana Pl. | 808-886-7888 | 877-924-5656 | www.waikoloabeachgolf.com | 6566/5122; 71.6/70.0; 134/118

The course name may be a bit "misleading" since there are "very few holes on the ocean", but this "well-maintained" resort track still offers some "stunning" visuals, including "lava outcroppings" and two holes that head "into an ampitheater", making the RTJ Jr. design feel a bit "like playing racquetball on a golf course"; "spectacular" seaside vistas highlight the "beautiful 12th", a par-5 double dogleg.

Waikoloa Beach Resort, Kings'   23 | 23 | 22 | 19 | $165

Waikoloa | 600 Waikoloa Beach Dr. | 808-886-7888 | 877-924-5656 | www.waikoloabeachgolf.com | 7074/5459; 73.4/72.2; 135/120

The "more challenging of the two Waikoloa courses", this "well-kept" Weiskopf/Morrish design has "tighter fairways than the Beach", along with "soft greens" and "strong winds" that can nevertheless "help" on the homeward trip since the breeze is "at your back"; expect "tourists", "slow play" and mongoose sightings, along with a "friendly staff" that's "ready to help you with all of your needs."

Waikoloa Village   22 | 20 | 22 | 24 | $84

Waikoloa | 68-1792 Melia St. | 808-883-9621 | www.waikoloavillagegolf.com | 6813/5501; 73.9/71.1; 130/120

Nestled in the foothills of Mauna Kea, this Big Island "value" can be "a challenge" thanks to "windy conditions" that have earned it the nickname "'Waiko-blowa'" and a final hole that causes "first-timers" to "go for a swim" in the "huge lake running in front of the green"; otherwise, this RTJ Jr. design is "friendly to higher handicaps", so even if the pace is "slow at times", most agree "it's well worth the wait."

Kauai

Kauai Lagoons,   26 | 23 | 24 | 22 | $150
Kiele Mauka/Kiele Moana &

Lihue | 3351 Hoolaulea Way | 808-241-6000 | 800-634-6400 | www.kauailagoonsgolf.com | 7120/5377; 76.1/72.4; 141/124

Located near Lihue Airport, this "beautiful Jack Nicklaus course" in Kauai reopened in May 2011 with the old Kiele back nine in place, freshened by three new holes, one an ocean hole, plus TifEagle greens and white silica sand bunkers; back in play is the "gut-check" of a par-3 No. 14 (formerly 13), featuring a shot "right over the ocean to a spot of green" with harbor views.

Kiahuna   19 | 17 | 19 | 20 | $103

Koloa | 2545 Kiahuna Plantation Dr. | 808-742-9595 | www.kiahunagolf.com | 6925/4887; 73.5/64.4; 134/114

A "less expensive alternative to nearby Poipu Bay", this RTJ Jr. design in Poipu Beach is "not too difficult unless it's really windy", boasting "fast and true" "paspalum greens" as well as Kauai's only set of junior tees; the staff is "eager to help" at this "hidden gem", but because it lacks a "resort component", defenders feel it "gets short shrift, which it shouldn't"; P.S. "come early for a great breakfast" at Joe's on the Green.

	COURSE	FACIL.	SERVICE	VALUE	COST

⊠ Poipu Bay ⛳
27 | 26 | 26 | 22 | $240

Koloa | 2250 Ainako St. | 808-742-8711 | 800-858-6300 |
www.poipubaygolf.com | 7123/5372; 73.9/70.4; 134/122

"Stunning beauty" and a "challenging" layout provide an "awesome experience" for everyone from "average players to low handicappers" at this RTJ Jr. design on the cliffs of Kauai (former host of the PGA Grand Slam of Golf); although the "gorgeous views" "can be distracting" ("humpbacks breaching off the 17th tee") and the wind makes it "exhausting", it's still "great fun" to play, with new, faster paspalum greens, while a "top-drawer" restaurant and "outstanding service" seal the deal.

⊠ Princeville, Prince
28 | 27 | 25 | 22 | $200

Princeville | Hwy. 56 S. | 808-826-5001 | 800-826-1105 |
www.princeville.com | 7309/5346; 75.2/72.0; 140/127

"Golf at its finest" returns to Kauai's North Shore with the reopening of this "beautiful yet brutal" RTJ Jr. design that offers a "challenging" experience, with "tight fairways and jungle roughs on many holes"; nevertheless, the "extraordinary view makes up for the difficult terrain", and the service and clubhouse spa are "excellent" too; its sibling, Makai, reopened in 2010 after a redo that converted it from 27 holes to 18.

Puakea ⛳
21 | 13 | 21 | 25 | $99

Lihue | 4150 Nuhou St. | 808-245-8756 | 866-773-5554 |
www.puakeagolf.com | 6954/5225; 73.5/69.3; 135/113

At this "gorgeous" Robin Nelson track near Lihue Airport, "you'll be rewarded" with "great vacation value" on a layout that's "challenging for any skill", roaming through "tropical terrain" (it's where *Jurassic Park* was filmed) and featuring "beautiful design and top-notch maintenance"; "great aloha spirit" from the staff adds to the experience.

Wailua Golf Course
▽ 20 | 16 | 20 | 26 | $60

Kapaa | 3-5350 Kuhio Hwy. | 808-241-6666 | www.kauai.gov/golf |
6991/5974; 73.6/74.3; 130/127

Redesigned and expanded by Toyo Shirai in 1961, this muni is the "best $$$ you'll spend in a long time" thanks to a "spectacular back nine" and a front that "lets you play almost at beach level" to take in the "fabulous views"; still, while it's kept in "excellent shape", the "facilities are basic" and the "great-value" pricing can lead to "heavy play and frustrating delays"; P.S. "cash only."

Lanai

⊠ Challenge at Manele ⛳
28 | 28 | 27 | 23 | $225

Lanai City | 1 Challenge Dr. | 808-565-2222 | www.golfonlanai.com |
7039/5024; 73.7/68.8; 135/119

A "must-play" on Lanai, this "spectacular" seaside Jack Nicklaus design is a "challenge" indeed, with "punishing winds" making it "a monster" for "even experienced golfers", though "stunning" "ocean views from all 18 holes", including a "picturesque" par-3 12th that "plays over a cove", offer solace ("if you're having a tough day, at least you can watch the whales"); sure, it's "expensive", but it's "worth the investment for a golf game of a lifetime."

	COURSE	FACIL.	SERVICE	VALUE	COST

7 Experience at Koele 🏌

27 | 25 | 26 | 22 | $225

Lanai City | 1 Keomuku Hwy. | 808-565-4653 | www.golfonlanai.com | 7014/5425; 75.3/68.1; 141/123

It "can't get much better" than this "absolutely gorgeous" Ted Robinson/Greg Norman design on Lanai that's "unlike anything else in Hawaii", offering mountainous play through Cook pines, koa and eucalyptus trees, culminating in a "dramatic 200-plus-ft. drop" on the 17th; with a swift pace of play, "you can get 36 in before lunch" at the clubhouse, and the resort guest day rate allows unlimited play here or at the nearby Challenge at Manele.

Maui

Dunes at Maui Lani 🏌

23 | 19 | 21 | 22 | $112

Kahului | 1333 Maui Lani Pkwy. | 808-873-0422 | www.dunesatmauilani.com | 6841/4768; 74.1/64.9; 141/113

A wee bit of "Ireland comes to Hawaii" at this "superb" "local course" in Kahului, a "gorgeous" linkslike layout by Robin Nelson that's set on a "dune several hundred feet high" with "a lot of elevation changes" that "require some shot-making", especially "later in the day" when it gets "very windy"; it's an "out-of-the-way gem" that's "perfect for a last-minute round before heading to nearby Maui airport."

Kaanapali Golf Resort, Kaanapali Kai 🏌

20 | 19 | 21 | 19 | $195

Kaanapali | 2290 Kaanapali Pkwy. | 808-661-3691 | 866-454-4653 | www.kaanapali-golf.com | 6388/4522; 70.7/66.2; 135/109

Royal Kaanapali's "underrated" sibling (redesigned by Robin Nelson in 2005) is "not the ugly stepsister it's made out to be", offering "phenomenal" greens and a back side with "character"; while the "spectacular" scenery can be "distracting" and the "wind is a problem", the "wide-open" track is "friendlier" than big brother, and you "can't beat the location or the service."

Kaanapali Golf Resort, Royal Kaanapali 🏌

22 | 20 | 22 | 19 | $235

Kaanapali | 2290 Kaanapali Pkwy. | 808-661-3691 | 866-454-4653 | www.kaanapali-golf.com | 6700/5016; 74.2/70.1; 131/123

Though it's the "tougher of the two courses" at Kaanapali Golf Resort, this track is still "manageable for the average golfer" thanks to some "terrific downhill par 4s that allow you to bomb your driver"; still, you should "bring your wind game, good legs" and a "boatload of money", and pause to take in the "breathtaking" "views of the mountains and ocean", as well as the Sugar Cane Train.

Kahili 🏌

∇ 24 | 20 | 24 | 25 | $95

Wailuku | 2500 Honoapiilani Hwy. | 808-242-4653 | www.kahiligolf.com | 6570/5359; 72.3/71.4; 135/126

Fans are glad this "formerly private country club" in Wailuku was "converted into a public course", for the Robin Nelson/Rodney Wright design built on the side of the West Maui Mountains is "top-notch", with "no houses" to impede the "panoramic views" of "both sides" of the island; while the track can be "very playable", "lots of volcanic rock" and "challenging" trade winds can make it a "real test."

☒ Kapalua, Bay ⛳

| 25 | 25 | 25 | 20 | $208 |

Kapalua | 300 Kapalua Dr. | 808-669-8044 | 877-527-2582 |
www.kapaluamaui.com | 6600/5124; 72.1/69.6; 136/121

"Dolphins, whales and turtles, oh my!" – the "ocean holes are stunning" on Plantation's "li'l sister", an "excellent layout" many consider the "friendliest course" on the "north end of Maui"; it's "well maintained" and a "good test" for "players of all skills", and "wonderful" service adds to an "enjoyable" experience that's well "worth the price of admission."

☒ Kapalua, Plantation ⛳

| 29 | 27 | 26 | 22 | $268 |

Kapalua | 2000 Plantation Club Dr. | 808-669-8044 | 877-527-2582 |
www.kapaluamaui.com | 7411/5627; 75.6/73.2; 140/129

"As beautiful and breathtaking as they come", Hawaii's top-rated Course is a "beast no matter how you play" and a "model for wind power" that's "as tough as it looks on TV" at the PGA Tour's Hyundai Tournament of Champions; the staff is "helpful and attentive" while the "facilities, especially the restaurant, measure up to the golf" (if not "the famous 18th" hole, the longest on the Tour), and sure it's "expensive", but all agree it's "worth every penny."

Makena, North ⛳

| 25 | 20 | 23 | 21 | $185 |

Makena | 5415 Makena Alanui | 808-891-4000 | 800-321-6284 |
www.makenagolf.com | 6914/5303; 73.6/70.5; 138/120

An "out-of-the-way gem" just south of the airport, this "Maui favorite" is "worth the drive" thanks to a "tough" "but fair" RTJ Jr. resort design featuring "gorgeous views of the ocean" and Molokini Island, "plenty of volcanic rock" and "some of the best greens around, fast with little grain"; what's more, you can expect "first-rate service" – *mahalo!* – and a clubhouse that's "wonderful for drinks afterward."

Wailea Golf Club, Emerald ⛳

| 26 | 26 | 25 | 23 | $190 |

Wailea | 100 Wailea Golf Club Dr. | 808-875-7450 | 888-328-6284 |
www.waileagolf.com | 6825/5256; 71.7/69.5; 130/114

It's an "expensive jewel", but the "view is worth the money alone" at this RTJ Jr. resort course that's "always a pleasure" thanks to its "immaculate" conditions and "female-friendly" layout; while there are "not a lot of forced carries", "tough rough" can make it "penal if you're off the fairway", so "expect a slow round", and "bring your camera" to snap photos of the "whales frolicking off the coast."

Wailea Golf Club, Gold ⛳

| 26 | 26 | 25 | 22 | $190 |

Wailea | 100 Wailea Golf Club Dr. | 808-875-7450 | 888-328-6284 |
www.waileagolf.com | 7078/5442; 73.4/70.1; 137/119

"If you play one round on Maui, this has to be it" say swingers who insist this "challenging" RTJ Jr. design is "definitely the best of the bunch" in Wailea, site of the 2008 Champions Skins Game; the course is so "beautifully landscaped, you'll think you're in a botanical garden" as you also enjoy "fabulous" ocean views, "excellent conditions" and "exemplary service" and facilities.

Wailea Golf Club, Old Blue ⛳

| 23 | 23 | 24 | 21 | $170 |

Wailea | 120 Kaukahi St. | 808-875-7450 | 888-328-6284 |
www.waileagolf.com | 6765/5208; 71.7/69.3; 130/114

"Hit the driver and let it fly" at this "extremely playable" course, the oldest and "cheapest" of the three Wailea tracks, which is "kept in excellent condition" and offers "amazing views" of "lush greenery, the blue Pacific and jagged lava rocks"; "friendly" service is another plus, and while it's "windy", the "wide-open" fairways "will keep your ball in play."

Oahu

Ala Wai Golf Course

14 | 13 | 14 | 19 | $49

Honolulu | 404 Kapahulu Ave. | 808-733-7387 |
www.co.honolulu.hi.us/des/golf | 5861/5095; 66.8/67.2; 115/110
Purportedly the "most played municipal in the U.S.", this "well-used course" on the edge of Waikiki is in "decent shape" nonetheless, with a "forgiving" layout that's "flat" and "short" but can also be "tricky"; it's "the furthest thing from a resort experience" and "play can be slow on weekends", but it's a "fun" "sandbagger's paradise" and besides, "where else can you play by the ocean for this little?"

Ewa Beach Golf Club

18 | 18 | 21 | 19 | $140

Ewa Beach | 91-050 Fort Weaver Rd. | 808-689-6565 |
www.ewabeachgc.com | 6312/4894; 71.0/64.1; 131/114
Though it "doesn't get much attention", this Robin Nelson design in Ewa Beach is a "challenging" links-style "treat" that's kept in "wonderful condition" – it's one of the first courses in Hawaii to boast eco-conscious seashore paspalum grass; "terrific service" adds to the "fun", and while the earth-friendly rough "might not look intimidating", you may need a "wrist brace" to slash your way through it.

Hawaii Kai, Championship ⌘

19 | 18 | 20 | 17 | $110

Honolulu | 8902 Kalanianaole Hwy. | 808-395-2358 |
www.hawaiikaigolf.com | 6500/5065; 71.4/70.0; 123/113
"Take your camera" to this William F. Bell layout on Oahu, where the views of the Pacific and the Makapuu cliffs "can't be beat"; relatively short at 6,500 yards, "with a few strange holes due to housing", it's nonetheless "challenging enough for intermediate players" with "lots of roll on typically dry" but "well-maintained" fairways, and players can sharpen their short game on RTJ Sr.'s 18-hole par-3 executive course.

Hawaii Prince ⌘

22 | 22 | 21 | 20 | $160

Ewa Beach | 91-1200 Fort Weaver Rd. | 808-944-4567 |
www.princeresortshawaii.com
A/B | 7117/5275; 73.8/65.5; 137/115
B/C | 7255/5205; 74.8/65.4; 136/110
C/A | 7166/5300; 74.1/65.4; 137/113
A "beautifully kept course" and "outstanding facilities and staff" all help to make Oahu's Hawaii Prince Hotel an "amazing place to stay", with three nine-hole routes "designed by Arnold Palmer" (and Ed Seay) that "offer a variety of challenging holes", including "several with water in play"; a few complain that they all "tend to have the same look" and the course names could've used a "little more imagination" – "come on, A, B and C?"

Kapolei ⌘

21 | 21 | 20 | 22 | $150

Kapolei | 91-701 Farrington Hwy. | 808-674-2227 | www.kapoleigolf.com |
7001/5490; 74.3/71.8; 135/124
Located 25 miles west of Waikiki, this "former stop on the LPGA Tour" is a "challenging and entertaining" "Ted Robinson setup", with agua on

12 of its holes and a lake on the 18th; a few critics find it "too expensive", but many surveyors insist the "well-maintained" layout, "totally renovated" clubhouse and "must-use" driving range and practice green all make it a "good value for visitors."

Ko'olau 🏌

25 | 21 | 21 | 23 | $145

Kaneohe | 45-550 Kionaole Rd. | 808-247-7088 | www.koolaugolfclub.com | 7310/5102; 75.7/72.9; 152/129

For the "chance to play golf in a rainforest backed up to a mountain range", "don't miss" this "magnificent", if "brutal", "favorite" with "one of the highest slope ratings in the U.S.", where "even skilled golfers" should "bring a healthy supply of balls" to deal with the "many forced carries over ravines" and dense jungle; a convenient location "close to Honolulu" helps to make it a "must-play" for those who "want to challenge themselves."

Ko Olina

23 | 23 | 23 | 19 | $179

Kapolei | 92-1220 Aliinui Dr. | 808-676-5309 | www.koolinagolf.com | 6815/5147; 73.3/71.8; 133/126

A "wonderful gem on Oahu's West Shore", this "nicely kept" Ted Robinson design is a "treat", with a signature 18th featuring a man-made waterfall that's "gimmicky" but "cute"; there are "some challenging holes spread throughout" ("watch the wind"), but if you "hit it straight, you can score", and the "relaxing" "paradise" setting is perfect for "consuming a few cocktails" afterward.

Makaha Valley Country Club 🏌

21 | 17 | 17 | 21 | $85

Waianae | 84-627 Makaha Valley Rd. | 808-695-9578 | www.makahavalleycc.com | 6369/5720; 70.8/71.6; 123/120

"All greens break to the ocean" at this William F. Bell layout located on the "far end of Oahu", a "must-play for golfers of any caliber", if only "to see putts break five feet uphill"; while it's an "interesting layout", it's the "awesome" setting, with "beautiful" "views of the ocean and surrounding mountains", that makes it both a "getaway for locals" and one of the "best values on the island" for visitors.

Pearl Country Club 🏌

19 | 18 | 21 | 19 | $120

Aiea | 98-535 Kaonohi St. | 808-487-3802 | www.pearlcc.com | 6787/5536; 72.7/71.5; 136/124

While "not as scenic as most Hawaiian courses", this "well-maintained", "interesting" track offers "great views of Pearl Harbor" from the slopes of the Ko'olau mountains (about a 20-minute drive from Waikiki); home to the annual Pearl Open, it "challenges" players with "fast greens, tough fairways", "windy" conditions and "lots of hills" that keep roundsmen "on a slant on almost every hole", while "very good" service helps justify the "expense."

Royal Hawaiian (fka Luana Hills) 🏌

25 | 17 | 21 | 21 | $125

Kailua | 770 Auloa Rd. | 808-262-2139 | www.royalhawaiiangolfclub.com | 6164/4654; 71.0/67.4; 134/129

"Like playing golf in *Jurassic Park*", this "beautiful" Pete Dye design nestled in a valley between Kailua and Waimanalo "tests how straight you can hit the ball" on a "thinking man's" layout that's "just as hard" as the nearby Ko'olau course but with "a bit more flash and finesse", so "leave your driver in the bag"; "the back nine is tougher than the front", so "ask the pro for playing tips" and then enjoy this "unique" "gem" that "everyone should experience."

Royal Kunia ⚶

22 | 12 | 17 | 20 | $140

Waipahu | 94-1509 Anonui St. | 808-688-9222 | www.royalkuniacc.com | 7007/4945; 73.6/68.1; 132/113

Long known as the 'ghost course' of Hawaii, this "fun" Robin Nelson design – which was completed in 1994 but opened eight years later – was certainly worth the wait: it's a "well-designed and well-maintained", "wide-open" track with a nearly 600-yard 9th hole overlooking "all of Oahu's South Shore" and Diamond Head; while the "restaurant is very modest", the clubhouse has a "friendly" staff and you can't beat a "replay for half price."

Turtle Bay, Arnold Palmer

26 | 22 | 22 | 20 | $175

Kahuku | 57-049 Kuilima Dr. | 808-293-8574 | www.turtlebayresort.com | 7218/4851; 74.4/64.3; 143/121

It may have "more wide-open fairways than you would expect at an LPGA" layout, but this "beautiful", "well-maintained" site of the 2009 SBS Open is still a "long, tough", "classic" Arnold Palmer design that can "physically and mentally drain you", especially "if the wind is blowing"; highlighted by the signature 17th, with a "scenic" oceanside finish, it's "well worth" the long drive to Oahu's North Shore, and a particularly good value "at the afternoon rate."

Turtle Bay, George Fazio

18 | 20 | 19 | 19 | $125

Kahuku | 57-049 Kuilima Dr. | 808-293-8574 | www.turtlebayresort.com | 6535/5355; 71.2/70.2; 131/116

George Fazio's only Hawaiian layout is "not the Palmer course" but it's still a "decent course for the money", and "not as expensive" as its big brother while still offering all the benefits of Oahu's North Shore – it's "wild hearing the waves pound" on the three oceanside holes; what's more, the "terrific back nine" may reveal to you why the course was host of the inaugural Senior Skins Game.

Idaho

Boise

Quail Hollow

24 | 21 | 23 | 20 | $35

Boise | 4520 N. 36th St. | 208-344-7807 | www.quailhollowgolfclub.com | 6325/4494; 70.7/66.1; 129/116

Located at the base of the Boise foothills with scenic valley views, this Robert von Hagge/Bruce Devlin design is a "tight and sporty" yet "forgiving" layout with "a number of elevation changes"; though some find it "difficult to walk", to others it's a "nice change."

Tamarack Resort, Osprey Meadows ⚶

- | - | - | - | $62

Donnelly | 311 Village Dr. | 208-325-1030 | 877-826-7376 | www.tamarackidaho.com | 7319/5003; 74.9/63.6; 143/111

Bordered by Idaho's Payette River Mountains near Lake Cascade about 100 miles north of Boise, this "challenging" "masterpiece by RTJ

Jr." is "so compelling" some "can't get enough" and "try to play 36 in a day" "to do it justice"; it's "demanding but fair", with "great greens" and "amazing scenery", so try to "keep the balls on the fairway or the wildflowers will eat them!"

Coeur d'Alene

⚡ Circling Raven ⛳   28 | 26 | 27 | 27 | $95

Worley | 37914 S. Nukwalqk Rd. | 800-523-2464 | www.cdacasino.com | 7189/4708; 74.0/66.0; 144/116

With a Gene Bates design that "aced the natural canvas" and used its "beauty" to "define the setting", this birdie of a course located at a casino and resort just a half hour south of Coeur d'Alene challenges players of any handicap, despite its lengthy yardage of 7,189; the "majestic back nine" features "long holes over mountainous terrain", and fans promise "you'll never forget the scenery."

Coeur d'Alene Resort   25 | 25 | 26 | 21 | $270

Coeur d'Alene | 900 Floating Green Dr. | 208-667-4653 | 800-688-5253 | www.cdaresort.com | 6803/4448; 71.1/64.4; 119/105

Set in a "unique lakeside" location in the foothills of the Rocky Mountains, this "incredibly beautiful, forgiving" and "classy" Scott Miller design may be "costly" but it's "definitely worth playing"; you "ride the launch from the hotel to the course", where the signature 14th – with an islandlike "floating green" – is "everything it's advertised to be", and it's complemented by "impeccable service" and "excellent facilities."

Sun Valley

Sun Valley Resort, Trail Creek ⛳   23 | 21 | 22 | 20 | $165

Sun Valley | 1 Sun Valley Rd. | 208-622-2251 | 800-786-8259 | www.sunvalley.com | 6941/5950; 72.5/70.7; 141/127

"Seeing the ball go so far" in the thin air "will make you feel like Tiger" at this RTJ Jr. redo of a 1936 original set atop Bald Mountain; although some say the track "has seen better days", it has a solid "reputation" and "great bones" that include a 58,000-sq.-ft. clubhouse, a nine-hole course called White Clouds and a putting course.

Illinois

TOP COURSES IN STATE
29   WeaverRidge | *Peoria*
28   TPC Deere Run | *Moline*
    Eagle Ridge, General | *Galena*
27   Annbriar | *St. Louis Area*
26   ThunderHawk | *Chicago*

Chicago

Aldeen   24 | 21 | 20 | 24 | $45

Rockford | 1900 Reid Farm Rd. | 815-282-4653 | 888-425-3336 | www.aldeengolfclub.com | 7131/5075; 74.2/69.1; 130/117

About an hour's drive from Chicago, this "model parkland course" is an "unbelievable value for a municipal", with a "private club feel",

COURSE | FACIL. | SERVICE | VALUE | COST

"friendly" service and "first-rate" practice facilities; the Dick Nugent layout is in "excellent condition", and while it can be "tight at times", it mostly sports "wide fairways with uneven lies" and "great greens"; P.S. it's a "real test from the tips."

Big Run
23 | 15 | 19 | 21 | $69

Lockport | 17211 W. 135th St. | 815-838-1057 | www.bigrungolf.com | 7028/5420; 74.4/71.9; 138/128

A big run, and a "long, challenging" walk as well, this "unheralded surprise in the south suburbs of Chicago" is "not for the faint of heart", but "so much fun", with "150-ft. putts", "soaring trees" and "massive elevation changes and hills that'll make you think you're in West Virginia"; while some grouse about "no driving range" and a clubhouse that "needs updating", to others it's a "well-maintained" course with "a lot of character."

Cantigny 斗
25 | 25 | 24 | 22 | $95

Wheaton | 27 W. 270 Mack Rd. | 630-668-3323 | www.cantignygolf.com
Hillside/Lakeside | 6831/5183; 72.8/70.4; 136/122
Lakeside/Woodside | 7055/5425; 74.2/71.8; 140/128
Woodside/Hillside | 7012/5236; 73.8/71.0; 139/126

With three "excellent, well-conditioned" nines, a "wonderful practice facility" and an "outstanding" staff clad in "knickers", this "fabulous public" in Chicago's western suburbs "feels like a private club"; while the "Hillside is nice", many prefer the Lakeside/Woodside combo, the former boasting a bunker shaped like Dick Tracy in a fedora; Woodside's 2nd, a par 5 that'll "scare you straight", is under renovation until May 2012.

Chalet Hills
21 | 17 | 17 | 21 | $75

Cary | 943 Rawson Bridge Rd. | 847-639-0666 | www.chaletgolf.com | 6877/4934; 73.6/69.1; 137/121

Many think this "underrated" course in Cary is "worth the trek" from Chicago and a "great value for the price", offering a "wonderful" layout that's "challenging off the tee", even if a few find some of the holes "a little tricked-up"; the "very nice" clubhouse with a vaulted ceiling and stone fireplace compensates somewhat for the "tiny locker room with limited shower facilities."

Cog Hill, No. 2 (Ravines) 斗
23 | 22 | 22 | 23 | $57

Lemont | 12294 Archer Ave. | 630-257-5872 | www.coghillgolf.com | 6639/5610; 71.8/72.3; 124/123

Fans tout "Baby Dubs" (aka Ravines) as an "excellent alternative" to Cog Hill's famous Dubsdread and a "better deal for the money"; "scenic, well-conditioned and challenging in its own right", this "shot-makers paradise" is a "good test for the average to above-average player", and while a few grumble that the "rangers need to be more diligent", many find the service "excellent" and the practice facilities among "the best anywhere."

Cog Hill, No. 4 (Dubsdread) 斗
- | - | - | - | $155

Lemont | 12294 Archer Ave. | 630-257-5872 | 866-264-4455 | www.coghillgolf.com | 7554/5367; 77.8/72.4; 151/133

In 2008 Rees Jones revamped Dick Wilson and Joe Lee's original design of Cog Hill's most famous course, host of the PGA Tour's BMW

Championship from 2009–2011; highlights include a pond to carry on the 7th and a whopping 500-yard par-4 finisher that's sure to thrill even the most experienced players.

Glen Club 术

25	25	24	17	$180

Glenview | 2901 W. Lake Ave. | 847-724-7272 | www.theglenclub.com | 7149/5324; 74.8/71.7; 140/127

Although it's "hard to imagine", this "great parkland layout" by Tom Fazio "was once an airfield", but now it's a "first-class course" boasting "short, challenging par 4s and monster par 4s", with greens that are "tough to read at times", so "only serious golfers need apply"; it's a frequent stop on the Nationwide Tour, and while a few find it "way overpriced for the Chicago market", to others it's a "joy to play."

Harborside International, Port 🏖

24	22	22	21	$95

Chicago | 11001 S. Doty Ave. | 312-782-7837 | www.harborsideinternational.com | 7164/5164; 74.8/74.8; 136/136

Lake Michigan inspires the nautical theme of this "excellent facility" with dual Dick Nugent "links-style" designs offering "great views of the Chicago skyline"; many call this "challenging" course the "harder of the two", where "tall grass and fescue will take all errant shots" and the "Windy City wind" will require you to "bring your punch shots."

Harborside International, Starboard 🏖

25	22	22	22	$95

Chicago | 11001 S. Doty Ave. | 312-782-7837 | www.harborsideinternational.com | 7166/5110; 74.7/66.4; 136/116

Port's sibling is a "long and always windy" track with "more sand than Waikiki Beach", and while some find the greens "hard to read", the "impeccable maintenance" and "unique surroundings" (with "incredible views of the skyline from many tee boxes") compensate; "excellent practice facilities" and "reasonable prices" seal the deal.

Heritage Bluffs

▽ 23	15	18	23	$48

Channahon | 24355 W. Bluff Rd. | 815-467-7888 | www.heritagebluffs.com | 7171/5035; 74.1/69.0; 138/120

Insiders plead "don't tell anyone" about this "out-of-the-way" course less than an hour southwest of Chicago, where Dick Nugent has fashioned another "interesting layout" traversing a variety of terrains, with "complex greens" and "tricky holes" that'll "push your game", but also fairways "wide enough to allow for errant drives"; it's "extremely well maintained", and you "can't beat the price."

Oak Brook

20	20	20	21	$55

Oak Brook | 2606 York Rd. | 630-368-6400 | www.oak-brook.org | 6541/5341; 71.1/70.7; 126/120

Located a half hour west of Chicago, this "well-conditioned municipal" is a "great place to hone your game", with "lots of water and doglegs" to negotiate, a "very good practice area and range" and ample "tee time availability"; "low" fees are another plus, and "you can always imagine that you're playing the adjacent [and private] Butler National."

Orchard Valley

26	22	21	24	$60

Aurora | 2411 W. Illinois Ave. | 630-907-0500 | www.orchardvalleygolf.com | 6745/5162; 72.4/70.0; 134/123

"Worth the [45-mile] drive from Chicago", this Ken Kavanaugh "gem" "might be the best golf experience for the money in the entire

Metro area"; "precision shot-placement is a must" on this "tough course" where, after an "easy 1st", the "opening holes" are "killers" with "water galore"; "top-quality conditioning" that's "way better than expected of a municipal" and "outstanding service" make it "friendly for all players."

Pine Meadow

25 | 16 | 19 | 21 | $84

Mundelein | 1 Pine Meadow Ln. | 847-566-4653 | www.pinemeadowgc.com | 7297/5272; 74.8/65.8; 138/115

"Reasonably priced" and "always in perfect condition", this course owned by the Jemsek family (Cog Hill) is "one of the best publics in the Chicago area", set on former seminary grounds where there are "no homes to be found"; it's a "tough challenge" even with its "wide fairways", so "choose your tee box soberly", and while a few think the "facilities need work", the "knowledgeable" staff and "nice" practice area add to its "good value."

Plum Tree National

- | - | - | - | $65

Harvard | 19511 Lembcke Rd. | 800-851-3578 | www.plumtreegolf.com | 6695/5710; 72.6/73.0; 133/129

This rural Joe Lee course in McHenry County is a "long ride" from Chicago, but fans insist it's a "great value", especially "in the spring or fall when rates are lower"; the 6,695-yard design, boasting bentgrass fairways, more than 4,000 trees and 105 bunkers in play, often serves as a qualifying venue for both the U.S. Amateur and U.S. Open.

Prairie Landing

26 | 25 | 24 | 22 | $84

West Chicago | 2325 Longest Dr. | 630-208-7600 | www.prairielanding.com | 6950/4859; 73.8/68.8; 139/118

"Well-designed" and "impeccably maintained", this RTJ Jr. "links-style" design near DuPage Airport is "difficult" but a "joy to play", with "plenty of open space" on the "almost treeless" course and "windy conditions" that can make it a "bear"; "nice practice facilities", including "three holes to play while waiting to tee off", and a "great clubhouse" add to its "good value."

Ruffled Feathers

25 | 24 | 23 | 20 | $95

Lemont | 1 Pete Dye Dr. | 630-257-1000 | www.ruffledfeathersgc.com | 6898/5273; 73.7/71.5; 140/131

Those unruffled by this "typical" Pete and P.B. Dye course say it's a "wonderful choice", "slightly short but challenging", with "lots of pot bunkers", "some blind shots" and "contoured greens and small landing areas that require precision shot-making" (read: "lots of lost balls"); it's "impeccably maintained" and the staff is "usually helpful", but some think it's "a little pricey compared to other courses in the area."

Schaumburg

- | - | - | - | $52

Schaumburg | 401 N. Roselle Rd. | 847-885-9000 | www.parkfun.com
Baer/Players | 6603/4839; 71.3/67.6; 129/114
Players/Tournament | 6435/4874; 70.6/68.0; 128/119
Tournament/Baer | 6644/4855; 71.7/67.6; 130/119

"Playable by any handicap", this "underrated" park district layout comprising three nines is "one of the better municipal courses around", with bentgrass fairways that "make the ball seem like it's on a tee" and "quick" greens; what's more it's "usually easy to get on", and you can also have an "inexpensive, relaxing meal" après-round at Chandler's Chophouse.

Seven Bridges

| 19 | 21 | 19 | 17 | $107 |

Woodridge | 1 Mulligan Dr. | 630-964-7777 | www.sevenbridges.com | 7111/5262; 74.4/76.4; 140/138

It only "seems as if there are seven bridges on every hole" at this Dick Nugent municipal track southwest of Chicago, with a "whole lotta water" in play on the back nine and a woodsy front; many praise the "wide fairways", but others find them "too small and tilted", causing balls to "roll to both edges and into a treacherous creek", and while the course is "always in good shape", some critics insist you "can find better value for the cost."

Shepherd's Crook

| ▽ 24 | 18 | 22 | 25 | $42 |

Zion | 351 N. Greenbay Rd. | 847-872-2080 | www.shepherdscrook.org | 6769/4901; 72.1/67.7; 128/115

Architect Keith Foster had Scotland in mind with this "natural" "links-style" public course boasting greens that "make you think you're putting at Augusta" with "lots of slope and undulation"; the "wind always has a say" here (queasy critics warn "watch out when it's blowing over the garbage dump" down the road), and while "no driving range" is a "downer", many still deem it an "unbelievable value."

Steeple Chase

| 20 | 17 | 17 | 20 | $58 |

Mundelein | 200 N. La Vista Dr. | 847-949-8900 | www.mundeleinparks.org | 6827/4831; 71.3/67.9; 139/119

"Not your typical suburban course", this Ken Killian design in a "nice park district facility" is a "good test of golf" with water in play on 13 holes and "huge", "excellent greens" that require "your flat stick A-game"; critics complain of "numerous O.B. stakes", "no driving range" and a clubhouse they regard as "dated", but many others still call it a "great value in the Chicago area."

Stonewall Orchard

| 25 | 21 | 21 | 21 | $77 |

Grayslake | 25675 Hwy. 60 W. | 847-740-4890 | www.stonewallorchard.com | 7124/5375; 74.7/71.7; 148/130

Admirers aver it's "worth the drive to the country to play" this "tough but extremely well-maintained" Arthur Hills design an hour north of Chicago, where you need to "be long and accurate", with "some holes reminding you of the Carolinas" and all of them "challenging the best and average players from the middle tees" (it has hosted a U.S. Open Qualifier); most agree it's "one of the best courses in the area."

ThunderHawk

| 26 | 23 | 25 | 25 | $85 |

Beach Park | 39700 N. Lewis Ave. | 847-968-4295 | www.lcfpd.org | 7031/5046; 73.8/69.2; 136/122

Hawks are frequent fliers over this "slice of heaven" in the Lake County Forest Preserve an hour from Chicago, where "good scoring opportunities" produce birdies of another feather, but where "you'll be punished for carelessness" as well; the RTJ Jr. design is "well maintained" and "especially beautiful in late summer", and the staff is "very

	COURSE	FACIL.	SERVICE	VALUE	COST

friendly" – in sum, it's "one of the best public courses in Northern Illinois" and "one of the best golf values" anywhere.

Water's Edge
∇ 23 | 20 | 24 | 25 | $66

Worth | 7205 W. 115th St. | 708-671-1032 | www.watersedgegolf.com | 6904/5332; 72.9/70.4; 131/122

Designer Rick Robbins and former Tour pro Gary Koch collaborated on this "sporty" muni southwest of Chicago that will take "beginners and accomplished players" alike to the edge, with water in play on 10 of the 18 holes, including the signature 11th, a 570-yard par 5 bracketed by a channel and a large lake; the practice facilities include chipping and putting areas and a lighted driving range.

Galena

⚡ Eagle Ridge, General
28 | 25 | 24 | 23 | $155

Galena | 444 Eagle Ridge Dr. | 815-777-2444 | www.eagleridge.com | 6820/5337; 73.8/66.7; 137/119

"Beautiful yet evil", Eagle Ridge's "must-play gem" is one of the best courses in the state thanks to a design by Roger Packard and U.S. Open winner Andy North that's "not for the faint of heart"; "spectacular vistas" enhance the "magnificent layout" boasting "dramatic elevation changes" and "deep" roughs that "can easily swallow golf balls whole", and many call it the "best resort course you've never heard of."

Eagle Ridge, North
24 | 24 | 24 | 24 | $140

Galena | 444 Eagle Ridge Dr. | 815-777-2444 | www.eagleridge.com | 6875/5578; 73.2/72.1; 132/125

"Challenging but fair", this Roger Packard–designed "Midwest gem" at the Eagle Ridge resort is "not too hard for the average duffer", and autumn play, when the "leaves are turning", is "just breathtaking"; while a few find it "ho-hum" "compared to the General", it's "cheaper" than its better known sibling, and many deem it "just as nice – for the price"; P.S. "great golf packages are available."

Eagle Ridge, South
∇ 22 | 20 | 22 | 21 | $140

Galena | 444 Eagle Ridge Dr. | 815-777-2444 | www.eagleridge.com | 6762/5609; 72.7/72.3; 134/129

While Eagle Ridge's South track may "not be as difficult as the General", many say it's still a "wonderful test of golf", offering a "nice" design through heavy hardwood stands, with a meandering stream in play on 11 holes; insiders advise you'll "need to play more than once to figure out" the "well-maintained" dance floors.

Moline

⚡ TPC Deere Run
28 | 27 | 25 | 27 | $88

Silvis | 3100 Heather Knoll | 309-796-6000 | 877-872-3677 | www.tpc.com | 7258/5179; 75.6/70.3; 145/127

"You get to play where the pros play" on this "beautiful" TPC course east of Moline, site of the annual PGA John Deere Classic; designed by native son D.A. Weibring, the "tight layout" has a "good variety of holes" and the course and facilities are "top-notch and immaculate", which is why many consider it a "great $$$ value" and "worth the drive from anywhere in the Midwest."

	COURSE	FACIL.	SERVICE	VALUE	COST

Peoria

☑ WeaverRidge

29 | 24 | 24 | 21 | $79

Peoria | 5100 Weaverridge Blvd. | 309-691-3344 | www.weaverridge.com | 7030/5046; 73.1/68.9; 136/115

The top-rated Course in Illinois, this "great find" in Peoria includes "two distinct nines" with "lots of visual interest", though the relatively flat front features "well-guarded greens and large landing areas", while the return trip is more of a "challenge" with its "dramatic elevation changes"; facilities that include a grass driving range and learning center make it even more "enjoyable to play."

Springfield

Piper Glen

▽ 23 | 21 | 21 | 23 | $32

Springfield | 7112 Piper Glen Dr. | 217-483-6537 | 877-635-7326 | www.piperglen.com | 7005/5138; 73.5/65.4; 132/116

Always "superbly conditioned", this Springfield spread makes for "exciting risk/reward golf", particularly on "devilish greens" that "can challenge any level" and on the 9th, a double dogleg par 5 that brings a creek into play; the "corporate-oriented country club" has an "ownership that cares", resulting in "awesome service" and "good-value" pricing.

St. Louis Area

Annbriar

27 | 20 | 24 | 26 | $45

Waterloo | 1524 Birdie Ln. | 618-939-4653 | 888-939-5191 | www.annbriar.com | 6863/4792; 72.8/66.4; 136/110

The "best daily fee golf course in the greater St. Louis area" is how fans describe this Michael Hurdzan design that's "15 minutes from Downtown, yet feels worlds away"; there's "not a condo in sight" of the "two drastically different nines", with "links on the front" and a "fantastic", "very hilly" back featuring the signature 11th, with a creek that winds across the fairway and a looming sycamore tree.

Gateway National

22 | 16 | 18 | 19 | $44

Madison | 18 Golf Dr. | 314-421-4653 | 800-482-8856 | www.gatewaynational.com | 7178/5187; 75.0/64.5; 138/109

Located next to the Gateway International race track, this Keith Foster design lets you "view the Gateway Arch" and Downtown St. Louis as you play a "tough links-style" route featuring "bentgrass tees, fairways and greens" that are "well maintained"; play from the tips and it's a "good long course", and while some dismiss the facilities as "unexceptional", at least the service is "friendly."

Spencer T. Olin

▽ 22 | 17 | 20 | 23 | $55

Alton | 4701 College Ave. | 618-465-3111 | www.spencertolingolf.com | 6941/5049; 73.5/65.6; 135/110

A "real sleeper course" 30 minutes from St. Louis, this Arnold Palmer design is "not punitive", but "will give you all you can handle", offering "challenges for every level of player"; "friendly" service helps many overlook the "spartan clubhouse and locker room", and insiders recommend "taking advantage of their promotions", but with the caveat that the "all-you-can-play specials slow things way-y down."

	COURSE	FACIL.	SERVICE	VALUE	COST

Stonewolf ⌂

▽ 22 | 20 | 21 | 18 | $50

Fairview Heights | 1195 Stonewolf Trail | 618-624-4653 | 877-721-4653 |
www.stonewolfgolf.com | 6943/4849; 73.4/68.2; 136/114

Less than a half hour from St. Louis, this "excellent" Jack Nicklaus design "takes no prisoners from the back tees", with plenty of elevation changes requiring you to "drive it long" and "put it in the right spot in the fairway", or else your "approach shots will be killers"; still, a few find the "upkeep not up to par."

Indiana

Cincinnati Area

Belterra ⌂

- | - | - | - | $110

Florence | 777 Belterra Dr. | 812-427-7783 | 888-235-8377 |
www.belterracasino.com | 6925/5102; 73.3/68.3; 136/122

One of the "best courses to play if you're in the area" (about an hour southwest of Cincinnati), this "excellent" Tom Fazio design with views of the Ohio River and Log Lick Creek is "very hard for high handicappers", with "a lot of forced carries" that "provide fun and headaches"; for a change of pace, there's gaming, entertainment and a bar/grill at the adjacent Belterra Casino Resort & Spa.

French Lick

French Lick, Donald Ross

25 | 21 | 23 | 24 | $120

French Lick | 8670 W. State Rd. 56 | 812-936-9300 | 888-936-9360 |
www.frenchlick.com | 7030/5050; 72.3/69.6; 135/120

"Lovingly restored" by architect Lee Schmidt, this "classic 1917 Donald Ross course" is "not to be missed" even if it "looks a lot easier on the scorecard than it plays" thanks to "many sidehill and downhill lies" and greens that are "tough to putt"; though "difficult", it's "golf as it should be", with "no tricks or gimmicks."

NEW French Lick, Pete Dye

- | - | - | - | $125

French Lick | 8670 W. State Rd. 56 | 812-936-9300 | 888-936-9360 |
www.frenchlick.com | 8102/5151; 80.0/70.5; 148/120

Celtics legend Larry Bird grew up in French Lick and you'll need something like his long-range touch to cope with this 8,100-yard, Pete Dye–designed beautiful brute built in 2009, which plays atop ridges and through valleys in the pristine, rolling southern Indiana countryside; survive the rough-covered sidehill lies and a fistful of volcano bunkers and the reward is a muscle-flexing finish, the 301-yard, par-3 16th (with water in play), the 518-yard, par-4 17th and the 657-yard, par-5 18th.

Indianapolis

Brickyard Crossing

24 | 20 | 23 | 21 | $90

Indianapolis | 4400 W. 16th St. | 317-484-6572 |
www.brickyardcrossing.com | 6994/5038; 74.0/68.8; 143/127

A "unique golf experience" awaits at this Pete Dye design adjacent to the Indianapolis Motor Speedway, with four of its holes located "in the infield of the track"; the "awesome venue" comes with a "great staff", and it's a particular "treat if you're there on a day when cars are running" ("if you like Indy racing", then "go under the track and look around – just be sure to inhale" first).

Fort, The
26 | 22 | 24 | 25 | $69

Indianapolis | 6002 N. Post Rd. | 317-543-9597 | www.thefortgolfcourse.com | 7148/5045; 74.4/69.2; 139/122
"One of the gems of Indy", this "wonderful" municipal designed by Pete Dye is set "on an old army base" just minutes from Downtown Indianapolis; with tree-lined holes, "large, undulating greens" and "elevation changes that are hard to come by in Indiana", it "has enough challenge for most golfers", so be sure to bring extra balls; P.S. the "fantastic" experience includes quaint lodgings at the seven-room Harrison House.

Heartland Crossing
– | – | – | – | $55

Camby | 6701 S. Heartland Blvd. | 317-630-1785 | www.heartlandcrossinggolf.com | 7267/5536; 75.4/69.0; 134/121
A collaboration between Steve Smyers and PGA Tour veteran Nick Price, this links-style layout just southwest of Indianapolis is a "gem" that has "generous fairways" but "plays really hard" thanks to "tons of bunkers" and a design that "puts a premium on the approach shot"; it's also "very nicely maintained" and relatively inexpensive, so fans urge "do not miss it if playing in Indy."

Otter Creek
∇ 23 | 15 | 21 | 23 | $79

Columbus | 11522 E. 50 N. | 812-579-5227 | www.ottercreekgolf.com
East/North | 7274/6286; 75.8/70.7; 132/120
North/West | 7349/5363; 75.7/71.2; 136/120
West/East | 7167/5155; 75.1/70.3; 132/118
Located in the serene countryside near Columbus, this 27-holer is a father-son collaboration: Robert Trent Jones Sr. created the North and West tracks back in 1964 and son Rees added the East in 1995; it's a "scenic, playable", "traditional" "muni at a bargain price", making it a "hidden gem" that's "well worth the drive from Indy."

Prairie View
∇ 25 | 24 | 24 | 23 | $75

Carmel | 7000 Longest Dr. | 317-816-3100 | www.prairieviewgc.com | 7073/5203; 74.3/70.6; 134/122
True to its name, this "amazing" RTJ Jr. design has prairie grass as a distinguishing feature; created for golfers of all abilities, the 206-acre spread features five lakes, 90 bunkers, towering sycamores and a meandering stream that weaves through four holes, and while a few fret that it's "overpriced for the market", the large clubhouse, grass driving range and other facilities help to compensate.

☒ Purgatory
28 | 24 | 22 | 24 | $55

Noblesville | 12160 E. 216th St. | 317-776-4653 | www.purgatorygolf.com | 7754/4562; 78.1/66.9; 142/115
"The name says it all" at Indiana's top-rated Course, this "must-play" just north of Indianapolis that's also the longest track in the state, stretching nearly 7,800 yards; it can "bring even the best of golfers to their knees" with "outstanding visual intimidation" (including bunkering and "great water holes"), but if you "bring your A+ sand game" and "play the right tees", it's a "fair challenge."

	COURSE	FACIL.	SERVICE	VALUE	COST

Rock Hollow
▽ 26 | 12 | 20 | 26 | $49

Peru | 669 S. County Rd. 250 W. | 765-473-6100 | www.rockhollowgolf.com | 6944/4967; 74.0/69.1; 136/118

A "wonderful track that winds through an old rock quarry" about 90 minutes north of Indianapolis, this "out-of-the-way" layout is "well worth the drive" to play a challenging but fair design from Pete Dye protégé Tim Liddy that mixes forests, wetlands and rocky sections; sparse facilities mean it's "all about the golf here", but it's a "great value" given that the course is "not overly played" and thus in "awesome condition."

Trophy Club
23 | 20 | 20 | 25 | $39

Lebanon | 3887 Hwy. 52 N. | 765-482-7272 | www.thetrophyclubgolf.com | 7317/5050; 75.3/69.3; 138/118

A "favorite in the Indianapolis area", this "wonderful, challenging" "links-style" "gem" designed by Tim Liddy is an "outstanding test", with "manicured fairways" that "make you play all the shots" and "large greens that require accurate approaches"; all in all, it's a "solid" track that's a "good value" – "weekend afternoons are a steal."

Iowa

Cedar Rapids

Amana Colonies 🏨
24 | 19 | 19 | 21 | $67

Amana | 451 27th Ave. | 319-622-6222 | 800-383-3636 | www.amanagolfcourse.com | 6824/5228; 73.3/70.0; 142/115

Who knew "there were so many hills and trees in the middle of Iowa?" ponder fans of this "gem" "tucked away" in a cluster of historic villages 15 minutes south of Cedar Rapids; "lots of elevation changes", a few "blind tee shots" and "many holes through the woods" with "relatively narrow fairways" make it "hard for first-timers", so "bring extra balls" – and your thirst for some post-round suds at the local brewery.

Des Moines

Harvester, The
▽ 29 | 25 | 26 | 26 | $109

Rhodes | 1102 330th St. | 641-227-4653 | www.harvestergolf.com | 7365/5180; 76.0/68.9; 140/120

Expect a "warm Midwestern welcome" to "start your challenging day" at "one of Iowa's finest" publics, this Keith Foster layout located "in the heartland" northeast of Des Moines; the "beautiful" design is "second-to-none", "with lightning-fast greens that roll and break with the best" and par 4s that require terrific "tee ball strategy", making it an "absolute must-play" that'll leave you "smiling."

Tournament Club of Iowa
- | - | - | - | $54

Polk City | 1000 Tradition Dr. | 515-984-9440 | www.tcofiowa.com | 7043/5039; 74.0/69.2; 145/122

"Make it a point to schedule a golf trip" to this Arnold Palmer design in Polk City or you'll be "missing the boat" insist fans; although it may be "too target golf" for some, most consider it a challenging but fair option at a "reasonable cost", with a "beautiful" routing through hills, bluffs and five man-made lakes.

Iowa City

Finkbine

▽ | 21 | 14 | 15 | 22 | $42

Iowa City | 1386 W. Melrose Ave. | 319-335-9246 | www.finkbine.com | 7239/5163; 74.6/69.4; 134/117

A "solid" circa-1930 design, the Hawkeyes' home track is in "surprisingly good condition", with "bentgrass greens and fairways" that "enhance its character"; a "wonderful traditional Midwestern" venue, it features "elevation changes", "fast greens, sand and trees" to make it "a real challenge", and while the sparse facilities are a "drawback" to some, "there are plenty of dining options nearby."

Pleasant Valley

▽ | 23 | 20 | 22 | 23 | $20

Iowa City | 4390 SE Sand Rd. | 319-337-7209 | www.pleasantvalleyic.com | 6472/5067; 70.7/68.7; 127/119

For "Florida golf in the middle of the cornfields of Iowa", head to this "tight little" "treat" that's a "must-play if you're in the vicinity" of Iowa City; "short but accessible", the layout sports "wonderful greens that are moderately fast" and "water that comes into play on roughly nine of the 18 holes" – there's also "great food in the clubhouse."

Riverside Casino & Golf Resort, Blue Top Ridge

- | - | - | - | $80

Riverside | 3184 Hwy. 22 | 877-677-3456 |
www.riversidecasinoandresort.com |
7432/5145; 77.6/66.0; 146/117

"Rees Jones designed it and that's all you need to know" about this track located 20 minutes south of Iowa City at a resort casino; it "will test your mettle" with "dramatic elevation changes" and "over 200 traps" even as it wows you with breathtaking scenery and diverse terrain; flooding forced the construction of four new holes (Nos. 2–5), but the original holes have been rebuilt and can be played separately.

Kansas

Garden City

Buffalo Dunes

- | - | - | - | $25

Garden City | 5685 Hwy. 83 S. | 620-276-1210 | www.buffalodunes.org | 6767/5631; 72.8/69.5; 128/118

While it may be a "surprise to find a course of this quality" in "out-of-the-way" rural southwest Kansas, this "interesting" muni is "well worth" the trek to Garden City to traverse a layout that's wide-open to the southerly winds; it's "well cared for by the staff and players alike."

Kansas City

Alvamar Public

23 | 17 | 19 | 20 | $45

Lawrence | 1809 Crossgate Dr. | 785-842-1907 | www.alvamar.com | 7092/4892; 74.5/68.1; 130/112

"If you like to push the limits on risk/reward", check out this "first-rate" option in Lawrence, "home to the U. of Kansas golf team"; it's "always in shape due to the thick zoysia grass", and if some find the clubhouse "spartan", a well-stocked pro shop adds to the overall "value."

| | COURSE | FACIL. | SERVICE | VALUE | COST |

Deer Creek
23 | 21 | 20 | 20 | $59

Overland Park | 7000 W. 133rd St. | 913-681-3100 | www.deercreekgc.com | 6811/5126; 74.5/68.5; 137/113

Nestled in a "picturesque setting" just south of Kansas City, this "outstanding RTJ Jr. course" utilizes a "natural creek to great effect" in a "challenging" setup that fans find "perfect in every detail"; the "well-kept" layout, "nice pro shop" and "friendly, knowledgeable staff" make it reminiscent of a "quiet country club in the suburbs", albeit one that "should really have a driving range."

Falcon Ridge
24 | 21 | 21 | 20 | $65

Lenexa | 20200 Prairie Star Pkwy. | 913-393-4653 | www.falconridgegolf.com | 6820/5160; 72.8/69.2; 130/123

"Gorgeous to look at" but "hell to play", this Lenexa layout remains a "favorite in the Kansas City area", even if one "must play more than once to learn some of the holes" due to "very undulating terrain"; with multiple tees and markers, it's "a challenge for the better golfer, but forgiving enough for the novice", and the "superb conditions" and "beautiful" views ensure "you get your money's worth."

Ironhorse
∇ 21 | 21 | 21 | 20 | $69

Leawood | 15400 Mission Rd. | 913-685-4653 | www.ironhorsegolf.com | 6889/4745; 73.8/67.6; 140/119

After an 18-month renovation, this Michael Hurdzan design (now a Troon course) in suburban Leawood reopened in 2008 with refurbished greens, new bunkers, a creek reinforcement and a new irrigation system; meandering through oaks, over water and around rock outcroppings, the layout features numerous holes that play downhill to generous fairways, and there's a bonus three-hole par-3 practice circuit.

Prairie Highlands
∇ 23 | 18 | 20 | 21 | $42

Olathe | 14695 S. Inverness Dr. | 913-856-7235 | www.prairiehighlands.com | 7066/5122; 74.6/70.3; 134/122

This "first-rate" Olathe course is a "nice surprise in Kansas", but "you'd better bring some extra balls" because "if you're not straight off the tee, you'll be borrowing some" – or digging them out of 60 bunkers; the former U.S. Senior Open qualifying site was designed to be walkable, but on such a long, hilly track, why walk "with GPS in the carts?"

Sycamore Ridge
∇ 26 | 20 | 21 | 26 | $49

Spring Hill | 21731 Clubhouse Dr. | 913-592-5292 | www.sycamoreridgegolf.com | 7081/4877; 76.2/65.4; 150/118

This "first-rate" Spring Hill municipal is actually "two courses in one" – a wide-open, "links-style front" followed by a "woodlands nine" where you're sure to lose some balls as you try "to steer [them] down the fairways"; it "provides every shot in the bag" for a reasonable fee, making it "outstanding for the money."

Topeka

Colbert Hills 🖧
∇ 28 | 19 | 25 | 25 | $80

Manhattan | 5200 Colbert Hills Dr. | 785-776-6475 | www.colberthills.com | 7525/4982; 77.5/69.4; 152/116

Designed by Kansas State alum Jim Colbert (with Jeff Brauer), this "challenging" "gem" in Manhattan "can be a terror when the wind is

	COURSE	FACIL.	SERVICE	VALUE	COST

up", so "bring extra balls" and select appropriately from the "wide range of tees"; views of the "rolling terrain" and "surrounding grasslands" backed by "outstanding service" and a fairly new clubhouse make it "worth a special trip", especially for alumni, students and school staff, who get a discount.

NEW Firekeeper
| - | - | - | - | $65 |

Mayetta | 12524 150 Rd. | 785-966-2100 | www.firekeepergolf.com | 7560/4790; 77.1/68.8; 137/114

The first golf course designed by a Native American on tribal-owned land, this collaboration between Notah Begay III, a four-time PGA Tour winner, and veteran architect Jeff Brauer is a nature-first, lay-of-the-land spread north of Topeka built for the Prairie Band Potawatomi Nation; with its blend of open and forested holes, short and long, there's something for everyone, and if the double-fairway, 455-yard, par-4 18th yields a high number on your scorecard, you can try to recoup your losses at the resort casino across the street.

Wichita

Sand Creek Station
| - | - | - | - | $51 |

Newton | 920 Meadowbrook Dr. | 316-284-6161 | www.sandcreekgolfclub.com | 7359/5165; 76.3/71.9; 133/124

Blending re-created holes from St. Andrews and North Berwick with more modern efforts, this Jeff Brauer layout embraces the old and the new on a "flat, open-prairie course" just north of Wichita; it's an "enjoyable challenge", with a long par-5 10th that requires you to negotiate water on all three shots, especially for those who "love trains, as one comes through" regularly on a track dividing the front and back nines.

Kentucky

Lexington

Bull at Boone's Trace
| - | - | - | - | $37 |

Richmond | 175 Glen Eagle Blvd. | 859-623-4653 | 877-662-4653 | www.thebullgolf.com | 6659/5615; 71.6/66.8; 136/126

Nestled in the heart of Kentucky horse country, this "must-play" course within a gated Richmond community is named for Daniel Boone, who first settled the Bluegrass State, and for the abolitionist Cassius Clay, who once ran one of the namesake beasts over a local precipice; the track is a "bucking bull" in its own right, a "challenging but fair" layout in which all of the fairways "have a slope to [maneuver] your ball in or out of position."

Kearney Hill Golf Links
| ∇ 26 | 20 | 22 | 26 | $33 |

Lexington | 3403 Kearney Rd. | 859-253-1981 | www.lexingtonky.gov | 7079/5367; 73.5/65.5; 131/115

"It doesn't get any better than this" Lexington municipal that's "one of the best for the buck in Kentucky" thanks to a Scottish links–style layout from father-son collaborators Pete and P.B. Dye; although some say the "links design doesn't quite work 1,000 miles from the ocean" (it's "hard to bump-and-run on bentgrass"), most laud the course as "just pure golf" with "no trick holes" to be found, although there are "several that will challenge."

Marriott's Griffin Gate ⌂   ∇ 19 | 19 | 19 | 18 | $75

Lexington | 1720 Newtown Pike | 859-288-6193 | www.marriott.com | 6784/5053; 72.2/68.6; 133/122

A "nice way to get away from the horses" while in the Bluegrass State, this Rees Jones resort course offers "a good mix of birdie holes and 'hang-on' holes" on a layout that "plays rather easy" but "feels cramped and tight" to some (it "looks better from afar"); the "clubhouse is a little tired", but the "attentive staff", "gourmet restaurant" and convenient location just minutes from Downtown Lexington compensate.

Old Silo   ∇ 26 | 21 | 21 | 25 | $49

Mount Sterling | 350 Silver Lake Dr. | 859-498-4697 | www.oldsilo.com | 6977/5509; 74.5/67.8; 139/125

"One of the top public courses in Kentucky", this "fabulous" Graham Marsh "jewel" is nestled in "a nice pastoral setting" about 30 minutes east of Lexington, boasting an "interesting layout" that's "challenging to all", with a meandering creek and "tough, undulating greens" as well as "lots of sand" (there are 98 bunkers) and "plenty of hills and water"; what's more, it's "so cheap, you'll feel like you're playing for free."

Louisiana

Baton Rouge

Bluffs, The ⌀   25 | 21 | 20 | 21 | $72

Saint Francisville | 14233 Sunrise Way | 225-634-5222 | www.thebluffs.com | 7003/4669; 73.9/67.2; 136/111

This laid-back Arnold Palmer design 40 miles north of Baton Rouge may feel like it's "in the boondocks" (it's "difficult to find even if you have a map"), but it's a "quirky" "little hidden gem" and a "solid target course" that's "worth the ride" for "some spectacular holes" offering a "good test" of skills; since it was intended for championship play, the flexible design makes it appealing to average golfers too.

Carter Plantation   22 | 22 | 22 | 19 | $64

Springfield | 23475 Carter Trace | 225-294-7555 | www.carterplantation.com | 7104/5057; 73.9/69.0; 133/117

LSU alum and 2001 PGA Championship winner David Toms created this "beautiful, well-designed" track located less than an hour from Baton Rouge, and the consensus is that it's a "great course in the middle of nowhere"; although some find it "uninspiring", most praise the layout's "strong holes", which are "in decent shape" – "as is everything" on the state's Audubon Golf Trail.

Copper Mill   - | - | - | - | $48

Zachary | 2100 Copper Mill Blvd. | 225-658-0656 | www.coppermillgolf.com | 6866/4693; 73.0/63.2; 131/99

Located in a residential community about 25 miles north of Baton Rouge, this "interesting 6-6-6 layout" is a "solid challenge", with six par 3s, six par 4s and six par 5s all offering "some very long carries"; planned with both the golfer and homeowner in mind, there's ample playing space surrounding the "well-maintained" course, while residents have front row seats.

Lake Charles

Gray Plantation

`-` | `-` | `-` | `-` | $65

Lake Charles | 6150 Graywood Pkwy. | 337-562-1663 |
www.graywoodllc.com | 7191/4514; 75.0/71.9; 137/128

It's "worth your time to visit" this "fun" option in southwestern Louisiana near Lake Charles thanks to a solid layout featuring tree-lined fairways, heavily bunkered greens and water on 12 holes; although a few feel there are only "three or four good holes", others insist it's "one of the best public courses you can play" at this price level.

New Orleans

TPC Louisiana

23 | 24 | 22 | 18 | $189

Avondale | 11001 Lapalco Blvd. | 504-436-8721 | 866-665-2872 |
www.tpc.com | 7399/5121; 76.6/69.7; 138/119

This "tough, flat" track in Avondale "has come back nicely" post-Katrina and now hosts the PGA Tour's Zurich Classic; although some consider it "uninspiring" ("many holes look the same"), many consider the "hard and fast" Pete Dye design one of the "best in the area", and it's run by a "great staff."

Maine

Central Maine

⊠ Belgrade Lakes ⅄

27 | 18 | 23 | 23 | $150

Belgrade Lakes | 46 Clubhouse Dr. | 207-495-4653 |
www.belgradelakesgolf.com | 6723/5168; 72.2/64.1; 135/126

"One more reason to love Maine", this "spectacular" spread sports "drop-dead views" "overlooking the lakes" on a layout routed over "rugged, extremely hilly terrain" about 25 minutes north of Augusta; "rocks along the fairways provide some interesting shots" but can make it "too penal for the mid-handicapper", and while there's a "friendly, helpful staff", the lack of a driving range causes some to suggest "such a nice course deserves better facilities."

Kebo Valley

▽ 19 | 13 | 20 | 19 | $99

Bar Harbor | 136 Eagle Lake Rd. | 207-288-3000 | www.kebovalleyclub.com |
6131/5473; 69.5/72.6; 124/128

"History and great golf combine for a wonderful experience" at this "quirky" 1888 links design by Herbert Leeds and A.E. Liscombe that's part of the country's eighth-oldest golf club, located in Bar Harbor; while it offers some "interesting holes", some say the "poor course conditions" and spartan facilities mean "old and rustic may be an understatement."

Sugarloaf

26 | 21 | 20 | 23 | $120

Carrabassett Valley | 5092 Access Rd. | 207-237-2000 | 800-843-5623 |
www.sugarloaf.com | 6910/5289; 74.8/72.5; 146/131

"It's all about the golf" at this "excellent design" from RTJ Jr. that will "challenge every aspect of your game" with a "hard, intimidating and at times cold" layout routed over "scenic, undulating" terrain in north-western Maine; the "well-maintained" track is "simply amazing", as is the clubhouse, a 5,500-sq.-ft. facility that includes a spacious pro shop, a bar/grill overlooking the 10th and 11th tees, and panoramic views of Bigelow Mountain.

Sunday River ⛳

▽ 26 | 24 | 22 | 22 | $120

Newry | 18 Championship Dr. | 207-824-4653 | 800-543-2754 | www.sundayrivergolf.com | 7130/5006; 75.2/65.2; 146/118

Another "spectacular mountain course" from RTJ Jr., this 2004 track nestled on the edge of the Sunday River Valley in western Maine is sur-rounded by wilderness, with "breathtaking views" of the Mahoosuc Range "from just about every tee"; it's "not for the faint of heart" or "those who have trouble with forced carries", but "if your game is on, you will score" – and you can reward yourself at the nearby Sunday River Brewing Company.

Southern Maine

Dunegrass ⛳

▽ 22 | 19 | 19 | 21 | $53

Old Orchard Beach | 200 Wild Dunes Way | 207-934-4513 | 800-521-1029 | www.dunegrass.com | 6684/4818; 72.1/68.0; 137/113

Nestled on more than 300 acres of scenic seaside terrain in the greater Portland area, this "feast for the eyes" looks "very similar to a Myrtle Beach course" thanks to its "great location near the coast"; although it's not that long, it "can be tough, depending on the wind" and on how well you can negotiate "narrow, tree-lined fairways with natural blind hazards throughout."

Ledges, The

24 | 17 | 21 | 21 | $75

York | 1 Ledges Dr. | 207-351-3000 | www.ledgesgolf.com | 6981/4997; 73.9/70.9; 138/126

A "mix of hazards" makes this "beautiful", "wonderfully challenging course", hewn from rock atop a rugged hillside about 50 miles from Portland, one "tough" nut; the "difficult but fun greens" are "humped, bumped and fast", and if the facilities are wanting, the "well-maintained" course conditions, ubiquitous wildlife and "nice staff" help make it one of the "best courses in southern Maine."

Old Marsh Country Club

- | - | - | - | $69

Wells | 445 Clubhouse Rd. | 207-251-4653 | www.sundayrivergolf.com | 6523/4847; 71.5/68.7; 131/116

Fans of classical design will embrace this throwback effort from resto-ration specialist Brian Silva, whose original creation evokes the talents of C.B. Macdonald and Seth Raynor thanks to his use of yawning, ran-domly scattered bunkers, enormous, rolling fairways and massive, un-dulating greens; situated at the southern tip of Maine, it features a fistful of modern-looking lakes that add contemporary flair.

Samoset

25 | 23 | 23 | 21 | $140

Rockport | 220 Warrenton St. | 207-594-2511 | 800-341-1650 | www.samoset.com | 6548/5083; 70.8/70.2; 133/120

A "must if you're in Maine", this redesign of a 1902 Rockport original sports "knockout holes with ocean views", particularly "on the front nine", including the signature par-5 4th alongside Penobscot Bay, enhanced by a stone seawall; the "back nine isn't bad, either", and you can expect "well-manicured" conditions and "luxury surroundings."

Maryland

TOP COURSES IN STATE

28 Bulle Rock | *Baltimore*
   Links at Lighthouse Sound | *Ocean City*
26 Whiskey Creek | *Frederick*
25 Rum Pointe | *Ocean City*
24 Queenstown Harbor, River | *Easton*

Baltimore

⚡ Bulle Rock 🏌   28 | 26 | 25 | 21 | $130

Havre de Grace | 320 Blenheim Ln. | 410-939-8887 | 888-285-5375 |
www.bullerock.com | 7375/5426; 76.4/72.0; 147/126
Again rated the "best in Maryland", this "terrific" "Pete Dye classic", which played host to the LPGA Championship, is a "complete bear" of a course with some of the "best public greens you will putt on" as well as "unbelievably dense rough – you can be standing on top of your ball and not see it"; it's "pricey for a remote town" northeast of Baltimore, but you can expect a "first-rate facility" complete with a "beautiful clubhouse" and "memorable service."

Greystone   23 | 19 | 21 | 25 | $78

White Hall | 2115 White Hall Rd. | 410-887-1945 |
www.baltimoregolfing.com | 6925/4800; 73.9/67.5; 141/112
At this "wonderful muni" run by Baltimore County, Bill Love tweaked Joe Lee's design to the tune of a $2 million bunker renovation, and it's now one of the "best values around", boasting a "challenging", "well-maintained" layout that's "all you'll want from the tips"; the clubhouse and other facilities "might not be much", but the chance to play "secluded", "scenic golf" more than compensates.

Waverly Woods   23 | 22 | 18 | 20 | $84

Marriottsville | 2100 Warwick Way | 410-313-9182 |
www.waverlywoods.com | 7024/4834; 74.0/68.1; 135/116
A "pleasure to play" just 30 minutes west of Baltimore, this Arthur Hills design strikes some as "maybe too challenging for a public track" with its "fast greens" and "difficult pin placements", but rest assured the "greens roll smooth", it's "fairly open off the tee" and it's "kept in top condition most of the time"; the "good practice facility" is another reason it's "well worth" a visit, making "the only downer [the fact] that more houses keep getting built here."

Cumberland

Rocky Gap Lodge 🏨   ▽ 25 | 22 | 23 | 21 | $90

Flintstone | 16701 Lakeview Rd. NE | 301-784-8500 | 800-724-0828 |
www.rockygapresort.com | 7000/5198; 74.2/70.0; 145/129
"You will love this Jack Nicklaus layout in the mountains of western Maryland" predict fans who are "surprised it's not more frequented" given its "hilly", picturesque location next to Rocky Gap State Park; the

resort lodge overlooking 243-acre Lake Habeeb and the Youth Golf Academy make it an ideal spot to "bring the family."

DC Metro Area

Lake Presidential

| - | - | - | - | $99 |

Upper Marlboro | 3151 Presidential Golf Dr. | 301-627-8577 | www.lakepresidential.com | 7230/4800; 74.4/69.6; 149/125

Located 20 miles southeast of the White House, this walker-friendly layout in Upper Marlboro is draped across heaving, densely forested terrain that's slashed by streams and punctuated by the namesake 30-acre lake; built by the folks behind PGA West and Kiawah Island's Ocean course, among others, it's sure to attract golfers of all political bents.

Swan Point

| ∇ 25 | 23 | 23 | 26 | $79 |

Issue | 11550 Swan Point Blvd. | 301-259-0047 | www.swanpointgolf.com | 6859/4992; 73.1/69.3; 130/116

"Great golf is not an issue in Issue" quip fans of this "beautiful" Bob Cupp design that delivers "spectacular marsh and Chesapeake inlet scenery" on a "challenging" layout with "interesting hazards" and "immaculate" conditioning; nestled "not far from DC" on the southern shore of the Potomac, it's a "quiet and relaxed" experience that some hope will "stay undiscovered" by "Beltway bandits."

Easton

Hog Neck

| 22 | 16 | 18 | 23 | $55 |

Easton | 10142 Old Cordova Rd. | 410-822-6079 | 800-280-1790 | www.hogneck.com | 7106/5477; 74.4/66.4; 132/118

A "hidden gem" off Route 50 north of Easton, this "well-kept" Lindsay Bruce Ervin design is "tough but fair", with a "links-style front" that's "wide-open off the tee" and a "wooded back nine" that's routed "through mature trees in a quiet environment"; "don't expect a lot of service" or other amenities, but its "value" pricing and nine-hole executive course make it "popular with locals."

Queenstown Harbor, Lakes (fka Atlantic Golf at Queenstown Harbor, Lakes)

| 22 | 18 | 20 | 17 | $72 |

Queenstown | 310 Links Ln. | 410-827-6611 | 800-827-5257 | www.ghgolf.com | 6569/4606; 71.0/66.6; 124/111

Native son Lindsay Bruce Ervin designed both of the 18-hole tracks at this "lovely" site near Easton, and although some consider the Lakes to be a "small step down from the River", it's still a "nice course" with "old-world charm"; it "can get very windy" and the "clubhouse leaves a bit to be desired", but the "picturesque" Chesapeake Bay views make it a "don't-miss" "Maryland experience."

Queenstown Harbor, River (fka Atlantic Golf at Queenstown Harbor, River)

| 24 | 20 | 23 | 19 | $119 |

Queenstown | 310 Links Ln. | 410-827-6611 | 800-827-5257 | www.ghgolf.com | 7096/4978; 74.2/69.0; 138/123

All of the greens were redone at this "sleeper" near Easton, but while the course "renovations only add to its appeal", the "move to make it

COURSE · FACIL. · SERVICE · VALUE · COST

a little more upscale than its sister" has "raised the price" such that it's "not anywhere near the value it used to be"; still, it's "a good place for a golfing buddies trip" (though it can be "difficult in the wind"), with "views of the Chester River adding to the greatness of the immaculately maintained layout."

River Marsh 🏌

▽ 24 | 24 | 24 | 22 | $134

Cambridge | 100 Heron Blvd. | 410-901-6397 | www.rivermarshgolfclub.com | 6801/4780; 72.5/67.8; 127/111

Affiliated with the Hyatt Regency Chesapeake Bay resort, this 2002 Keith Foster design has "matured nicely", developing into a fairly "wide-open course" that's "great for women golfers" even as it "penalizes the overaggressive"; it plays around "picturesque scenery, with water on most holes", notably the signature 17th, a "long par 3" that traverses Shoal Creek, and a "fun 18th" featuring the Choptank River "running the length of the hole."

Frederick

Maryland National 🏌

24 | 21 | 19 | 20 | $99

Middletown | 8836 Hollow Rd. | 301-371-0000 | www.marylandnational.com | 6811/4844; 73.1/68.3; 137/120

"Set in the hills of central Maryland", this "challenging" Arthur Hills design "gets the blood pumping" with plenty of "elevation changes" along with "trees and rough [that] will eat your drives if you aren't accurate", but "not much water"; a few find it "more picturesque than playable", but most agree it's both "fair and good enough to play over and over", especially when you factor in the "great views" of the Catoctin Mountains.

P.B. Dye

21 | 21 | 20 | 18 | $89

Ijamsville | 9526 Doctor Perry Rd. | 301-607-4653 | www.pbdyegolf.com | 6724/5107; 72.2/68.3; 136/123

The eponymous designer is a "master magician", and "you will either love or hate" his "tough", "take-no-prisoners" creation near Frederick, where the "signature railroad ties" and "small, terraced greens" add up to an "exceptional challenge"; it seems "tricked up" and "harshly penal" to some, but they admit it's a "distinctive design with lots of potential", especially if management continues to "soften it around the edges."

Whiskey Creek

26 | 23 | 22 | 22 | $75

Ijamsville | 4804 Whiskey Ct. | 301-694-2900 | 888-883-1174 | www.whiskeycreekgolf.com | 7001/5296; 74.6/70.5; 138/121

A "tremendous design" from J. Michael Poellot and consultant Ernie Els, this "challenging" Frederick-area "winner" at the foot of the Catoctin Mountains is "big, beautiful and distinctive", with "lots of elevation and interesting topography"; crisscrossed by a creek once used to float barrels of moonshine (the clubhouse boasts a "good whiskey selection"), it "ends with a spectacular 18th."

Worthington Manor

21 | 17 | 20 | 21 | $69

Urbana | 8329 Fingerboard Rd. | 301-874-5400 | 888-917-2582 | www.worthingtonmanor.com | 7034/5206; 74.4/70.1; 144/116

Nestled in the "scenic" hills near Frederick, this "terrific, fair" track is a "real test" that's "worth playing again" thanks to "an interesting mix of holes" featuring "elevation changes" and "some of the toughest greens you will ever play", which is why it's hosted the U.S. Open Qualifier nine times since 1999; while a few feel the "well-maintained" layout "could be better", most are convinced it's the "best buy in the area."

Ocean City

Eagle's Landing

21 | **18** | **20** | **22** | **$79**

Berlin | 12367 Eagles Nest Rd. | 410-213-7277 | 800-283-3846 | www.eagleslandinggolf.com | 7003/4896; 73.6/64.0; 129/108

For "tidal golf at its best", head to this "unique" Michael Hurdzan "must-play" offering "beautiful scenery" and "eagles overhead" combined with "wonderful high risk/reward shot-making possibilities" – expect "long drives, for both ball and cart, over wetlands"; just minutes from Ocean City, it features "gorgeous views" of the Sinepuxent Bay on an inbound nine that also boasts "some killer holes", like the short par-4 closer, dubbed the Beast of the East.

Links at Lighthouse Sound 🏌

28 | **25** | **23** | **21** | **$179**

Bishopville | 12723 St. Martins Neck Rd. | 410-352-5767 | 888-554-4557 | www.lighthousesound.com | 7031/4553; 73.3/67.1; 144/122

The "best course at the Maryland beaches" is this "primo" Arthur Hills design that delivers "stunning views of the Ocean City skyline" from a "challenging", "well-conditioned" course where there's "whipping wind" and many a carry "over hazards, so bring lots of spare balls"; it's "a value at twilight" for $69 but is "worth every penny even at full price"; P.S. it also boasts the "longest golf cart bridge in the country."

Ocean City Golf Club, Newport Bay

20 | **18** | **19** | **19** | **$95**

Berlin | 11401 Country Club Dr. | 410-641-1779 | 800-442-3570 | www.ocgolfandyacht.com | 6657/5205; 71.0/71.5; 126/119

Completely redesigned by Lester George in 1998, this "lovely marshland" layout is ideal "for the casual player" looking for an "enjoyable afternoon of golf and dining" accompanied by "beautiful views of the Intracoastal Waterway"; some grouse that it "charges resort fees for an average course", and that there are "better places to play in the Ocean City area", but "friendly" service helps to compensate.

River Run 🏌

21 | **17** | **19** | **20** | **$119**

Berlin | 11605 Masters Ln. | 410-641-7200 | 800-733-7786 | www.riverrungolf.com | 6705/4818; 72.1/73.1; 136/117

An "enjoyable" "Gary Player design minutes from Ocean City", this "well-kept" course delivers "pretty scenery" on a "widely varied layout" that can "lull you to sleep" on the open, links-style front, then "challenge you" on a wooded return that requires you "to hit accurate long irons"; it can get "windy", but the "average golfer can score well", and while the facilities "leave something to be desired", the staff is "very pleasant."

Rum Pointe 🏌

25 | **21** | **22** | **23** | **$149**

Berlin | 7000 Rum Pointe Ln. | 410-629-1414 | 888-809-4653 | www.rumpointe.com | 7001/5276; 72.6/70.3; 122/120

A "beautiful course with equally beautiful views" of the Sinepuxent Bay (from all holes save one), this Ocean City–area "must-play" was "well planned" by Pete and P.B. Dye to be "a nice, long track that plays much tougher than its slope rating", with "heavy rough" and sturdy winds ensuring it's "always a challenge"; the "facilities are nice" and the staff is "accommodating", but insiders advise "make sure to bring plenty of bug spray."

Massachusetts

TOP COURSES IN STATE

27 Taconic | *Berkshires*
   Pinehills, Jones | *Boston*
   Pinehills, Nicklaus | *Boston*
26 Crumpin-Fox | *Berkshires*
   Farm Neck | *Martha's Vineyard*

Berkshires

Crumpin-Fox
26 | 18 | 19 | 22 | $77

Bernardston | 87 Parmenter Rd. | 413-648-9101 | 800-943-1901 | www.golfthefox.com | 7007/5432; 73.8/71.5; 141/131

"What's a nice course like you doing in a place like this?" quip supporters of "one of the finest tracks" in the state, a "fantastic Roger Rulewich" design "tucked in the woods near Vermont"; perhaps the "hardest in the Northeast", it's a "bear" boasting "tough greens", numerous carries and rolling, forested terrain, so even if the facilities and course are "in need of a little TLC", it remains a solid "value."

ⓩ Taconic ⊕
27 | 17 | 21 | 23 | $145

Williamstown | 19 Meacham St. | 413-458-3997 | www.taconicgolf.com | 6808/5143; 73.5/71.4; 136/122

"Simply the finest golfing experience in Massachusetts", the state's top-rated Course is this "short but absolutely gorgeous" Berkshires "classic" dating from 1896, where you "feel like you're in heaven" as you "relax, walk it" and take in the ambiance of a "New England college town"; it's "expensive" (except for Williams College students, staff and alumni, who get steep discounts), but it offers some of the "best conditioning" around, so "make the drive" because this is "as good as it gets."

Boston

Atlantic Country Club
25 | 23 | 22 | 22 | $76

Plymouth | 450 Little Sandy Pond Rd. | 508-759-6644 | www.atlanticcountryclub.com | 6728/4918; 73.0/68.3; 131/116

A "hidden gem in Plymouth", this "classic course" "comes highly recommended" thanks to a "beautifully manicured" layout that can be "difficult and at times frustrating", with "some challenging holes" that make "staying in the fairway a must"; add "views that can't be beat" and "impeccable service" (you're "treated like royalty") and you have a "great value for the price."

Granite Links at Quarry Hills ⌨ ⊕
22 | 24 | 20 | 17 | $125

Boston | 100 Quarry Hills Dr. | 617-689-1900 | www.granitelinksgolfclub.com
Granite/Milton | 6818/5001; 73.4/70.6; 141/124
Granite/Quincy | 6735/4723; 73.3/68.4; 137/123
Quincy/Milton | 6873/4980; 73.9/69.8; 139/118

The "price of the greens fees is surpassed only by the views" of the Boston skyline at this "magnificent course" that was "built on an old

	COURSE	FACIL.	SERVICE	VALUE	COST

quarry" just south of the city; the three nines are "wide-open" and "very hilly", with "almost no trees", so "even the slightest of breezes feels like a hurricane" and will present you with some "challenging decisions as you select your clubs"; you need to check ahead to see which holes are open to the public.

Olde Scotland Links
18 | **10** | **16** | **20** | **$49**

Bridgewater | 695 Pine St. | 508-279-3344 | www.oldescotlandlinks.com | 6790/4649; 72.6/68.4; 126/111

Although "neither olde nor Scottish nor links", this "challenging" Bridgewater municipal is an "interesting" design that "looks like a links-style course but plays like a parklander", with "more forced carries" than you would expect from the name; the sparse facilities "bring this place down a little" and some say it's "unremarkable", but most insist the "price is right" for a track that's both "enjoyable" and in "good shape."

☑ Pinehills, Jones
27 | **27** | **26** | **24** | **$110**

Plymouth | 54 Clubhouse Dr. | 508-209-3000 | 866-855-4653 | www.pinehillsgolf.com | 7175/5380; 73.8/71.2; 135/125

"Bring your A-game" to this "wonderful" Rees Jones design, because while some find it "the prettier of the two at Pinehills" ("stunning vistas"), as with many pretty faces, it "presents more issues" – "surprising elevation changes" and fairways that can be "punishing if you're off"; still, it's "outstanding all around", with "top-notch conditions", "amazing facilities" and "excellent service."

☑ Pinehills, Nicklaus
27 | **27** | **26** | **23** | **$110**

Plymouth | 54 Clubhouse Dr. | 508-209-3000 | 866-855-4653 | www.pinehillsgolf.com | 7243/5185; 74.3/69.4; 135/123

A "must-play on any list", this "top-tier track" in Plymouth represents the "golden mean of Nicklaus design", putting a "premium on approach shots" (via tricky wetlands and "pine tree–lined fairways") while being "more forgiving than the Jones"; it was designed by the Golden Bear's son to be "as pretty" as its sibling, with "big, true greens" kept "in excellent shape", plus a "nice clubhouse" and a "beautiful range and practice facilities."

Poquoy Brook
20 | **15** | **18** | **24** | **$49**

Lakeville | 20 Leonard St. | 508-947-5261 | www.poquoybrook.com | 6762/5415; 72.4/71.0; 128/114

"One of the best values south of Boston", this "hidden gem" just 30 minutes from the city is a "true test", not only because of its tricky, "well-guarded greens" but also because of the blackflies that swarm the fairways in spring, "taking away from the enjoyment" for some ("bring bug spray"); it "can be slow on the weekends", but overall it offers "nice, conditioned golf" at a "reasonable price."

Cape Cod

Ballymeade 🏳
18 | **19** | **19** | **17** | **$80**

North Falmouth | 125 Falmouth Woods Rd. | 508-540-4005 | www.ballymeade.com | 6928/4871; 74.7/69.5; 140/123

"Incredible views" of Buzzards Bay from several holes distinguish this "beautiful" Jim Fazio/Chi Chi Rodriguez redesign located some 15 minutes from the Bourne Bridge; the layout is kept in "good shape", but what some call "too much risk on approach shots to the greens", as well as tight fairways lined with thick scrub pine, can make it "difficult for the average golfer."

Brookside

▽ 18 | 20 | 19 | 21 | $55

Bourne | 11 Brigadoon Rd. | 508-743-4653 | www.thebrooksideclub.com | 6337/5152; 71.1/69.6; 126/118

Located less than two miles from the Bourne Bridge, this "enjoyable" course offers scenic views of the Cape Cod Canal on a "short" layout that's in "good condition"; some suggest the design is "gimmicky" and "awkward", with holes that appear "forced based on the available land", but the majority considers it "challenging yet fair" and "decent for its value."

Captains, Port

22 | 18 | 19 | 23 | $76

Brewster | 1000 Freemans Way | 508-896-1716 | 877-843-9081 | www.captainsgolfcourse.com | 6724/5282; 73.5/71.1; 130/119

It's "easy to par if you don't count all of your strokes" at this "tight", "well-maintained" track where "pine tree-lined fairways, well-guarded greens" and several "elevation changes" add up to a "challenging" course; it's part of an "excellent" municipal facility offering "beautiful scenery", but given that it's a Cape Cod "value", it can be "overbooked and not well-rangered, so expect a long round."

Captains, Starboard

21 | 18 | 19 | 22 | $76

Brewster | 1000 Freemans Way | 508-896-1716 | 877-843-9081 | www.captainsgolfcourse.com | 6776/5359; 72.6/71.2; 130/116

For "Cape Cod golfing at its best", head to this muni in Brewster, where Brian Silva refashioned some of his original 18 holes into two courses, one of which is this "user-friendly" layout that's "less challenging than the Port"; although "not exceptional, it's a solid, fair" test "for the price", and some fancy the "nautical cleats used for tee box markers" – they "anchor the feet", allowing players to "swing from the yardarms."

Cranberry Valley

24 | 19 | 21 | 23 | $65

Harwich | 183 Oak St. | 508-430-5234 | www.cranberrygolfcourse.com | 6761/5568; 73.4/73.0; 133/127

An "enjoyable" "little gem run by the town of Harwich", this "old-style course on the Cape" pleases fans with a "beautiful", "interesting layout" featuring "some really challenging holes, particularly the closing three" and "excellent" conditioning – "it's so green and serene", you may be tempted to "take off your shoes before playing"; despite "minimal facilities", it's a "favorite", making it "difficult to get a tee time" some days.

Dennis Pines

20 | 17 | 18 | 20 | $66

East Dennis | 50 Golf Course Rd. | 508-385-8347 | www.dennisgolf.com | 7000/5567; 74.6/73.1; 135/133

A "favorite on Cape Cod", this vintage 1965 municipal is "beautiful but challenging", meandering amid the pines with a "long and narrow" layout that's "much harder than it looks" ("if you're not in the fairway, you're in jail"); a "solid clubhouse" and "nicely manicured" conditions add to its "great value", but expect "slow rounds because of its difficulty" ("bring a chair for those five-hour summer" circuits).

	COURSE	FACIL.	SERVICE	VALUE	COST

Olde Barnstable Fairgrounds

23 | 18 | 19 | 22 | $61

Marstons Mills | 1460 Rte. 149 | 508-420-1141 | www.obfgolf.com | 6479/5122; 69.1/69.7; 128/119

"As good a course as you'll find on the Cape", this "classic" Mark Mungeam design is "one of the best-kept public tracks" in the area and boasts a layout that's "equal to the privates in quality" and a "challenge for any handicap"; although "a bit tight" in some spots, it's considered "playable" and "easy to walk", so given the reasonable greens fees, you "cannot beat the price."

Martha's Vineyard

Farm Neck

26 | 23 | 24 | 22 | $150

Oak Bluffs | 1 Farm Neck Way | 508-693-3057 | www.farmneck.net | 6815/4987; 72.8/64.3; 135/118

"Still a great track after all these years", this "fabulous Martha's Vineyard" "favorite" "starts in the pines and moves out toward the Sound", with several "beautiful" "holes overlooking the ocean"; the "only public (from April to December) championship course on the island", it's "worth the ferry ride" (and the relatively high "price of admission") for both its "grand, scenic setting" and "difficult" design.

Nantucket

Miacomet

▽ 20 | 15 | 19 | 18 | $110

Nantucket | 12 W. Miacomet Rd. | 508-325-0333 | www.miacometgolf.com | 6890/5145; 73.6/64.0; 128/123

After the original nine was "upgraded" in 2008, this "cool links-style layout" on Nantucket is a "pleasant" 18-hole option; although it's "not terribly challenging", it's "always windy" (thus "never plays the same way") and the "raised greens and tee boxes make it slightly more difficult" than before, so while many consider it "pricey for what it is", it's nevertheless "a great way to start the day before heading to the beach."

Springfield

Ranch, The

26 | 24 | 23 | 21 | $110

Southwick | 65 Sunnyside Rd. | 413-569-9333 | 866-790-9333 | www.theranchgolfclub.com | 7171/4983; 75.4/70.7; 143/127

More of an old farm than a ranch, complete with a yellow barn that "serves as a nice clubhouse", this "challenging", "scenic" spread in Pioneer Valley west of Boston has so "much elevation change" "you would swear you're in the mountains of North Carolina"; a few feel it's "expensive", but the "well-conditioned" greens and fairways, "wonderful staff" and "excellent restaurant" are all reasons it's "worth the trip."

Worcester

Blackstone National

24 | 19 | 20 | 18 | $75

Sutton | 227 Putnam Hill Rd. | 508-865-2111 | www.bngc.net | 6909/5203; 74.6/71.8; 139/129

This "demanding" Rees Jones design "may be called Blackstone, but it's a gem", with "pretty woodland vistas" complementing an "excellent layout" that provides a "challenging test of accuracy" as it travels over hilly terrain near Worcester – you'd "have to be a billy goat to walk it"; it's "well maintained" and especially "gorgeous in the fall", but some find it "a bit pricey" and a "long ride" from Boston.

Cyprian Keyes
24 | 23 | 22 | 21 | $59

Boylston | 284 E. Temple St. | 508-869-9900 | www.cypriankeyes.com | 6871/5029; 74.4/71.2; 136/126

"Threading back and forth" through the central Massachusetts woods, this "extraordinarily challenging target golf" track is "no pushover" given a "tight", hilly Mark Mungeam design with "lots of trouble off the fairways", so "choose the right tee box", "bring an extra sleeve of balls" and "leave your ego behind, as laying up is mandatory"; "many picturesque holes" and a "superb par-3 course" round out the "complete package."

Red Tail
26 | 20 | 22 | 19 | $99

Devens | 15 Bulge Rd. | 978-772-3273 | www.redtailgolf.net | 7006/5049; 73.9/69.4; 138/120

At this "wonderful" "gem" (site of the the 2009 U.S. Women's Amateur Public Links Championship) located on a former army base north of Worcester, "you can hit into a real bunker" on a "challenging yet fair layout" that "plays tougher than its rating", with hazards that "abound for wayward balls" and a 7th hole that "can make you weep"; while some find it "mighty pricey", the twilight rate is a "great deal."

Shaker Hills
24 | 20 | 18 | 19 | $85

Harvard | 146 Shaker Rd. | 978-772-2227 | www.shakerhills.com | 6850/4999; 74.0/69.8; 137/122

"Especially gorgeous during leaf season", this "eye-poppingly beautiful course" just 35 miles from Boston "will humble the average golfer" with a "number of challenges", including tree-framed fairways, rock walls, wetlands and elevation changes (the 5th hole, a 606-yard uphill par 5, is a "beast"); although a few gripe that the "clubhouse is tired" and the staff is "not very friendly", most consider it a "solid" option that's "worth the ride and the $$$."

Stow Acres, North
20 | 17 | 17 | 19 | $66

Stow | 58 Randall Rd. | 978-568-8690 | www.stowacres.com | 7035/4400; 74.2/74.4; 131/132

An "old standby" in Stow, this "solid design" is ideal "for a quick local game" since it's "tough but fair", "always enjoyable" and "never too busy"; regulars suggest it "could use better conditioning" ("with a little TLC, it could be a primo public links"), but all in all, it's "a value"; it was the site of the first national African American men's championship and, more recently, the 70th U.S. Amateur Public Links Championship.

Wachusett
▽ 20 | 17 | 17 | 22 | $65

West Boylston | 187 Prospect St. | 508-835-2264 | www.wachusettcc.com | 6567/5573; 71.7/74.6; 124/121

A "classic" 1927 Donald Ross design outside Worcester, this "scenic layout" promises an "enjoyable round" "without a whole lot of trouble"; those who "grew up" on it call it a "great learning course" that's kept "in excellent condition", and "reasonable prices" make it a real "value", especially for "walkers before 9 AM on weekdays."

Michigan

TOP COURSES IN STATE

29 Arcadia Bluffs | *Traverse City*
St. Ives Resort, Tullymore | *Grand Rapids*
28 Bay Harbor | *Petoskey*
27 St. Ives Resort, St. Ives | *Grand Rapids*
Treetops, Robert Trent Jones Masterpiece* | *Gaylord*

Bay City

Lakewood Shores, Gailes   ▽ 25 | 17 | 20 | 22 | $62

Oscoda | 7751 Cedar Lake Rd. | 989-739-2073 | 800-882-2493 |
www.lakewoodshores.com | 6954/5246; 75.0/72.2; 138/122

Devotees call this lakeside layout some two hours north of Bay City "one of the best links-style courses in the States", so successfully modeled on the coastal greats that some feel like they're "back in Scotland"; purists insist it "must be played on a windy day to really appreciate its character", and the "wonderful package deals" and uncrowded setup add to its appeal.

Red Hawk ⌂   23 | 18 | 21 | 20 | $69

East Tawas | 350 W. Davison Rd. | 989-362-0800 | 877-733-4295 |
www.redhawkgolf.net | 6589/4883; 71.6/69.0; 139/120

Part of the Arthur Hills Michigan Golf Trail, this northeast course is "a real delight", "playable and fair" with a view that's "worth the drive" 90 minutes north of Bay City; though it's "in nice shape", "a few holes are over the top" and some say it's "a little too hilly with a lot of development around the course."

Detroit

Majestic at Lake Walden ⌂   26 | 18 | 23 | 24 | $69

Hartland | 9600 Crouse Rd. | 810-632-5235 | 800-762-3280 |
www.majesticgolf.com
10/27 | 6904/4896; 73.8/69.5; 138/123
1/18 | 7009/5081; 74.1/70.3; 135/120
19/9 | 6749/5033; 72.7/69.8; 136/122

At this 27-holer designed by Jerry Matthews, "each of the nines offers a different look" – the first 18 are a "scenic trip around the lake" while a newer nine plays around a marsh "cut out of the Michigan wilderness" near Detroit; swingers "take a boat across the lake between nines", which can lead to "ver-r-ry slow play."

Orchards, The   25 | 21 | 21 | 23 | $70

Washington | 62900 Campground Rd. | 586-786-7200 | www.orchards.com |
7036/5158; 74.5/70.3; 136/123

A "bit of a hike from the city", this "high-end course northeast of Detroit" is a "challenging, well-maintained" and "inspiring" Robert Trent Jones Jr. design; although visitors may "need to play it a few times" in order to avoid bunkers aplenty (88), the extensive practice area, "gorgeous clubhouse and friendly staff" always add up to an "enjoyable experience."

---

* Indicates a tie with property above

Shepherd's Hollow

27 | 25 | 24 | 23 | $85

Clarkston | 9085 Big Lake Rd. | 248-922-0300 | www.shepherdshollow.com
10/27 | 7235/4982; 76.1/70.4; 144/120
1/18 | 7236/4906; 76.0/69.7; 147/120
19/9 | 7169/4960; 75.5/69.7; 143/120

The "best course in the Detroit area" is this 27-hole Arthur Hills track "tucked back in the woods right off I-75", which "makes you feel like you are in northern Michigan" or in "another place and another time" altogether; there are "plenty of elevation changes", "rolling hills, pine and other trees" on this "true test of golf" that forces players to "use all the clubs."

Gaylord

Black Forest at Wilderness Valley

▽ 25 | 19 | 24 | 26 | $75

Gaylord | 6500 Nicklaus Dr. | 231-585-7090 | www.blackforestgolf.com | 7044/4556; 74.5/71.4; 145/127

Located just north of his Traverse City design headquarters is this "early Tom Doak course", a "hidden gem" that's "worth playing" thanks to a typically minimalist design made "super-tough" with "ample sand traps and doglegs" plus "surprisingly fast" and "tricky greens", so "don't get above the pin or you'll pay dearly"; it's "demanding but fair", and particularly scenic in the "fall, when the leaves are spectacular."

Black Lake

▽ 24 | 21 | 21 | 23 | $65

Onaway | 2800 Maxon Rd. | 989-733-4653 | www.blacklakegolf.com | 7046/5058; 74.4/70.1; 138/120

The United Auto Workers commissioned Rees Jones to design this "hidden gem of northern Michigan" that may be in the "middle of nowhere" but is "worth the effort to visit" in order to play a "wall-to-wall lush" layout "nestled among towering eucalyptus trees" with "lots of wildlife"; it's a "treat for all handicap levels", and the presence of an "attentive staff" and nine-hole pitch-and-putt course (also designed by Jones) adds to one of the "best values" around.

Elk Ridge

▽ 29 | 28 | 26 | 28 | $75

Atlanta | 9400 Rouse Rd. | 989-785-2275 | 800-626-4355 | www.elkridgegolf.com | 7072/5261; 75.8/74.2; 145/133

"Go for the golf, stay for the sandwiches" at this layout owned by the CEO of the HoneyBaked Ham chain, a fact which helps to explain why this "nice course" located in out-of-the-way Atlanta has "pig-shaped bunkers" (look for one on the downhill par-3 10th); it's an "underrated and overlooked" track that "will challenge your game", and it's surrounded by "so much woodland", it will seem "like your group is the only one" there.

☒ Forest Dunes

27 | 27 | 25 | 21 | $155

Roscommon | 6376 Forest Dunes Dr. | 989-275-0700 | www.forestdunesgolf.com | 7141/5032; 74.8/69.8; 142/128

"Michigan's best-kept secret", this "fabulous" Tom Weiskopf creation is "one of the finest designs in America", with a "beautiful" layout in which "each hole is unique" "but hard – be prepared for trudging through sand"; less-skilled players are advised to "swallow their pride and play the whites", and although some "can't believe the money they put into this place", the result was an "immaculate" setup; an ownership change in 2012 may outdate the scores.

Treetops, Rick Smith Signature 🔒 | 27 | 25 | 24 | 24 | $135 |

Gaylord | 3962 Wilkinson Rd. | 989-732-6711 | 888-873-3867 |
www.treetops.com | 6653/4604; 72.6/66.9; 136/125

One of the game's great teachers has his signature all over this resort five miles east of Gaylord – as the owner, head of the golf academy and designer of this "well-maintained" course; all of the tracks on-site "are the lushest imaginable", routed "over rolling terrain" that seems like it "was invented for" the game, so "hit it straight" or this "classic" "must-play" will be "a nightmare."

Treetops, Robert Trent Jones Masterpiece 🔒 | 27 | 25 | 25 | 24 | $135 |

Gaylord | 3962 Wilkinson Rd. | 989-732-6711 | 888-873-3867 |
www.treetops.com | 7007/4980; 75.0/70.4; 143/126

The "entire resort is top-notch", and this Robert Trent Jones Sr. track is praised as "one of the best in Michigan", a "great course in a magnificent setting" and a "destination everyone should experience"; it's the "toughest of Treetops'" options "with a lot of elevation changes" and "oblong" greens that are "hard to reach and hold", and "playing on the ridge has the feel of being on top of the trees."

Treetops, Tom Fazio Premier 🔒 | 27 | 26 | 26 | 26 | $135 |

Gaylord | 3962 Wilkinson Rd. | 989-732-6711 | 888-873-3867 |
www.treetops.com | 6832/5039; 73.6/69.8; 134/122

A "beautiful" course that some call the "easiest" of the Treetops' offerings, this Tom Fazio track is considered "extremely fair, well designed and fun to play", with "outstanding elevation changes"; high-scorers lament "tough penalties" but nonetheless recommend playing it "on a trip"; there's also a notable nine-hole, par-3 layout by Rick Smith called Threetops.

Grand Rapids

Pilgrim's Run | ▽ 26 | 22 | 22 | 26 | $65 |

Pierson | 11401 Newcosta Ave. | 231-937-7505 | 888-533-7742 |
www.pilgrimsrun.com | 7093/4863; 74.3/67.7; 138/114

No alcohol is sold or permitted on-site, but it's "no bother" because the "course is intoxicating enough" say sober swingers who venture 30 minutes north of Grand Rapids to this "real gem" with "greens built by Mike DeVries"; it's a "wooded layout" where "every hole has that added touch", and players consider it a "challenging but fair" "bargain that's always in good shape."

St. Ives Resort, St. Ives 🔒 | 27 | 25 | 27 | 24 | $125 |

Stanwood | 9900 St. Ives Dr. | 231-972-4837 | 800-972-4837 |
www.tullymoregolf.com | 6702/4821; 73.3/68.7; 140/120

"If you're going to play 36 in a day, this and sibling Tullymore" – located about an hour north of Grand Rapids – are "two of the best courses together anywhere"; the design by native son Jerry Matthews is "friendly but challenging" and "requires precision with some severe drop-offs", and the "excellent facilities and a top-notch staff" are pluses.

	COURSE	FACIL.	SERVICE	VALUE	COST

⊡ St. Ives Resort, Tullymore

| 29 | 22 | 26 | 26 | $160 |

Stanwood | 11969 Tullymore Dr. | 231-972-4837 | 800-972-4837 |
www.tullymoregolf.com | 7148/4668; 74.9/68.8; 148/115

"Every hole is calendar-worthy" on Jim Engh's "truly magnificent" design, a "beautiful Michigan gem" boasting blue tees that are "hard with accuracy and some significant carries required" and "tough greens" with "a lot of undulation and sloping", plus a "wide-open" appearance that can "lull you into a false sense of security"; amenities include a clubhouse with an Irish pub and a separate fine-dining room.

Kalamazoo

NEW Harbor Shores

| - | - | - | - | $125 |

Benton Harbor | 400 Klock Rd. | 269-927-4653 |
www.HarborShoresGolf.com | 6861/4932; 74.7/69.1; 143/123

Some of the most wildly contoured greens Jack Nicklaus has ever sculpted grace this short but rugged 2010 Nicklaus Signature design that zigzags through hardwoods, wetlands, tattered-edge bunkers and enormous sand dunes along the shores of Lake Michigan; intended to recharge a depressed area of southwest Michigan, it's already attracted the 2012 and 2014 Senior PGA Championships.

Lansing

Eagle Eye ⌕

| ▽ 28 | 28 | 26 | 25 | $89 |

East Lansing | 15500 Chandler Rd. | 517-641-4570 | 888-411-4295 |
www.hawkhollow.com | 7318/5109; 76.4/69.6; 145/124

"A must-play if you're in the Lansing area", this Chris Lutzke/Pete Dye collaboration is a "well-kept links design" that "keeps you in the game" (i.e. "no tricks"), though its "fast, challenging greens" require you to "plan every shot"; "the 17th is the closest you'll get to the 17th at TPC Sawgrass' Stadium course" – "sans the $300 greens fees" – while the "friendly staff" and "great replay rate with Hawk Hollow" add to its "excellent value."

Forest Akers MSU, West

| - | - | - | - | $45 |

East Lansing | Harrison Rd. | 517-355-1635 | www.golf.msu.edu |
7013/5278; 74.0/70.3; 136/123

Home of the Spartans golf team, "MSU's championship course" is an "excellent university" track that's "well maintained" and "always in great condition" – the turf and grounds management benefits from a student-developed Environmental Stewardship Program; alum Arthur Hills did a redesign of the original Bruce Matthews layout in 1992, making it a "tough test" that'll make you "use every club in your bag."

Hawk Hollow ⌕

| - | - | - | - | $81 |

Bath | 15101 Chandler Rd. | 517-641-4295 | 888-411-4295 |
www.hawkhollow.com
10/19 | 6693/4962; 73.0/69.1; 140/120
1/10 | 6974/5078; 73.9/69.1; 140/121
19/1 | 6487/4934; 71.9/68.8; 135/123

"You won't be disappointed" after a visit to this "excellent" Jerry Matthews design, a 27-holer that's routed over woodland terrain in

MICHIGAN

COURSE
FACIL.
SERVICE
VALUE
COST

Bath just north of Lansing; there are a "good variety of holes for each level of play", with plenty of risk/reward throughout, and there's also a golf academy, nine-hole executive track and par-54 putting course to help you sharpen your skills.

Pohlcat

▽ 23 | 23 | 23 | 23 | $59

Mt. Pleasant | 6595 E. Airport Rd. | 989-773-4221 | 800-292-8891 | www.pohlcat.net | 6954/5140; 74.2/70.5; 140/128

Named after its designer, tour veteran Dan Pohl, this "excellent course with a lot of diversity" located near Soaring Eagle Casino & Resort in central Michigan shows its claws if you aren't careful in the "placement of your shots", thanks to "lots of water"; while some of the layout is "fairly pedestrian", it's "good-value", "high-standard golf" and the "finishing holes are really special."

Petoskey

✚ Bay Harbor ⌂

28 | 28 | 26 | 23 | $159

Bay Harbor | 5800 Coastal Ridge Dr. | 231-439-4028 | 800-462-6963 | www.bayharborgolf.com
Links/Quarry | 6762/4319; 73.0/67.4; 145/117
Preserve/Links | 6773/4215; 72.9/65.5; 142/113
Quarry/Preserve | 6693/4040; 73.1/65.1; 146/116

"One of the best that northern Michigan has to offer", this "spectacular" Arthur Hills creation features "three unique nines" that are all "outstanding", although the "scenic" "Links/Quarry is the combination to play", with its "memorable views of Lake Michigan"; it's "challenging" but "fair", with a "natural design" and "lush, green turf", and it also boasts a "wonderful clubhouse" where you can "lunch on the patio between rounds."

Boyne Highlands, Arthur Hills ⌂

23 | 23 | 23 | 23 | $99

Harbor Springs | 250 Heather Dr. | 231-526-3028 | 800-462-6963 | www.boynehighlands.com | 7310/4811; 76.4/68.5; 144/117

All of the Boyne Highlands courses are a "value and in excellent condition", but some fans feel this "gem" is an "especially" "great bargain", offering a typical Arthur Hills design (read: "always well above average"); you'll want to "be on your game when you play" the "challenging", "hilly" track that's nonetheless "fair" and "fun", and given its location "up north" near Petoskey, you can expect a particularly "scenic" woodlands setting.

Boyne Highlands, Donald Ross Memorial ⌂

26 | 23 | 23 | 23 | $89

Harbor Springs | 250 Heather Dr. | 231-526-3028 | 800-462-6963 | www.boynehighlands.com | 6814/4935; 73.4/68.7; 138/122

A "fantastic golf experience" that pays tribute to the architect Donald Ross, this Boyne Highlands replica course may bring visitors as close as they will come to playing legendary privates such as the Inverness Club, Oakland Hills and the Seminole Golf Club (there are a "number of trophy holes" from each); it's "enjoyable" if "a bit incongruous" at times, with "beautiful" scenery and "friendly" service – and a "price that matches the quality."

	COURSE	FACIL.	SERVICE	VALUE	COST

Boyne Highlands, Heather
26 | 23 | 23 | 23 | $99

Harbor Springs | 1343 Heather Dr. | 231-526-3029 |
800-462-6963 | www.boynehighlands.com |
7118/4845; 74.6/68.7; 141/117

Part of a 72-hole resort once featured on the Golf Channel's *Big Break*, this "challenging" Boyne Highlands "test" designed by RTJ Sr. (and renovated in 2007) features championship tee boxes and "lots of water" on most of its holes; many tab it as their "favorite at the resort", and report that it's "prettiest in the fall", when you may want to take advantage of the caddy program and walk (advance booking required).

Boyne Highlands, Moor
∇ 23 | 23 | 22 | 25 | $79

Harbor Springs | 250 Heather Dr. | 231-526-3138 | 800-462-6963 |
www.boynehighlands.com | 6850/5100; 73.7/70.8; 141/123

Michigan designer Bill Newcombe put together this "well-thought-out" "risk/reward" layout that's "not too crazy", opting instead for a laid-back, "open style of golf" that makes it the "best of the Boyne" courses for some – perhaps because it's the "easiest"; it offers some doglegs, marshes and water holes, but some caution "it plays more slowly than the others."

Dunmaglas ⌘
- | - | - | - | $89

Charlevoix | 9031 Boyne City Rd. | 231-547-4653 | www.dunmaglas.com |
6901/5175; 75/69.8; 139/123

Winding "through the woods" in view of Lake Michigan and Charlevoix, this "challenge" offers "nice elevation changes" but remains "lots of fun" as you tackle its rolling front and links-style back; it's the type of course that should "fit into all Michigan travel plans", especially since management cleared brush and sodded bunkers to make it more playable.

Traverse City

❷ Arcadia Bluffs 🏌
29 | 27 | 26 | 25 | $180

Arcadia | 14710 Northwood Hwy. | 231-889-3001 | 800-494-8666 |
www.arcadiabluffs.com | 7300/5107; 75.4/70.1; 147/121

The state's top-rated Course is this "golf nirvana" on the bluffs above Lake Michigan, one of "the most beautiful courses you will ever play", with "spectacular views" from every hole on a "fantastic links-style" layout that offers "a wee bit of Scotland", "from the heather to the bagpipes at sunset"; the "howling winds" and tricky greens ("like elephants buried under satin") "will bring you to your knees", and while it's "expensive", all agree this "magnificent jewel is worth every penny."

Grand Traverse, The Bear ⌘
26 | 24 | 23 | 20 | $140

Acme | 100 Grand Traverse Village Blvd. | 231-534-6000 |
800-236-1577 | www.grandtraverseresort.com |
7078/5281; 76.3/73.4; 148/139

Asked to build a "tough" course, Jack Nicklaus did just that: a 139 slope from the 5,281-yard tees tells the tale of this "bear" that's been "tamed since its creation" in 1985; often credited with igniting Michigan's golf boom, "one of the brightest jewels of the north" is "manicured to the hilt" and "still worth a visit" – as long as "you're indifferent to losing golf balls and your temper."

	COURSE	FACIL.	SERVICE	VALUE	COST

Shanty Creek, Cedar River 🖾 | - | - | - | - | $99 |

Bellaire | 5780 Shanty Creek Rd. | 231-533-8621 | 800-678-4111 |
www.shantycreek.com | 6989/5315; 73.6/70.5; 144/128

Located at a resort about an hour from Traverse City, this Tom Weiskopf
design is a "fun, playable but challenging golf course", with some of
the former PGA star's signature short par 4s – like the 285-yard 13th –
making it an especially appealing test; the rolling, wooded layout with
views of the Cedar River is a "must-play every year", and you "can't
beat the spring and fall rates."

Shanty Creek, The Legend 🖾 | 27 | 23 | 23 | 21 | $99 |

Bellaire | 5780 Shanty Creek Rd. | 231-533-8621 | 800-678-4111 |
www.shantycreek.com | 6764/4953; 73.6/69.6; 137/124

With "high overlooks of Lake Bellaire", this "fabulous course" is "wonderful to play on a fall day", as Arnold Palmer took advantage of the
"picturesque" site to put together "maybe the best combination of
playability, scenery and strategy in all of Michigan"; while the price
might be "a bit" much, this one's "top-notch"; P.S. beware the "high
vertical wall of underbrush" looming off the second tee.

Upper Peninsula

Marquette, Greywalls | - | - | - | - | $130 |

Marquette | 1075 Grove St. | 906-225-0721 | 866-678-7171 |
www.marquettegolfclub.com | 6828/4631; 73.0/66.0; 144/121

Set on over 200 acres of woodland, this Upper Peninsula layout is "one of
the most unique in the Midwest"; scenic views include towering trees
and Lake Superior in the distance, plus what fans call a glimpse at what
the "revered architects" of yore "might have designed in today's world."

Minnesota

Brainerd

**Ⓩ Grand View Lodge,
Deacon's Lodge** 🖾 | 29 | 26 | 27 | 25 | $114 |

Pequot Lakes | Breezy Point, 9348 Arnold Palmer Dr. | 218-562-6262 |
886-801-2951 | www.grandviewlodge.com |
6964/4766; 73.8/68.6; 146/119

"Is this heaven?" ask devotees of this "fantastic" Arnold Palmer "must-
play", voted Minnesota's top-rated Course thanks to a "challenging but
fair" layout with eye-opening "elevation changes", "awesome greens"
and "wide fairways"; named after his father, the track is kept in "excellent
condition" and is run by a "super staff that helps along the way"; P.S. it's
useful to go "more than once to gain familiarity with the course."

Grand View Lodge, Pines | ▽ 23 | 24 | 26 | 25 | $104 |

Nisswa | 23521 Nokomis Ave. | 218-963-8755 | 866-801-2951 |
www.grandviewlodge.com
Lakes/Woods | 6874/5134; 73.8/70.4; 143/128
Marsh/Lakes | 6837/5112; 73.8/70.5; 143/130
Woods/Marsh | 6883/5210; 73.6/70.7; 143/126

All three of the courses at this Northwoods resort are "fun and well
kept", and you can choose from a trio of "distinctly different and inter-

esting nines" aptly named for their topography; with such "variety, you'll never get bored", like one zealot who "golfed 54 holes" and summed it up as "a good day."

Grand View Lodge, Preserve ▽ 26 | 25 | 23 | 24 | $104

Nisswa | 5506 Preserve Blvd. | 218-963-8755 | 866-801-2951 | www.grandviewlodge.com | 6601/4816; 72.5/68.6; 137/121

Woodlands, wetlands and 11 elevated tees are preserved on this "well-maintained" course that's perhaps "not as famous as the Pines", but is "actually better" according to some; it's "challenging but playable", with "severe elevation changes" that make for "really interesting terrain"; luckily, there are "forgiving fairways" and "wonderful" if "very quick greens", and when you add in the "great vistas", it's a "beautiful" option that comes "highly recommended."

Madden's on Gull Lake, Classic 27 | 25 | 26 | 23 | $119

Brainerd | 11266 Pine Beach Peninsula | 218-829-2811 | 800-642-5363 | www.maddens.com | 7102/4859; 75.0/69.4; 143/124

"One of the best" and "most beautiful in Minnesota", this resort track boasts "spectacular", "panoramic views all over", but just be sure to "check your ego at the gate" and seek out the "correct set of tees", for the "great bunkering, plenty of water holes and severe greens" can "bring the average player to his knees"; yes, it's "pricey", but most regard it as a "pure delight."

Duluth

Giants Ridge, Legend 🏌 ▽ 27 | 24 | 25 | 25 | $89

Biwabik | 6325 Wynne Creek Dr. | 218-865-8030 | 800-688-7669 | www.giantsridge.com | 6930/5084; 73.7/70.3; 133/126

With the "Sleeping Giant" footprint-shaped bunker on the 3rd among its signatures, this resort course an hour north of Duluth enchants players with an "absolutely awesome" though "difficult" layout routed through lakes, massive boulders and woods; "every hole is beautiful", making it "just a great way to spend a day" – or more, if you stay at the attractive Giants Ridge lodge.

Giants Ridge, Quarry ▽ 29 | 23 | 24 | 26 | $84

Biwabik | 6325 Wynne Creek Dr. | 218-865-8030 | 800-688-7669 | www.giantsridge.com | 7201/5119; 75.6/70.8; 146/125

"Jeff Brauer turned an old quarry into a gem of a course", this "unique" layout that's "one of the most scenic in Minnesota" thanks to features such as open mine pits and "elevation changes galore"; it "can give any woodlander in the country a run for its money" with a variety of "hole layouts that are challenging and fun", and it's "immaculately maintained", so the "steep price" is "not insane for what you get."

Wilderness at Fortune Bay - | - | - | - | $96

Tower | 1450 Bois Forte Rd. | 218-753-8917 | 800-992-4680 | www.thewildernessgolf.com | 7207/5324; 75.3/71.7; 142/129

Though this Jeff Brauer design is a "long way north" from the Twin Cities (and 90 miles from Duluth), it's "worth the drive" to play "one of the top courses in the state" – and maybe the "prettiest" with its views of

Lake Vermilion; players "can't wait to go back" as "you couldn't find a better value anywhere", especially the "beverage cart in 40 degree weather – only in Minnesota."

Minneapolis

Baker National
▽ 21 | 16 | 18 | 21 | $38

Medina | 2935 Parkview Dr. | 763-694-7670 | www.bakernational.com | 6762/5313; 73.9/72.7; 135/128

Just "20 minutes from the center of Minneapolis", this "well-maintained" muni is a "wonderful deal for very good golf" in a "pretty" regional park; winding through "rolling hills and wooded valleys", it provides a "decent test" in a "low-key atmosphere", and "there's nothing better" than the backdrop for the first green, "the famous red-barn hole."

Chaska Town
26 | 20 | 21 | 25 | $66

Chaska | 3000 Town Course Dr. | 952-443-3748 | www.chaskatowncourse.com | 6817/4853; 73.8/69.4; 140/119

An "Arthur Hills gem at a public course price", this muni "adjacent to Hazeltine National" is a "top, challenging" layout "that could host many a tournament" (it co-hosted the 2006 U.S. Amateur); it's a "real test" that's "more open on the front nine and then wanders through woods and marshes on the back", and since it's "clock conscious", it's "not for dawdlers."

Dacotah Ridge
- | - | - | - | $52

Morton | 31042 County Hwy. 2 | 507-697-8050 | 800-946-2274 | www.dacotahridge.com | 7109/5055; 73.9/68.9; 134/121

This "scenic links-type layout" from Rees Jones is an "outstanding track in good condition" with "lots of water" and a "great stretch of finishing holes"; yes, it's 110 miles from the Twin Cities – and it can be "windy" with "distracting livestock odors" – but it's close enough to the Jackpot Junction Casino Hotel to make it a "nice destination for two rounds of golf and some blackjack."

Edinburgh USA 🏌
22 | 24 | 23 | 22 | $62

Brooklyn Park | 8700 Edinbrook Crossing | 763-315-8550 | www.edinburghusa.org | 6888/5319; 74.2/71.5; 149/133

A golf academy adds to the "wonderful facilities" at this "interesting" RTJ Jr. track with "abundant water and sand and a number of wooded holes"; further touches such as the massive stone clubhouse and one-acre putting surface shared by the 9th, 18th and practice greens make it a "good place to play overall."

Legends Club
▽ 27 | 26 | 26 | 24 | $74

Prior Lake | 8670 Credit River Blvd. | 952-226-4777 | www.legendsgc.com | 7063/5095; 74.2/71.3; 142/127

Less than half an hour from Downtown Minneapolis, this track is regarded by many as one of the "best public access courses in the Twin Cities", boasting a "superb layout through woods and wetlands" featuring "lots of interesting holes", including "spectacular" par 3s, plus greens that are "fast" and huge, averaging 6,500 sq. ft.; there's a "great bar and dining area to relax in afterwards" and a "very helpful staff."

	COURSE	FACIL.	SERVICE	VALUE	COST

Les Bolstad University of Minnesota Golf Course

▽ 16 | 13 | 17 | 23 | $33

St. Paul | 2275 Larpenteur Ave. W. | 612-627-4000 | www.uofmgolf.com | 6278/5478; 70.0/66.4; 119/111

Designed by Seth Raynor and Tom Vardon, this "fun, old-style course" has accrued "lots of history" as "Patty Berg's home" base and the site where U. of Minnesota alum Tom Lehman took his licks; swingers warn "you get what you pay for here" – i.e. a track that's "short by today's standards" with "lots of mature trees", some "beat-up" turf and a queue "waiting to tee off."

Meadows at Mystic Lake ⌂

▽ 23 | 23 | 19 | 20 | $85

Prior Lake | 2400 Mystic Lake Blvd. | 952-233-5533 | www.mysticlake.com | 7144/5293; 74.6/71.2; 146/131

The Shakopee Mdewakanton Sioux Community "spent a fortune on landscaping" the old Long Pine Golf Club "and it shows" in a layout that's "as good as it gets" ("aside from the no-beer" or other alcohol policy); the track is "wide-open so you can spray your drives", leading up to an "exhilarating tee shot on the par-3 17th, over a lake to the green", and if that's not risky enough, there's also a casino on the property.

Rush Creek

▽ 26 | 27 | 25 | 21 | $109

Maple Grove | 7801 County Rd. 101 | 763-494-8844 | www.rushcreek.com | 7306/5405; 75.0/72.0; 148/130

There's "something for everyone" at this Bob Cupp/John Fought collaboration, a "fabulous public facility comparable in quality to an excellent private club course", with an "interesting layout" that "winds through marshes and trees", so one "needs to be accurate with drives and irons" – and if not, there are "superb practice and teaching facilities"; it's "well maintained", with a "great clubhouse" and "helpful pro shop staff", all adding up to a "pure golf experience."

StoneRidge

▽ 28 | 25 | 25 | 24 | $84

Stillwater | 13600 Hudson Blvd. N. | 651-436-4653 | www.stoneridgegc.com | 6992/5247; 74.2/70.7; 142/126

It's "Scotland in Minnesota" for navigators of this "challenging, immaculate" Bobby Weed design east of St. Paul where "many changes in elevation and fast greens add difficulty" – it can be "tough to score on", but it's "tons of fun"; while some warn of "slow play", "great hamburger sliders" afterward will reward your patience.

Wilds, The

27 | 26 | 22 | 21 | $80

Prior Lake | 3151 Wilds Ridge Ct. NW | 952-445-3500 | www.golfthewilds.com | 7025/5118; 74.5/71.1; 152/132

"You need to think your way through" this "fantastic" Weiskopf/Morrish design, one of the "top public courses in the Twin Cities", although a few gripe over "too many houses" "too close to the course"; the fall and spring "Pay the Temperature plan" is hailed as "a great offering", and there's also a "nice clubhouse" and casino for after-golf relaxing.

⊠ Willingers

27 | 18 | 21 | 27 | $48

Northfield | 6900 Canby Trail | 952-652-2500 | www.willingersgc.com | 6809/5166; 74.4/71.8; 150/135

Make the drive "45 minutes from the Twin Cities" to perhaps the "best value in Minnesota", this "all-around gem" "located on a former tree

	COURSE	FACIL.	SERVICE	VALUE	COST

nursery", where the "front nine is open and cuts through marshes", while the woody back is "extremely quiet" with "tremendous scenery (especially in autumn)"; it's geared for those who "enjoy a challenge", so "you can't play it just once" – it simply has "too many secrets."

Mississippi

Gulfport

Beau Rivage Resort, Fallen Oak 🏌 ⛳   ▽ 28 | 27 | 26 | 22 | $200

Saucier | 24400 Hwy. 15 N. | 228-386-7015 | 877-805-4657 |
www.fallenoak.com | 7487/5362; 76.5/71.1; 142/127

"Expensive, but absolutely first-class", Tom Fazio's handiwork at the Beau Rivage Resort attracts "high rollers" with a "wonderful", if "unbelievably tough" course in "phenomenal shape" and "amenities that are off the charts"; the staff "treats you like a rock star" to round out what many deem one of their "top five golf experiences."

Bridges at Hollywood Casino ⛳   ▽ 20 | 19 | 18 | 20 | $99

Bay Saint Louis | 711 Hollywood Blvd. | 228-467-9257 |
www.hollywoodbsl.com | 6841/5108; 72.5/70.1; 139/126

Opinions are split over whether this Arnold Palmer design is "better than ever after Hurricane Katrina" or "not as nice as it was", but it remains a "tough course" regardless; the wetlands layout is "unfair at times", with a setup on which "you don't need your driver on all shots" but you will need "lots of balls", and there's always the chance of playing "around alligators and snakes on the green."

Grand Biloxi, Grand Bear   25 | 25 | 24 | 22 | $109

Saucier | 12040 Grand Way Blvd. | 228-539-7806 | 888-524-5695 |
www.golfgrandbear.com | 7204/4802; 75.5/68.4; 143/120

"Everything you'd expect from a Jack Nicklaus" design, this "deserving" Katrina survivor, an "amenity of the Grand Biloxi Casino", is "routed through pines" and wetlands in the "unspoiled natural surroundings" of the DeSoto National Forest; the "challenging and fun" track is in "excellent condition" and "lengthy enough", and there's an "immaculate practice green and driving range" plus a "gorgeous, homey clubhouse."

Oaks, The   23 | 19 | 22 | 24 | $79

Pass Christian | 24384 Club House Dr. | 228-452-0909 |
www.theoaksgolfclub.com | 7006/4691; 72.5/66.4; 131/107

The regal live oaks that dot this Gulf Coast track have scenic sidekicks in the form of lively "real Hooters girls" manning the refreshment carts; diversions aside, ball-whackers say that although the course might not be "in the shape it was years ago", the "greens are great" and it's "still a test" "for all levels of experience."

Jackson

☑ Dancing Rabbit, Azaleas ⛳   29 | 26 | 24 | 25 | $135

Choctaw | 1 Choctaw Trail | 601-663-0011 | 866-447-3275 |
www.dancingrabbitgolf.com | 7128/4909; 74.4/68.6; 135/115

One of two Tom Fazio/Jerry Pate designs at this casino-resort "getaway" northeast of Jackson, this track "hits the jackpot" as one of the "best courses in Mississippi" thanks to a "mesmerizing layout" with "fantastic holes" that "set up easy" but can come back to "bite you"; otherwise, "you'll feel like you're in Wonderland", especially if you swing "when the azaleas have bloomed" and it becomes like "Augusta in [terms of] beauty and charm."

Dancing Rabbit, Oaks ▱   ▽ 28 | 26 | 25 | 26 | $135

Choctaw | 1 Choctaw Trail | 601-663-0011 | 866-447-3275 |
www.dancingrabbitgolf.com | 7076/5097; 74.6/69.0; 139/123

"Almost as good as Azaleas", this Tom Fazio/Jerry Pate design is "one of the top in Mississippi" thanks in part to a splendidly "isolated location"; it "couldn't play more differently" than its sibling, "which is the beauty and genius" of this Choctaw facility, whose resort-class amenities and casino enhance its two golfing options.

Pascagoula

Shell Landing ▱   ▽ 23 | 19 | 23 | 21 | $110

Gautier | 3499 Shell Landing Blvd. | 228-497-5683 |
866-851-0541 | www.shelllanding.com |
7024/5047; 73.8/69.6; 134/118

Players just "love this Davis Love III design", a "diverse" layout that "weaves through tall pines, wetlands and sandy terrain" midway between Biloxi and Pascagoula, revealing "all the beauty of the Mississippi countryside"; "challenging for any handicap" with "great sand bunkers and greens", it comes complete with a "nice driving range" and "excellent service", and the "price is right too."

Missouri

Kansas City

Stone Canyon Golf Club   - | - | - | - | $55

Blue Springs | 22415 E. 39th St. | 816-228-3333 |
www.stonecanyongolfclub.com | 7059/5852; 75.2/68.5; 144/129

Originally slated to be private, this 2009 suburban Kansas City retreat is instead a public-access paradise (for the foreseeable future), boasting a Greg Norman design that features rock walls and outcroppings that frame many of the holes, notably at the par-4 3rd, where the green sits in an amphitheater of rocks; other Norman signature touches include handsome, lacy-edged bunkers as well as closely mown chipping areas around the greens, which allow for multiple short-game options.

Tiffany Greens ▱   ▽ 27 | 26 | 22 | 21 | $66

Kansas City | 6100 NW Tiffany Springs Pkwy. | 816-880-9600 |
www.tiffanygreensgolf.com | 6977/5391; 74.4/71.3; 136/121

Routed over rolling hills northwest of Kansas City and "close to KC International Airport", this RTJ Jr. design "gives the average to above-average golfer a good challenge" thanks to a layout with "decent length", lots of water and some interesting shots; it's "always one of the best-conditioned in the area" – perhaps because it's "not heavily overplayed" – and it also boasts ample practice facilities and a "nice clubhouse."

	COURSE	FACIL.	SERVICE	VALUE	COST

Lake of the Ozarks

Lodge of Four Seasons, Cove ⌂

▽ 25 | 25 | 25 | 24 | $95

Lake Ozark | Horseshoe Bend Pkwy. | 573-365-8544 |
800-843-5253 | www.4seasonsresort.com |
6553/5172; 71.3/70.8; 139/124

"You won't be disappointed teeing it up" at this resort course that's "capable of putting a lump in your throat" thanks to an RTJ Sr. design in which "position is everything" – it's "quite difficult off the back tees, especially when windy", so "sensible decisions will be rewarded"; relatively recent renovations added new greens, bunkers, cart paths, a putting area and a clubhouse.

Lodge of Four Seasons, Ridge ⌂

23 | 21 | 22 | 21 | $80

Lake Ozark | Horseshoe Bend Pkwy. | 573-365-8544 | 800-843-5253 | www.4seasonsresort.com | 6447/4617; 71.4/67.2; 130/115

"What golf was meant to be, set in the beautiful hills of the Lake of the Ozarks", this Ken Kavanaugh design is a "long, tough" "throwback" that makes a "great complement" to the Cove; "play can be slow", but there's a "wide variety of holes" with "well-manicured greens", plus a "friendly staff", and, as a bonus, limited tee times are available for lodge guests at the otherwise private Nicklaus-designed Club at Porto Cima.

Old Kinderhook ⌂

27 | 23 | 24 | 24 | $89

Camdenton | 20 Eagle Ridge Rd. | 573-346-4444 | 888-346-4949 | www.oldkinderhook.com | 6855/4962; 72.8/69.5; 137/128

"One of the better courses in the Lake of the Ozarks area", this "must-do" designed by Tom Weiskopf is "well worth the drive from St. Louis" to tackle a "challenging", "fantastic layout" with rugged terrain and elevation changes (walking is discouraged, although not forbidden); bentgrass greens that are kept in "great condition", scenic views and on-site cottages help make it a "real treat."

Osage National ⌂

▽ 24 | 19 | 20 | 20 | $89

Lake Ozark | 400 Osage Hills Rd. | 573-365-1950 | 866-365-1950 | www.osagenational.com
Links/River | 7102/5026; 74.6/69.1; 141/120
Mountain/Links | 7165/5076; 74.7/69.9; 139/121
River/Mountain | 7149/5016; 75.6/69.2; 145/119

"Another Lake of the Ozarks gem", this "roller-coaster ride above the Osage River" is a "great 27-hole experience"; some suggest the Arnold Palmer–designed "Mountain and River courses are much better than the Links", but all boast scenic vistas, and there's also a "huge porch" for "relaxing after a long day."

Tan-Tar-A, The Oaks ⌂

18 | 20 | 21 | 19 | $69

Osage Beach | 1524 State Rd. KK | 573-348-8521 | 800-826-8272 | www.tan-tar-a.com | 6432/3931; 72.1/62.5; 134/92

A "favorite" of many, this course "can't be beat for play in the area" thanks to an "all-around good" design from Bruce Devlin and Robert von Hagge with plenty of trees, scenic vistas and water on 11 holes as it skirts the Lake of the Ozarks; it's both junior- and women-friendly, and part of a family-oriented resort that also features a nine-hole track as well as a spa, indoor water park and other amenities.

Springfield

☒ Branson Creek

28 | 11 | 18 | 25 | $99

Hollister | 1001 Branson Creek Blvd. | 417-339-4653 |
www.bransoncreekgolf.com | 7036/5032; 73.0/68.6; 133/113

"Tom Fazio nailed it" when designing this "scenic" "must-play", a "tough, long", "outstanding layout" on "the high Ozark ridges overlooking Branson" that boasts a "variety of tee lengths for all handicaps", "excellent conditions" and "incredible views"; yet, many feel "this course deserves better" than "sorry service" and the "lack of a 19th hole."

St. Louis

Missouri Bluffs

23 | 20 | 20 | 18 | $95

St. Charles | 18 Research Park Circle | 636-939-6494 | 800-939-6760 |
www.mobluffs.com | 7047/5191; 73.2/69.2; 131/115

Tom Fazio will call your bluff at this course that's "like no other in Missouri", a "scenic" spread that "can be very long with wind" but features "forgiving" "U-shaped fairways"; set "outside the bustle and noise of St. Louis", it offers "breathtaking holes" with "abundant wildlife", making for a "relaxing round" that's "not too easy and not too hard."

Pevely Farms

19 | 18 | 19 | 18 | $65

Eureka | 400 Lewis Rd. | 636-938-7000 | www.pevelyfarms.com |
7088/5219; 74.2/69.4; 135/114

Nestled on a former dairy farm southwest of St. Louis, this "challenging" Arthur Hills design is "tough yet scenic", with "nice views" and a "quiet" ambiance broken only by the "noise of wild turkeys"; the hilly layout features lots of "elevation changes" and "heavily sloped" fairways, and some complain the "tee boxes are the only level lie."

Montana

Butte

Old Works

▽ 29 | 20 | 24 | 28 | $57

Anaconda | 1205 Pizzini Way | 406-563-5989 | 888-229-4833 |
www.oldworks.org | 7705/5348; 75.8/65.0; 135/103

"You'll see right away" why this Jack Nicklaus design is "so unique" and "striking" – "winding through an old copper smelting site", it features "visually memorable bunkers" filled with "black copper slag"; the "interesting terrain" is also strewn with mining memorabilia, so although it's located "out of the way" 30 minutes northwest of Butte, it's a "fantastic value" that's "worth the journey to play it."

Kalispell

Big Mountain

- | - | - | - | $62

Kalispell | 3230 Hwy. 93 N. | 406-751-1950 | 800-255-5641 |
www.bigmountaingolfclub.com | 7015/5421; 72.4/69.2; 126/114

Tucked into the "rolling hills" two miles north of Kalispell, this junior- and women-friendly design from Roger Packard and U.S. Open champion Andy North combines a wide-open, links-style outward nine and an inward nine that winds through towering pines along the Stillwater

River; picturesque views of the Flathead Valley and surrounding mountains and a generous practice area enhance the experience.

Eagle Bend
- | - | - | - | $96

Bigfork | 279 Eagle Bend Dr. | 406-837-7310 | 800-255-5641 | www.eaglebendgolfclub.com | 6711/5075; 71.9/68.8; 130/123

Located just a few minutes from Flathead Lake near Bigfork, this "nice course" includes 18 holes designed by William Hull in the '80s along with a newer nine from Jack Nicklaus Jr.; some find the layout to be "uninspiring", but everyone will appreciate the grand views of Glacier National Park and the Swan Mountains, as well as amenities that include extensive practice facilities and a spacious clubhouse with several decks.

Whitefish Lake, North
- | - | - | - | $61

Whitefish | 1200 Hwy. 93 W. | 406-862-4000 | www.golfwhitefish.com | 6869/5476; 71.2/69.9; 125/126

Still the only 36-hole facility in Montana, this 1936 WPA project boasts "two courses that may be the best value in the country"; the North layout is lined with pine and birch and offers "gorgeous views" of Whitefish Lake and the surrounding mountains, and the "great facilities" and "wildlife all around" ("sometimes on the fairways") are quite "a bonus."

Whitefish Lake, South
- | - | - | - | $56

Whitefish | 1200 Hwy. 93 W. | 406-862-4000 | www.golfwhitefish.com | 6551/5361; 71.6/71.2; 131/126

Winding through houses and along the banks of Lost Coon Lake, this "user-friendly" 1992 design boasts "interesting fairways" featuring mounding and well-bunkered greens; "rustic scenery" abounds, so expect mountain views plus bird and wildlife sightings, an experience that has one golfer begging "don't go there, I want it all to myself."

Nebraska

North Platte

Wild Horse
25 | 18 | 21 | 22 | $38

Gothenburg | 41150 Rd. 768 | 308-537-7700 | www.playwildhorse.com | 6955/4688; 73.6/67.5; 134/109

A "gem in the middle of nowhere", this "mid-Nebraska delight" is a "must for anyone passing through" the Gothenburg area thanks to a links layout on which "beauty and nature are everywhere"; what's more, the "greens are very true", the "fairways are plush" and the "rates are reasonable", and though some find the facilities and clubhouse "sparse", "you aren't playing the clubhouse", after all.

Omaha

Indian Creek
- | - | - | - | $49

Elkhorn | 3825 N. 202 St. | 402-289-0900 | www.golfatindiancreek.com
Black Bird/Gray Hawk | 7179/5282; 74.7/70.4; 135/126
Black Bird/Red Feather | 7182/5040; 74.7/70.3; 133/121
Gray Hawk/Red Feather | 7041/5120; 73.8/70.4; 130/122

Frank Hummel designed this "well-maintained" 27-hole layout just west of Omaha and "all three nines are very strong", with lakes, creeks, mounding and bunkers providing a "challenging" test no matter which combination you choose; it's "not overly crowded, so tee times are easier to come by", and after your round, be sure to take advantage of the "nice practice facilities, which include a grass range."

Iron Horse
▽ 21 | 19 | 18 | 19 | $59

Ashland | 900 Clubhouse Dr. | 402-944-9800 | www.golfironhorse.com | 6500/4411; 71.4/66.1; 128/106

"Built around a lake in an old rock quarry" some 30 miles southwest of Omaha, this Gene Bates design is "one of the most beautiful courses" around, with "elevation changes, undulating fairways" and scenic vistas creating a round you'll "never forget"; the daunting 10th features a tee shot to a peninsula surrounded by water and wetlands, and the "top-notch clubhouse" adds to its "good value."

Quarry Oaks
▽ 27 | 23 | 24 | 25 | $73

Ashland | 16600 Quarry Oaks Dr. | 402-944-6000 | 888-944-6001 | www.quarryoaks.com | 7010/5068; 74.7/72.3; 139/124

This "impeccably maintained" track near Omaha is a "great value" and "as solid as it gets", "requiring your A-game" to deal with a "tremendous set of holes", some of which "run along the Platte River"; the "beautiful scenery" and "passing freight trains make for a fine Midwestern vista", and seeing as how "it's Nebraska, all male golfers wear red shirts" (don't underestimate "Cornhuskers madness").

Tiburon
▽ 18 | 23 | 19 | 17 | $34

Omaha | 10302 S. 168th St. | 402-895-2688 | www.tiburongolf.com
Great White/Hammerhead | 6560/6107; 73.8/71.4; 131/121
Hammerhead/Mako | 6427/5095; 71.4/70.9; 129/121
Mako/Great White | 6530/6107; 73.5/71.5; 130/120

Contrary to the names of the nines, this 27-holer in Omaha was designed not by Greg Norman (The Shark), but Dave Barrett and Larry Hagewood, who created a "nice course" that's "not as challenging as others" in the area but still offers holes that are difficult "for even the accomplished golfer"; a few consider it "gimmicky" and "not worth the money", but even they admit the clubhouse is "fantastic."

Valentine

NEW Prairie Club, Dunes ⛳ ⏱
- | - | - | - | $185

Valentine | 88897 State Hwy. 97 | 888-402-1101 | www.theprairieclub.com | 6838/5752; 71.7/72.0; 128/126

Unbelievably wide fairways highlight this 2010 Tom Lehman/Chris Brands design set into a rustic, wind-blown tract in Nebraska's northwest corner; despite the ample width and dearth of trees, however, wayward tee shots are punished by firm, heavily contoured landing areas surrounded by thick native grasses and gigantic, boldly sculpted 'blowout' bunkers, while the massive, undulating hyper-fast greens also demand touch and precision.

Prairie Club, Pines ⛳ ⏱
- | - | - | - | $185

Valentine | 88897 State Hwy. 97 | 888-402-1101 | www.theprairieclub.com | 7403/5346; 75.1/70.9; 133/117

Compared to its wide-open, links-like sibling Dunes, this tree-studded, canyon-laced 2010 Graham Marsh design is more traditional American parkland, with its dramatic combination of sand, forest, wind and contour; still, a windmill pump behind the third green and rugged bunkers etched into the terrain make it an unmistakably prairie experience; the two courses on the property alternate daily as public courses.

Nevada

TOP COURSES IN STATE

<u>28</u> Wolf Creek | *Las Vegas*
 Cascata | *Las Vegas*
<u>27</u> Shadow Creek | *Las Vegas*
 Las Vegas Paiute, Sun Mountain | *Las Vegas*
 Las Vegas Paiute, Wolf | *Las Vegas*

Las Vegas

Angel Park, Mountain

| 19 | 18 | 19 | 18 | $155 |

Las Vegas | 100 S. Rampart Blvd. | 702-254-4653 | 888-446-5358 |
www.angelpark.com | 6722/5150; 71.1/69.1; 130/114

It may be "nothing fancy", but this "well-maintained" design from Arnold Palmer and Ed Seay provides "pretty good bang for the buck" – "for Las Vegas", that is; a combo of "crazy blind shots", extreme greens and "generous fairways" are "tough but not impossible" (suitable for "beginners to pros"), and bonuses like "beautiful views" and a "cool 9-hole putting course" make it a "good warm-up" only minutes from the Strip.

Angel Park, Palm

| 17 | 18 | 19 | 19 | $155 |

Las Vegas | 100 S. Rampart Blvd. | 702-254-4653 | 888-446-5358 |
www.angelpark.com | 6525/4570; 70.9/66.8; 129/110

A "solid" option near Summerlin, this "urban" track is deemed "well conditioned and playable", with "generous" landing areas and "mostly fair greens" updated with "new hole designs to conserve water"; it's ideal "for locals" owing to the "excellent pace of play", while tourists will appreciate the "views of Vegas", and all benefit from an "always courteous" staff, "surprisingly good" restaurant and "value" prices.

Badlands ⌂

| - | - | - | - | $145 |

Las Vegas | 9119 Alta Dr. | 702-363-0754 | www.badlandsgc.com
Desperado/Diablo | 6450/5100; 70.4/69.3; 142/116
Desperado/Outlaw | 6200/5100; 69.5/68.4; 142/116
Diablo/Outlaw | 6400/5200; 70.6/69.5; 140/120

Cacti, canyons, forced carries and rocks ensure that 'desert' and 'target' are never far from golfers' minds at this rough-and-tumble 27-holer near Vegas designed by Johnny Miller (with an assist from Chi Chi Rodriguez); given a setup that requires accuracy, if you don't want to be desperado, you'd better make sure you bring a saddlebag of ammunition.

Bali Hai ⅍

| 21 | 22 | 23 | 15 | $325 |

Las Vegas | 5160 Las Vegas Blvd. S. | 702-450-8000 | 888-427-6678 |
www.balihaigolfclub.com | 7002/5535; 73.0/71.5; 130/122

This "tropical"–themed "oasis right off the Strip" is "challenging enough for even the most avid golfer" thanks to a "tough", "stunning" layout sprinkled with bunkers "so bright, sunglasses are needed"; despite "constant" "noise from McCarran Airport" and a "less-than-memorable practice range", there are plenty of perks, including an "accommodating staff", "nice clubhouse" and notable restaurant – but cognoscenti quip you "better have a good day at the tables to pay for the round."

Bear's Best Las Vegas ⌕ | 23 | 22 | 23 | 17 | $249 |

Las Vegas | 11111 W. Flamingo Rd. | 702-804-8500 | 866-385-8500 | www.bearsbestlasvegas.com | 7194/5043; 74.0/68.7; 147/116

Eighteen "noteworthy holes" pieced together from Jack Nicklaus' extensive portfolio is the "interesting concept" behind this "excellent experience"; the "rare sight of black-sand bunkers" is a "unique" touch on a layout that offers "variety" and "challenge", but there's debate over cost ("fair by Vegas standards" vs. "too pricey for anyone who hasn't hit the jackpot") and not everyone is glad that it "dropped the forecaddie program"; P.S. "play it now before the houses devour it."

Boulder Creek | - | - | - | - | $75 |

Boulder City | 1501 Veteran's Memorial Dr. | 702-294-6534 | www.golfbouldercity.com

Coyote Run/Desert Hawk | 7628/4984; 75.8/68.2; 142/117
Coyote Run/Eldorado Valley | 7525/5110; 75.1/69.0; 137/117
Desert Hawk/Eldorado Valley | 7582/4984; 75.4/68.5; 136/117

Owned by the city of Boulder, this sometimes riotous Mark Rathert municipal comprises three nines – the youngest, Eldorado Valley, is more traditionally grassed (and played) than its high risk/reward desert siblings; although there's lots of water, sand and length among the 27 diverse holes, it also provides options off the tee and into the green, allowing players to balance their strategic and heroic sensibilities.

☑ Cascata ⌕ | 28 | 29 | 29 | 20 | $375 |

Boulder City | 1 Cascata Dr. | 702-294-2000 | www.golfcascata.com | 7137/5591; 74.6/67.2; 143/117

"Golf heaven" is how devotees describe this Rees Jones "stunner", voted No. 1 for Facilities thanks to a clubhouse with a "Tuscany look" as well as a river running through it – you feel like it's "your own private country club"; "carved out of rock" in the hills outside Boulder City, the layout boasts "spectacular elevation changes", "endless views" and "incredible man-made streams", while a "knowledgeable" staff "treats you like gold", and yes, it's "expensive", but most agree "it's more fun than you'll have at any gaming table."

NEW Conestoga Golf Club ⌕ | - | - | - | - | $140 |

Mesquite | 1499 Falcon Ridge Pkwy. | 702-346-4292 | www.conestogagolf.com | 7232/5017; 74.9/64.9; 147/120

True to its name, this course harnesses the spirit of the Old West in fine fashion, thanks to a Gary Panks design that crackles with rough-hewn terrain, flashy bunkers and mountain panoramas; situated an hour-plus north of Las Vegas within the confines of the Sun City Mesquite community, this two-year-old layout isn't easy to get to, but its deep canyons, enormous sandstone mesas and dramatic elevated tees are worth the journey.

	COURSE	FACIL.	SERVICE	VALUE	COST

Coyote Springs
- | - | - | - | $175

Coyote Springs | 3100 State Rte. 168 | 877-742-8455 |
www.coyotesprings.com | 7471/5288; 75.8/70.5; 141/127

If you want to chase down this 2008 Jack Nicklaus design, just drive
50 miles due north from the Strip through barren, if eerily attractive, desert; your reward will be this terrific challenge that combines fast, undulating greens and an army of strategically deployed
bunkers with just enough bells and whistles in the form of lakes, waterfalls and mountain views.

Falcon Ridge
- | - | - | - | $115

Mesquite | 1024 Normandy Ln. | 702-346-6363 | www.golffalcon.com |
6546/4423; 71.6/66.2; 138/112

Set within an emerging housing development on Mesquite's west
side, this 'birdie' has fashioned itself after the town's famed golf
giant, Wolf Creek, climbing over ridges and valleys with a daring
mix of sharp doglegs, blind shots and parachute drops; as is standard
practice in the region (where homes frequently determine routing),
play is carts-only.

Las Vegas Paiute Golf Resort, Snow Mountain
27 | 25 | 25 | 24 | $149

Las Vegas | 10325 Nu Wav Kaiv Blvd. | 702-658-1400 | 866-284-2833 |
www.lvpaiutegolf.com | 7146/5341; 73.3/70.4; 125/117

There are "no houses to hit" or waterfalls, "just golf and the desert" at
the Las Vegas Paiute Resort's original course, a Pete Dye "gem in the
middle of nowhere", on which players "grip it and rip it" while trying
"not to be distracted by the impressive view of the surrounding mountains"; it's tough to "find one blade of grass out of place" on this
"amazing" course that's in "excellent condition", and most agree it's
"expensive, but worth it."

Las Vegas Paiute Golf Resort, Sun Mountain
27 | 26 | 24 | 24 | $149

Las Vegas | 10325 Nu Wav Kaiv Blvd. | 702-658-1400 | 866-284-2833 |
www.lvpaiutegolf.com | 7112/5465; 73.3/71.0; 130/123

Some swear it's the "quietest course they have ever played", this
"hideaway" in a "perfect, nearly exotic location" about a half hour
northwest of the city, where many "hate to take a divot" from a "wonderfully maintained" Pete Dye layout that's "hard", but "not as brutal as
some others in Vegas"; "awesome" views, "attentive" service and a
"first-rate" grass driving range add to the "high-quality golf experience."

Las Vegas Paiute Golf Resort, Wolf
27 | 24 | 24 | 23 | $169

Las Vegas | 10325 Nu Wav Kaiv Blvd. | 702-658-1400 |
866-284-2833 | www.lvpaiutegolf.com |
7604/5130; 76.3/68.5; 149/116

A game here "will leave you howling for more", especially since this
"beautifully maintained" Pete Dye "gold standard" is routed through
the high desert where it "seems like your group is the only one on the
course", with nary a housing development in sight; like the other
Paiute courses, "wind can take a big bite out of any game", but recovery is only steps away at the clubhouse with "stunning views."

Legacy, The ⌖

| 22 | 22 | 22 | 22 | $119 |

Henderson | 130 Par Excellence Dr. | 702-897-2187 | 888-446-5358 |
www.thelegacygc.com | 7233/5340; 74.0/70.5; 139/117

"Who wouldn't want to hit off a diamond, heart, club or spade tee box?" gush gamblers who double down on this "enjoyable" track in Henderson that boasts "interesting holes" and "all the challenge you could want" on a desert design from Arthur Hills; it's a "great value" in a competitive market, offering a "fast pace of play", "reasonable" facilities and "friendly" service that really "impresses."

Mojave Resort ⌖

| - | - | - | - | $109 |

Laughlin | 9905 Aha Macav Pkwy. | 702-535-4653 |
www.mojaveresortgolfclub.com | 6939/5520; 73.6/72.2; 136/124

Located just south of Laughlin, down California way, this Schmidt/Curley design is often overlooked even though it plays in a scenic setting of sandy dunes that were created by Colorado River floods and later reclaimed by thickets of mesquite and tamarisk; if the many water hazards and walls of trees get you down, head to the adjoining Avi Resort and Casino, where you can lift your spirits as you try to recoup your greens fee.

Oasis, Canyons ⌖

| 23 | 21 | 22 | 21 | $85 |

Mesquite | 100 Palmer Ln. | 702-346-7820 | www.theoasisgolfclub.com |
6408/4739; 71.3/67.3; 129/112

If you "want a little challenge", fans recommend this "interesting" track near Mesquite; it's a test "not so much for distance" but "accuracy", with "incredible views" and "great elevation changes", and while some sniff "it's not the best course" around, it's "fun" and "cheap", and many "would go back anytime."

Oasis, Palmer ⌖

| 26 | 19 | 23 | 22 | $145 |

Mesquite | 100 Palmer Ln. | 702-346-7820 | www.theoasisgolfclub.com |
6633/4227; 71.5/64.2; 133/106

Showcased on the Golf Channel's *Big Break,* this "fantastic" Arnold Palmer design is a "great layout", with "smooth greens" and a "picturesque" setting routed "through slot canyons"; the key to this "playable" but "tough" desert track is "keeping the ball on the fairway", otherwise "you could hit a really nice house."

Primm Valley, Lakes ⌖

| 26 | 24 | 23 | 23 | $135 |

Nipton | 1 Yates Well Rd. | 702-679-5510 | 800-386-7837 |
www.primmvalleygolf.com | 6444/4842; 71.2/68.5; 130/121

A "must-play on every trip to Vegas", this "beautiful, challenging" Tom Fazio course in the heart of the Mojave Desert is an "excellent test of golf", boasting "long, wide fairways", short par 4s and doglegging in both directions, with nary a house in sight; the watery, pine-filled layout is "always in superb shape" and the service is "fantastic", while the 22-acre practice area and cozy clubhouse are pluses.

Revere, Concord ⌖

| 24 | 22 | 20 | 18 | $169 |

Henderson | 2600 Hampton Rd. | 702-259-4653 | 877-273-8373 |
www.reveregolf.com | 7069/5171; 73.3/69.7; 151/119

"Often overlooked" in a market of "more famous (read: expensive) courses", this Henderson layout is "well worth the money", offering "big elevation changes, tight holes" and a "desert style" that "can punish a bad shot severely"; the 23,300-sq.-ft. clubhouse includes a highly regarded pro shop and a full-service restaurant, and you can get "some good deals" if you play in the summer and book online.

Revere, Lexington 🏖

23 | 24 | 23 | 19 | $235

Henderson | 2600 Hampton Rd. | 702-259-4653 | 877-273-8373 | www.reveregolf.com | 7143/5216; 73.5/69.6; 139/119

"Desert golf in its most diabolical joy" is how fans describe this Henderson track that's a "blast to play" with "tons of elevation changes" and "classic rock blaring at the bag drop"; the staff is "helpful", and the layout offers "incredible views of Las Vegas and the Strip", but critics complain there are "too many houses too close to the course."

Rio Secco 🏖

26 | 25 | 22 | 19 | $275

Henderson | 2851 Grand Hills Dr. | 702-889-2400 | 888-867-3226 | www.riosecco.net | 7314/5760; 75.7/70.0; 153/127

You can "play where Tiger once did" (when he was a student of on-site guru Butch Harmon) at this "spectacular" Rees Jones playground in the foothills of suburban Henderson; it's a difficult "desert layout" with "impressive views" and "enough challenges to make you want to come back and do it better", and while some critics find the service "haphazard" and complain about "all the new homes going up", most insist "you can't go wrong" here.

Royal Links 🏌

21 | 20 | 21 | 14 | $199

Las Vegas | 5995 Vegas Valley Dr. | 702-450-8123 | 888-446-5385 | www.royallinksgolfclub.com | 7029/5142; 73.7/69.8; 135/115

"If the euro exchange is preventing you" from traveling across the pond, try this "interesting, links-style" course boasting "great replicas of British Open holes" with "true pot bunkers that'll make you shudder"; critics find it "overpriced" for "muni-type service and conditions", and while single-malts in the "castlelike clubhouse" add an authentic note, skeptics sigh "you still feel like you're in Vegas"; P.S. "unless you're Tiger", "hit out sideways from the rough."

Shadow Creek 🏌 ⚬⚬

27 | 26 | 27 | 21 | $500

North Las Vegas | 3 Shadow Creek Dr. | 702-791-7161 | 866-260-0069 | www.shadowcreek.com | 7560/6626

Though it's currently unrated by the USGA, MGM Mirage's "expensive", "spectacular" course is an "amazing architectural achievement" "crafted out of dust and sand", boasting so much flora and water that "you wouldn't know you're playing in the middle of the desert"; "amazing" facilities, including a "wonderful locker room and bar area", round out this "once-in-a-lifetime experience" (which may be all most of us can afford).

Siena 🏖

21 | 22 | 23 | 20 | $139

Las Vegas | 10575 Siena Monte Ave. | 702-341-9200 | 888-689-6469 | www.sienagolfclub.com | 6843/4978; 71.7/68.2; 131/114

"Affordable" and "fun", this Lee Schmidt/Brian Curley track on the red rock side of the Vegas valley has a surprising amount of vertical and horizontal movement given the surrounding terrain; though "not overly long", free-form bunkering, patches of native desert, uneven lies and water make it a "nice resort course."

TPC Las Vegas
25 | 23 | 23 | 21 | $249

Las Vegas | 9851 Canyon Run Dr. | 702-256-2500 | www.tpc.com/lasvegas | 7080/4963; 73.4/67.8; 136/117

"Challenging tee shots" over "frightening chasms" to "perfectly groomed fairways" and "to-die-for greens" plus lots of "risk/reward holes where a carry can put you in birdie range" make for a "fun round" on this "quintessential desert course" and former PGA Tour stop; "stunning views" of the Strip and surrounding red-and-purple-tinted mountains, "top-notch practice facilities" and a "staff that puts a capital 'S' in service" round out the "awesome experience."

☑ Wolf Creek ⚑
28 | 22 | 23 | 24 | $195

Mesquite | 403 Paradise Pkwy. | 866-252-4653 | www.golfwolfcreek.com | 6939/4101; 75.4/61.0; 154/106

"Strategy and accuracy are vital" on Nevada's top-rated Course, this "roller coaster" "hewn out of desert canyons" that resemble the "face of the moon" (if the moon's greens roll 10 on the Stimpmeter, that is); "signing the waiver to drive a cart" gives some indication of the "adventure" that awaits on this "total hoot of a layout" complemented by a "fantastic" clubhouse and golf shop, and the only knock is on the marshals for "doing little to move groups along."

Wynn Las Vegas ⚑⚏
24 | 26 | 26 | 17 | $500

Las Vegas | 3131 Las Vegas Blvd. S. | 702-770-3575 | 888-320-9966 | www.wynnlasvegas.com | 7042/6464; 69.3/69.2; 131/130

"Just out the back door" of the Wynn Las Vegas, this "excellent" Tom Fazio/Steve Wynn design is an "oasis in the desert" that's "maintained like Augusta National" and it's now open to non-resort guests; the "top-of-the-line" staff "aims to please" and chances are you'll "run into celebrities", and while critics carp about fees that amount to a "month's car payment", "if you're a high roller, it is well worth it."

Reno

Edgewood Tahoe ⚐
26 | 23 | 22 | 20 | $220

Lake Tahoe | 100 Lake Pkwy. | 775-588-3566 | 888-881-8659 | www.edgewood-tahoe.com | 7545/5567; 75.5/71.3; 144/136

Fans are in "paradise" playing on what they call "one of the best mountain courses" around (home to the American Century Celebrity Golf Championship), a "spectacular" spread set against the "breathtaking backdrop" of Lake Tahoe; you'll "use all your clubs and then some" and, thanks to the high-altitude air, "you can have a career drive on nearly every hole"; P.S. "don't miss the malts at the turn."

New Hampshire

Northern New Hampshire

Balsams, Panorama
▽ 22 | 22 | 21 | 24 | $96

Dixville Notch | 1000 Cold Spring Rd. | 603-255-4961 | 800-255-0600 | www.thebalsams.com | 6804/4978; 72.8/69.3; 127/116

"You'll get your exercise on the 18th hole alone" warn whackers familiar with this "tranquil, remote" 1912 Donald Ross design near the

Canadian border, where even the forward tees on the "long uphill par 3s" "offer little advantage"; perks at this "stay-and-play resort" include "unlimited rounds on the house", "dizzying vistas" and "moose [sightings] on the fairways in the mornings."

Mount Washington Hotel & Resort
∇ 17 | 21 | 21 | 18 | $100

Bretton Woods | Rte. 302 | 603-278-4653 | www.mtwashington.com | 6974/5138; 73.7/70.2; 124/120

This "beautifully designed" 1915 Donald Ross course is a "true classic" that may be the "most challenging in the state" and is a "must-play just for the experience"; the original layout was "thankfully preserved" during a 2007 restoration, and putters can ponder "breathtaking views of Mt. Washington" as they get cozy in a northern New Hampshire hotel with "old-world" charm.

Owl's Nest ⌂
∇ 24 | 21 | 24 | 23 | $64

Campton | 40 Clubhouse Ln. | 603-726-3076 | 888-695-6378 | www.owlsnestgolf.com | 6818/5174; 73.3/69.8; 136/115

A "great find" with scenic views of the White Mountains, this aptly named track has "elevated tees" on its "somewhat hilly" layout – and since you'll be "hitting downhill", "you'll be pleased with the length of some drives"; the course can be divvied into three sections – six links-style holes, six that meander through fields and a pond, and six set atop Sunset Hill – and despite "several blind shots", it's considered a "wonderful course" overall.

Southern New Hampshire

Atkinson Resort & Country Club
- | - | - | - | $62

Atkinson | 85 Country Club Dr. | 603-362-5681 | www.atkinsonresort.com | 6580/4867; 73.1/68.6; 135/117

Tucked away in southeastern New Hampshire, this "sure winner" has a "terrific layout", opening with a "straight and uncomplicated" 1st followed by "17 holes of constant challenge"; despite the modest length, short hitters will be in for a "long day", but the "incredible clubhouse and amenities", which include a grass range and a 65-yard short-game practice hole, make it a "pleasant" experience overall.

Breakfast Hill ☉
- | - | - | - | $48

Greenland | 339 Breakfast Hill Rd. | 603-436-5001 | www.breakfasthill.com | 6493/4994; 71.5/64.8; 131/109

Set on former farmland several miles from the coast in Greenland, NH, this short Brian Silva design is a rolling, tree-lined track that can be "a challenge" (requiring tactics more than heroics) yet it manages to "accommodate everyone" with "lots of tee choices"; reasonable rates and "plush fairways" that are kept "in great shape" also make it a "joy."

Bretwood, North
∇ 22 | 15 | 18 | 24 | $44

Keene | 365 E. Surry Rd. | 603-352-7626 | www.bretwoodgolf.com | 6976/5140; 73.7/70.1; 136/120

A good "argument for turning the old family farm into a golf course", this "scenic, challenging" spread stretches to nearly 7,000 yards as it plays along the Ashuelot River, with an island par 3, multiple ponds and plenty of trees; if some are less impressed ("don't see what the fuss is all about"), it's a "well-maintained course" at a "fair price", with

	COURSE	FACIL.	SERVICE	VALUE	COST

play-all-day specials to make it an even better "value"; P.S. weekday reservations are not required.

Portsmouth Country Club ☉

| 22 | 19 | 21 | 18 | $85 |

Greenland | 80 Country Club Ln. | 603-436-9719 | www.portsmouthcc.net | 7133/5134; 73.6/64.8; 123/108

"A must-play in New England", this "great old Donald Ross course" sits about an hour north of Boston, offering an "interesting layout" with "a number of holes on the water", some of which can be difficult "if the wind blows"; a few surveyors suggest it's "expensive for public play", but it remains an "enjoyable" option; P.S. bring bug spray to ward off the pesky mosquitoes.

Shattuck, The

| 23 | 15 | 18 | 21 | $67 |

Jaffrey | 53 Dublin Rd. | 603-532-4300 | www.sterlinggolf.com | 6764/4632; 73.5/69.0; 153/115

Carved from "the base of Mt. Monadnock", this "beautiful" "beast" "must have been designed by a masochist" given "long carries over marshes" ("bring a few dozen golf balls, then buy some more") and "lots of tricky holes" that a few feel "border on being unplayable"; still, given that it boasts "spectacular views", this "extremely difficult track" is "worth the challenge", so choose the right tees and then "listen carefully to the clues."

New Jersey

TOP COURSES IN STATE

27] Hominy Hill | *Freehold*
26] Crystal Springs, Ballyowen | *NYC Metro*
  Shore Gate | *Atlantic City*
25] Twisted Dune | *Atlantic City*
  Neshanic Valley | *Bridgewater*

Atlantic City

Atlantic City Country Club 🏌 🏓 ☉

| 24 | 24 | 23 | 18 | $225 |

Northfield | 1 Leo Fraser Dr. | 609-236-4400 | www.accountryclub.com | 6577/5349; 72.3/71.5; 133/127

For "golf as it used to be and how it still should be today", head to this "old classic", which was "nicely renovated" by Tom Doak in 1998, yielding an "amazing course" that provides a "real challenge" to go with the "country-club atmosphere" and "attentive service"; while the greens fees are "steep", most agree the "scenic views across the bay", "timeless design" and "rich history" make it "worth the price of admission."

Ballamor Golf Club 🏓

| - | - | - | - | $105 |

Egg Harbor Township | 6071 English Creek Ave. | 609-601-6220 | www.ballamor.com | 7098/5238; 74.2/70.3; 136/125

Though the name sounds vaguely Scottish or Irish, there's nothing links-like about this all-American track near the Jersey Shore that rolls through dense tree cover amid sparkling lakes, large splashes of sand and multi-tiered greens; the 11-year-old Ault, Clark & Associates design was private until 2010, but now all comers can tackle some of the most compelling risk/reward holes in the Garden State, including the sporty par-4 17th and the reachable par-5 18th.

Blue Heron Pines 🏌

22 | 20 | 21 | 20 | $99

Cologne | 550 W. Country Club Dr. | 609-965-4653 | 888-478-2746 | www.blueheronpines.com | 6557/5053; 71.5/69.2; 133/120

"Get a good night's sleep before you leave your casino", because this "solid, well-designed" layout near the Atlantic City Boardwalk is "reasonably difficult" ("if you like sand, this is your course"), but still "fun for all handicaps" and "lady-friendly" to boot; while a few feel the "price is a little high", the course is "always kept in nice shape" and the staff is "helpful."

Harbor Pines 🏌

21 | 20 | 21 | 18 | $109

Egg Harbor Township | 500 St. Andrews Dr. | 609-927-0006 | www.harborpines.com | 6827/5099; 72.3/68.8; 131/118

You can let the big dog out at this Egg Harbor Township "ego-booster", since "most of the fairways seem as wide as they are long", but the "huge, fast greens" can be "tough" indeed – it's "very easy to three-putt if you're on the wrong side of the pin"; laid out "amongst the pines" just outside Atlantic City, it's a "beautiful" course that makes for a "great first or last round" of a trip.

McCullough's Emerald Golf Links 🏌

21 | 14 | 18 | 22 | $89

Egg Harbor Township | 3016 Ocean Heights Ave. | 609-926-3900 | www.mcculloughsgolf.com | 6535/4962; 71.7/67.2; 130/118

"Ireland comes to the Jersey Shore" at this "bang for the buck" that "reclaims a former landfill" with its "replicas of holes from England, Scotland" and the Green Isle, so "let it transport you" – "at a discount"; the "unique, links-style" layout is "wide-open", and though it's "not terribly long", the "elevated design brings the wind into play" ("hold on to your hat"), and most concur it's "worth a shot if you're in the area."

Sea Oaks ⏱

23 | 23 | 21 | 20 | $95

Little Egg Harbor Township | 99 Golf View Dr. | 609-296-2656 | www.seaoakscc.com | 6950/5150; 73.3/69.6; 139/127

Despite its location in Little Egg Harbor, this "tactical course" is "no day at the beach" given "windy" conditions that "can make it a monster" and "huge greens" that can lead you to "three-putt all day"; a "courteous staff" and "great facilities" – including "a driving range right next to the first tee" – also make it "worth a stopover if you're on your way down to Atlantic City."

Seaview Resort, Bay

22 | 24 | 23 | 20 | $109

Galloway | 401 S. New York Rd. | 609-748-7680 | 800-932-8000 | www.seaviewgolf.com | 6247/5017; 70.4/69.5; 124/120

A "timeless classic" from "golf master Donald Ross", this links-style LPGA Tour host challenges players with "small greens", "ball-eating rough" and "lots of wind" – when the breeze is up, "you'll need a howitzer to get it home" – even as it treats them to the "salty air" and "views of glitzy Atlantic City"; it can get "buggy by the bay", however, so "take repellent for the summer months", or retreat into the "Taj Mahal of clubhouses", where the golf shop and locker rooms were completely renovated in 2011.

	COURSE	FACIL.	SERVICE	VALUE	COST

Seaview Resort, Pines

22	23	22	19	$109

Galloway | 401 S. New York Rd. | 609-748-7680 | 800-932-8000 |
www.seaviewgolf.com | 6731/5276; 72.1/70.7; 126/121

The "better of the two" at the "Gatsby-esque" Seaview Resort, this "narrow", "traditional" track "carved out of the pines" features "tough", "tight fairways" that make it a "must-play" "for single-digit handicappers"; although some say it's "not as beautiful as the Bay", bugs are also less of a problem, and the "excellent practice and clubhouse facilities" give it the "heritage and ambiance of a gentlemen's club."

Shore Gate 🏳

26	18	19	20	$120

Ocean View | 35 School House Ln. | 609-624-8337 |
www.shoregategolfclub.com | 6794/5284; 72.7/71.1; 134/126

With "more sand and water than nearby Sea Isle City", this "little-known gem" "can bring you down to your knees" with "real risk/reward" holes featuring "tough", "tight fairways" and "super-fast greens", making it "difficult to play if you don't know the course"; but while there are "bunkers all over the place", some suggest the facilities "could use a facelift", but not the "don't-miss burgers at the halfway house."

Twisted Dune

25	15	19	21	$99

Egg Harbor Township | 2101 Ocean Heights Ave. | 609-653-8019 |
888-894-7839 | www.twisteddune.com | 7339/5026; 75.2/69.0; 132/120

You'll "feel like you just landed in Scotland" at this "beautiful links-style course", a "long, sandy, punishing diamond-in-the-rough" where "giant dunes" "framing the fairways provide a great visual"; you'll need to "bring your A-game and thinking cap" to tackle the "tall grass", "long par 3s and uphill holes", and while the "facilities are modest", "Atlantic City is right down the road."

Vineyard Golf at Renault

22	20	21	21	$89

Egg Harbor | 72 N. Bremen Ave. | 609-965-2111 |
www.vineyardgolfatrenault.com | 7213/5176; 75.3/68.8; 132/117

This "hidden treasure" in Egg Harbor is "unique for New Jersey", with "half of [the layout] running through vineyards" that "don't come into play much" but do "produce the grapes for the wonderful local wines"; it's "pretty" and "well kept", with the lack of a driving range the only "detraction" from what's become a "real winner."

Bridgewater

Neshanic Valley

25	23	21	24	$85

Neshanic Station | 2301 S. Branch Rd. | 908-369-8200 |
www.somersetcountyparks.org
Lake/Meadow | 7069/5096; 73.7/70.2; 128/126
Meadow/Ridge | 7036/5013; 73.4/70.0; 129/126
Ridge/Lake | 7065/5061; 73.5/69.9; 127/119

"You can't get much better in NJ for the price, even if you're not a Somerset County resident", than this "magnificent 27-hole muni" that's "a treasure, a pleasure and a challenge" with its "imaginative layout", "narrow fairways" and "sloping greens"; "friendly service", "outstanding practice facilities" and an "on-site Callaway Performance Center" render it "a complete facility" that "would have no trouble finding members if it were a country club."

	COURSE	FACIL.	SERVICE	VALUE	COST

Royce Brook, East 𝅘 𝄞

21 | 22 | 21 | 20 | $115

Hillsborough | 201 Hamilton Rd. | 908-904-4786 | 888-434-3673 |
www.roycebrook.com | 6946/5062; 73.6/69.6; 132/121

A "solid track" nestled in the pines near Hillsborough, this "beautiful course" "adapts to all levels", with "wide-open" fairways, "fast greens" and "a lot of beaches" ("bring suntan lotion") to make it "especially challenging if the wind blows"; some find it "pricey", but it boasts "friendly" service and some of the "nicest non-country club facilities in New Jersey", including an "amazing clubhouse" and "excellent" practice area.

Camden

Scotland Run

23 | 23 | 21 | 20 | $99

Williamstown | 2626 Fries Mill Rd. | 856-863-3737 | www.scotlandrun.com |
6810/5010; 73.3/69.5; 134/120

An old quarry in Williamstown is the "unusual setting" for this "visually pleasing" collection of holes that presents players with "sand, sand and more sand", including a tee shot on the 16th "over a waste area with an airplane" fuselage inside; yes, it's "frustrating if you don't stay on the fairway", but it's nonetheless a "well-groomed" course that "doesn't have houses throughout" and "comfortable facilities" to boot.

Cape May

Cape May National

20 | 16 | 18 | 20 | $85

Cape May | Fairway Ave. & Rte. 9 | 609-884-1563 | www.cmngc.com |
6905/4711; 73.4/67.6; 136/117

Encircling a private bird sanctuary, this "lovely" layout with "immense natural beauty" offers "a nice variety of holes" featuring "tough" greens and a number of forced "carries over waste areas"; it's "one of the better courses in the area", and while there's "not much of a clubhouse" and the track "needs a bit more care", the "beautiful Cape May" location allows you to "swing your clubs near the beach and the birds."

Sand Barrens

21 | 21 | 21 | 20 | $105

Swainton | 1765 Rte. 9 N. | 609-465-3555 | 800-465-3122 |
www.sandbarrensgolf.com
North/South | 6969/4946; 72.7/68.0; 133/120
South/West | 6895/4971; 71.7/68.3; 130/119
West/North | 7092/4951; 73.2/67.9; 135/119

The "name is apropos" for this "unique", "beautifully maintained" layout on the Jersey Shore, where the "imaginative" holes with "large waste areas" and "sand traps you'll never forget" make "target golf a must", so "bring your A-game" and "don't complain" if you "shape a shot over a fairway bunker only to find another immediately behind it"; you'll "have a great time", even if it "can be hot and buggy during the summer."

Freehold

Charleston Springs, North

24 | 19 | 17 | 23 | $72

Millstone Township | 101 Woodville Rd. | 732-409-7227 |
www.monmouthcountyparks.com | 7011/5071; 73.4/69.7; 126/117

This "links-style" "gem" is routed through berms of native grasses that "penalize errant shots", "gobbling up your ammo" and "bringing your confidence down a peg"; a few feel the "reservations system needs to be changed", but the "well-manicured course" offers "enough surprises and challenges to keep 'em coming back"; P.S. it's the "best deal around if you're a resident" of Monmouth County and an "excellent value" for everyone else.

Charleston Springs, South

24 | 19 | 17 | 23 | $72

Millstone Township | 101 Woodville Rd. | 732-409-7227 |
www.monmouthcountyparks.com | 6953/5153; 73.2/69.7; 125/118
Although "a little easier than the North", this "well-kept" county-owned course is a "long", "tough" parkland track that will have you "scratching your head" as you tackle the "narrow fairways lined with tall grass"; "don't look for service" here, but you can expect "great" practice facilities – in sum, it's a "real steal"; P.S. "walking is doable", but it's "hilly enough that you'll wish you took a cart."

Eagle Ridge

19 | 19 | 19 | 18 | $98

Lakewood | 2 Augusta Blvd. | 732-901-4900 | www.eagleridgegolf.com
Links/Pines | 6976/5039; 73.6/67.2; 140/118
Links/Ridge | 6976/5049; 73.6/69.3; 139/117
Pines/Ridge | 6976/4898; 72.7/71.0; 138/123
Still "relatively young", this "short", "tight", "hilly track" near the Jersey Shore has a "classic feel", and though "wrapped around housing", the "pine forest holes" are "enjoyable from any of the tee boxes"; the "grounds crew does an amazing job", and the rest of the staff is "friendly and informative", rounding out an altogether "worthwhile" experience.

Hominy Hill

27 | 17 | 18 | 23 | $72

Colts Neck | 92 Mercer Rd. | 732-462-9223 |
www.monmouthcountyparks.com | 7049/5793; 73.8/73.6; 131/129
Jersey's top-rated Course, this "jewel of the Monmouth County collection" "could convert to a high-end country club in about a week", with its "fabulous", "classic RTJ Sr. design" that's "tough" from all tees and "a real challenge from the back"; the "facilities and service leave a bit to be desired", and "getting a tee time is next to impossible" for non-residents, but it's sure "worth it when you get one."

Howell Park

22 | 12 | 15 | 24 | $60

Farmingdale | 405 Squankum-Yellowbrook Rd. | 732-938-4771 |
www.monmouthcountyparks.com | 6964/5698; 73.0/72.5; 126/125
An "alternative to pricier" courses in the area, this "nice muni" near Farmingdale is a "well-built and well-maintained" layout that's "pleasant for an enjoyable round" – "if you can hit 'em far, you can play well here"; it's a "real value", particularly for Monmouth County residents, and while some say "they need to do a better job" with the facilities, it's fine if you come to "play golf and don't worry about amenities."

NYC Metro

Architects

25 | 21 | 21 | 21 | $110

Phillipsburg | 700 Strykers Rd. | 908-213-3080 | www.thearchitectsclub.com |
6863/5233; 72.5/71.2; 131/126
"This is what golf is all about" say fans of this "gem in western NJ" where "each hole has a different style" reflecting the "signature" elements of "golf architecture's royalty", from Alister MacKenzie to

Donald Ross and beyond; some suggest it's a "novelty" track, but all agree it's a "well-done" and "imaginative" "treat for the mind" that strikes a "good balance between difficulty and playability" – in short, it's "worth the [70-mile] drive from New York City."

Berkshire Valley 🏌

24 | 18 | 18 | 23 | $90

Oak Ridge | 28 Cozy Lake Rd. | 973-208-0018 | www.morrisparks.net/golf | 6354/4647; 71.1/66.9; 120/113

"Not your everyday muni", this "hidden gem" is perhaps "Morris County's prettiest course", with its opening holes set "along a mountain ridge" for a "challenging start" that offers "spectacular views" while requiring players to "sacrifice distance for hitting it straight" (it "gives new meaning to the term 'out of bounds'"); although the two nines are "very different", they combine to create a "beautiful" and "unique" "little course" that's "no pushover."

🄿 Crystal Springs, Ballyowen 🏌

26 | 25 | 24 | 20 | $137

Hamburg | 105-137 Wheatsworth Rd. | 973-827-5996 | www.crystalgolfresort.com | 7094/4903; 73.6/68.7; 131/123

"Leave the driver in the bag" at this "real test and treat", a "beautiful, remote links course" that channels the "spirit of Scotland", from "brutal fescue that will eat any stray shot" and "bagpipes at sunset" "all the way down to a staff in kilts"; it can prove a "big challenge for once-a-year-types", but everyone will appreciate the "excellent putting area", "great grass driving range" and "friendly" service; P.S. the "cart-path-only rule" can make for an "exhausting" round.

Crystal Springs, Black Bear 🏌

19 | 19 | 19 | 20 | $89

Franklin | 138 Rte. 23 N. | 973-827-5996 | www.crystalgolfresort.com | 6673/4785; 72.2/67.7; 130/116

"Watch out for bears" at this "forgiving" course located in a "beautiful setting in the mountains of NJ", where a "fairly pedestrian front nine" is paired with a "more challenging back"; although less than 6,700 yards from the tips, the "surrounding woods" and "clever bunker placement help to lengthen" a layout that "offers something for all golfers", including "reasonable rates" that are lower than its "neighboring brothers."

Crystal Springs, Crystal Springs Course 🏌

19 | 22 | 20 | 18 | $100

Hamburg | 1 Wild Turkey Way | 973-827-5996 | www.crystalgolfresort.com | 6808/5111; 74.1/70.5; 137/123

"A true shot-makers course", this "tight, challenging layout" has a "reputation for being too difficult", with "penal moguls just off the fairways", "too many houses to bounce balls off of" and "uneven lies" "no matter where you hit it"; nevertheless, many consider it to be "quirky and fun", with "spectacular views of the mountains" and "awesome facilities" that include an "elaborate clubhouse with a fine restaurant."

Crystal Springs, Great Gorge 🏌

20 | 16 | 18 | 20 | $92

McAfee | Rte. 517 | 973-827-7603 | www.crystalgolfresort.com
Lakeside/Quarryside | 6710/5354; 72.7/71.8; 133/128
Quarryside/Railside | 6758/5502; 72.9/72.6; 129/130
Railside/Lakeside | 6852/5518; 73.3/72.8; 132/129

Located in the state's "rolling foothills" on a site that's also "home to the former Playboy Club", this 27-hole "true golfers' paradise" offers a "mature", "traditional, tree-lined" setting that's a "pleasing contrast" to its nearby siblings; the "elevated tees", "undulating fairways", "ample water hazards" and "difficult greens add to the challenge", and although the "facilities leave a lot to be desired", the "picturesque holes" boast "amazing views."

Crystal Springs, Wild Turkey 🗺   24 | 24 | 23 | 22 | $122

Hamburg | 1 Wild Turkey Way | 973-827-5996 | www.crystalgolfresort.com | 7202/5024; 74.8/69.0; 131/118

"Unlike its brutal brother Ballyowen", this "interesting" course is "enjoyable for many levels" with a "wide-open", "forgiving" layout that still "offers some challenge" in the form of "elevation changes"; kept in "excellent condition", it boasts "breathtaking vistas of the New Jersey highlands", and the "friendly" "Scottish-clad" staff and "upscale" facilities are two more reasons many "would go back again and again."

Flanders Valley, Red/Gold   21 | 12 | 15 | 25 | $58

Flanders | 81 Pleasant Hill Rd. | 973-584-5382 | www.morrisparks.org | 6770/5540; 72.6/73.1; 129/130

An "outstanding value for Morris County residents", this "wonderful" muni "warms you up on the flat, forgiving" front nine and then "aerobically challenges you" on a "scenic" back where "walkers need a little bit of mountain goat" to tackle the "rolling hills and elevated tees"; the "facilities are a bit tired" but "recent tree harvests and drainage improvements" have restored course conditions to their "former glory" - now "the only thing missing is a driving range."

Flanders Valley, White/Blue   22 | 12 | 16 | 26 | $58

Flanders | 81 Pleasant Hill Rd. | 973-584-5382 | www.morrisparks.org | 6765/5534; 72.9/72.5; 128/128

"Cut out of the woods" near Flanders, this "first-rate" member of "the Morris County system" offers a "solid routing", with two nines that "fit very nicely together" and are kept in "above-average condition for a municipal"; although detractors dismiss the "small pro shop", "nonexistent service" and "slow" pace of play, it's "an incredible value" that's "wonderful to play, particularly in the fall as the leaves are turning."

High Bridge Hills ⏱   23 | 12 | 16 | 20 | $80

High Bridge | 203 Cregar Rd. | 908-638-5055 | www.highbridgehills.com | 6640/4928; 72.0/68.9; 130/116

A "hidden gem" in "rural" "northwestern New Jersey", this "links-style layout" "has character": with a design nod to Ireland and Scotland, it "looks more open than it is", with "lots of blind shots", "elevation changes" and other hazards ("fescue abounds") to make it "tough for the high-handicapper"; yes, you can expect "six-hour rounds on weekends", but "immaculate grooming", a "great" clubhouse and a "friendly" staff help to compensate.

Sunset Valley   21 | 14 | 17 | 22 | $58

Pompton Plains | 47 W. Sunset Rd. | 973-835-1515 | www.morrisparks.net/golf | 6368/5157; 71.5/70.2; 128/122

"Another Morris County gem", this "short", "tight", "terrific municipal" boasts "perhaps the state's toughest finishing holes", which "can make or break your round", as can the "quick, true", "glasslike greens" that are "some of the largest" around, with "clever pin placements making for long putts if your approach is off"; the facilities are bare-bones, but course "improvements happen constantly", making it a "great value."

New Mexico

Albuquerque

Black Mesa

26 | 17 | 20 | 26 | $67

Española | 115 State Rd. 399 | 505-747-8946 | www.blackmesagolfclub.com | 7307/5157; 73.9/71.2; 141/125

"About as good as it gets" according to surveyors, this "tough but fair" layout offers a "great mix of holes" as it travels through the foothills of Española; "blind tee shots" and "heavy, brutal wind" add up to a "wild challenge", and the "other-worldly views" – a "unique", "pristine desert" landscape with arroyo-edged fairways and mountain panoramas – make up for the decidedly "no-frills" facilities.

🔢 Paa-Ko Ridge

29 | 25 | 25 | 26 | $114

Sandia Park | 1 Clubhouse Dr. | 505-281-6000 | 866-898-5987 | www.paakoridge.com
Back/New | 7667/5846; 75.8/71.9; 139/134
Front/Back | 7562/5702; 75.2/71.7; 137/134
New/Front | 7579/5896; 75.6/72.2; 137/134

"The best golf experience in New Mexico, bar none", is this "absolutely beautiful" "must-play" that "rivals Pebble Beach for scenery" with its "mystical" setting "high in the mountains" outside Albuquerque ("bring your camera"); "extreme elevation changes" and "difficult greens" make it "a tough course for those who aren't accurate", but it's an "interesting" 27-holer that remains "fair" and "playable – even for women"; P.S. an "excellent pro shop" and service that's "second to none" add to "the wow factor."

Sandia

▽ 22 | 22 | 22 | 20 | $71

Albuquerque | 30 Rainbow Rd. NE | 505-798-3990 | www.sandiagolf.com | 7759/5112; 76.0/68.4; 133/115

Architect Scott Miller, who also designed Coeur d'Alene and We-Ko-Pa Cholla, is the talent behind this high desert track located on the Sandia Pueblo north of Downtown Albuquerque; play here is "fun for all levels depending on the tee box used" (it's particularly "challenging for women") and a "value" to boot, and it's part of a "great facility" that boasts resort accommodations, a casino and scenic views of the surrounding mountains.

Santa Ana

- | - | - | - | $47

Santa Ana Pueblo | 288 Prairie Star Rd. | 505-867-9464 | www.santaanagolf.com
Cheena/Star | 7145/5060; 73.0/68.3; 135/118
Star/Tamaya | 7187/4936; 73.1/67.3; 134/121
Tamaya/Cheena | 7298/5034; 74.1/68.2; 133/122

Set "above the Rio Grande River" with "wonderful views of the Sandia Mountains", this "very nice" desert course is "well laid out" and ideal for walking, with three "links-style" nines featuring native grasses;

some suggest it's "living on past glory", but the "friendly staff" and famous Prairie Star restaurant help to compensate.

Twin Warriors

| 25 | 25 | 25 | 21 | $125 |

Santa Ana Pueblo | 1301 Tuyuna Trail | 505-771-6155 |
www.mynewmexicogolf.com | 7736/5100; 75.4/67.0; 140/116

Routed through the high desert an hour north of Albuquerque, this "long" layout "provides outstanding views" of the Rio Grande River Valley, along with superior "hole perspective, as almost every tee box is elevated"; there are arroyos and canyons everywhere, and "the winds blow hard", so "bring your low game" and be prepared to open your wallet, as it's "expensive for the area", although a "super staff" and an "accommodating" replay policy help make it "worth" the relatively high greens fees.

University of New Mexico Championship

| 27 | 17 | 19 | 26 | $58 |

Albuquerque | 3601 University Blvd. SE | 505-277-4546 |
www.unmgolf.com | 7562/5381; 75.4/69.1; 135/128

"Worth the challenge", this 42-year-old "Albuquerque monster" is a "nice change from the moderns", sporting "length from the tips" on a "tough" layout that also features "plenty-wide fairways" and greens that are "fast and difficult to read"; home to the U. of New Mexico's golf teams and a longtime host of numerous "collegiate championships", it's a "high-value choice", and its location "next door to the airport" puts it in easy reach, but also means it's "under the landing pattern."

Farmington

Piñon Hills

▽ | 28 | 22 | 26 | 28 | $41 |

Farmington | 2101 Sunrise Pkwy. | 505-326-6066 | www.pinonhillsgolf.com |
7198/5428; 73.9/70.6; 139/125

Although it seems like it's "a four-hour drive from anywhere", this "perfect gem in northwestern New Mexico" is "worth the detour" thanks to a "fantastic" Ken Dye design that can be stretched to a knee-buckling 7,200 yards (hint: there's an altitude assist); full of canyon crossings, dramatic elevation and "tricky greens", it's "awesome" and "well maintained", despite being a true municipal owned by the city of Farmington.

New York

TOP COURSES IN STATE

30| Bethpage, Black | *Long Island*
28| Turning Stone, Atunyote | *Finger Lakes*
27| Leatherstocking | *Albany*
26| Saratoga National | *Albany*
    Bethpage, Red | *Long Island*
    Montauk Downs | *Long Island*
25| Turning Stone, Shenendoah | *Finger Lakes*
    Turning Stone, Kaluhyat | *Finger Lakes*
    Grossinger, Big G | *Catskills*
24| Sagamore | *Adirondacks*

| | COURSE | FACIL. | SERVICE | VALUE | COST |

Adirondacks

Lake Placid Club, Links 🏌

| 22 | 20 | 22 | 22 | $75 |

Lake Placid | 88 Morningside Dr. | 518-523-2556 | 800-874-1980 |
www.lakeplacidcp.com | 7052/4964; 73.6/65.0; 129/108

Dating back to 1918, this "challenging" track offers a "links feel in the mountains" on a layout that looks "deceptively easy on the scorecard" but has "one- to two-club winds that blow almost every day"; given its "magnificent views", it's no wonder it's a "favorite among the historic Adirondacks courses" and a "reason why Lake Placid is a good destination for something other than skiing."

Lake Placid Club, Mountain 🏌

| 21 | 18 | 21 | 20 | $75 |

Lake Placid | 88 Morningside Dr. | 518-523-2556 | 800-874-1980 |
www.lakeplacidcp.com | 6501/4693; 71.6/68.0; 127/110

The "elevation changes are sure to present a challenge" on this "above-average course in gorgeous surroundings", so "practice your aim" because multiple "blind shots put a premium on accuracy, distance and courage"; "spectacular scenery" that reveals "the Adirondacks in its true glory" "makes up for any stress you experience during play", as does an "après-golf drink" in the "terrific clubhouse."

Sagamore, The

| 24 | 22 | 22 | 19 | $150 |

Bolton Landing | Frank Cameron Rd. | 518-644-9400 |
www.thesagamore.com | 6800/5176; 73.8/66.2; 138/131

"If you like old classic layouts, you must play" this "wonderful, fully restored" "Donald Ross gem", an "interesting, challenging design" that "teaches humility" with risk/reward holes and "thick rough" ("word to the wise: keep it in the fairway!"); it has a "gorgeous setting in the Adirondacks" at a resort "near Lake George", but regulars reveal that it offers "fewer views" than you might expect: you glimpse the lake "only once, on the 1st hole."

Whiteface

| ∇ 19 | 18 | 21 | 20 | $100 |

Lake Placid | 373 Whiteface Inn Lane | 518-523-2551 | 800-422-6757 |
www.whitefaceclubresort.com | 6451/5305; 71.1/71.5; 123/125

You'll "feel the history" as you play "one of the oldest layouts in the Adirondacks", this Lake Placid "charmer" that's "not long" but is "memorable", "especially in autumn" when you'll have "spectacular scenery" to "distract you"; the "epitome of a mountain course", it "hardly ever gives a level lie unless you're on the green", and while it's "an enjoyable golf experience overall", keep in mind that "it can be cool and windy, even in July."

Albany

Leatherstocking

| 27 | 22 | 24 | 21 | $99 |

Cooperstown | 60 Lake St. | 607-547-9931 | 800-348-6222 |
www.otesaga.com | 6401/5180; 71.0/70.2; 133/122

"Don't go to the National Baseball Hall of Fame without playing" this "great old course", a "hidden gem" in "beautiful Cooperstown" that surveyors say is "not long" but is "still challenging" thanks to a rolling layout on which "the only flat lies are on the tees" and the greens are "tough to read" and "well protected"; laid out "on the shore of Lake

Otesaga", it boasts "wonderful vistas" and a "pleasant" staff; P.S. extend your trip by basking in the "old-time" "comfort of the Otesaga Resort Hotel."

Saratoga National 🏌 🏞

| 26 | 25 | 25 | 20 | $150 |

Saratoga Springs | 458 Union Ave. | 518-583-4653 | www.golfsaratoga.com | 7265/4954; 75.7/69.3; 147/121

For a "wonderful walk" in Saratoga Springs, head to this "immaculate but brutally difficult course" that offers "risk/reward" holes with "extremely long carries" over wetlands and water, so "bring your A-game" and "at least a dozen extra balls"; a "beautiful" setting and "amazing facilities" combine with "superb food, drinks and service" to make it a "true mecca", and while it's "a little pricey", it can be a "value when it's not racing season."

Saratoga Spa, Championship

| 22 | 17 | 19 | 23 | $37 |

Saratoga Springs | 60 Roosevelt Dr. | 518-584-2006 | www.saratogaspagolf.com | 7145/5514; 74.4/71.1; 130/119

"A nice way to begin a new season before tackling the more difficult layouts", this "enjoyable" state park property is considered by some to be "one of the best values" in upstate New York, offering a "well-manicured", "very walkable" track with "pine tree–lined fairways" that can induce the "sounds of swearing" over many "lost balls"; the "bare-bones" municipal facilities are more than offset by the "picturesque" setting and "easy-to-get tee times."

Catskills

Grossinger, Big G

| 25 | 14 | 17 | 21 | $85 |

Liberty | 127 Grossinger Rd. | 845-292-9000 | www.grossingergolf.net | 7004/5750; 74.7/74.1; 139/136

"Now obscure but once well-known", this "great, scenic" track "continues to be the best in the Catskills" – "long and challenging, with an interesting variety of holes", "lots of water" and "tricky greens"; this "old course" has managed to "stand the test of time", and while the "facilities are outdated", "just ignore the abandoned resort" and enjoy the "friendly staff" and "value."

Finger Lakes

Bristol Harbour

| 22 | 18 | 18 | 21 | $65 |

Canandaigua | 5410 Seneca Point Rd. | 585-396-2460 | 800-288-8248 | www.bristolharbour.com | 6662/5482; 73.4/72.5; 136/132

This "pleasant surprise" "in the heart of the Finger Lakes" is a RTJ Sr. "beauty" – and a "tale of two nines with links on the front, and a mountain course on the back" where things "tighten up, providing a good challenge"; for all the solid play, post-rounders revel in the "killer 19th hole view from your Adirondack chair", and when autumn rolls around, the setting "almost makes you forget how nice the course is."

Chenango Valley State Park 🏞

| ∇ 21 | 11 | 15 | 25 | $25 |

Chenango Forks | 153 State Park Rd. | 607-648-9804 | www.nysparks.com | 6271/5279; 70.4/69.4; 125/127

A state-owned course 15 minutes north of Binghamton that "can't be beat for the price", this track scampers through the "hills and woods of Chenango County" playing "short" and "enjoyable" – though the "fairways can be tricky" and there are "some blind shots" too; on the down side, the "typical-for-a-park facilities need a retrofit."

Conklin Players Club ▽ 26 | 23 | 23 | 24 | $55 |

Conklin | 1520 Conklin Rd. | 607-775-3042 | www.conklinplayers.com | 6772/4699; 72.5/67.8; 127/116

Situated not far north of the Pennsylvania border, this "hilly, real golfers'" track signs in with a "fun and interesting layout" that "never disappoints", even if it occasionally slips into the "goofy" realm; conditioning is "always immaculate" here, and when you add "friendly" service and amenities such as GPS-equipped carts, the value is "awesome."

Greystone ▽ 25 | 22 | 20 | 22 | $59 |

Walworth | 1400 Atlantic Ave. | 315-524-0022 | 800-810-2325 | www.234golf.com | 7215/5277; 74.3/70.4; 128/118

"Off the beaten path" east of Rochester, this track is considered a "favorite public course in the area", with "changing elevations" that make for a "challenging round" and some "picturesque holes", including the "signature 18th with the last 125 yards over stone-lined water"; the staff is "friendly and helpful", and you can relive your round over rounds at the Scottish-themed Stoney's Pub overlooking the shared green of the 9th and 18th holes.

Links at Hiawatha Landing ▽ 26 | 22 | 25 | 24 | $63 |

Apalachin | 2350 Marshland Rd. | 607-687-6952 | 800-304-6533 | www.hiawathalinks.com | 7104/5101; 74.4/69.8; 133/118

You'll find "excellent value for the money" at this "tough, classic links course" that offers plenty of "risk/reward tee shots" and tall fescue ("bring lots of balls") as it travels along the "beautiful" Susquehanna River; the "top-notch track" is "usually in great shape", and the "nice staff" is yet another reason it's one of "the best in Upstate" New York – so "play it if in the area."

Ravenwood 24 | 21 | 23 | 22 | $63 |

Victor | 929 Lynaugh Rd. | 585-924-5100 | www.ravenwoodgolf.com | 6546/4880; 72.1/68.5; 130/120

"Growing into a fine golf course", this "beautiful, challenging" Robin Nelson design offers a variety of "very nice holes" that are suitable "for all levels" of play – "keep it in the fairway and you can score" here; the facilities and "grass driving range" also receive kudos, which may be why supporters say it's "high on the list of public courses to play" in the Finger Lakes area.

Seneca Hickory Stick 🏌 - | - | - | - | $69 |

Lewiston | 4560 Creek Rd. | 716-754-2424 | www.senecahickorystick.com | 7016/5417; 73.6/70.7; 129/120

Named for the rare Shellbark Hickory trees on-site, this tranquil Robert Trent Jones Jr. design owned by the Seneca Gaming Corporation is nevertheless more closely associated with water, perhaps no surprise given its location, 10 miles from Niagara Falls; most notable may be its unusual par-3 finish, a tiny, 152-yard, lake-guarded terror, as well as liquid peril on 10 other holes, but if the water doesn't sink you, the shaggy native grasses and cunningly placed bunkers just might.

	COURSE	FACIL.	SERVICE	VALUE	COST

Seven Oaks ☉
▽ 26 | 16 | 17 | 25 | $80

Hamilton | 13 Oak Dr. | 315-824-1432 | www.sevenoaksgolf.com | 6915/5252; 74.6/71.6; 143/128

Yet another "reason to send your kids to Colgate", this RTJ Sr. "gem in Hamilton" is owned by the university and is "easily the best value around", with a "fantastic layout" that "makes you hit great shots and rewards you" for them; a "meandering stream" adds to the "beautiful but demanding" design, so even if the facilities are "minimal", it's considered "a wonderful public course"; P.S. the "great prices" are even better for students, faculty and staff.

☒ Turning Stone, Atunyote ⚘
28 | 27 | 25 | 23 | $225

Verona | 5218 Patrick Rd. | 315-829-3867 | 800-771-7711 | www.turningstone.com | 7315/5120; 75.6/69.8; 140/120

A "gem" by Tom Fazio (and former PGA Tour event host), this "immaculate" layout is set amid "quiet farmland surroundings", with "wide, sweeping fairways and fast, undulating greens"; the "fantastic conditions" and "top-notch facilities" make it "feel like a private course", and the "excellent" service and hotel/casino "provide a phenomenal atmosphere before and after the round" – "you just need to win big at the blackjack tables to pay for the greens fees."

☒ Turning Stone, Kaluhyat ⚘
25 | 26 | 24 | 22 | $125

Verona | 5218 Patrick Rd. | 315-361-8518 | 800-771-7711 | www.turningstone.com | 7105/5293; 75.5/71.7; 150/134

Perhaps the "toughest of the three gems" at Turning Stone, this "beautiful" RTJ Jr. design is "very demanding from the back tees", with "challenges at every turn", including "tight fairways" and tricky "shots to finicky greens" that lead some to conclude it's "not for average golfers"; it's "pricey" but "worth every penny" given facilities and service that "rival some of the best private courses around", so "make a weekend of it and play its sisters as well."

☒ Turning Stone, Shenendoah ⚘
25 | 27 | 25 | 22 | $150

Verona | 5218 Patrick Rd. | 315-361-8518 | 800-771-7711 | www.turningstone.com | 7129/5185; 75.1/70.8; 146/126

The "original course at Turning Stone", this "nice track" can be "challenging" at points but is generally considered the "least interesting and most playable of the three" layouts on-site, with "a few gimme holes" that are sure to help you score; still, it's affiliated with "one of the top golf destinations" in upstate New York, which means you can expect "beautiful" scenery and "fantastic" conditioning, along with high-end facilities and service.

Hudson Valley

Garrison Golf Club
20 | 15 | 17 | 20 | $90

Garrison | 2015 Rte. 9 | 845-424-4747 | www.garrisongolfclub.com | 6497/4902; 71.3/69.3; 130/122

"Even on a bad day you can't beat the outrageous views" of the river and West Point at this Hudson Valley course that "will prove a challenge" "if you spray the ball"; the "very narrow front nine" is "more intriguing" than the "more open" inward nine, and to score, players "must hit the correct sides of the sloping fairways"; while some feel the clubhouse needs work, others contend that in fall, this place is "better than a trip to Vermont."

Links at Union Vale

| 23 | 21 | 21 | 22 | $76 |

LaGrangeville | 153 N. Parliman Rd. | 845-223-1000 |
www.thelinksatunionvale.com | 6954/5198; 73.4/71.3; 138/122

A "challenging links-style layout nowhere near the sea", this "hidden gem" "rests on old farmland" an "hour north of NYC" and offers an "Irish flavor" – "from the front gate's Gaelic greeting" to the "helpful staff" to the "deep sod bunker" on 15, "you feel as though you've been transplanted across the pond"; it's "punishing" (especially "when the wind is up") but still "playable for all" and, in a nod to the *auld* game, they even "allow you to walk."

Town of Wallkill Golf Club

| 19 | 16 | 17 | 22 | $49 |

Middletown | 40 Sands Rd. | 845-361-1022 | www.townofwallkill.com |
6470/5125; 72.5/70.7; 125/118

"Hidden about 70 miles north of NYC" in the Hudson Valley, this municipal "gem" is a "tight, hilly", "ingenious layout through the woods" with a total yardage that's certainly "not long" – "put away the driver and use irons for better placement" – and plays even shorter given the many doglegs; it's "reasonably priced [even] for out-of-towners", so when you factor in the "accommodating staff" and "convenient" location, it's a "surprise find" and a "terrific value."

Long Island

☑ Bethpage, Black 🏌

| 30 | 20 | 18 | 28 | $150 |

Farmingdale | 99 Quaker Meeting House Rd. | 516-249-0700 |
www.nysparks.com | 7468/6223; 76.6/77.0; 144/152

"An extraordinary, physically grueling test", this Farmingdale host of the 2009 U.S. Open is the U.S.'s top-rated Course thanks to a "monster" layout designed by A.W. Tillinghast on which "challenges abound, from hellacious rough and lightning-fast greens" to "brutal length and multiple sand traps"; the cart-free spread "is a bear to walk but worth every step", and since it "remains the public-course standard of excellence", those already initiated insist "you haven't golfed until you've played the Black."

☑ Bethpage, Blue

| 22 | 19 | 17 | 25 | $30 |

Farmingdale | 99 Quaker Meeting House Rd. | 516-249-0700 |
www.nysparks.com | 6638/6158; 71.7/72.0; 124/118

This "underestimated course at Bethpage" is the "best choice for the average golfer who is not out to prove something"; a high-value play, it has surprisingly "reasonable rates" for such a "solid" option that's in "country club condition" since the USGA started bringing the Open to its more famous sister; P.S. expect "five- to six-hour rounds."

Bethpage, Green 🏌

| 20 | 19 | 18 | 25 | $30 |

Farmingdale | 99 Quaker Meeting House Rd. | 516-249-0700 |
www.nysparks.com | 6378/5826; 70.6/73.7; 126/125

"A gentler version of the Black" that gives "higher handicappers a taste" of that notorious layout while being "easier on the ego", this course is perhaps the Bethpage club's most "all-around" offering, and it's one that "lets duffers feel like they are playing"; the "great value" is "pleasing in these financially down times", but "prepare for a nice long round" that proceeds at a "worse-than-molasses pace."

🄯 Bethpage, Red 🕏   26 | 19 | 17 | 28 | $96

Farmingdale | 99 Quaker Meeting House Rd. | 516-249-0700 | www.nysparks.com | 7014/6206; 72.2/75.0; 127/126

Being "second-best at Bethpage" still puts this A.W. Tillinghast design ahead of "most any other course in New York"; "not for the faint-hearted or the short hitter", "Baby Black" is a layout that makes players "work the ball the whole round", "using a driver on every par 4 and par 5" and smacking second shots with "fairway woods and long irons"; all in all, "this is one tough track in a world-class facility."

Harbor Links   22 | 20 | 19 | 19 | $113

Port Washington | 1 Fairway Dr. | 516-767-4807 | www.harborlinks.com | 6927/5465; 73.1/69.1; 127/121

Architect Michael Hurdzan fashioned a Port Washington quarry into this "well-laid-out" "links-style course" where "split fairways", "native grasses", "old sand pits" and "multiple options" add up to one "excellent public track" that'll "challenge" you "without inducing club-throwing or other tantrums"; in addition to the "elegant" spread, there's a nine-hole executive course and miniature golf on-site.

Island's End   19 | 14 | 17 | 20 | $60

Greenport | Rte. 25 | 631-477-0777 | www.islandsendgolf.com | 6655/5017; 71.2/68.9; 123/115

"While it won't be mistaken for its prestigious South Fork neighbors", this short, "flat" layout "far out on the end of the North Fork" is filled with "character", "especially on the back" along the Long Island Sound ("can't beat the views from the 16th"); while some find the facilities "tired", it's the type of "playable gem at a great price" that regulars "hope doesn't get too popular"; a post-Survey redo of all the bunkers may not be reflected in the Course score.

Long Island National 🏌   22 | 20 | 20 | 18 | $99

Riverhead | 1793 Northville Tpke. | 631-727-4653 | www.longislandnationalgc.com | 6838/5006; 73.6/70.7; 132/119

"A delight to the eye and a challenge to the game", RTJ Jr.'s "sleeper of a links-style course" in Riverhead sports "great double greens and shared fairways" along with "evil fescue" and wind that "blows at all times of the year" and can "add 10 strokes to your score"; it "gets a lot of play" and is "a little pricey for the area", but it's "usually well main-tained" and is perfect "for Hamptonites looking to get away from the scene for an afternoon."

🄯 Montauk Downs   26 | 17 | 18 | 25 | $96

Montauk | 50 S. Fairview Ave. | 631-668-1100 | www.montaukdowns.org | 6988/5541; 75.3/74.3; 141/135

For "a dreamy day on the links", head to RTJ Sr.'s "breathtaking" sea-side "gem at the tip of Long Island", an "underrated", "championship-caliber" municipal that's in the process of being reworked by the designer's son, Rees Jones; it's "challenging in many ways", but "if the wind is up, it's brutal", and while "amenities are sparse" and it can get "real crowded", it's "a tremendous value" that's "well worth" the "long hike" to "scenic, beautiful" Montauk.

	COURSE	FACIL.	SERVICE	VALUE	COST

Oyster Bay Town Golf Course
20 | **17** | **15** | **19** | **$73**

Woodbury | 1 Southwoods Rd. | 516-677-5980 | www.oysterbaytown.com |
6376/5101; 71.5/69.4; 131/119

Built on "a former estate with a nature preserve", this Tom Fazio municipal may be "short", "but don't be fooled by the yardage", as it's a "tight" "test of accuracy", with "multiple doglegs" and "narrow, tree-lined fairways" ("each hole has a personality of its own"); it's a "great value" if you live in Oyster Bay, but a few feel it's too "costly for non-residents."

Rock Hill
20 | **16** | **17** | **21** | **$39**

Manorville | 105 Clancy Rd. | 631-878-2250 | www.rockhillgolf.com |
7050/5390; 73.6/70.7; 133/120

"If you're out on the east end of Long Island", try this "standby" where the "elevation changes", "windy" conditions and "length can challenge" but "wide-open" landing strips mean "you can score" – "if you can't hit the fairways here, you won't be able to anywhere"; yes, the staff "could be friendlier", but it remains a "beautiful" and "enjoyable experience."

Smithtown Landing
19 | **15** | **17** | **20** | **$38**

Smithtown | 495 Landing Ave. | 631-979-6534 | 800-444-0565 |
www.michaelhebron.com | 6114/5263; 69.3/69.7; 125/117

A "short but tough test" in Smithtown, this "challenging" municipal boasts a layout with "no flat lies, even in the middle of the fairways", and "small greens" that "you need to hit"; it's kept "in relatively good shape", and while it's "often crowded", it's "enjoyable" "for what it is", and the facility, which includes a nine-hole par-3 course and a golf school with teaching pro Mike Hebron, helps make it a "value even for non-residents."

Swan Lake
19 | **16** | **17** | **17** | **$42**

Manorville | 388 River Rd. | 631-369-1818 | www.swanlakegolf.com |
7035/5264; 73.7/69.4; 125/114

"Have fun putting" on "massive greens" "the size of city blocks" at this "flat" Suffolk County course that's otherwise "playable", with "wide-open pastures" on which the "rough isn't too rough"; a few surveyors feel the "tired" layout and "poor facilities" "need upgrading", but it's nevertheless "very well kept" and serves as a "nice standby" "for a pleasant enough outing."

NYC Metro

Blue Hill
20 | **16** | **18** | **22** | **$57**

Pearl River | 285 Blue Hill Rd. | 845-735-2094 |
www.orangetown.com
Lakeside/Pines | 6500/5500; 70.8/69.6; 128/122
Pines/Woodland | 6400/5200; 70.8/69.6; 128/122
Woodland/Lakeside | 6400/5100; 70.8/69.6; 128/122

"NYC-close" and "one of the best values in the area", this "always crowded" 27-holer is like a "poor man's country club" that serves up the "best possible conditions" despite "a lot of use"; gripes include "some redundant holes", "no driving range" and "good luck getting on it if you don't know a town member"; post-Survey renovations to the locker rooms may not be reflected in the Facilities score.

| | COURSE | FACIL. | SERVICE | VALUE | COST |

Centennial

23 | 22 | 21 | 19 | $135

Carmel | 185 Simpson Rd. | 845-225-5700 | 877-783-5700 |
www.centennialgolf.com
Fairways/Meadows | 7050/5208; 74.2/70.2; 137/122
Lakes/Fairways | 7133/5208; 75.3/69.9; 145/126
Lakes/Meadows | 7115/5208; 74.7/70.1; 136/126

This "roller coaster in the foothills of the Catskills" near Carmel is comprised of "three very different nines that "make every round an adventure"; choose tees wisely, as the layout "can be a beast if you're forever trying to carry the ball over trouble" and you'll want a shot at the "risk/reward reachable par 4s"; it "isn't cheap", but "being able to play in less than six hours within a drive of the city" adds to the "great value."

Hudson Hills 🏌

20 | 15 | 18 | 18 | $115

Ossining | 400 Croton Dam Rd. | 914-864-3000 | www.hudsonhillsgolf.com |
6935/5102; 73.3/68.6; 129/117

"Just the right amount of hills and woods" makes this "beautiful Hudson Valley" municipal "challenging without being impossible", as long as you safely negotiate the "many blind shots", "uneven lies, cliffs and water and tall grass"; although a "good value if you're a county resident", some say it's "a little overpriced" for visitors, especially given the occasionally "slow service" and "lack of a driving range."

Mansion Ridge 🏌

23 | 19 | 18 | 17 | $129

Monroe | 1292 Orange Tpke. | 845-782-7888 | www.mansionridge.com |
6134/4788; 70.1/67.9; 131/121

The only Jack Nicklaus course in the state that's open to the public, this "subtly difficult" design "puts the emphasis on accuracy and course management" thanks to a "hilly", "narrow" layout with "lots of carries over protected areas" and some "long par 4s"; it can seem "unfair" at times, and a few feel the maintenance is "just too spotty to spend all that money", but it sports "some spectacular views" – at least in the areas where there aren't "too many houses."

Pound Ridge 🏌

21 | 12 | 16 | 12 | $235

Pound Ridge | 18 High Ridge Rd. | 914-764-5771 | www.poundridgegolf.com |
7165/5151; 76.1/70.0; 146/130

A "phenomenal" course near the Connecticut border, this 2008 Pete Dye design is "both scenic" and "extremely challenging from just about every tee box", with "many elevation changes", waste bunkers and other "tiring" obstacles; a few feel it's "tricked up" and "not ready" for prime time, but most insist it "will be stunning" in time; P.S. "facilities are still being built", which can make it "tough to swallow the $235 price tag", although new price options such as nine-hole rates should be a bit more palatable.

Spook Rock

20 | 14 | 15 | 21 | $65

Suffern | 233 Spook Rock Rd. | 845-357-6466 | www.ramapo.org |
6806/4880; 72.9/70.9; 139/120

"What you see is what you get" at this "straightforward" course in Suffern, a "solid muni within an hour of NYC" that features "tight fairways", "strategic bunkering" and "massive greens with huge breaks"; it's the "best deal in town" for Ramapo residents, and the lighted driving range and practice facility "add value" for visitors.

North Carolina

TOP COURSES IN STATE

29 Pinehurst, No. 2 | *Pinehurst*
28 Ocean Ridge, Leopard's Chase | *Myrtle Beach Area*
27 Ocean Ridge, Tiger's Eye | *Myrtle Beach Area*
   Pinehurst, No. 8 | *Pinehurst*
   Pine Needles Lodge, Pine Needles | *Pinehurst*
   Pinehurst, No. 4 | *Pinehurst*
   Linville | *Asheville*
   Tanglewood Park, Championship | *Winston-Salem*
   Tobacco Road | *Pinehurst*
26 Rivers Edge | *Myrtle Beach Area*

Asheville

Grove Park Inn

| 20 | 23 | 24 | 20 | $129 |

Asheville | 290 Macon Ave. | 800-438-5800 | www.groveparkinn.com |
6720/5001; 69.5/64.2; 125/113

Channeling another era, this "delightful", "old-school" Asheville track
was redesigned by Donald Ross in 1924 – and it takes only one round
to be "reminded why he is a legend"; "well-kept", it's "breathtaking in
fall and spring" and benefits from fine service and "excellent
facilities" – but note that there's no driving range, and some claim play
is "secondary" to the "fabulous" on-site hotel and "excellent spa."

Linville 🏌 ⚲

| 27 | 24 | 24 | 25 | $120 |

Linville | 175 Linville Ave. | 828-733-4363 | www.eseeola.com |
6620/4948; 72.2/69.1; 135/122

A "fantastic Donald Ross original not touched in eight decades", this
"charmer" 90 minutes northeast of Asheville allows players to use
"the same ball almost all day" – if they watch out for the "classic collection areas that grab anything but precise approach shots"; "you'll
see everyone from scratch golfers to little old ladies to duffer dads
with kids in tow" at this "family-friendly" club "in the mountains."

Mt. Mitchell

| – | – | – | – | $85 |

Burnsville | 11484 Hwy. 80 S. | 828-675-5454 |
www.mountmitchellgolfresort.com | 6495/4965; 70.0/68.8; 131/120

Serving up views of the mountains as it runs through the Toe River
Valley, this track has charmed surveyors into calling it "one of the
most beautiful courses anywhere"; though named after the highest
point east of the Mississippi, the course is essentially flat, which is a
boon to walkers, and at less than 6,500 yards it's no marathon, leaving
ample time for post-round libations at Hawtree's Pub.

NEW Sequoyah National at Harrah's Cherokee, Sequoyah National 🏌

| – | – | – | – | $110 |

Whittier | 79 Cahons Rd. | 828-497-3000 | www.sequoyahnational.com |
6602/4692; 71.3/64.2; 139/103

An amenity for Harrah's Cherokee Hotel & Casino located 45 minutes
west of Asheville, this narrow but spectacular Robert Trent Jones
II/Notah Begay III–designed track plunges from breezy bluffs into tree-
choked valleys in the steep foothills of the Great Smoky Mountains;

Troon Golf Management capably takes care of the bluegrass fairways and bentgrass greens, but you'll have to take care of the multiple forced carries yourself, though après-golf relief is available on the outdoor clubhouse deck with mountain views.

Chapel Hill

UNC Finley
24 | 18 | 20 | 24 | $82

Chapel Hill | Finley Golf Course Rd. | 919-962-2349 |
7349/6231; 75.0/70.1; 141/127

"One of the nation's top universities has a course befitting its reputation", this "enjoyable" "gem" "laid out with intelligence" near the Chapel Hill campus; "a fair test of golf", it's "a bear of a track from the back tees" and "does not disappoint", especially when it comes to the "wonderful staff" – it "prides itself on perfecting your golfing experience."

Charlotte

Highland Creek 🏌
▽ 18 | 17 | 17 | 15 | $52

Charlotte | 7101 Highland Creek Pkwy. | 704-875-9000 |
www.highlandcreekgolfclub.com | 7043/5080; 73.9/70.1; 138/125
Ball blasters must "watch out for the ever-present Highland Creek" at this "well-manicured" course with "fast, smooth greens" in Charlotte; "some fun holes" mix it up with "several challenging" and "ok" ones, producing a "decent track" that's best navigated on a "Carolina Trails Card" for "special rates and e-mailed discounts."

Rock Barn,
Robert Trent Jones, Jr. 🏌 ⏲
▽ 29 | 27 | 26 | 26 | $79

Conover | 3791 Clubhouse Dr. | 828-459-9279 | www.rockbarn.com |
7182/5122; 74.7/72.0; 140/128
"Down home meets highbrow" at this RTJ Jr. track in the Blue Ridge foothills that exudes a "feel of woodsy excellence" and hits "all the marks" according to surveyors; "difficult but playable" with "no two holes alike", it's "not your average course", but this "real sleeper" probably won't be "kept secret" much longer, since the Champions Tour makes an annual visit for the Greater Hickory Classic; call ahead for public tee times.

Greensboro

Bryan Park, Champions 🏌
▽ 26 | 18 | 18 | 27 | $59

Greensboro | 6275 Bryan Park Rd. | 336-375-2200 | www.bryanpark.com |
7265/5395; 75.4/71.3; 140/123
Rees Jones designed this city of Greensboro offering that insiders call a "great course for the price" that's "more fun and in better shape than some exclusive private clubs in the area"; the "outstanding layout" (site of the 2010 U.S. Amateur Public Links Championship) has water in play on 13 holes, so plan the pre-round trip to the golf shop accordingly and keep in mind that it's "crowded on weekends."

Tot Hill Farm 🏌
▽ 27 | 21 | 24 | 26 | $64

Asheboro | 3185 Tot Hill Farm Rd. | 336-857-4455 | 800-868-4455 |
www.tothillfarm.com | 6543/4556; 72.1/67.9; 144/120
"Another Mike Strantz gem", this "visually stunning" "can't-miss" course 30 minutes south of Greensboro "makes you think before you

hit your next shot" with its "narrow fairways, small greens", "uneven lies" and "two-club elevation changes"; it's "a must-play to appreciate this type of golf", so even if a few feel it's "just not fun", most consider it a "superb design" that will "challenge anyone's game" and is boosted further by its "outstanding conditions."

Myrtle Beach Area

Bald Head Island 🔊 ⊙

| 22 | 20 | 21 | 21 | $125 |

Bald Head Island | 1 Saltmeadow Trail | 910-457-7310 | 866-657-7311 | www.bhiclub.net | 6821/4810; 73.7/68.7; 143/119

"Beautiful views" grace this "difficult" course that provides a "unique challenge" as it "winds through maritime forest" and runs out to serve up "holes exposed to ocean winds" along with "tough green placements" throughout; look out for "lots of wildlife" – perhaps even "more gators than on the Discovery Channel" – and "count on taking most of your day getting there and back", though the ferry ride to Bald Head Island is a "big treat"; post-Survey renovations by architect Tim Cate may not be reflected in the Course score.

🆕 Cape Fear National at Brunswick Forest 🔊

| - | - | - | - | $110 |

Leland | 1281 Cape Fear National Dr. | 910-383-3283 | 888-342-3622 | www.capefearnational.com | 7217/4802; 74.3/67.9; 143/114

Part Lowcountry (think low-lying wetlands and fairways bracketed by oaks, pines and crepe myrtle) and part neo-modern design (rock-studded creeks and vast waste bunkers) sums up this Wilmington-area Tim Cate design; as a real estate development course, it features long treks from hole to hole, but the tranquil lakes and sturdy challenges, including a formidable opening stretch, make it worth the effort.

Carolina National 🔊

| 22 | 20 | 20 | 22 | $75 |

Bolivia | 1643 Goley Hewett Rd. SE | 910-755-5200 | 888-200-6455 | www.carolinanationalgolf.com
Egret/Heron | 7017/4738; 74.2/67.6; 140/120
Heron/Ibis | 6961/4675; 73.7/66.6; 140/114
Ibis/Egret | 6944/4737; 73.9/67.4; 140/120

"Carved out of woods and threaded through marshes" in Bolivia, this 27-hole facility designed by Fred Couples is a "great links-style", "shot-makers" course with "large, fast greens" and "always immaculate" conditions; players "love the nature, the track and the different tee locations" – five for each hole – that "add a degree of challenge each time", making this layout "worth a visit" or two.

Ocean Ridge Plantation, Leopard's Chase 🔊

| 28 | 23 | 26 | 23 | $148 |

Ocean Isle Beach | 6330 Castlebrook Way | 910-579-5577 | 800-233-1801 | www.big-cats.com | 7155/5458; 74.1/67.3; 142/114

The "newest of the big cats at Ocean Ridge" (opened in 2007) displays some of the "raw" qualities of a kitten, but swingers expect it "will become exceptional as it matures" – and when it upgrades its temporary clubhouse; "difficult for the average golfer", the course is better suited to low handicappers who can handle the "plentiful hazards", "elevation changes" and "long carries"; P.S. the "waterfall on 18 is a sight to behold."

	COURSE	FACIL.	SERVICE	VALUE	COST

Ocean Ridge Plantation, Lion's Paw 🏌

| 22 | 25 | 25 | 24 | $73 |

Ocean Isle Beach | 351 Ocean Ridge Pkwy. | 910-287-1703 | 800-233-1801 | www.big-cats.com | 7003/5872; 74.1/67.5; 132/118

"Above-average play in an area with lots of great courses" is what fans find at this "challenging track" known for "an exceptional pro shop and great customer service"; part of the litter at Ocean Ridge Plantation, it comes "highly recommended" as a daily-double second play to "Tiger's Eye, its better sister course."

Ocean Ridge Plantation, Panther's Run 🏌

| 24 | 25 | 26 | 24 | $81 |

Ocean Isle Beach | 351 Ocean Ridge Pkwy. | 910-287-1703 | 800-233-1801 | www.big-cats.com | 7089/5546; 73.5/67.5; 141/111

"Another great" track near Myrtle Beach, this big cat prowls "old woods" to offer "challenge", "fun" and "visual interest"; it's a fine "alternative to the others" at Ocean Ridge, but be sure to "bring lots of balls" in preparation for the water hazards, and after you've conquered it, retire to Tamer's Grill for an earned respite.

Ocean Ridge Plantation, Tiger's Eye 🏌

| 27 | 26 | 24 | 24 | $119 |

Ocean Isle Beach | 360 Ocean Ridge Pkwy. | 910-287-7228 | 800-233-1801 | www.big-cats.com | 7014/5136; 73.3/65.0; 141/103

"Long and challenging is the best way to describe" the top cat of Ocean Ridge, "a real gem with teeth" whose "lovely modern course design" offers "drama, natural beauty, variety and value"; "you'll feel the butterflies when faced with a 225-plus-yard shot over water (and it's a par 4)" promise players who rank it "a staple on any trip to Myrtle Beach", adding they'd "play it again and again" if they could.

Oyster Bay 🏌

| 25 | 20 | 22 | 22 | $115 |

Sunset Beach | 614 Lakeshore Dr. | 910-579-3528 | 800-552-2660 | www.legendsgolf.com | 6685/4665; 72.1/66.8; 136/118

Dan Maples' "classic parkland layout" has "lovely vistas" along with "surprisingly dramatic holes that present considerable challenge" say swingers who nonetheless lament that "maintenance and facilities are not quite up to the area's best"; but players are rewarded with "plenty of wildlife", including "gators – so watch your step", and afterwards, try "the best barbecue on the Strand."

Porters Neck Country Club ⏱

| ▽ 22 | 19 | 21 | 21 | $120 |

Wilmington | 8403 Vintage Club Circle | 910-686-1177 | 800-947-8177 | www.portersneckcountryclub.com | 7112/5145; 74.8/70.4; 138/121

Expect the wide shoulders and narrow necks of a Tom Fazio design at this "semi-private course"; the track winds through a residential Wilmington community, and the crew keeps the rolling fairways and greens "in good shape – especially given how much play it gets."

Rivers Edge

| 26 | 22 | 23 | 23 | $115 |

Shallotte | 2000 Arnold Palmer Dr. | 910-755-3434 | 877-748-3718 | www.river18.com | 6909/4692; 72.7/67.1; 140/118

"A prettier setting cannot be found in this region" than at this course on the Shallotte River's edge that provides "ample opportunity to try a bunch of different shots and not just grip-it-and-rip-it"; Arnold

Palmer's design team crafted a "dynamic layout" with "marsh views" and a "spectacular" front-side closer that alone is "worth the price of admission"; add in a "friendly staff" and prepare for a "great outing."

Sea Trail, Dan Maples 🔊   22 | 20 | 21 | 19 | $50

Sunset Beach | 210 Clubhouse Rd. | 910-287-1122 | 800-546-5748 | www.seatrail.com | 6797/5110; 71.5/68.6; 135/117

Perhaps the "best of the Sea Trail courses", this Dan Maples design boasts a scenic setting amid the pines and oaks 30 minutes north of Myrtle Beach; with five of its holes laid out along Calabash Creek, you're sure to see swamp snappers, osprey and other wildlife, and if the facilities don't wow everyone, there's "wonderful service" to compensate.

Sea Trail, Rees Jones 🔊   21 | 18 | 20 | 18 | $109

Sunset Beach | 75 Clubhouse Rd. SW | 910-287-1122 | 800-546-5748 | www.seatrail.com | 6761/4912; 72.8/68.9; 132/119

"You will enjoy your round" at this "well-maintained" Rees Jones design that some consider "the best of the lot" at Sea Trail; pot bunkers, large mounds and water on 11 holes will test your skills, but a few feel "there's simply nothing new or exciting" at what they dub an "average course", while others point to sparse facilities while noting it's "a bit overpriced."

Sea Trail, Willard Byrd 🔊   ∇ 21 | 21 | 20 | 19 | $65

Sunset Beach | 75 Clubhouse Rd. SW | 910-287-1122 | 800-546-5748 | www.seatrail.com | 6750/4697; 72.6/68.3; 132/109

A traditional woodland layout designed by Willard Byrd, this "wide-open" option at Sea Trail is oriented around several lakes, with "large", undulating greens that "let the ball land softly and bite"; although there's perhaps "nothing that memorable" here, it's still an "enjoyable" course to "hit on the drive north from Myrtle", so "should you have the chance to play it, do!"

Outer Banks

Currituck 🔊   24 | 21 | 22 | 18 | $170

Corolla | 620 Currituck Clubhouse Dr. | 252-453-9400 | 888-453-9400 | www.thecurrituckgolfclub.com | 6885/4766; 73.9/68.7; 136/117

A "long, winding course along the Sound", this Rees Jones looker "plays as beautifully as the views" and presents hitters with "target golf and lots of wind", causing the savvy to "leave the driver in the trunk" and fall back on "iron control"; among the Outer Banks options, "this one earned its reputation and everything about it says upper class" – and it's priced accordingly, so "even in a gentle breeze" prepare to "hold onto your wallet."

Nags Head 🔊   20 | 20 | 19 | 17 | $120

Nags Head | 5615 S. Seachase Dr. | 252-441-8073 | 800-851-9404 | www.nagsheadgolflinks.com | 6126/4415; 70.2/67.7; 138/117

This "links-style course" "on the bay side of the Outer Banks" elicits a range of emotions, from "more fun, more playable and almost as scenic" as world-famous Kiawah to "overpriced and underwhelming"; wind might have something to do with the extremes, adding an "intimidation" factor that can make for an enjoyable "challenge" or produce scenarios in which your threesome has "30 lost balls"; P.S. "five-plus-hour rounds" are not out of the question.

| | COURSE | FACIL. | SERVICE | VALUE | COST |

Pinehurst

Carolina Club

| 25 | 20 | 22 | 22 | $55 |

Pinehurst | 277 Ave. of the Carolina | 910-949-2811 | 888-725-6372 | www.thecarolina.com | 6928/4828; 73.7/68.8; 149/123

There's "enough variation to keep all levels happy" at this Arnold Palmer layout in Pinehurst that's "very challenging for players with handicaps above 12 and not easy for" better ball whackers, thanks in part to "huge greens" with cascading elevation changes; good management and conditioning, a "lovely setting" through marsh and wetlands, and "great Southern hospitality" outshine "not much of a clubhouse", making it definitely "worth checking out."

NEW Dormie Club 𝍲

| - | - | - | - | $195 |

Pinehurst | 6033 Beulah Hill Church Rd. | 910-215-4587 | www.dormieclub.net | 6988/5189; 74.0/70.4; 140/126

Master design duo Bill Coore and Ben Crenshaw crafted this impressive layout in 2010 that gives its historic neighbor, Pinehurst No. 2, a run for the money; wide, pine-framed fairways, multiple forced carries over wetlands and sprawling bunkers unfold over 309 roomy acres amid more than 150 feet of elevation change, but most memorable are the undulating green surrounds and the quick, gigantic putting surfaces, which require tremendous creativity and ground-game prowess.

Legacy 🏌

| 24 | 22 | 23 | 26 | $99 |

Aberdeen | 12615 Hwy. 15/501 S. | 910-944-8825 | 800-344-8825 | www.legacygolfnc.com | 7004/4946; 73.9/68.7; 133/120

The "excellent staff" stands out at this secluded Sandhills track designed by Jack Nicklaus Jr. to be a "beautiful, classic Pinehurst-style course" that makes players "feel like the only group out there" and features a mix of "tight tree-lined holes" with "challenging water" and more "open risk/reward" opportunities; while some say the layout can be "tough for the girls", the consensus is that it's "always a pleasure to play."

Little River

| ▽ 22 | 19 | 21 | 21 | $134 |

Carthage | 500 Little River Farm Blvd. | 910-949-4600 | 888-766-6538 | www.littleriver.com | 7018/4850; 74.2/67.9; 140/120

"Major improvements" are the name of the game at this little Carthage track (established by course architect Dan Maples) where "upgrades" appear to "happen daily", shaping it into an "up-and-coming secret in the Sandhills"; the "fair but not too difficult" layout has "outstanding greens" and "charm beyond comparison", which has players predicting "you'll enjoy" this "cheaper alternative" to others in the area.

Mid Pines Inn 𝍲

| 25 | 23 | 24 | 23 | $180 |

Southern Pines | 1010 Midland Rd. | 910-692-2114 | 800-323-2114 | www.pineneedles-midpines.com | 6528/5504; 71.3/65.9; 127/116

Purists profess this "Donald Ross original is as good as it gets" - from the "classic Southern amenities" to a "beast" of a back nine, it's a throwback to "what the game should be" and makes it easy to "see why" the designer's "courses are worshiped", given a "subtle and beautiful" layout where "positioning is extremely important"; post-round libations in one of the "white rocking chairs overlooking the 18th" add to the aura of "one of the most relaxing places to play."

Pinehurst Resort, No. 1 ⚑ ⏱

22 | 27 | 26 | 21 | $120

Pinehurst | 1 Carolina Vista Dr. | 910-295-6811 | 800-795-4653 | www.pinehurst.com | 6093/5214; 68.7/69.6; 118/116

"Start your adventure off in order" at this "short" but "challenging" 1898 "gem" that was "recently restored to its original Donald Ross design"; whether you choose it as a "warm-up for the tougher courses at Pinehurst" or because it's "the most playable" "for higher handicaps", remember that the "benign" look gives way to "lurking trouble" like the signature "crowned greens"; P.S. the resort has "something for families and non-golfers" too.

Pinehurst Resort, No. 2 ⚑

29 | 28 | 27 | 22 | $420

Pinehurst | 1 Carolina Vista Dr. | 910-295-6811 | 800-795-4653 | www.pinehurst.com | 7495/5240; 76.4/70.2; 141/129

"Feel the history as you walk the fairways" of North Carolina's top-rated Course, this "Donald Ross masterpiece" that's arguably the "most subtly difficult course in the country", where "it's all about the green complexes", as "balls roll off every side" of the "thrilling" "turtlebacks"; in sum, this two-time U.S. Open venue (and site of the 2014 Men's and Women's Opens) is "worth all of the hype" and the "steep price"; a Bill Coore/Ben Crenshaw renovation in 2011 may not be reflected in the Course score.

Pinehurst Resort, No. 3 ⚑

23 | 28 | 28 | 21 | $120

Pinehurst | 1 Carolina Vista Dr. | 910-295-6811 | 800-795-4653 | www.pinehurst.com | 5682/5232; 67.3/70.2; 115/116

It's perhaps "the most approachable of the Pinehurst courses" with its "short" length and "wide fairways", but this 1910 layout "will take your pants off in a minute" as you tackle "some of the longest par 3s" around plus "those classic Donald Ross greens" ("make sure you have a short game"); it's tailor-made "for a second 18 if you're doing 36 in a day."

Pinehurst Resort, No. 4 ⚑

27 | 28 | 27 | 23 | $230

Pinehurst | 1 Carolina Vista Dr. | 910-295-6811 | 800-795-4653 | www.pinehurst.com | 7117/5217; 74.2/69.6; 135/119

Originally built by Donald Ross and "nicely redone by Tom Fazio" in 2000, this "relatively unknown jewel of Pinehurst" is a "dramatic, scenic" "championship track" – it co-hosted the 2008 U.S. Amateur – with "extremely tough rough", "classic crowned greens" and "bunkers galore"; it's a "real test of golf" that's perhaps "more eye-catching than No. 2", adding up to an "incredible experience" that "will make you want to come back for more."

Pinehurst Resort, No. 5 ⚑

22 | 27 | 26 | 22 | $120

Pinehurst | 1 Carolina Vista Dr. | 910-295-6811 | 800-795-4653 | www.pinehurst.com | 6848/5248; 73.2/70.3; 135/121

A "decent little parklander" that "doesn't present the challenges" of its brethren, this "enjoyable" RTJ Sr. redesign has a "local feel", "like the kind of course you can find in any city in America"; still, it can be "challenging for the short game and irons", and it boasts "all the Pinehurst trappings": "beautiful surroundings" and "awesome facilities and service."

	COURSE	FACIL.	SERVICE	VALUE	COST

Pinehurst Resort, No. 6 ⛳

| 25 | 23 | 25 | 23 | $230 |

Pinehurst | 1 Carolina Vista Dr. | 910-295-6811 | 800-795-4653 |
www.pinehurst.com | 6990/5001; 74.4/70.0; 139/121

Looks can be deceiving on this "winning" Tom Fazio redesign, an "un-expected" "sleeper" that "gives the sense there is no bad shot" ("huge greens", "wide fairways") but requires accurate "drive and approach shots to have any chance of a great score"; although "elevated tees" produce "nice views", it's routed over hills and through a development "not on the Pinehurst property", which has players protesting about "way too many homes lining the course."

Pinehurst Resort, No. 7 ⛳

| 25 | 24 | 26 | 22 | $230 |

Pinehurst | 1 Carolina Vista Dr. | 910-295-6811 | 800-795-4653 |
www.pinehurst.com | 7216/5183; 75.5/71.7; 149/127

Although "often overlooked in the Pinehurst mix", this Rees Jones "de-light" (he tweaked his original design in 2002) offers "bold drama" in the form of "significant elevation changes", "tough doglegs", "well-protected greens" and "water and natural areas that come into play"; it's "the narrowest" of the eight layouts and therefore a "place to try after a few warm-up rounds", and while it's "off by itself with a sepa-rate clubhouse", it's "definitely worth the trip."

Pinehurst Resort, No. 8 ⛳

| 27 | 27 | 27 | 23 | $230 |

Pinehurst | 1 Carolina Vista Dr. | 910-295-6811 | 800-795-4653 |
www.pinehurst.com | 7092/5177; 74.1/69.7; 138/121

"Modern features ensure a challenge while a classic layout provides the mid-Carolina charm you would expect from the home of U.S. golf", so "if you like Fazio, you will love" this "outstanding" "must-play" con-sidered the "second best at Pinehurst"; it's set "in a nature preserve with no homes" around, so it's just "you, Mother Nature and a chal-lenging course" that's really "like a walk in the park" – "a long walk" with "demanding shots."

Pine Needles Lodge, Pine Needles ⛳

| 27 | 23 | 25 | 24 | $235 |

Southern Pines | 1005 Midland Rd. | 910-692-8611 |
800-747-7272 | www.pineneedles-midpines.com |
7015/5513; 73.5/66.8; 135/115

"A true test of golf from the Donald" – as in Ross – this piney home to multiple U.S. Women's Opens southeast of Pinehurst "gives all you can handle and does so with graciousness"; "lightning-fast greens that roll truer than any", "laid-back elegance" and "just the right" amount of "punishment" combine with "great history", "excellent value" and "some of the nation's best teaching pros" to make for a complete scorecard, leaving players "in awe" and itching "to go back."

Pinewild, Holly ⛳

| ▽ 24 | 22 | 22 | 25 | $150 |

Pinehurst | 6 Glasglow Dr. | 910-295-5145 | 800-523-1499 |
www.pinewildcc.com | 7021/4574; 73.1/67.3; 137/117

This Gary Player signature design is a "shot-makers masterpiece" as it threads through mixed-wood forests, lakes, ponds and streams, mak-ing players "think" ahead, while its "huge greens make knowing the pin placements critical"; the club's Golf Academy offers schools for all ages, and there's an additional regulation-length course and a nine-hole par-3 layout on-site.

	COURSE	FACIL.	SERVICE	VALUE	COST

Talamore 🏌

24 | 22 | 23 | 24 | $119

Southern Pines | 48 Talamore Dr. | 910-692-5884 | 800-552-6292 | www.talamore.com | 6840/4977; 73.2/68.7; 140/120

"An unpretentious experience" awaits at this "true test from Rees Jones", a "tight", "challenging course" near Pinehurst that "will eat you up", unless you "hit the ball well" and "stay out of the bunkers"; it's "very hilly", so use the "unique" club-carriers – llamas – which are available in winter on a limited basis; P.S. the "hospitable staff" helps make it a "great buddy trip choice, especially if staying in the adjacent villas."

Tobacco Road

27 | 21 | 24 | 25 | $134

Sanford | 442 Tobacco Rd. | 919-775-1940 | www.tobaccoroadgolf.com | 6532/5094; 73.2/66.1; 150/115

"So untraditional that you will either love it or hate it", this "visually intimidating course" was crafted by the late Mike Strantz – who surveyors suggest "was either a genius or crazy or both" – in an "off-the-beaten-path" location 40 minutes north of Pinehurst; "carved out of an old quarry", the layout "masterfully weaves together" "lots of blind shots" and other "demonic" twists and turns that "force creativity" and make this "wild and wonderful" ride "worth every minute and every penny."

Raleigh-Durham

Duke University Golf Club

24 | 22 | 21 | 23 | $100

Durham | 3001 Cameron Blvd. | 919-681-2288 | www.washingtondukeinn.com | 7154/5288; 73.9/72.2; 141/126

Designed by Robert Trent Jones Sr. and reworked decades later by his son Rees, this Duke institution earns praise as a "classic" "old South course" that suggests "Augusta with its rolling hills and tall pine trees"; players say this "great layout for walkers" explains why the school "has some of the best male and female teams in the country", adding "it's almost worth going back to college" for; P.S. "stay for lunch" or do an overnight at the "fabulous inn."

NEW Lonnie Poole at NC State University

- | - | - | - | $75

Raleigh | 1509 Main Campus Dr. | 919-833-3338 | www.lonniepoolegolfcourse.com | 7358/4869; 74.8/68.2; 145/121

Wake Forest alum Arnold Palmer has endowed in-state rival North Carolina State with a beautifully balanced test, complete with enormous greens, five par 3s, views of the Raleigh skyline and a heroic Pine Valley-ish closing par 4; it's named after State benefactor and garbage magnate Lonnie Poole, so don't feel too bad if you trash your scorecard on the brutal 665-yard, par-5 11th.

Winston-Salem

Tanglewood Park, Championship 🏌

27 | 22 | 21 | 24 | $48

Clemmons | 4061 Clemmons Rd. | 336-778-6300 | www.tanglewoodpark.org | 7101/5119; 75.4/69.8; 142/126

"A delight for the eyes", this county-owned "classic" just southwest of Winston-Salem is "one of the greatest courses a lot of people don't know about", an "unfussy" option where it "appears as if RTJ Sr. just laid the holes over the existing land forms"; with its 99 bunkers, "you'll think you're spending a day at the beach", which is one of the reasons this value-priced track hosted the 1974 PGA Championship won by Lee Trevino.

Tanglewood Park, Reynolds

- | - | - | - | $26

Clemmons | 4061 Clemmons Rd. | 336-778-6300 | www.tanglewoodpark.org | 6537/4709; 72.5/68.0; 136/116

Although perhaps "not as much fun as the Championship", this "challenging", "parklands-style" spread is a "fine" RTJ Sr. design that "will test you but not beat you up"; a "beautiful", "mature" track "with lots of trees", it's suitable for "players of all abilities", and most consider it one of the "best golf deals in the Carolinas."

North Dakota

Bismarck

Bully Pulpit

- | - | - | - | $79

Medora | 3731 Bible Camp Rd. | 701-623-4653 | 800-633-6721 | www.medora.com | 7166/4750; 75.4/68.3; 138/113

"A diamond in the North Dakota rough", this Michael Hurdzan design travels through the Badlands, with a "fantastic layout" featuring 200-ft. elevation changes and holes nestled amid dunes, creeks, canyons and plateaus; the moniker refers to Teddy Roosevelt's nickname for the White House (he once lived in Medora), and it's exactly the type of rough-riding course that one true believer "would build if [he] were to make a ton of money."

Hawktree

- | - | - | - | $70

Bismarck | 3400 Burnt Creek Loop | 701-355-0995 | 888-465-4295 | www.hawktree.com | 7085/4868; 75.2/69.7; 137/116

"Bring your A-game and lots of balls" to this "well-designed course" in the middle of North Dakota that doesn't need an ocean to be linksy; the long, "tough" design from Jim Engh settles in as part of the terrain, with holes surrounded by rusty native grasses as well as black coal slag traps that "are unique" – and protect against sand going airborne in the ever-present winds.

Ohio

Akron

Blue Heron, Highlands/Lakes 🏌

21 | 20 | 20 | 19 | $69

Medina | 3225 Blue Heron Trace | 330-722-0227 | www.golfblueheron.com | 6932/5031; 74.7/70.1; 144/125

Routed over forested land west of Akron, this "beautiful" 27-holer is "one of the best" and "toughest" in the area, with a "difficult target-golf" orientation that features ravines and water in play on many holes, with some requiring "a longer second shot than [was needed] on your first"; what's more, the layout is kept "in great shape", and there are also five sets of tees, GPS-equipped carts and a clubhouse with an outdoor patio overlooking the course.

	COURSE	FACIL.	SERVICE	VALUE	COST

Boulder Creek
24 | 18 | 19 | 19 | $64

Streetsboro | 9700 Page Rd. | 330-626-2828 | www.bouldercreekohio.com | 7462/5586; 74.7/72.1; 140/130

Nestled in a "beautiful setting" with "lots of trees" and water, this "tough but playable" track is "worth the [30-minute] drive from Cleveland" thanks to a set of "very interesting holes", including a par-3 17th with an island green; what's more, the course's "excellent conditioning" helps compensate for the "no-frills clubhouse and service."

Windmill Lakes
▽ 23 | 21 | 24 | 26 | $55

Ravenna | 6544 Rte. 14 | 330-297-0440 | www.golfwindmilllakes.com | 6936/5368; 73.8/70.4; 128/115

An "example of the high quality of courses in the Akron area", this "classic, brutish design complete with long par 4s and huge greens" is tough enough to be "the home of the Kent State U. golf team"; "always in good shape", it requires the occasional thread-the-needle shot and is an overall value, even if the "excellent pro shop" entices players to pull out their wallets again.

Cincinnati

Shaker Run ⌖
27 | 21 | 20 | 21 | $74

Lebanon | 1320 Golf Club Dr. | 513-727-0007 | 800-721-0007 | www.shakerrungolfclub.com
Lakeside/Meadows | 6991/5046; 73.7/68.4; 136/118
Meadows/Woodlands | 7092/5161; 74.1/69.6; 134/119
Woodlands/Lakeside | 6953/5075; 74.0/68.8; 138/121

"Bring your A-game or bring plenty of balls" when tackling the "course where Michelle Wie challenged" the guys at the 2005 U.S. Amateur Public Links Championship, because this "difficult but fair" track will "challenge all facets of your game regardless of handicap"; "the original 18 designed by Arthur Hills is the best" (Woodlands/Lakeside), but all three of the "well-maintained" nines contribute to its status as a "must-play when in southern Ohio."

Stonelick Hills
- | - | - | - | $61

Batavia | 3155 Sherilyn Ln. | 513-735-4653 | www.stonelickhills.com | 7145/5116; 73.2/69.8; 134/121

Located a half hour east of Cincinnati, this former host of an LPGA Futures Tour event was designed by architect and owner Jeff Osterfeld, who routed the course over forested hills and around lots of water, which comes into play - or at least into view - on 11 holes, making it "tough but rewarding if you're striking it well"; what's more, it's kept "in great shape", with a "beautiful setting" devoid of housing.

Vineyard, The
20 | 17 | 19 | 21 | $31

Cincinnati | 600 Nordyke Rd. | 513-474-3007 | www.greatparks.org | 6789/4747; 72.3/66.7; 131/116

This "enjoyable course" owned by the Hamilton County Park District "keeps you coming back" and is "always a good challenge" given "well-maintained" fairways lined with "lots of big old trees" (look for "beautiful foliage" in the fall) and greens that strike some as being "too tiered for the average golfer"; although play can be "slow on weekends", a "friendly staff" and "excellent rates" help to make it a "very good value."

Cleveland

Avalon Lakes

23 | 21 | 19 | 18 | $135

Warren | 1 American Way NE | 330-856-8898 | www.avalongcc.com |
7551/4904; 76.9/68.5; 143/119

An early Pete Dye design nestled midway between Cleveland and
Pittsburgh, this "classic, tree-lined Midwestern course" underwent a
revamp in 2000 and is now a "real treat" that hints at the architect's
more recent work; suitable "for players of all levels", the layout also
features "nice service and amenities", and while a few find it "fairly expensive for this part of Ohio", that seems not to have deterred the
LPGA Tour, which has held several events here.

Fowler's Mill

26 | 21 | 23 | 24 | $69

Chesterland | 13095 Rockhaven Rd. | 440-729-7569 |
www.fowlersmillgc.com
Lake/Maple | 6618/5630; 72.1/68.0; 128/113
Maple/River | 6385/5712; 70.7/66.6; 125/110
River/Lake | 7025/5815; 74.7/71.8; 136/118

A "solid Pete Dye track" that was "originally built as a private course",
this "first-rate" 27-holer in Chesterland is "one of the nicest in the
state", offering a "good experience for the daily player" and serving as
host to several U.S Open Qualifiers; although a few feel it's "expensive", "you won't be disappointed" thanks to a "beautiful" setting with
abundant "trees and hills" and a level of conditioning that's kept high
"even though [the track] gets a great deal of play."

Little Mountain ☼

∇ 26 | 21 | 21 | 24 | $77

Concord | 7667 Hermitage Rd. | 440-358-7888 | www.littlemountaincc.com |
6616/4982; 72.7/68.3; 131/115

"Surrounded by beautiful luxury homes and the hills" of northeast
Ohio, this "top public course" in Concord "will satisfy even the lowest
handicap player" with "challenging", "mountainous" terrain and
greens that are "like billiard tables"; although it's "a little expensive"
for the area, you can expect "great service from the starters", a "nice
clubhouse" and practice facilities that have been updated to include a
grass driving range.

Reserve at Thunder Hill

∇ 26 | 19 | 20 | 24 | $49

Madison | 7050 Griswold Rd. | 440-298-3474 | www.thunderhillgolf.com |
7504/4769; 78.5/68.5; 152/121

Nestled in northeastern Ohio, this "monster" of a course has water
hazards on every hole, including several long carries, so be sure to hit
it straight and "bring an extra dozen balls – you'll need them"; yes, it's
one of the most difficult courses in the area, but it can be "fun when
played from the right set of tees."

Sawmill Creek

∇ 20 | 18 | 18 | 21 | $69

Huron | 600 Mariner Village | 419-433-3789 | 800-729-6455 |
www.golfsawmillcreek.com | 6702/5074; 72.3/69.4; 128/115

One of Tom Fazio's earliest designs, this resort "layout on the shores
of Lake Erie" is short, "tight" and "compact", with the "main defense"
to scoring being "the speed and contours of its greens"; some take issue with holes that were "rerouted to make way for condos" ("the
original layout was better"), while others fret about the "small prac-

tice green" and lack of a driving range, but overall, this "nice facility" boasts "a good price for the quality."

Columbus

Cooks Creek
22 | 17 | 19 | 23 | $40

Ashville | 16405 Hwy. 23 | 740-983-3636 | 800-430-4653 | www.cookscreek.com | 7071/5095; 73.7/68.2; 131/120

Though it's in the "middle of nowhere", this "nice public facility" is "worth the drive 30 minutes south of Columbus" to play 18 "challenging holes that require all the clubs" in your bag as you tackle a "variety of lengths" and "very fast greens"; it's "in a flood area, so can easily be underwater" at times, but there are "no houses on the course", which makes it "pleasing to the eye" and helps make it a "good value."

Eaglesticks
▽ 23 | 18 | 21 | 22 | $56

Zanesville | 2655 Maysville Pike | 740-454-4900 | 800-782-4493 | www.eaglesticks.com | 6508/4233; 70.7/63.7; 123/107

With an "unassumingly good design" by Michael Hurdzan, this "short course" is "worth the ride to Zanesville" to play a layout that's "fun for all levels" but will "test your skills", requiring "lots of different shots" to deal with the "elevation changes" and "punitive rough"; it's relatively cozy, however, so "hit it straight" – and "don't forget your hard hat to protect against getting bombed from another fairway."

Granville
- | - | - | - | $42

Granville | 555 Newark Rd. | 740-587-0843 | www.granvillegolf.com | 6559/5197; 71.3/69.6; 128/123

A 1920s-era "classic" from Donald Ross, this "central Ohio favorite" tucked away in "a quaint little college town" is "worth the ride from Columbus" to tackle a "nice old layout" with a "variety of holes"; redesigned in later years to "make it more challenging" (although perhaps "not as authentic"), it features "significant elevation changes" – particularly on the signature 18th, which drops more than 100 feet from tee to fairway – to go with its "great vistas."

◪ Longaberger
29 | 28 | 28 | 24 | $99

Nashport | 1 Long Dr. | 740-763-1100 | www.longabergergolfclub.com | 7243/4985; 75.2/67.9; 140/115

"Owned by the company that sells exclusive baskets", this Nashport track is "the best public course you'll find in Ohio" – it's ranked No. 1 in the state – thanks to a "lovely Arthur Hills design" that's "fair" but "challenging" (in fact, it could "make a basket case out of you"); it's also "top-notch for women" and "the ultimate in eye candy": the "well-groomed layout" is set on "a beautiful piece of land" and boasts an "awesome clubhouse with sweeping views."

Dayton

Yankee Trace, Championship
▽ 24 | 24 | 21 | 21 | $30

Centerville | 10000 Yankee St. | 937-438-4653 | www.yankeetrace.org | 7139/5204; 74.1/70.6; 136/121

Expect "country-club conditioning" when visiting this Centerville-owned facility that's "challenging but fair", with "great fairways, greens and bunkers", as well as "some tricky shots" that may make it helpful to "play with someone who's familiar with the course"; its "nice facilities", which include an indoor practice area and a short, watery par-36 nine-hole track, also help to make it a "terrific value."

Toledo

Maumee Bay ⌂   ▽ 24 | 17 | 19 | 24 | $45

Oregon | 1750 State Park Rd. #2 | 419-836-9009 |
www.maumeebaystateparklodge.com | 6941/5221; 73.5/70.4; 131/120
Routed over 1,850 acres of wetlands inside Maumee Bay State Park, this links "beauty" designed by Arthur Hills may have "no trees" but it has a "variety of holes" with "lots of water" and bunkers that "appear out of nowhere", so "bring plenty of balls"; it's "often overlooked" and thus "uncrowded", so when you factor in the adjacent lodge and Lake Erie setting, you may discover this "wonderful" state-owned facility is a "great value for the money."

Red Hawk Run   ▽ 28 | 18 | 21 | 25 | $53

Findlay | 18441 Rte. 224 E. | 419-894-4653 | 877-484-3429 |
www.redhawkrun.com | 7129/4875; 74.0/68.6; 133/119
"Arthur Hills turned a flat piece of farmland" into a "very nice" course with "a Scottish links" feel ("sand and burns abound") at this "wonderful find in rural Ohio" where the first two holes are some of the "toughest openers" around but the rest of the course is "acceptably challenging" too as players contend with woods, lakes and a creek; yes, it may be "in the middle of nowhere" nearly an hour south of Toledo, but it's really "a treat to play."

Oklahoma

Oklahoma City

Jimmie Austin University of Oklahoma   _ | _ | _ | _ | $54

Norman | 1 Par Dr. | 405-325-6716 | www.ougolfclub.com |
7387/5216; 76.2/69.9; 132/117
Considered "one of the better university courses in the Midwest", the home of the U. of Oklahoma Sooners is a "long, challenging" Bob Cupp redesign that's kept "in good shape" and was "improved" in preparation for the 2009 U.S. Amateur Public Links Championship; a "large variety of tee lengths makes it great for all skill levels", although everyone will have to find a way to deal with "very fast greens."

Stillwater

Karsten Creek   ▽ 28 | 26 | 23 | 23 | $300

Stillwater | 1800 S. Memorial Dr. | 405-743-1658 | www.karstencreek.com |
7407/4906; 77.2/73.2; 152/134
Perhaps the "hardest course in America that will never host a major", this Stillwater "star" designed by Tom Fazio is "a magnificent layout completely set in the trees", with undulations that are "totally unexpected" given "the flat Oklahoma terrain"; the "practice facilities are amazing" too, and "if it were set on the ocean or a mountain, everyone would know about it"; P.S. it's "no wonder the Oklahoma State golf team is so good" since this is its home course.

Tulsa

Forest Ridge - | - | - | - | $70

Broken Arrow | 7501 E. Kenosha St. | 918-357-2443 | www.forestridge.com | 7083/5341; 74.8/73.3; 137/132

"One of the nicest semi-private courses you can play", this "challenging" layout just east of Downtown Tulsa is "long" and "narrow", with some "very difficult holes" to make it a "true test of golfers' ability"; the "houses they are putting in around the course" "take away from the beauty of the land", while the "above-average conditions", "excellent facilities" (including a "great clubhouse") and "competent staff" add to the overall experience.

Oregon

TOP COURSES IN STATE

Bend

Black Butte Ranch, Big Meadow 24 | 24 | 24 | 23 | $75

Black Butte | 13020 Hawks Beard | 541-595-1500 | 800-399-2322 | www.blackbutteranch.com | 7002/5485; 71.6/70.1; 125/126

An "outstanding" outing can be had at this "walkable" Robert Muir Graves design that's "quietly tucked" into a "wonderful" central Oregon setting; updated tee boxes and bunkers highlight the "long, challenging hole layouts" that suit "all handicaps", and you can turn to the "good pro staff" for pointers on how to avoid the stands of pine and aspen through which the course is traced; P.S. it's closed in winter.

Black Butte Ranch, Glaze Meadow ▽ 26 | 25 | 26 | 22 | $75

Black Butte | 13020 Hawks Beard | 541-595-1500 | 800-399-2322 | www.blackbutteranch.com | 6574/5545; 71.3/71.7; 124/130

Shorter, tighter and with more undulation than its older sibling, this "quirky" "mountain course" with views of Mt. Washington is best suited to mid-handicappers and lower; its unique design offers holes individually framed with towering pines, a setup that mimics the feel of a private golf experience, and it's particularly "beautiful in fall", with "bargain" pricing to boot; it's currently under renovation, with the front nine scheduled to reopen on Memorial Day, and the entire course by late June 2012.

Pronghorn Club, Nicklaus - | - | - | - | $197

Bend | 65600 Pronghorn Club Dr. | 541-693-5365 | 866-372-1003 | www.pronghornclub.com | 7379/5256; 75.2/70.8; 151/131

After several years as a private club, this 2004 Jack Nicklaus Signature Design finally opened up to outside play in 2010, thus wowing a wider audience with its ancient lava rock ridges, firm, fast-playing conditions and panoramic vistas of snow-capped mountain peaks; the dry desert climate and 3,200-ft. elevation usually make for perfect summer conditions, but it's seldom a smooth journey negotiating the par-4 13th, which horseshoes around a lake, or the back-to-back back-breaking par 5s on 15 and 16.

Sunriver, Crosswater 👤 ⛳

| 28 | 26 | 24 | 18 | $175 |

Sunriver | 17600 Canoe Camp Dr. | 541-593-1000 | 800-547-3922 | www.sunriver-resort.com | 7683/5359; 76.5/71.1; 153/133
Considered by some to be the "best course in the Bend area", this "magnificent" "links-style" design from Bob Cupp and John Fought (host of the JELD-WEN Tradition Championships from 2007–2010) is "extremely challenging" even for the "most competent players" thanks to "tough" rough and "water everywhere" over 600 acres of woodlands; "stunning scenery" and "impeccable facilities" round out the "surprisingly wonderful" experience, which is open seasonally to resort guests only.

Sunriver, Meadows 👤

| 19 | 23 | 24 | 19 | $140 |

Sunriver | 1 Center Dr. | 541-593-1000 | 800-547-3922 | www.sunriver-resort.com | 7012/5287; 72.9/70.4; 131/131
"If your game isn't up to snuff, play here, not Crosswater" advise veterans who've tackled this "narrow and fun" John Fought design, a creation that pays tribute to American courses from the '20s and '30s; it's "well laid out with a moderate amount of challenge" and lots of variety, and while a few holes are "still pretty difficult", you can soothe yourself with the compelling views of snow-tipped volcanoes.

Sunriver, Woodlands 👤

▽ | 22 | 23 | 24 | 19 | $140 |

Sunriver | 1 Center Dr. | 541-593-1000 | 800-547-3922 | www.sunriver-resort.com | 6933/5341; 73.4/70.4; 142/135
You'll "love hitting the ball at 4,000-plus feet" at this RTJ Jr. design set on the high east side of the Cascades, with enough water and lava rock outcroppings to ensure it's "not easy" even as it remains "fair" and "not too challenging for average players"; part of a "lovely" seasonal retreat "for golfers and [their] families", it's "heavily played" but nevertheless a "beautiful, well-groomed" "favorite."

Tetherow 👤 ⏱

| - | - | - | - | $175 |

Bend | 61240 Skyline Ranch Rd. | 541-388-2582 | www.tetherow.com | 7298/5342; 74.8/70.1; 144/129
A slice of Scotland in the mountains of central Oregon, this high desert layout from David McLay Kidd traverses two distinct ridgelines in view of nine different peaks, with firm, fast fairways and shaved-down green complexes requiring a reliance on the ground game even at Bend's 3,900-ft. elevation; manzanitas and sagebrush add to the British heathland feel, but the snow-capped mountains will keep you grounded in the heart of the Pacific Northwest.

Blue River

Tokatee

| - | - | - | - | $45 |

Blue River | 54947 McKenzie Hwy. | 541-822-3220 | 800-452-6376 | www.tokatee.com | 6806/5018; 72.8/68.3; 125/114
Separated from the scenic McKenzie Highway by rows of tall fir trees, this "true gem" is a convenient stop for tourists motoring to central Oregon; designed by Ted Robinson over four decades ago, it weds

meadows and woodlands on a walkable layout that boasts gorgeous views of the west Cascades foothills and Three Sisters volcanos.

Central Coast

Salishan
24 | 20 | 20 | 22 | $69

Gleneden Beach | 7760 Hwy. 101 N. | 541-764-2371 | 800-890-0387 | www.salishan.com | 6470/5237; 72.2/71.3; 134/128

Located in "remote" coastal Oregon, this redesigned layout is "like two different courses" in one: a wooded front precedes a "back nine that plays like a links course, especially the holes along the ocean", which feature "beautiful Pacific vistas" along with "brutal" wind; it's "pricey", but it's affiliated with a "first-class hotel, restaurant and spa"; P.S. for "a unique experience, play it in the AM before the fog burns off."

Sandpines
▽ 24 | 20 | 23 | 25 | $69

Florence | 1201 35th St. | 541-997-1940 | www.sandpines.com | 7190/5323; 75.2/72.2; 131/127

A "beautiful" Rees Jones design on the central Oregon coast, this "links-and-target combo" keeps players honest "with many uneven lies and challenges", not the least of which is wind "that picks way up in the afternoon" ("don't play from the tips"); it's a "great way to start a trip", and its routing through trees and grassed dunes makes it a particularly "good warm-up for Bandon."

Coos Bay

Bandon Crossings
26 | 17 | 23 | 26 | $75

Bandon | 87530 Dew Valley Ln. | 541-347-3232 | www.bandoncrossings.com | 6855/5030; 74.3/70.5; 136/126

A "cheaper alternative to the Bandon Dunes courses", this "hilly" track is routed "near, but not on, the coast", with play dictated by "wetlands and forest" and "long gaps between holes" that make a "cart useful"; the staff is "friendly", and while some gripe that the "facilities are meager", others insist "you don't need any" at this "beautiful must-play."

⊠ Bandon Dunes, Bandon Dunes Course 於
29 | 27 | 27 | 26 | $275

Bandon | 57744 Round Lake Dr. | 541-347-4380 | 888-345-6008 | www.bandondunesgolf.com | 6732/5072; 74.1/72.4; 143/128

"Awe-inspiring natural beauty and commitment to the concept of pure enjoyment" are hallmarks of this "extraordinarily challenging yet playable" David McLay Kidd design hard by the Pacific Ocean, where walking (no carts) the "magnificent" track is a "must for every golfer"; "incomparable" service "without the pretentious air of most resorts" and "world-class" facilities add to the "incredible experience"; P.S. "be prepared for the wind – very prepared."

⊠ Bandon Dunes, Bandon Trails 於
26 | 27 | 27 | 25 | $275

Bandon | 57744 Round Lake Dr. | 541-347-4380 | 888-345-6008 | www.bandondunesgolf.com | 6765/5064; 73.7/70.8; 133/122

"Play starts in the dunes and moves into the trees" at this "underrated" Ben Crenshaw/Bill Coore design that offers a "fascinating counterpoint to the other" Bandon Dunes courses; "fast, undulating" greens are set within a forest of "slopes and gathering areas" that are "as tough as they come", and any downside from being inland is offset by its "outstanding architecture and rustic layout", not to mention the "gorgeous" (and mandatory) "walk through the woods."

⚡ Bandon Dunes, Pacific Dunes 术 | 29 | 27 | 27 | 26 | $275

Bandon | 57744 Round Lake Dr. | 541-347-4380 | 888-345-6008 | www.bandondunesgolf.com | 6633/5088; 73.0/69.8; 142/128

Voted Oregon's top-rated Course, "genius" Tom Doak's "jewel" set "along high cliffs jutting into the sea" offers "golf the way it was meant to be": a "lovingly maintained" track with "best-ever views" and "eat-you-alive gorse", where "wind is the wild card", changing par 3s "from pitching wedge to a 3-iron" depending on the day; add "beautiful facilities" and "superior" service, including "fabulous caddies, and you have the makings of an "otherworldly experience."

NEW Bandon Dunes Golf Resort, | - | - | - | - | $275
Old Macdonald 术

Bandon | 57744 Round Lake Dr. | 888-345-6008 | www.bandondunesgolf.com | 6978/5044; 74.1/70.4; 133/118

The fourth course at Bandon Dunes pays homage to pioneering American architect C.B. Macdonald, with a 2010 design by Tom Doak and Jim Urbina offering near-replicas of classic Macdonald template holes such as 'Biarritz,' 'Alps,' and 'Redan'; highlights include firm, lumpy, but roomy fairways, enormous, wildly undulating greens, towering dune ridges and glimpses of the Pacific, while the pro shop in a converted stable is a play on the name.

Eugene

Diamond Woods | - | - | - | - | $33

Monroe | 96040 Territorial Hwy. | 541-998-9707 | 800-559-4653 | www.diamondwoods.com | 7036/4968; 74.5/71.1; 143/128

Co-owned by former baseball player Jeff Doyle, this aptly named track was laid out by his brother, amateur golf designer Greg Doyle, in an off-the-beaten-path location northwest of Eugene; players will need to contend with an open, watery front that's routed through a meadow as well as a rolling return featuring tricky, tree-lined holes.

Emerald Valley | - | - | - | - | $50

Creswell | 83301 Dale Kuni Rd. | 541-895-2174 | www.emeraldvalleygolf.com | 7165/5186; 74.6/70.1; 133/131

Currently in the midst of a multiyear renovation project to improve irrigation, renew hazards and replace tees, this layout may look less familiar to regulars returning for a bout with its tall trees, fast greens and snaking fairways; located on the Coast Fork of the Willamette River near Eugene, it lures U. of Oregon players, who can often be found spraying sand at the far end of the club's renovated practice facility.

Klamath Falls

Running Y Ranch | - | - | - | - | $79

Klamath Falls | 5790 Coopers Hawk Rd. | 541-850-5580 | 888-850-0261 | www.runningy.com | 7138/4847; 73.4/66.8; 132/120

The "one to play when in the Crater Lake area", this "beautiful course" makes everyone feel like Bubba Watson, with enough altitude to en-

OREGON

COURSE
FACIL.
SERVICE
VALUE
COST

sure that "your ball will go far"; designed by Ed Seay, it also offers an "interesting", "relaxing environment" that'll entice you to "stop and admire the beauty of the woods" (even if it "distracts you from your play"), but while walking is permitted, it's not recommended by the club.

Portland

Heron Lakes, Great Blue

| 23 | 14 | 16 | 23 | $30 |

Portland | 3500 N. Victory Blvd. | 503-289-1818 | www.heronlakesgolf.com | 6902/5258; 74.0/71.3; 139/131

"If you're in Portland, make time to play" this "solid" RTJ Jr. municipal that's "well maintained", with "thick rough and many water hazards" to make it "very challenging"; it's "lacking in clubhouse facilities", but the tradeoff is a "beautiful setting" that's "close to the Downtown area", with "views of Mt. Hood and Mt. St. Helens" adding to its "great value."

Langdon Farms

∇ | 22 | 22 | 22 | 23 | $79 |

Aurora | 24377 NE Airport Rd. | 503-678-4653 | www.langdonfarms.com | 6931/5246; 74.1/70.7; 135/128

Forest fringe and a farmland heart are the setting for this "well-maintained" "links course" "right off the freeway" about 30 minutes south of Portland; although a few find it "a bit spendy for the area", it remains "a favorite", with "fast greens" and "undulating fairways" adding "interesting" challenges to an "otherwise flat" layout; the Big Red Barn clubhouse is patterned after the original circa-1916 barn, which is now in play on the 8th hole.

Pumpkin Ridge, Ghost Creek

| 27 | 24 | 24 | 22 | $150 |

North Plains | 12930 NW Old Pumpkin Ridge Rd. | 503-647-9977 | 888-594-4653 | www.pumpkinridge.com | 6839/5111; 74.0/70.7; 145/128

Nestled just west of Portland, this "tough but beautiful" Bob Cupp design promises "good memories" thanks to a "lush", "challenging" layout routed over gently rolling terrain, with a creek that reappears throughout; it's a true championship track that's hosted two Nationwide Tour Championships, so you're advised to "play it – so you can say you did"; P.S. walkers are rewarded with a "good workout" and should keep an eye out for plentiful wildlife.

Reserve Vineyards, North

∇ | 25 | 28 | 25 | 24 | $85 |

Aloha | 4805 229th Ave. SW | 503-649-8191 | www.reservegolf.com | 6845/5146; 73.8/71.2; 130/127

An "underrated course" from Bob Cupp, this "fun" linksy layout in Aloha once hosted the Champions Tour JELD-WEN Tradition event; the "9th and 18th holes are both memorable", and while some suggest the design can be "a little Mickey Mouse" at times (as if they had "enough land for 16 holes and put 18 on it"), it's noteworthy for its "excellent staff" and "strong facilities", from the "great clubhouse" to the equally impressive food.

Reserve Vineyards, South

∇ | 23 | 26 | 24 | 23 | $85 |

Aloha | 4805 229th Ave. SW | 503-649-8191 | www.reservegolf.com | 7172/5189; 74.7/70.4; 142/128

Part of a 36-hole facility in the Willamette Valley, this John Fought design is a "tough course" featuring "consistently challenging holes"; set within tall stands of forest, with lots of rough, sand traps and water, it's an en-

PENNSYLVANIA

COURSE
FACIL.
SERVICE
VALUE
COST

joyable option that also offers "great" facilities and service; the two tracks alternate between public and private play every half-month.

Pennsylvania

TOP COURSES IN STATE

<u>27</u> Golf Course at Glen Mills | *Philadelphia*
Olde Stonewall | *Pittsburgh*
Nemacolin Woodlands, Mystic Rock | *Pittsburgh*
Penn National, Founders | *Gettysburg*
<u>25</u> Wyncote | *Lancaster*

Allentown

Club at Morgan Hill
| 19 | 21 | 22 | 19 | $69 |

Easton | 100 Clubhouse Dr. | 610-923-8480 | www.theclubatmorganhill.com | 6749/5166; 72.8/70.9; 135/125
"Players either love or hate" this "interesting experience" on the PA-NJ border, a "short" mountainside track made "challenging" with "great elevation changes", "many blind shots" and "few flat lies anywhere"; critics claim it's "too tricked-up", with five-hour rounds a "painful" reality, but most agree "it's worth playing at least once" given the "nice clubhouse" and "dramatic views of the Lehigh Valley."

Olde Homestead
| 23 | 18 | 21 | 24 | $60 |

New Tripoli | 6598 Rte. 309 | 610-298-4653 |
www.oldehomesteadgolfclub.com | 6800/4953; 73.2/68.2; 137/116
Former farmland in the Lehigh Valley provides an "open setting" for this "challenging track" that's "worth the trip" thanks to "serious elevation changes" and "fantastic views" of the mountains "on virtually every hole"; "well-maintained" course conditions, "helpful personnel" and an "awesome" in-cart GPS system add to its "unbeatable value"; P.S. the "excellent" facilities include a nine-hole par-3 course with distances ranging from 80 to 208 yards.

Whitetail
| 17 | 16 | 17 | 18 | $60 |

Bath | 2679 Klein Rd. | 610-837-9626 | www.whitetailgolfclub.com | 6432/5152; 70.6/68.5; 128/117
"A diamond in the rough", this "short but well-laid-out" Lehigh Valley track is a "fun" choice for locals given that it's "convenient" to Allentown and "never seems crowded"; it's "well maintained" and "affordable" (a "value for the price"), and while there are some "long, narrow holes on the back", the "nice starters" are willing to "explain potential problems."

Bedford

Omni Bedford Springs Resort & Spa, The Old Course
| ∇ 25 | 25 | 24 | 20 | $149 |

Bedford | 2138 Business Rte. 220 | 814-623-8100 |
www.bedfordspringsresort.com | 6785/5106; 73.4/69.8; 140/122
This "restoration of a classic layout with holes by Spencer Oldham, Donald Ross and A.W. Tillinghast" can serve as notice to "current architects designing tricked-up" tracks as to "what a real golf course should be"; though it's "a little pricey", it's "great to step back in time

and play" an "excellent course in fine condition", and the affiliated resort is just as "fabulous", with "first-class facilities and service" and a scenic Cumberland Valley location.

Gettysburg

Bridges, The
22 | 18 | 20 | 22 | $59

Abbottstown | 6729 York Rd. | 717-624-9551 | www.bridgesgc.com | 6713/5134; 72.4/70.4; 136/118

"Nicely laid out" near Gettysburg, this "pleasant" course offers "interesting" "variation in hole design", with "fast, undulating greens" that require golfers to "hit to the correct portion" yet remain "playable" and "fair"; there are also "nice" hotel rooms and facilities on-site, and since it's set in Pennsylvania Dutch country, you can expect a "warm reception" and plenty of "area attractions for the family", making it an "all-around good value."

Liberty Mountain Resort, Carroll Valley
– | – | – | – | $57
(fka Carroll Valley Resort, Carroll Valley Course)

Fairfield | 78 Country Club Trail | 717-642-8211 | 800-548-8504 | www.libertymountainresort.com | 6688/5022; 72.3/68.8; 128/116

"Surrounded by mountains that are ski slopes in the winter", this woodland layout just southwest of Gettysburg has water in play on 10 of its holes and "requires some thinking", as the "wrong choices can leave you with difficult shots to the greens"; the course is "much improved", and there are "nice rooms" and "great packages" to entice you to "stay-and-play", leading most to conclude it's "worth a shot."

Links at Gettysburg
23 | 21 | 19 | 21 | $78

Gettysburg | 601 Mason-Dixon Rd. | 717-359-8000 | 888-793-9498 | www.thelinksatgettysburg.com | 7069/4977; 74.1/68.8; 144/120

A "beautiful layout" located just south of the namesake Civil War battlefield, this "enjoyable" option offers "decent scenery" in the form of the surrounding Blue Ridge Mountains and red rock cliffs; it's a "great value" that "you can't play just once", which may be helpful since some swingers say you'll "need to know the course in order to score", especially when tackling the "six very tough finishing holes" featuring "fast greens" and "some well-placed ponds."

Penn National, Founders
27 | 23 | 26 | 26 | $79

Fayetteville | 3720 Club House Dr. | 717-352-3000 | 800-221-7366 | www.penngolf.com | 6972/5360; 73.9/71.4; 139/123

With "tree-lined fairways, good bunkering and fast greens", this "traditional" track designed by Ed Ault in 1968 seems to "get better each year", offering a strong "contrast" to its Iron Forge sibling; it's one of the "best values" in the area, so "make a day of it and play both courses" for a "nice 36-hole experience" that includes a "highly professional staff" and "first-class" accommodations.

Penn National, Iron Forge
∇ 25 | 22 | 24 | 25 | $79

Fayetteville | 3720 Club House Dr. | 717-352-3000 | 800-221-7366 | www.penngolf.com | 7009/5246; 73.8/70.3; 133/120

The younger of the two courses on-site, this "decent links track" has "more trouble than meets the eye" on a "challenging layout" that may be nearly treeless but sports "fast, undulating greens" and large bunker complexes; a few focus on "a couple of uninteresting holes", but those who "like it better than Founders" praise its "very good conditions" and scenic views.

Harrisburg

Hershey, East 🔂 ⛳

22 | 22 | 21 | 18 | $130

Hershey | 1000 E. Derry Rd. | 717-533-2464 | 800-437-7439 | www.hersheygolfcollection.com | 7061/5645; 74.5/73.6; 136/128

"Get away from the Hershey amusements" and tackle this "classic" George Fazio design, on which "every hole feels like you're hitting uphill" and "the greens are tougher than they look", which may explain why this rolling layout has been host to several Nationwide Tour events; if you want to "play golf with the scent of chocolate in the air", don't delay, for the iconic factory on East Chocolate Avenue is slated to cease operations some time in 2012.

Hershey, West 🔂 ⛳

24 | 24 | 24 | 22 | $150

Hershey | 1000 E. Derry Rd. | 717-533-2464 | 800-437-7439 | www.hersheygolfcollection.com | 6860/5598; 72.6/72.6; 130/129

Once the site of the 1940 PGA Championship (as well as regular LPGA events), this "old-style course" remains "a must-play if you're in the area" thanks to a "super" design featuring "terrain changes" and "beautifully rolling greens"; it's a "great way to work off the extra calories Milton Hershey has made us consume."

Hershey Links 🔂

∇ 25 | 18 | 21 | 24 | $125

Hummelstown | 101 Hanshue Rd. | 717-533-0890 | www.hersheygolfcollection.com | 7009/4764; 73.6/69.1; 137/122

Hershey's newest course ambles along natural bluffs and ravines in a "wide-open" links format featuring a Redan-style par-3 11th, "tall grasses edging the fairways", cross bunkers and a judicious application of water; the track itself is kept in "great condition", and the 12,500-sq.-ft. clubhouse, which was completed post-Survey, boasts a full-service restaurant, a pro shop and views of the 18th hole.

Lancaster

Reading Country Club

∇ 21 | 21 | 18 | 23 | $55

Reading | 5311 Perkiomen Ave. | 610-779-1000 | www.readingcountryclub.com | 6162/5131; 69.4/70.2; 128/121

"Now the gem of Berks County golf", this Exeter Townshop municipal has a "historic background": it was designed by Alex Findlay in the 1920s as a private "country-club" course and was "once home to Byron Nelson" (he was the venue's first golf pro); "a must-visit only an hour from Philadelphia", it's an "old classic" that may be "a bit short" but nevertheless delivers a "pleasant", "enjoyable round."

Wyncote

25 | 21 | 22 | 22 | $71

Oxford | 50 Wyncote Dr. | 610-932-8900 | www.wyncote.com | 7148/5454; 74.3/71.6; 140/126

"An amazing links course" that seems "transplanted from Great Britain", this "remarkable value" in Oxford, PA, may have "no trees" but it features "challenging fairways and greens" with "tall fescue", "lateral

| | COURSE | FACIL. | SERVICE | VALUE | COST |

hazards in environmental areas" and "the wind blowing hard over the fields"; in short, it "can be scorable or a killer", and there's a "fabulous clubhouse" and pub to make it "well worth the rather long drive."

Philadelphia

Downingtown

| 18 | 19 | 17 | 17 | $63 |

Downingtown | 85 Country Club Dr. | 610-269-2000 | www.golfdowningtown.com | 6642/5771; 72.0/67.7; 129/122

A "traditional, tree-lined layout" located 45 minutes east of Philly, this "really short" "George Fazio classic" has an "old-style" aesthetic to go with "challenging holes" "where shot-making is more important than power"; it's "easy to walk" with a "quick pace of play", but some suggest the "greens fees are too high given other local values" and the "lack of a good warm-up facility."

Golf Course at Glen Mills

| 27 | 20 | 23 | 24 | $95 |

Glen Mills | 221 Glen Mills Rd. | 610-558-2142 | www.glenmillsgolf.com | 6636/4703; 72.3/67.3; 138/116

Set "on a perfect piece of land" outside of Philadelphia, this "beautiful, pristine golf oasis" is Pennsylvania's top-rated Course, a "links-meets-mountaintop" "masterpiece" from Bobby Weed that "feels like it's been there since the turn of the last century"; "maintained at a much higher level than others in the area", it "has everything, from deep bunkers to water" to "lovely views", and if it seems "a little pricey", it's "for a great cause": it's affiliated with a school that trains troubled youth in golf course management and maintenance.

Hickory Valley, Presidential

| ▽ 22 | 14 | 16 | 23 | $68 |

Gilbertsville | 1921 Ludwig Rd. | 610-754-9862 | www.hickoryvalley.com | 6721/5269; 72.6/70.9; 136/125

With plenty of "variation in its holes", this Gilbertsville layout is a "challenge for all players" but it can be particularly "difficult for high-handicappers" given that there are "a lot of carry shots and opportunities to lose balls" on a newer, "well-laid-out" front nine and a tighter, tree-lined back; although a few note that the "pace of play is not maintained" and the "people could be nicer", the track itself is "in great shape" and is a "nice course for the value."

Lederach

| 20 | 19 | 19 | 20 | $75 |

Harleysville | 900 Clubhouse Dr. | 215-513-3034 | www.lederachgolfclub.com | 7023/5034; 73.9/64.3; 137/110

It may be "one of the goofiest courses" around, but this "refreshingly well-designed links-style" affair is also "well worth" the 30-minute drive north from Philly, even if "you'll be scratching your head in disbelief" at the "devilish greens complexes" – "severely sloped and undulating" – and "grassy, penal mounds"; a few find it "too tricked-up" and others point to "spotty rough", but "nice facilities" and a "pleasant staff" help to compensate.

Raven's Claw

| 20 | 18 | 19 | 21 | $71 |

Pottstown | 120 Masters Dr. | 610-495-4710 | www.ravensclawgolfclub.com | 6739/4824; 71.0/67.1; 130/112

"Some unique hazards" and "risk/reward" opportunities mean you should "not take any of the holes for granted" at this "beautifully maintained" course routed over rolling hills and through woods "about 45 minutes outside of Philadelphia"; it's "a nice addition" to the area, but some suggest it's just "not memorable" and take issue with a layout "crammed" around "more houses than Fannie Mae."

Turtle Creek

23 | 13 | 17 | 21 | $50

Limerick | 303 W. Ridge Pike | 610-489-5133 | www.turtlecreekgolf.com | 6702/5131; 72.1/68.6; 127/115

"A delight for walkers", this "wide-open", "almost treeless" course is located in a "farmlike setting" in Limerick and has become a "local favorite" thanks to a "challenging", "well-kept" layout that's defended by "thick rough" yet still allows you to "bring the driver and bomb away"; yes, "the facilities are lacking, but that's not what you come here for"; the adjacent Waltz Golf Farm offers a par-3 course, miniature golf and batting cages.

Pittsburgh

Chestnut Ridge Resort, Chestnut Ridge Course

- | - | - | - | $49

Blairsville | 132 Pine Ridge Rd. | 724-459-7180 | www.chestnutridgeresort.com | 6242/5080; 70.2/69.7; 127/119

Part of a 36-hole facility just 45 minutes east of Pittsburgh, this short track serves up "lots of variety" on a layout that's loaded with "challenging shots" and picturesque views of the Laurel Mountains; since it's "always in great shape" and the rates are "very fair", the majority insists it's "worth spending the day" at this "favorite local resort."

Chestnut Ridge Resort, Tom's Run ⌕

∇ 23 | 21 | 21 | 18 | $59

Blairsville | 132 Pine Ridge Rd. | 724-459-7180 | www.chestnutridgeresort.com | 6812/5363; 73.0/71.0; 135/126

The newer of the two tracks at the Chestnut Ridge Resort, this "awesome" layout offers "variety and challenge" via greens that are "difficult to putt", waste areas that "have to be negotiated" and a Jekyll-and-Hyde quality wherein "each nine is different"; it's been host to a number of regional tourneys, so if you happen to be in the Pittsburgh area, "you should take the time to play this course."

Hidden Valley ⌕

17 | 14 | 17 | 16 | $60

Hidden Valley | 1 Craighead Dr. | 814-443-8000 | 800-458-0175 | www.hiddenvalleyresort.com | 6549/4929; 72.6/69.0; 133/123

"Beautiful scenery" and "great mountain golf" combine at this ski-by-winter, golf-by-summer resort in western Pennsylvania, where architect Russell Roberts has designed a short but "challenging course" that's "worth playing"; although a few feel the "tired" track "needs work", it's nonetheless a relatively "good value" offering "excellent ambiance."

⯐ Nemacolin Woodlands, Links

18 | 24 | 22 | 16 | $65

Farmington | 1001 Lafayette Dr. | 724-329-8555 | 800-422-2736 | www.nemacolin.com | 6658/4716; 72.6/67.7; 134/118

"Showcasing the beauty of the countryside", this "links-style course with mountain views" and "many interesting holes" makes for a "good warm-up" and an "excellent contrast" to its "much tougher and better sister"; although the layout is "nothing to write home about", it's "one of the prettiest courses in western Pennsylvania" and boasts the "same great amenities" as its sibling – "nice conditioning", "upscale" facilities – at a "much lower cost."

☑ Nemacolin Woodlands, Mystic Rock 🏌

27 | 27 | 25 | 19 | $149

Farmington | 1001 Lafayette Dr. | 724-329-8555 | 800-422-2736 | www.nemacolin.com | 7550/4848; 77.0/68.8; 149/125

"From the French-château beauty of the lodgings to the quality of the golf", this "delightful" "retreat" is a slice of "paradise in Pennsylvania"; the former site of the PGA Tour's 84 Lumber Classic, this "typical Pete Dye design" is "challenging but fun", with "top-conditioning" as well as the type of "friendly" service and "wonderful facilities" you might expect from a "superb resort with every amenity"; P.S. it's "pricey", so take out "a small mortgage before you go."

Olde Stonewall

27 | 26 | 26 | 22 | $150

Ellwood City | 1495 Mercer Rd. | 724-752-4653 | www.oldestonewall.com | 7103/5241; 74.2/69.6; 147/124

One of the "best golf experiences in the area", this "fantastic" layout "tests all skill levels" with "some very challenging holes" featuring "elevation changes, occasional narrow landing areas" and some of "the fastest greens [you'll] ever putt"; you'll need to "drive an hour north of Pittsburgh", but it will be "like having a private course all to yourself in the rolling hills of western Pennsylvania" – the "color changes on the trees" alone make it "worth the price."

Quicksilver

22 | 16 | 18 | 20 | $70

Midway | 2000 Quicksilver Rd. | 724-796-1594 | www.quicksilvergolf.com | 7083/5059; 75.7/68.6; 145/115

Playing this former Senior PGA and Nationwide Tour host "from the tips can be brutal" thanks to a design with "lots of bunkers" and "fast", "sloped greens", but it's nevertheless a "difficult but fair" test with "large fairways that make driving the ball fun"; a few feel it's "past its prime", but others deem it "a must-play in the Pittsburgh area."

Seven Springs Mountain 🏌

∇ 23 | 20 | 22 | 22 | $33

Champion | 777 Waterwheel Dr. | 814-352-7777 | 800-452-2223 | www.7springs.com | 6560/4946; 72.5/69.7; 130/115

Located at an all-season family resort in western Pennsylvania, this "enjoyable" course offers "very good mountain golf" thanks to a "really nice" layout featuring "wide fairways" and "a great deal of variety"; what's more, it's "not crowded" so play moves at a "relaxed pace", allowing you to pause at the "elevated tees" and enjoy "scenic" three-state views.

Poconos

Hideaway Hills 🏌

23 | 16 | 19 | 22 | $59

Kresgeville | 5590 Carney Rd. | 610-681-6000 | www.hideawaygolf.com | 6933/5047; 72.7/68.4; 127/116

For a "scenic round of golf", head to this "underrated" track that's cast out across 300 acres of rolling foothills in the Poconos; it's "challenging and long", with "elevated tees and greens" as well as a few "difficult uphill holes", but what really makes it a "value for the price" are the "spectacular views", especially in the fall, when the changing leaves create "a visual treat."

Shawnee Inn 🏌

| 19 | 18 | 19 | 17 | $90 |

Shawnee-On-Delaware | 1 River Rd. | 570-424-4000 | 800-742-9633 | www.shawneeinn.com
Blue/Red | 6800/5650; 72.8/72.5; 129/123
Blue/White | 6665/5398; 72.4/71.1; 131/121
Red/White | 6589/5424; 72.2/71.4; 132/121

A "storied venue" that has hosted both a PGA and NCAA Championship, this "blast from the past" is "A.W. Tillinghast's first U.S. design", an "old-school" "classic" in which 24 of the 27 holes play on an island in the Delaware River; although a few point to "inconsistent" conditions when they suggest it's "priced too high", most find it to be a "decent golfing experience", with some "great par 3s hitting over the river" and four-season resort amenities.

State College

Toftrees

| 21 | 21 | 18 | 18 | $74 |

State College | 1 Country Club Ln. | 814-234-8000 | 800-252-3551 | www.toftreesgolf.com | 7107/5320; 74.8/72.2; 140/125

Located "out in the middle of Nowhere, PA", this resort track offers "tight", tree-lined "mountain golf" that strikes some as "a bit too targety" but nevertheless boasts a "nice layout, pace of play and upkeep"; although the "ridiculous greens fees" seem "pricey for this area", you can expect a "well-maintained course", "pleasant" service and an "excellent restaurant."

Puerto Rico

Dorado

Dorado Beach Resort, East 🏌

| 23 | 22 | 21 | 20 | $195 |

Dorado | 500 Plantation Dr. | 787-626-1006 | www.kempersports.com | 7192/5479; 75.1/72.7; 135/126

"Still one of the best in the Caribbean" despite being "orphaned" after the "closing of the hotel facilities", this "old-fashioned" 1958 RTJ Sr. design on a former Puerto Rican palm tree plantation reopened in 2011 after a renovation by RTJ Jr. (which may not be reflected in the Course score); it pairs "incredible" ocean views with "stunning holes", including a par-5 4th that affords strong players a "reachable" green in two shots "over two water hazards" (amateurs can opt for a more cautious route).

Dorado Del Mar 🏌

| 23 | 21 | 20 | 20 | $102 |

Dorado | 200 Dorado Del Mar | 787-796-3070 | www.embassysuitesdorado.com | 6940/5245; 75.2/71.9; 138/125

A "scenic" Chi Chi Rodriguez design located at the Embassy Suites some 25 miles from San Juan, this "interesting layout" is "worth a visit compared to pricier options" thanks to a "back nine with breathtaking views of the Caribbean Sea", most notably on the 10th hole; although the course is a draw in itself, it merits "the ride [just] to view the nature and foliage" – or to partake of the hotel's four restaurants, gym, tennis courts and pool.

Las Croabas

El Conquistador Resort 🏨 ⏱

| 23 | 24 | 23 | 19 | $210 |

Las Croabas | 1000 El Conquistador Ave. | 787-863-6784 | www.elconresort.com | 6746/4939; 74.5/70.8; 141/126

"Bring a Sherpa with you" to navigate this "extremely challenging" mountain course at the Waldorf-Astoria Collection's El Conquistador, where "lots of elevation changes", "hilly lies", "blind tee shots" and "constant winds will be more than enough" for the average golfer; the "jungle borders the fairways", so "remember, the giant iguanas are your friends" on an Arthur Hills design that also offers "fabulous facilities" and 15 holes with "phenomenal" ocean views.

Rio Grande

Wyndham Rio Mar, Ocean 🏨

| 23 | 23 | 21 | 20 | $199 |

Rio Grande | 6000 Rio Mar Blvd. | 787-888-6000 | 888-627-8556 | www.wyndhamriomar.com | 6782/5450; 73.8/72.6; 132/126

This Rio Grande resort course is located in a seaside setting so "spectacular" it's "hard to concentrate on your round" (the "ocean view more than compensates" for the "construction on the back nine", so "bring your camera"); "one of the best on the island", it's "wide-open" with "nice greens" and "a quick pace of play", but the George and Tom Fazio design can be "challenging from the back tees", so "pray the wind isn't blowing."

Wyndham Rio Mar, River 🏨

| 22 | 23 | 22 | 20 | $199 |

Rio Grande | 6000 Rio Mar Blvd. | 787-888-6000 | 888-627-8556 | www.wyndhamriomar.com | 6945/5119; 74.5/69.8; 135/120

With a feel that's "completely different than its Ocean counterpart", this Greg Norman–designed "jungle experience" includes "lots of wildlife and beautiful views" along the Mameyes River near Rio Grande; the layout follows the natural terrain, so you can expect some "goofy" sections that are nonetheless "fun" and an overall experience that occasionally "plays tougher" than its sibling "because of narrower landing areas" and 12 holes with water (so mind your golf cart's GPS).

Rhode Island

Northern Rhode Island

Triggs Memorial

| ∇ 19 | 13 | 13 | 23 | $40 |

Providence | 1533 Chalkstone Ave. | 401-521-8460 | www.triggs.us | 6522/5392; 71.5/72.0; 129/124

Located "right in the city" of Providence, this 1932 Donald Ross-designed municipal is a "great", "challenging" layout featuring four demanding par 3s and a "winner" of a 10th, plus "a 19th hole to catch up on the local gossip", and while a few feel that "lackluster maintenance" "takes a toll on the experience", supporters say it has "a lot of potential"; public weekend play is determined by a Monday lottery.

COURSE · FACIL. · SERVICE · VALUE · COST

Southern Rhode Island

Exeter Country Club

| 21 | 15 | 16 | 22 | $40 |

Exeter | 320 Ten Rod Rd. | 401-295-8212 | www.exetercc.com |
6921/5706; 72.1/72.1; 125/115

"Worth a visit if you're in southern Rhode Island", this scenic 1969 course is "fun for all levels" thanks to a "long, wide and open" layout; a "covered wooden bridge" on the 13th hole is "an interesting feature", and while naysayers note "the facilities are a bit average" "with no amenities" (although there is a practice range and green), it's nonetheless a "decent", "reasonably priced" option.

Newport National, Orchard 🏨

| 27 | 16 | 21 | 21 | $150 |

Middletown | 324 Mitchell's Ln. | 401-848-9690 |
www.newportnational.com | 7244/5217; 74.4/68.8; 138/119

Soak in the scenery at this "idyllic, unspoiled" links-style layout that was "well designed" by Arthur Hills to be "difficult for beginners" but nonetheless "playable", with "native plants" and "wonderful views of the Atlantic Ocean" and Sakonnet Passage; a few feel the "facilities should be better", but the "friendly staff makes up for [having] no clubhouse or driving range", and while it's "pricey, it's worth it if you're in the Newport area."

Richmond Country Club

| 23 | 20 | 20 | 21 | $40 |

Richmond | 74 Sandy Pond Rd. | 401-364-9200 |
www.richmondcountryclub.net | 6817/4925; 72.1/70.4; 121/113

"You'll think you're on a private course" at this "casual, friendly", family-owned club that's sculpted out of a pine forest in a beautiful country setting in Richmond; the "fair but challenging" layout is supplemented with "nice facilities and staff" as well as a clubhouse with panoramic views of the ponds and footbridge, all at a "reasonable" price.

South Carolina

TOP COURSES IN STATE

29	Kiawah Island, Ocean	*Charleston*
28	Sea Pines, Harbour Town	*Hilton Head*
	Caledonia Golf & Fish Club	*Pawleys Island*
27	Tidewater	*Myrtle Beach*
26	Daufuskie Island, Melrose	*Hilton Head*
	Heritage Club	*Pawleys Island*
	Dunes Golf & Beach Club	*Myrtle Beach*
	Barefoot, Dye	*Myrtle Beach*
	Barefoot, Fazio	*Myrtle Beach*
25	Barefoot, Love	*Myrtle Beach*

Charleston

Charleston National 🏨

| 22 | 16 | 16 | 21 | $89 |

Mt. Pleasant | 1360 National Dr. | 843-884-4653 |
www.charlestonnationalgolf.com |
7064/5086; 74.6/70.3; 136/128

At this semi-private club 10 miles from the heart of historic Charleston, mossy oaks, Palmetto palm stands and "lovely holes with views" of the Intracoastal Waterway and Bulls Bay highlight Rees Jones' championship design set in Low Country marshland; the "laid-back", "enjoyable" course with five sets of tees and 14 water holes is "always in great condition", and is complemented by "typical, somewhat upscale" facilities.

Dunes West 🏌

22 | 21 | 20 | 20 | $85

Mt. Pleasant | 3535 Wando Plantation Way | 843-856-9000 |
www.duneswestgolfclub.com | 6859/5129; 73.0/69.6; 134/120
While the staff "thoughtfully puts out plenty of iced towels" on hot summer days, wags wager you can "put up a good score and not break a sweat" on this "mild" Arthur Hills design with "approachable greens and wide-open fairways"; the "pleasant" Low Country setting on the historic Lexington Plantation is filled with mossy oaks, and the "excellent" antebellum clubhouse exudes Southern charm.

Kiawah Island, Cougar Point 🏌

23 | 21 | 24 | 21 | $215

Kiawah Island | 1 Sanctuary Beach Dr. | 843-768-6000 | 800-576-1570 |
www.kiawahresort.com | 6875/4776; 74.0/67.6; 138/118
"Often overlooked because of its Ocean" counterpart, this "hidden gem" is "not as famous" or as difficult as its well-known sibling, but "Kiawah Island's oldest course" may be "more fun to play" thanks to a "solid" Gary Player redesign that offers a "pleasant mix of terrain", including some "beautiful holes over marshy areas" ("lots of gators"); "top-notch service" is a given, but a few wallet-watchers would rather "play Osprey or Turtle Point for [about] the same cost."

Kiawah Island, Oak Point 🏌

22 | 22 | 23 | 22 | $143

Johns Island | 4394 Hope Plantation Dr. | 843-768-6000 |
800-576-1570 | www.kiawahresort.com |
6701/4954; 72.4/69.8; 137/121
It may "not be up to the standards" of its siblings, but don't let this "great test of golf" "fall by the wayside", since "new players and juniors" alike will find the Clyde Johnston–designed layout to be "a real value" when compared to the more "expensive Kiawah properties"; the clubhouse is "beautifully situated" overlooking Haulover Creek, so if you're lucky, you may even catch sight of an Atlantic bottlenose dolphin.

⛳ Kiawah Island, Ocean 🏌

29 | 27 | 26 | 23 | $343

Kiawah Island | 1000 Ocean Course Dr. | 843-768-6000 | 800-576-1570 |
www.kiawahresort.com | 7356/5327; 77.3/72.7; 144/124
"In heaven, this is where you get to play golf every day" aver admirers of South Carolina's top-rated Course, a "once-in-a-lifetime experience" that's set to host the 2012 PGA Championship; it's "Pete Dye at his diabolical best", so "bring your A-game, wallet" and "lots of ammo" to play this "challenge by the sea" that's particularly "sadistic when the wind picks up", and expect "attentive" service at the "spectacular" clubhouse; P.S. "take a caddie" to play it "like the pros do", and keep in mind it's walking-only before noon.

Kiawah Island, Osprey Point 🏌

24 | 24 | 25 | 22 | $215

Kiawah Island | 700 Governors Dr. | 843-768-6000 | 800-576-1570 |
www.kiawahresort.com | 6932/5023; 73.3/70.0; 135/121
It may lack the seaside holes, but this equally "scenic" Tom Fazio "gem" is a "surprisingly strong challenger to the Ocean course for

playability and fun", with "great shot qualities and hole variety" on a layout that's routed through natural wetlands ("lots of water") and a forest full of "herons and alligators"; in fact, "many golfers prefer Osprey" to a "beat-down" from Ocean, especially when you factor in the "top-notch facilities" and "always friendly" staff.

Kiawah Island, Turtle Point ⚐ | 24 | 25 | 25 | 21 | $215 |

Kiawah Island | 1 Turtle Point Ln. | 843-768-6000 | 800-576-1570 | www.kiawahresort.com | 7061/5210; 73.6/71.5; 138/126
"Well worth playing while visiting Kiawah Island", this "truly fine" Jack Nicklaus design features three "fabulous" holes "right on the ocean" that may be "slightly out of character compared to the rest" of the track but are a "fantastic" diversion nonetheless; though "less challenging than the Ocean course", it's "tighter", with "tough green complexes", "plenty of wildlife and some water carries [that] make it a worthwhile adventure."

Wild Dunes, Harbor 🏨 | 24 | 24 | 24 | 21 | $110 |

Isle of Palms | 5757 Palm Blvd. | 843-886-2180 | 800-845-8880 | www.wilddunes.com | 6359/4907; 71.0/70.4; 133/120
Wild Dunes' cheaper yet "solid" Tom Fazio design is tough "but not gimmicky" and plays further inland than its sister course, providing a "great tour of the Intracoastal Waterway" and "saltwater marshes"; still, it's close enough to the ocean to warrant "bringing an anchor on gusty days", as well as a "ball retriever", thanks to all the marshes and dunes; P.S. "watch out for gators."

Wild Dunes, Links 🏨 | 25 | 23 | 23 | 22 | $165 |

Isle of Palms | 5757 Palm Blvd. | 843-886-2180 | 800-845-8880 | www.wilddunes.com | 6709/4907; 73.1/70.4; 132/120
Although this "beautiful, challenging" "Tom Fazio seaside links" design north of Charleston has "suffered a lot at the hands of Mother Nature", fans insist the last three holes are still "not to be missed", especially the restored 18th, which reopened in 2009; the "rest of the course is wonderful" as well, featuring towering dunes and 14 water holes.

Hilton Head

Country Club of Hilton Head 🏨 ⏲ | 23 | 22 | 22 | 21 | $155 |

Hilton Head Island | 70 Skull Creek Dr. | 843-681-4653 | www.hiltonheadclub.com | 6919/5373; 75.2/71.7; 143/128
Take a stab at Rees Jones' "difficult" but "playable" Hilton Head "classic" (circa 1986), the type of course "you'll want to play over and over again" thanks to its "excellent conditions", "multiple doglegs", "well-bunkered" greens and water on 13 holes; "beautiful facilities" and "public access with a private feel" also contribute to its "great bang for your buck" overall.

Daufuskie Island, Melrose | 26 | 24 | 23 | 23 | $139 |

Hilton Head Island | 421 Squire Pope Rd. | 843-422-6963 | 888-909-4653 | 7081/5575; 74.2/73.0; 140/131
It's an "all-day affair" at this "secluded", car-less island resort accessible only by a ferry ride that sometimes comes with a "dolphin escort"; Jack Nicklaus' "spectacular design" offers "excellent conditions" and "beauti-

ful views of the bay", not to mention what many regard as the "three best finishing holes on the East Coast."

Golden Bear At Indigo Run ⛳

21 | 19 | 21 | 20 | $92

Hilton Head Island | 72 Golden Bear Way | 843-689-2200 |
www.goldenbear-indigorun.com |
7014/5259; 73.7/66.4; 132/115

"Jack is the man" exclaim fans of Nicklaus' "long" "bear of a course" on Hilton Head Island sporting "lots of water" on 11 holes, "well-positioned trees" and "not-so-wide fairways", with shorter holes like the par-4 5th that offer "lots of challenges"; amenities include a "beautiful clubhouse", GPS-equipped golf carts and a "great staff", so the only gripe heard is that it "plays slow at peak times."

Hilton Head National ⛳

24 | 21 | 22 | 23 | $105

Bluffton | 60 Hilton Head National Dr. | 843-842-5900 |
www.golfhiltonheadnational.com
Player/Weed | 6730/4682; 72.7/66.0; 131/104

A "gem of a public", this Gary Player/Bobby Weed design in Bluffton is a "good starter course" that "gets you revved up for the tougher ones" on Hilton Head, with a "playable" layout that's "not too long" and "always well maintained", with "not a home or building visible from any fairway or green" (though you may spot a "few gators"); "friendly, courteous" service and "reasonable" fees up the ante.

May River at Palmetto Bluff ⛳ ⛳

- | - | - | - | $260

Bluffton | 476 Mount Pelia Rd. | 843-706-6580 |
www.palmettobluffresort.com | 7171/5223; 75.7/70.4; 143/118

This "pristine" Jack Nicklaus design is a "world-class experience", from the scenic "Low Country setting" overlooking the May River to the "fun", "fair" course featuring "great shot-making opportunities", right down to the short par-3 14th affording views of Downtown Bluffton; it's considered by some to be "expensive" (a caddie's required whether you walk or ride), but the "customer-focused staff" ensures "you get what you pay for."

Old South

21 | 18 | 20 | 21 | $95

Bluffton | 50 Buckingham Plantation Dr. | 843-785-5353 |
800-257-8997 | www.oldsouthgolf.com |
6772/4776; 72.7/68.2; 138/117

Partisans promise a "refreshing change from the typical Hilton Head course" at this Clyde Johnston design "just off the island" in Bluffton; it's a "great shot-makers course" with "island greens and fairways", rolling hills and scenic "bay views", "especially at high tide", and the "well-maintained" conditions and "friendly" service make it a "great value for the price."

Oyster Reef ⛳

23 | 19 | 21 | 21 | $135

Hilton Head Island | 155 High Bluff Rd. | 843-681-1750 |
800-234-6318 | www.heritagegolfgroup.com |
7018/5288; 74.7/71.1; 137/120

Though it's "not a household name", this Rees Jones "pearl" is a "favorite" of many Hilton Head "regulars", thanks to "three holes that could play at any course anywhere", including the 6th overlooking Port Royal Sound, "one of the best views you'll ever see"; the facilities are "very nice", and while some grouse that the "teaching pros are expensive", others say it delivers real "value" overall.

Palmetto Dunes, Arthur Hills 🏌 | 24 | 23 | 23 | 22 | $139 |

Hilton Head Island | 2 Leamington Ln. | 843-785-1140 |
800-827-3006 | www.palmettodunes.com |
6651/4999; 72.9/69.2; 129/119

It's the shortest of the Palmetto Dunes courses, but your "A-game is required" on this "amazingly hard" Arthur Hills design with "one great hole after another" featuring "narrow fairways", doglegs and "greens guarded by wide lagoons", plus a "natural beauty and serenity" that makes you "think you're in a deep forest"; fans give "kudos to pro Doug Weaver" and the "personable" staff, and "love the a-c on the carts."

Palmetto Dunes, George Fazio | 23 | 21 | 22 | 20 | $125 |

Hilton Head Island | 2 Carnoustie Rd. | 843-785-1130 |
800-827-3006 | www.palmettodunes.com |
6873/5273; 73.9/70.8; 135/127

The "least expensive", and some say the "easiest", of the Palmetto Dunes courses, this "beautiful" George Fazio design is well "worth the money" and "fun for all", thanks to "large landing areas" and a layout that "doesn't beat you up", though it does have its "challenges" – i.e. a "couple of long carries over the river" and "lots of sand"; it's "very well kept" and "they treat you right here", with amenities that include a pro shop and Segway scooters.

Palmetto Dunes, Robert Trent Jones | 24 | 22 | 22 | 21 | $139 |

Hilton Head Island | 7 Trent Jones Ln. | 843-785-1136 |
800-827-3006 | www.palmettodunes.com |
7005/5035; 74.7/65.7; 137/114

A "spectacular" par-5 10th takes you right out to the ocean, while the remainder of the course produces a "Low Country atmosphere" at this "traditional" and "somewhat overlooked" RTJ Sr. "treat" from 1969; Roger Rulewich's "necessary renovation" didn't make it "overly hard", so it remains "very straightforward" and "wide-open", with "friendly" service, a "great golf school" and kid-friendly tees adding to the experience.

Palmetto Hall, Arthur Hills 🏌 | 23 | 21 | 22 | 21 | $107 |

Hilton Head Island | 108 Fort Howell Rd. | 843-681-7717 | 800-234-6318 |
www.palmettohallclub.com | 6918/5006; 73.7/70.6; 136/123

One of two semi-private courses that flip-flop daily in terms of which is open to the public, this Arthur Hills design "is underplayed so is in excellent shape", offering a "good challenge" that twists through towering pines and scenic lakes on Hilton Head Island; while a few feel it's "not very memorable", others conclude it's an "interesting" experience that will require you to save some balls for the tight, long 18th featuring water on the left and O.B. on the right.

Palmetto Hall, Robert Cupp | - | - | - | - | $107 |

Hilton Head Island | 108 Fort Howell Rd. | 843-681-7717 | 800-234-6318 |
www.palmettohallclub.com | 7079/5220; 75.2/71.0; 149/123

This innovative 1993 Robert Cupp creation was plotted out on a computer, and the end result is full of bunkers and greens featuring

	COURSE	FACIL.	SERVICE	VALUE	COST

straight lines, sharp angles and shapes that are unusual in traditional golf course design; cutting through thick, Low Country woodlands with a championship slope, it's also one of Hilton Head Island's most difficult layouts; it alternates public play with the Arthur Hills course on a daily basis.

☑ Sea Pines, Harbour Town

| 28 | 25 | 25 | 20 | $259 |

Hilton Head Island | 11 Lighthouse Ln. | 843-363-8385 | 800-955-8337 | www.seapines.com | 6973/5208; 75.2/70.7; 146/124

Maybe it's "overpriced because it's a PGA Tour stop", but the consensus on this Pete Dye "classic" on Hilton Head is that it's a "once-in-a-lifetime course to play", with short "but tight fairways" and "postage-stamp greens" ("drivers who spray, stay away"); you'll need "all your clubs" at this "most enjoyable layout", considered "the real deal" right up to its oceanfront finishing holes, complete with an "awe-inspiring" lighthouse at the "majestic 18th."

Sea Pines, Heron Point

| 23 | 22 | 23 | 20 | $139 |

Hilton Head Island | 100 N. Sea Pines Dr. | 843-842-8484 | 800-955-8337 | www.seapines.com | 7103/5261; 75.2/66.4; 141/112

Fresh off of a 2007 redesign, this "excellent" "addition to an island full of good golf" is "nothing like the old Sea Marsh" course it replaced given a "tricky" new layout from Pete Dye that is "challenging to all" but is particularly "difficult for the average golfer", with its many bunkers, "undulating greens and rolling fairways with various lies"; it's "still young" and "a bit pricey", but most agree it shows "lots of promise" and is "well worth" the cost.

Sea Pines, Ocean

| 23 | 23 | 24 | 20 | $129 |

Hilton Head Island | 100 N. Sea Pines Dr. | 843-842-8484 | 800-955-8337 | www.seapines.com | 6906/5325; 73.5/71.1; 144/124

Still an "excellent test" that "rewards shot-making", this granddaddy of Hilton Head golf (built in 1960 and redesigned in 1995, it's the island's oldest course) is a "pleasurable experience" that, despite its name, has "only one hole on the ocean", the "scenic" signature par-3 15th; it's "a real challenge" with "tough greens" and "lots of water" in the form of lagoons, and while it's "pricey" enough, many find it an "inexpensive day out [compared to] Harbour Town."

Myrtle Beach

Arrowhead ⛳

| 22 | 20 | 21 | 22 | $112 |

Myrtle Beach | 1201 Burcale Rd. | 843-236-3243 | 800-236-3243 | www.arrowheadcc.com
Cypress/Lakes | 6668/4812; 71.4/69.1; 141/124
Lakes/Waterway | 6614/4698; 71.6/68.1; 140/117
Waterway/Cypress | 6644/4624; 71.6/67.8; 139/121

An "underrated gem" that "won't break the bank", this Tom Jackson and Raymond Floyd design offers three "enjoyable" nines – "each a little different in style" – featuring "a lot of water", "houses or O.B. no matter where you hit the ball"; it's a "well-maintained" spread with "nice views along the Intracoastal Waterway", and "since it's so close to the airport, it's good for the first or last day" of a "Myrtle Beach golf trip."

Barefoot Resort, Dye

26 | 26 | 25 | 22 | $185

North Myrtle Beach | 2600 Pete Dye Dr. | 843-399-7238 | 888-250-1793 | www.barefootgolf.com | 7343/5021; 76.0/69.8; 146/124

One of Barefoot Resort's "four gems", this "tough" track designed by "perilous Pete Dye" comes complete with "diabolical greens", "hazards galore" and "waste areas that will make you sweat", so "keep it in the grass"; "it will beat you up, but you'll love it" thanks to the "beautiful conditions", "first-class clubhouse", "top-notch staff" and expansive on-site practice facility – in sum, "it's hard to find anything wrong" here.

Barefoot Resort, Fazio

26 | 25 | 23 | 22 | $185

North Myrtle Beach | 4980 Barefoot Resort Ridge Rd. | 843-390-3200 | 888-250-1793 | www.barefootgolf.com | 6834/4820; 73.2/68.0; 145/115

A "typical Tom Fazio challenge" awaits at this "meticulously land-scaped" Barefoot Resort layout routed through a swath of Low Country filled with oaks, pines, sand and native grasses; with natural elevation changes adding to the drama, it's "less forgiving than the Love course", but while it may "look hard", "it plays easy", with "well-thought-out" waste areas and formal bunkers, and sure, it's "pricey", but it's "so much fun!"

Barefoot Resort, Love

25 | 25 | 24 | 22 | $185

North Myrtle Beach | 4980 Barefoot Resort Ridge Rd. | 843-390-3200 | 888-250-1793 | www.barefootgolf.com | 7047/5336; 75.1/71.1; 139/124

Low Country native Davis Love III has crafted a "user-friendly" course amid the re-created ruins of an old plantation home at this Barefoot Resort layout that features "large", "difficult greens" that "always roll true" since they're kept "in pristine shape"; there's plenty of "room off the tee" for free-swinging, but keep an eye out for the "wildlife and resident black bears"; P.S. try "the best burger in town" at the club-house overlooking the 18th hole.

Barefoot Resort, Norman

22 | 25 | 23 | 21 | $185

North Myrtle Beach | 4980 Barefoot Resort Ridge Rd. | 843-390-3200 | 888-250-1793 | www.barefootgolf.com | 7035/4953; 74.1/67.8; 140/113

Deemed "the stepchild of the Barefoot Resort", this Greg Norman de-sign is "the easiest" and, for some, "least interesting" of the four lay-outs, with a "straightforward front nine" followed up with a "back nine along the Intracoastal Waterway" that "gets sexy" at times; it's also "less scenic" than its sisters (in part due to "endless townhouse con-truction"), although it does boast a "good pace of play", "great facili-ties", a "beautiful clubhouse" and "very helpful staff."

Blackmoor

22 | 21 | 21 | 22 | $95

Murrells Inlet | 6100 Longwood Dr. | 843-650-5555 | 888-650-5556 | www.blackmoor.com | 6614/4807; 72.0/67.4; 129/109

Modest in length and "very playable", this "interesting" Gary Player design lets you be "wide off the tee" but features "lots of water holes", doglegs and "obstacles close to the green"; some suggest it's a "second-tier track for the Myrtle Beach area", but it offers a "fun" experience that includes "some wild turkey" and alligator sightings as well as a price point that makes it a "good value", especially for parents (juniors play for free with a paid adult).

Dunes Golf & Beach Club ⌂

26 | 23 | 23 | 22 | $200

Myrtle Beach | 9000 N. Ocean Blvd. | 843-449-5914 | 866-386-3722 | www.dunesgolfandbeachclub.com | 7195/5345; 75.7/71.4; 145/131

"You know you're someplace special" when you set foot on what many call the "grande dame" of Myrtle Beach courses, where "old school and old money" reign; this 1948 RTJ Sr. design, formerly home to the Senior Tour Championship, is a "true classic" that's "superbly maintained" and "visually stunning", with a famous par-5 13th dubbed Waterloo ("watch out for the gators") and the area's only beach-view hole on the par-3 9th.

Glen Dornoch Waterway ⌂

25 | 23 | 23 | 24 | $159

Little River | 4840 Glen Dornoch Way | 843-249-2541 | 800-717-8784 | www.glendornoch.com | 6890/5002; 73.1/69.8; 145/129

"Bring lots of balls" – at least enough to make it through the "dramatic" and "difficult" "best three-hole finish on the Grand Strand" – to this "unique layout" that offers "classic holes" and "perfect greens" but also some "tough up-and-downs" to "challenge the better golfer"; "excellent conditions", "breathtaking views of the Intracoastal Waterway" and "attentive" service lead many to conclude it's "worth the drive" north from Myrtle Beach.

Grande Dunes ⌂

25 | 25 | 24 | 20 | $174

Myrtle Beach | 8700 Golf Village Ln. | 843-449-7070 | 888-886-8877 | www.grandedunes.com | 7578/5353; 77.1/71.2; 142/123

Although "a bit pricey for Myrtle Beach", this "first-class" Roger Rulewich design is a "great value" thanks to an "immaculate", "challenging" "but fair" layout that's routed along the Intracoastal Waterway, with "terrific" par 3s to go with a few "tricked-up holes", and six sets of tees for golfers of all levels; "you'll want to play it over and over" claim cognoscenti keen on its "wide fairways", "huge greens" and clubhouse with a "nice veranda off the restaurant."

Heather Glen ⌂

25 | 22 | 22 | 24 | $139

Little River | 4650 Heather Glen Way | 843-249-9000 | 800-868-4536 | www.heatherglen.com
Blue/Red | 6771/5053; 73.3/69.8; 138/112
Red/White | 6783/5101; 73.4/70.0; 134/113
White/Blue | 6822/5082; 73.0/70.0; 135/116

A "perennial favorite" in North Myrtle Beach, this "delightful" 27-hole "gem" offers a "beautiful", "unique Scottish links layout", with "well-thought-out holes" featuring "lots of trees and variation in elevation" along with "great bunkering"; it's "not a killer, but there are still plenty of challenges" to make it "enjoyable", so given that it's also "reasonably priced", most say they "would have no problem playing here again."

Legends, Heathland ⌂

24 | 25 | 23 | 23 | $135

Myrtle Beach | 1500 Legends Dr. | 843-236-9318 | 800-552-2660 | www.legendsgolf.com | 6800/4904; 72.8/71.0; 131/121

"Do not miss" your chance to head "back in time to the old country" at this "very playable" "Scottish links"–style design by Tom Doak that is perhaps "not as challenging as the other [two] on-site" but offers "the most fun at the Legends complex"; a "shot-makers paradise" full of "water, sand, moguls, waste bunkers" and "putt-able fairways", it's "a treat" that comes complete with "one of the best" covered and lighted driving ranges around.

Legends, Moorland ⛳   25 | 25 | 24 | 24 | $135

Myrtle Beach | 1500 Legends Dr. | 843-236-9318 | 800-552-2660 | www.legendsgolf.com | 6755/4811; 74.0/72.8; 140/121

"Fun, in a sadistic kind of way", this stadium-type "shot-makers course" designed by P.B. Dye is considered the "best of the Legends" trio for its "tough bunkers" with railroad ties, including the short par-4 16th (aka "Hell's Half Acre"), and "very tough greens" that can yield "spectacular scores"; "well-maintained" and "well-run" by a "helpful" staff, it's a "good value" in the Myrtle Beach area; P.S. don't miss the clubhouse's "wonderful breakfast buffet."

Legends, Parkland ⛳   23 | 25 | 24 | 24 | $135

Myrtle Beach | 1500 Legends Dr. | 843-236-9318 | 800-552-2660 | www.legendsgolf.com | 7108/5370; 74.9/72.0; 136/125

The longest of the three Legends courses is "totally different from the other two", boasting four sets of tees and a "challenging", tree-lined design with 10 water holes and "huge" bunkers; while a few find it a "little too repetitive", it's "always in great shape", and the "top-notch" clubhouse and practice facilities, "helpful" staff and golf school are further reasons fans rate it "head and shoulders above most" others.

Long Bay   22 | 22 | 21 | 21 | $122

Longs | 200 Long Bay Golf Pl. | 843-399-2222 | 800-344-5590 | www.mbn.com | 7025/4944; 74.6/69.5; 141/111

Nicknamed 'Jack's Sandbox', this "deceptively challenging" "target-golf" course located north of Myrtle Beach is Nicklaus "at his penal best", where "if you miss, you're dog meat" thanks to "seas of sand" so large you can drive your cart "through the massive fairway traps"; naturally, the signature 10th features "waste bunkers running the entire length of the hole on both sides of the fairway."

Myrtle Beach National, King's North ⛳   25 | 22 | 22 | 22 | $150

Myrtle Beach | 4900 National Dr. | 843-448-2308 | 800-344-5590 | www.mbn.com | 7017/4816; 74.2/67.0; 137/113

There's "never a dull moment" on this "gorgeously landscaped", "pristinely conditioned" Arnold Palmer design at Myrtle Beach National boasting six sets of tees and "a lot of hole variety", as well as bent-grass greens and "big fairways" that "let you swing away"; the popular island fairway on the par-5 6th, aka the Gambler, is a "fantastic" (some say "gimmicky") "challenge", and fans promise that if you "play it once, you'll play it again."

Myrtle Beach National, South Creek ⛳   20 | 23 | 23 | 20 | $80

Myrtle Beach | 4900 National Dr. | 843-448-2308 | 800-344-5590 | www.mbn.com | 6416/4723; 71.0/68.0; 128/117

This older, "midpriced" Myrtle Beach National course designed by Arnold Palmer and Francis Duane is a "good warm-up for King's

North", with houses on the "narrow" fairways ("watch out for O.B."), five water holes and four sets of tees; "great conditioning" and family-friendly pricing (children under 16 accompanied by an adult play free) add to its "value."

Tidewater 🏌

27 | 23 | 23 | 23 | $199

North Myrtle Beach | 1400 Tidewater Dr. | 843-913-2424 | 800-446-5363 | www.tidewatergolf.com | 7044/4648; 74.3/67.7; 144/123

Thanks to its "spectacular setting", this Myrtle Beach "must-play" boasts "beautiful", "well-maintained" holes along the salt marshes and Intracoastal Waterway, including the 3rd and 12th – "two of the best par 3s anywhere" – that'll make you "use every club" in your bag to play a "wide variety" of "tricky shots"; an "accommodating staff" enhances the "wonderful experience."

TPC Myrtle Beach

25 | 25 | 25 | 22 | $170

Murrells Inlet | 1199 TPC Blvd. | 843-357-3399 | 888-742-8721 | www.tpc-mb.com | 6950/5118; 74.2/70.3; 145/125

"See what the pros play" at this "heck of a track" crafted by Tom Fazio (along with consultant Lanny Wadkins) that was once a Senior Tour Championship site thanks to a "fantastic layout" featuring "glasslike greens", "fairways that are like hitting off of a carpet" and "some really fun par 3s"; yes, it's "a bit pricey", but "exceptional service" and a noteworthy clubhouse are two more reasons it should be "included in any Myrtle Beach trip."

Wachesaw Plantation East 🏌

23 | 22 | 22 | 22 | $140

Murrells Inlet | 911 Riverwood Dr. | 843-357-2090 | 888-922-0027 | www.wachesaweast.com | 6933/4995; 74.1/70.2; 135/123

This former LPGA tournament host – and woman-friendly venue – might not be a place to play "full tilt, but if you get a good deal, it's well worth it" say surveyors who appreciate the large, "excellent greens" and staff that will "treat you right"; the tight, Clyde Johnston design located in Murrells Inlet, just 20 minutes south of the Myrtle Beach International Airport, is built on a former rice plantation and weaves through a combination of residential communities and environmentally protected marshlands.

Wild Wing Plantation, Avocet 🏌

23 | 22 | 23 | 21 | $100

Myrtle Beach | 1000 Wild Wing Blvd. | 843-347-9464 | 800-736-9464 | www.wildwing.com | 7127/5298; 74.5/70.4; 132/118

Once part of a four-course resort, this "traditional" layout was spared from residential development, offering some "wonderful hole variation" on a "beautiful, wooded layout" that may "make you think more than you want to" thanks to 11 holes with water; it's kept in "great condition", with "plush fairways and greens that are very smooth", and its "huge facilities", including a nine-hole course on-site, help make it an all-around "well-run" setup.

Witch, The 🏌

22 | 18 | 20 | 21 | $112

Conway | 1900 Hwy. 544 | 843-448-1300 | www.mysticalgolf.com | 6796/4812; 71.2/69.0; 133/109

"With the fog lying low over the swamp and the sound of alligators chewing on tree stumps", this "quirky" "sleeper" is "worth playing at least once" for the "unique" wildlife preserve setting near Conway;

golfers traverse "lots of bridges" and 4,000 feet of "boardwalk over swamplands" on a Dan Maples–designed layout that's "excellent for all handicaps" but "requires placement off the tee"; P.S. "reasonable rates" help offset the "minimal facilities."

Wizard, The 🏌

| 19 | 20 | 20 | 20 | $106 |

Myrtle Beach | 4601 Leeshire Blvd. W. | 843-236-9393 | www.mysticalgolf.com | 6721/4972; 72.0/71.2; 129/121

There are "all sorts of different shots to make" on this "links-style" Dan Maples design boasting "wide-open fairways", "big greens" of bentgrass and "lots of mounds", plus "distances that can be deceiving on a windy day"; the "picturesque" course is "usually in good shape", but opinions are split over the "quirky" castle ruin clubhouse.

Pawleys Island

☑ Caledonia Golf & Fish Club

| 28 | 25 | 26 | 24 | $200 |

Pawleys Island | 369 Caledonia Dr. | 843-237-3675 | 800-483-6800 | www.fishclub.com | 6526/4957; 72.1/68.7; 140/122

"Be mesmerized by the beauty" of "one of the best" in the area, this Mike Strantz–designed "gem" on Pawleys Island that's "fabulous in every way", from the "pristine conditions" to the "dramatic bunkering" to a "challenging" 18th hole with an approach shot "over water" (and "dozens of people watching from the deck" nearby); the "plantation atmosphere" extends to the "friendly staff" and "excellent service", and makes up for "no driving range."

Heritage Club 🏌

| 26 | 24 | 25 | 24 | $123 |

Pawleys Island | 478 Heritage Plantation Dr. | 843-237-3424 | 800-552-2660 | www.legendsgolf.com | 7118/5201; 75.3/67.4; 145/119

Plenty of wildlife (including gators) and 400-year-old oaks are part of the "plantation" scenery at this Pawleys Island course that's "as beautiful a setting for golf as you'll find in the Low Country", with an "entrance like Augusta National" that leads you to a "challenging" layout with a "great stretch of holes around the huge lake on the back nine"; the "fantastic" clubhouse and "nice staff" exude plenty of "Southern charm" and help make it a "memorable experience."

Pawleys Plantation

| 25 | 23 | 23 | 22 | $146 |

Pawleys Island | 70 Tanglewood Dr. | 843-237-6200 | 800-367-9959 | www.pawleysplantation.com | 7026/4976; 74.5/70.1; 142/122

Still considered "one of Jack Nicklaus' best designs", this "oldie but goodie" on Pawleys Island is a "tough" track "with some stunning holes on the waterway", including a back nine that "plays along the marsh" and a "very short par-3 13th that [players] love to hate"; although a few grouse that it's "overpriced" and "overrated", loyalists laud it as an example of "true Southern golf", all the way down to the plantation-style clubhouse.

Tradition Club 🏌

| 23 | 21 | 22 | 23 | $98 |

Pawleys Island | 1027 Willbrook Blvd. | 843-237-5041 | 877-599-0888 | www.traditiongolfclub.com | 6875/5189; 73.1/70.1; 135/126

It might be overlooked relative to its better-known neighbors, but this "beautiful" Ron Garl design is the type of "favorably priced" track that you can "recommend to anyone" thanks to a "very fair" layout – with a few difficult spots, like the water-heavy par-3 15th – that's routed over former plantation land on Pawleys Island; some suggest it's "not memorable", but it's "always in shape", and an "amiable staff" and "good clubhouse" add to its "value."

True Blue
25 | 24 | 24 | 22 | $165

Pawleys Island | 900 Blue Stem Dr. | 843-235-0900 |
888-483-6801 | www.truebluegolf.com |
7126/4995; 74.3/65.4; 145/109

A "big, brawny" "beast" located on the Grand Strand on Pawleys Island, this "quirky" course designed by the late architect Mike Strantz "gets better each time you play" it thanks to a "challenging" layout that's "like a theme-park roller coaster", with "lots of blind shots" and elevation changes, and while the "huge fairways" can help you "throw up a great score", if you strike out, you'll be stuck in "acres of sand"; amenities include free range balls.

Willbrook Plantation
25 | 22 | 24 | 25 | $125

Pawleys Island | 426 Tidewater Circle | 843-237-4900 | 800-344-5590 |
www.mbn.com | 6292/4981; 70.3/67.7; 129/118

Treat yourself to "the high end of the affordable" at this "beautiful" Dan Maples design, a "super Low Country course" set on a "historic plantation" lined with centuries-old oaks that drip "with Spanish moss"; a "pleasant surprise" on the southern end of Myrtle Beach, it "just keeps getting better and better", offering "excellent shot values" (e.g. the island-green par-3 6th) and "one of the best staffs" around to help "keep play moving."

South Dakota

Rapid City

Golf Club at Red Rock
- | - | - | - | $49

Rapid City | 6520 Birkdale Dr. | 605-718-4710 | www.golfclubatredrock.com |
6586/5038; 71.4/69.6; 131/127

"Don't even think about walking" this Rapid City layout counsel congnoscenti who know that it's a "very hilly course" (it is in the Black Hills, after all) featuring dramatic elevation changes that will make you glad you're riding in a GPS-equipped cart; rolling fairways and links-style bunkers "will challenge your creativity", while a minimum of four tee placements per hole makes it suitable for players of all skill levels.

Meadowbrook
▽ 25 | 22 | 24 | 21 | $38

Rapid City | 3625 Jackson Blvd. | 605-394-4191 |
www.golfatmeadowbrook.com | 6933/5623; 72.4/71.5; 128/125

It may be a decades-old municipal set at the foot of the Black Hills, but admirers insist this "outstanding" Rapid City layout is "like playing in heaven" – or at least at a "very nice country club"; you simply "cannot beat the scenery" here (five holes feature Rapid Creek flowing through them), and it also boasts 60-plus "beautifully kept sand traps" along with large, undulating greens that some surveyors say are "like putting on glass."

Sioux Falls

Hillcrest Golf & Country Club

▽ 22 | 19 | 23 | 21 | $60

Yankton | 2206 Mulberry St. | 605-665-4621 | www.hillcrest.4t.com | 6874/5676; 74.1/74.0; 131/124

A classic course designed by Homer Fieldhouse in 1953, this flat parklander on the border of South Dakota and Nebraska may have a championship length of just under 6,900 yards but it still holds its own, hosting an annual Dakotas Tour event; houses dot some of the fairways, but keep an eye out for the signature par-5 17th featuring water down the full length of its right side, while a grass driving range and chipping and bunker practice areas enhance the experience.

Willow Run

- | - | - | - | $34

Sioux Falls | 8000 Hwy. 42 E. | 605-335-5900 | www.willowrungolfcourse.com | 6525/5060; 72.6/70.8; 135/124

After 20-plus years, this venerable Sioux Falls course "has matured gracefully", in part due to recent renovations that included the addition of new greens, bunkers and tees, which should "present a significant challenge to players of all levels"; it has a meandering creek, so you can expect 16 holes with water in play to help add to its "good value."

Vermillion

Bluffs, The

- | - | - | - | $27

Vermillion | 2021 E. Main St. | 605-677-7058 | www.thebluffsgc.com | 6684/4926; 72.4/68.5; 123/113

Four "interesting holes along the bluffs" overlooking the Missouri River Valley and prairie highlands are the highlight of this links-style layout that's partially routed through a residential area in the southeastern section of the state; host of the annual South Dakota Open, it's an "excellent value" featuring elevation changes and 16 holes with water in play, all of which helps compensate for the modest facilities and service.

Tennessee

Chattanooga

Bear Trace at Harrison Bay

- | - | - | - | $42

Harrison | 8919 Harrison Bay Rd. | 423-326-0885 | 877-611-2327 | www.tngolftrail.net/beartrace | 7313/5292; 74.9/70.3; 136/118

Part of the "great" Tennessee Golf Trail – it's the second of four Jack Nicklaus–designed layouts – and the host of a Nationwide Tour Qualifier, this "pretty" layout is routed through tall pine and hardwood forests north of Chattanooga; there's plenty of water to up the ante, but a few conclude this 1999 creation "fails to measure up."

Memphis

Mirmichi Golf Course ⛳

- | - | - | - | $71

Millington | 6195 Woodstock Cuba Rd. | 901-259-3800 | www.mirimichi.com | 7479/5072; 76.8/65.4; 138/118

No need to cry a river for the former Big Creek Golf Course, which was facing demolition until 6-handicap native son Justin Timberlake purchased his boyhood course, redesigned it with architect Bill Bergin and renamed it with a Native American word meaning 'place of happy retreat'; the long, well-bunkered layout sports water on 12 holes, notably on Timberlake's favorite, the par-3 11th, where only a shot hit on the green or long-left will avoid the lake.

Nashville

Gaylord Springs, Springhouse — 21 | 24 | 22 | 17 | $77

Nashville | 18 Springhouse Ln. | 615-458-1730 | 866-515-4657 | www.gaylordsprings.com | 6842/5040; 73.8/70.1; 136/115

A "lovely" faux Scottish links that follows the Cumberland River, this Nashville option offers up "gorgeous", "well-groomed" holes that are routed alongside protected wetlands and limestone bluffs; "top-notch facilities", "very good service" and a "beautiful clubhouse" cap the experience, and be sure to look for the namesake century-old springhouse next to the signature 4th; P.S. it can be "expensive", but there are "great resident rates."

Hermitage, General's Retreat — 23 | 19 | 22 | 24 | $59

Old Hickory | 3939 Old Hickory Blvd. | 615-847-4001 | www.hermitagegolf.com | 6832/5437; 72.3/70.8; 129/120

With a "completely different feel than its younger sister", this Nashville-area course is a "challenging" design that's "more scenic and less marshy" than President's Reserve; six sets of tees (including 'novice tees' for a 3,300-yard round) help it "cater to a ladies' game" (it once hosted the LPGA's Sara Lee Classic); with the same "friendly staff" and "reasonable rates" as its sibling, it's an "excellent value."

Hermitage, President's Reserve — ∇ 24 | 19 | 21 | 23 | $72

Old Hickory | 3939 Old Hickory Blvd. | 615-847-4001 | www.hermitagegolf.com | 7157/5138; 74.4/69.2; 132/117

Winding through 300 acres of natural wetlands along the Cumberland River, this Old Hickory option is "perhaps one of the best values in the country", with a Denis Griffiths–designed layout that's kept "in wonderful condition" despite "the heat in Nashville"; the staff is "incredibly friendly" too, so chances are one visit will "keep you wanting more."

Ross Creek Landing — - | - | - | - | $43

Clifton | 110 Airport Rd. | 931-676-3174 | www.rosscreeklandinggolfclub.com | 7131/5225; 74.7/71.6; 137/123

Formerly part of the Bear Trace collection of Jack Nicklaus Signature courses scattered across the state, this 2001 design two hours southwest of Nashville is now a stand-alone, but the great holes remain intact, including the par-5 8th that skirts the Tennessee River and the par-4 10th that forces an approach over a gorge; it boasts a mix of wide-open and tree-lined holes and to a cache of risk/reward tests that incorporate Ross Creek on drives or approaches.

Tennessean, The — - | - | - | - | $35

Springville | 900 Olde Tennessee Trail | 731-642-7271 | 866-710-4653 | www.tennesseanlife.com | 7183/4765; 74.6/68.6; 136/121

Situated within a new residential community about two hours west of Nashville, this "exceptional" Keith Foster design is spread over 1,100 acres and features 160 feet of elevation change plus five sets of tees to accommodate all levels of play; although one critic complains about "tricked-up greens", the course is generally "well maintained for the price", with a back nine that boasts some particularly impressive par 5s as well as a shorter risk/reward finish.

Texas

TOP COURSES IN STATE

28 Redstone, Tournament | *Houston*
Tribute | *Dallas*
Horseshoe Bay, Ram Rock | *Austin*
27 Barton Creek, Fazio Canyons | *Austin*
Barton Creek, Fazio Foothills | *Austin*
Texas Star | *Dallas*
26 Wolfdancer | *Austin*
Augusta Pines | *Houston*
La Cantera, Palmer | *San Antonio*
Cypresswood, Tradition | *Houston*

Austin

Barton Creek, Crenshaw Cliffside 차 ⊶ ⊕

| 22 | 25 | 23 | 20 | $165 |

Austin | 8212 Barton Club Dr. | 512-329-4653 | 800-336-6158 | www.bartoncreek.com | 6630/4726; 68.6/67.6; 116/110

This "sneaky" but "fun" spread in Austin's Barton Creek resort group receives mixed reviews: while some find it "the easiest" of the four courses and thus "enjoyable for all levels", others insist "the greens are tough to putt" and can be "too difficult for the average golfer"; either way, it's a winner for hotel guests who applaud the "spectacular facilities", including an upscale spa and pool area.

Barton Creek, Fazio Canyons 차 ⊶ ⊕

| 27 | 25 | 24 | 22 | $235 |

Austin | 8212 Barton Club Dr. | 512-329-4653 | 800-336-6158 | www.bartoncreek.com | 7153/5098; 75.1/70.6; 141/121

"Long, gorgeous and diabolical", this "outstanding" Tom Fazio design "challenges you with every shot and requires everything in your bag to score" on a layout that's perhaps "the prettiest" and "most fun" of the Barton Creek siblings; since it's two miles from the resort, with many holes "so isolated you can't see anyone else", expect "incredible views" and plenty of wildlife.

Barton Creek, Fazio Foothills 차 ⊶ ⊕

| 27 | 26 | 25 | 22 | $235 |

Austin | 8212 Barton Club Dr. | 512-329-4653 | 800-336-6158 | www.bartoncreek.com | 7125/5185; 74.0/69.4; 138/115

Fans of Tom Fazio's original Barton Creek course say it's "every bit as good if not better" than the Canyons and makes "subtle" use of the natural landscape: "one minute you're in the valleys, the next minute in woods", which tip-toe around the cliff-lined fairways, waterfalls and natural limestone caves; it's a classic that just "keeps getting better", with the "outstanding facilities" and "excellent service" you'd expect from a "premier resort" experience.

	COURSE	FACIL.	SERVICE	VALUE	COST

Barton Creek, Palmer Lakeside 🏌 o⇥ ⏱
22 | 20 | 22 | 20 | $145

Austin | 8212 Barton Club Dr. | 512-329-4653 | 800-336-6158 | www.bartoncreek.com | 6645/5047; 72.2/70.0; 133/124

"Always underrated" is how fans view this Arnold Palmer design that's an "ego-builder", even though it can "challenge all levels" with "several spectacular holes", including the signature 11th featuring "a 'special' waterfall" behind the green; "excellent service" and a "rolling Hill Country setting" with "some nice views" of Lake Travis also make it "worth" the 25-mile drive from the resort.

Forest Creek
19 | 17 | 20 | 19 | $59

Round Rock | 99 Twin Ridge Pkwy. | 512-388-2874 | www.forestcreek.com | 7147/5394; 73.8/71.9; 136/124

A "fine golf experience" just north of Downtown Austin, this host of the Central Texas Amateur Championship is "worth playing twice" thanks to a tree-lined and hilly Dick Phelps design that stretches to over 7,100 yards; what's more, the greens fees are "not too pricey", and there's also a three-tiered driving range and short game area to keep players busy.

Horseshoe Bay Resort, Apple Rock 🏞 o⇥
24 | 22 | 21 | 20 | $150

Horseshoe Bay | 2622 Bay West Blvd. | 830-598-6561 | 800-252-9363 | www.hsbresort.com | 6999/5536; 75.4/73.6; 136/128

Offering the "best views" of the Horseshoe Bay options ("the holes near Lake LBJ are superb"), this RTJ Sr. design "isn't as tight as Ram Rock", but it's "still a good test" and "well worth the visit"; a "practice area with several putting greens, a big range and a practice bunker" ensure that this Hill Country course gets what you would expect: "lots of resort play."

Horseshoe Bay Resort, Ram Rock 🏞 o⇥
28 | 24 | 24 | 23 | $150

Horseshoe Bay | 2622 Bay West Blvd. | 830-598-6561 | 800-252-9363 | www.hsbresort.com | 6926/5306; 75.6/72.7; 137/127

"One of the hardest in the state", this "demanding" Horseshoe Bay Resort layout "requires some shot-making to navigate" through narrow fairways and over natural rock outcroppings, so "bring your A-game" and be prepared to "use every club in your bag"; the bentgrass greens – not common in central Texas – make putting a fun time", and while a tee time here is expensive, "all three courses are worth the price" and this is "the best of the three."

Horseshoe Bay Resort, Slick Rock 🏞 o⇥
22 | 23 | 24 | 21 | $150

Horseshoe Bay | 1301 Hi Stirrup | 830-598-2561 | 800-252-9363 | www.hsbresort.com | 6834/5438; 72.8/72.7; 131/126

The oldest track at the Horseshoe Bay Resort, this 1971 RTJ Sr. design is the most "straightforward", "user-friendly" layout of the three, making it the one to try "if you can only play one – and you aren't a single-digit handicap"; set in "beautiful Texas Hill Country", it's "worth the drive from Austin", if only to "enjoy the 'Million Dollar' golf hole", a "famous" feature in which players ride a cart through a waterfall that spans 35 yards.

	COURSE	FACIL.	SERVICE	VALUE	COST

Wolfdancer

26 | 25 | 24 | 20 | $145

Lost Pines | 575 Hyatt Lost Pines Rd. | 512-308-9653 |
www.wolfdancergolfclub.com | 7205/4953; 76.1/69.1; 137/118

This "true sleeper nobody knows about" is a "young course" that will just "get better with age" and is already luring golfers to the "beautiful Hill Country" just a "short drive" from Downtown Austin; it offers "forgiving fairways" and "tricky but fair greens" that "get tougher as you head back into the trees" ("watch out for snakes"), and since it's part of the Hyatt Regency Lost Pines, it features the type of resort amenities that make it a "place to go with the kids in summer."

Dallas

Buffalo Creek 🏌

20 | 16 | 16 | 23 | $64

Heath | 624 Country Club Dr. | 972-771-4003 | www.americangolf.com |
7078/5209; 73.9/70.0; 136/113

"A gem when built" in 1992, this Weiskopf/Morrish design near Dallas "now needs updating" according to players who nonetheless profess it's "worth the money" to play a layout that was once a USGA Amateur qualifying site and is still an "excellent challenge" ("when it's in good shape") thanks to "a couple of blind tee shots" and two holes ranked among the city's hardest; a "large practice facility" and somewhat "small clubhouse" add to its "value for the price."

Cliffs, The 🏌

26 | 22 | 22 | 22 | $80

Graford | 160 Cliffs Dr. | 940-779-4520 | 888-843-2543 |
www.thecliffsresort.com | 6808/4876; 73.9/68.4; 143/124

Set at a "scenic" clifftop resort two hours west of Dallas, this "mustplay" will "keep you on the edge" with its ravines, rock outcroppings and cedar groves overlooking Possum Kingdom Lake; designed by tour pro Bruce Devlin and architect Robert von Hagge, it's as "challenging" as it is "beautiful", and while it's relatively short (at just over 6,800 yards), it remains one of Texas' toughest tracks; P.S. there are golf packages available for resort guests.

Cowboys

26 | 25 | 25 | 20 | $180

Grapevine | 1600 Fairway Dr. | 817-481-7277 | www.cowboysgolfclub.com |
7017/4702; 74.7/68.9; 138/114

For a "unique golf experience" with a "Dallas Cowboys theme", head to this "well-maintained" option that's a "fun place to play, especially for football fans", with its Hill Country elevation changes, "deep fairway bunkers" and "occasional sightings of Cowboys players and staff"; "it's pricey", but it's the "finest in Grapevine", "so get there very early and make a day of it"; P.S. VIP packages include complimentary "food and nonalcoholic drinks."

◪ Four Seasons at Las Colinas, TPC ⚲

25 | 28 | 27 | 21 | $195

Irving | 4150 N. MacArthur Blvd. | 972-717-2500 |
www.thesportsclubfourseasons.com |
7166/5030; 76.0/71.5; 142/135

Boasting "many improvements" after a 2008 redesign, this home of the PGA Tour's Byron Nelson Championship "lives up to the TPC reputation" with a layout that's now "in great condition" (and "much tougher" too); although "a little pricey", the course is part of a "first-class" complex just outside of Dallas, where the brand-new practice facilities are "top-notch" and the service is "as good as expected from a Four Seasons Resort."

NEW Old American Club, The Old American Club

— | — | — | — | $125

The Colony | 1001 Lebanon Rd. | 972-370-4653 | www.theoldamericangolfclub.com | 7174/5226; 75.8/72.8; 144/130

As a counterpoint to its elder sibling, the Tribute, an homage to some of the greatest holes in the British Isles, architect Tripp Davis crafted this retro layout (with former British Open champ Justin Leonard consulting) that conjures up images of American classics such as Shinnecock Hills and Prairie Dunes; like those, it emphasizes width, angles, thoughtful bunkering and imaginative contouring, while offering risk/reward decisions, wispy native fescue grasses and views of 23,000-acre Lake Lewisville.

Pine Dunes

▽ 27 | 12 | 18 | 25 | $79

Frankston | 159 Private Rd. 7019 | 903-876-4336 | www.pinedunes.com | 7117/5150; 74.4/71.3; 131/126

Perhaps "the best-kept secret in Texas" is this family-owned "oasis" about 90 miles east of Dallas that will make you "think you're playing Pinehurst" thanks to 100-ft.-tall pine trees lining most of the holes; it's a "fair test of golf", with nearly 90 sand traps, "a driveable par 4 on each side and a 254-yard par 3 with a 60-ft. drop", so even if it is "in the middle of nowhere", it's a "favorite" that's "worth seeking out."

Tangle Ridge

▽ 22 | 18 | 17 | 19 | $50

Grand Prairie | 818 Tangle Ridge Dr. | 972-299-6837 | www.tangleridge.com | 6835/5187; 73.4/70.6; 133/125

An "undiscovered gem" in a "beautiful" location just south of Dallas, this Grand Prairie municipal is "worth finding" thanks to a 250-acre spread featuring views of Joe Pool Lake and Hill Country–like elevation changes of over 50 feet; some say the switch to "Champions Bermuda" greens only added to the course's "great value."

Texas Star

27 | 20 | 21 | 25 | $77

Euless | 1400 Texas Star Pkwy. | 817-685-7888 | 888-839-7827 | www.texasstargolf.com | 6936/4962; 74.1/69.0; 136/120

One of the "most underrated courses in the Dallas/Ft. Worth area" is this "fabulous muni", a "beautiful" Keith Foster design featuring "challenging" terrain on its "risk/reward holes", including "great elevation changes" and "natural habitats [that are] protected in most places" ("watch out for cottonmouth snakes"); what's more, it's "well maintained and the service is equal to that of many private clubs", making the experience "worth every penny."

Tour 18 Dallas 🏳

22 | 20 | 18 | 19 | $95

Flower Mound | 8718 Amen Corner | 817-430-2000 | 800-946-5310 | www.tour18-dallas.com | 7033/5493; 74.5/74.0; 137/140

"You know you're not making it to Augusta, so why not play 'Amen Corner' in Dallas?" conclude those who've tried this "real treat" that duplicates "18 famous holes from around the country"; it's "not everyone's cup of tea", but many consider it "a great concept and lots of "fun", although you should "not expect a stroll in the park" – after all, "the reason these holes are famous is because they're all difficult."

⏏ Tribute
28 | 25 | 24 | 25 | $129

The Colony | 1000 Lebanon Rd. | 972-370-5465 | www.thetributegc.com | 7002/5352; 73.2/65.6; 128/111

"They've managed to capture a Scottish links course" right down to the "ever-present winds" at this replica track near Dallas that was designed by Tripp Davis to emulate 18 famous holes from the British Open (it's "as close as you're going to get in north Texas"); even if "100-degree temperatures spoil the illusion", it's nevertheless "very enjoyable" – the 1st, 17th and 18th are "a tribute" to St. Andrews' Old Course and "are worth the greens fees alone."

Westin Stonebriar, Fazio ⛳
23 | 24 | 24 | 22 | $122

Frisco | 5050 Country Club Dr. | 972-668-8748 | www.westinstonebriar.com | 7002/5208; 73.8/72.1; 137/129

"Worth the drive from Dallas" to Frisco, this "challenging" Tom Fazio resort course may wind through thick native grasses, but at least some of your drives should find the fairway thanks to "mounds [that] make everything bounce back to the middle"; you must be a member or resort guest to play, but that's a "nice change of pace" ("very little crowding").

El Paso

Butterfield Trail
- | - | - | - | $80

El Paso | 1858 Cottonwoods Dr. | 915-772-1038 | www.butterfieldtrailgolf.com | 6865/5053; 71.7/67.8; 127/129

Named after a historical trail from the mid-1800s that runs through the course, this "not-to-miss" Tom Fazio design is a "great addition to El Paso", with a "beautiful" setting that's convenient to the airport; the "lush green fairways stand in stark contrast to the desert" locale, but hitters needn't hop a covered wagon to play, since both carts and walking are allowed; P.S. the "helpful, knowledgeable staff" goes "above and beyond with their assistance."

Painted Dunes Desert
- | - | - | - | $35

El Paso | 12000 McCombs St. | 915-821-2122 | www.painteddunes.com
East/West | 6925/5701; 72.7/67.6; 134/122
North/East | 6904/5615; 72.3/66.6; 128/116
West/North | 6941/5662; 72.6/66.8; 131/120

"You'll be pleasantly surprised" by this El Paso–area municipal that comes "recommended by locals" who love playing 27 holes carved out of rolling Chihuahuan Desert terrain; with dramatic views of the Franklin Mountains, "immaculate rental clubs" and a "helpful, available staff", you may just feel like they all but "rolled out the red carpet."

Houston

Augusta Pines
26 | 25 | 23 | 24 | $79

Spring | 18 Augusta Pines Dr. | 281-290-1910 | www.tour18.com | 7041/5007; 73.6/68.5; 125/112

Enjoy a "championship course with a country-club feel" at this former Champions Tour host nestled north of Houston, where "tall pines line every hole" on an "outstanding" "risk/reward" design featuring "lightning"-fast dance floors – be sure to save enough balls for the back-to-back island greens on the 17th and 18th; what's more, the "staff is friendly" and "it has one of the best practice areas around", so "stop by the [on-site] Massengale Academy for a tune-up."

BlackHorse, North
23 | 24 | 22 | 22 | $95

Cypress | 12205 Fry Rd. | 281-304-1747 | www.blackhorsegolfclub.com | 7075/5640; 74.0/72.7; 131/132

"You won't be disappointed" by this "worthwhile" Jim Hardy/Peter Jacobsen design that's carved into a landscape of lakes, wetlands and trees in northwest Houston; the final nine are "a bit back and forth", but there's a "great front nine" plus "well-maintained" fairways dotted with numerous bunkers ("bring your sand wedge"); P.S. after your round, giddyap over to Jake's Grill for "good food and cold beer."

BlackHorse, South
23 | 25 | 23 | 23 | $95

Cypress | 12205 Fry Rd. | 281-304-1747 | www.blackhorsegolfclub.com | 6957/5473; 74.1/71.3; 134/128

Saddle up for the "trickier" of the two BlackHorse layouts, this "risk/reward" track that's "tighter, with trees" and more water than its relatively wide-open sibling ("watch out for the occasional alligator!"); despite its challenges, it's nonetheless a "very playable" course that offers "value for the money" given that it's part of a "darn good facility" that includes a 2,000-sq.-ft. pro shop.

Cypresswood, Tradition
26 | 18 | 19 | 23 | $69

Spring | 21602 Cypresswood Dr. | 281-821-6300 | www.cypresswood.com | 7220/4785; 74.7/67.8; 140/117

A "challenging" PGA Tour qualifying site, this "beautiful", "well-maintained" woodlander "tests all facets of your game" with a Keith Foster layout routed through the native forests north of Houston; while the facilities are "average", the course itself is "removed", creating "a pure golf experience" that's "never really crowded" and has "no homes to detract" from the views of "big, gorgeous pine trees."

Falls, The
24 | 20 | 21 | 22 | $75

New Ulm | 1750 N. Falls Dr. | 979-992-3123 | www.thefallsresort.com | 6765/5348; 73.1/71.9; 140/131

With scenery that's "worth the drive" from Houston to New Ulm, this "Cadillac of courses" is at its "best in the cool weather because it's surrounded by trees" that produce colorful fall foliage; it's made "challenging" by undulating terrain and 11 water holes (you'll "need to hit it straight"), and although it's "in the middle of nowhere", you won't have to face the long trip home if you "stay in one of the cabins" – they're perfect for a "weekend golf trip."

Meadowbrook Farms
19 | 19 | 20 | 20 | $89

Katy | 2323 Meadowbrook Farms Club Dr. | 281-693-4653 | www.meadowbrookfarmsgolfclub.com | 7100/5000; 74.4/70.6; 135/119

"You will get your money's worth" at this "challenging and fun" Greg Norman design that's "always in great shape", weaving in and out of trees, creeks, lakes and wetlands 30 minutes west of Houston; although the "pro shop and restaurant are minimal", it's "a must-see" thanks to an "imaginative" layout.

	COURSE	FACIL.	SERVICE	VALUE	COST

Memorial Park

	20	15	15	25	$38

Houston | 1001 E. Memorial Loop | 713-862-4033 |
www.memorialparkgolf.com | 7305/5459; 73.0/70.7; 122/114

This "amazing public course minutes from Downtown" Houston fills
the bill for a "typical muni course", with "wide" and "forgiving fairways"; "it may not be the nicest" around (though some say it's in
"great shape"), but it's "very playable" and a "good value for your
money", thus it's "always crowded" and "getting a tee time" can be
hard (it's closed on Tuesdays), though "walk-ups are usually
available – especially for a single player."

ⓩ Redstone, Tournament

	28	27	26	20	$150

Humble | 5860 Wilson Rd. | 281-459-7800 | www.redstonegolfclub.com |
7422/5926; 76.0/71.3; 144/125

"You won't find a better experience" than at the top-rated Course in
Texas, this "fantastic" host of the Shell Houston Open that's one of
only 10 non-resort PGA Tour venues that are open to the public; a
2005 Rees Jones design with fairways that are "nice and wide" and
greens that are large, "tough and fast" ("make sure to get a pin
sheet"), it can be "pricey", but you can expect "perfect conditions"
and facilities and service that are "over the top."

Tour 18 Houston 🏯

	21	20	19	21	$109

Humble | 3102 FM 1960 Rd. E. | 281-540-1818 | www.tour18golf.com |
6782/5380; 72.7/71.3; 129/129

Featuring 18 "famed holes from around the country", this replica course
may be "kind of gimmicky", but it's "a hoot to play" and "the reproduc-
tions are pretty good", even if "it's hard to get Augusta's elevation
changes in Houston"; a few fret that it's "overplayed" and "not as well
maintained as the Dallas version", but most consider it "worth playing
once, especially if you've seen some" of the original courses.

Lubbock

Rawls Course at Texas Tech University

	▽ 20	15	18	20	$64

Lubbock | 3720 Fourth St. | 806-742-4653 | www.therawlscourse.com |
7349/5493; 75.3/67.2; 139/116

It's "amazing what they did in the middle of flat Lubbock" when Texas
Tech moved over a million cubic yards of earth to emulate local valleys
and canyons; designed by architect Tom Doak and funded by alum
Jerry Rawls, it's "tough", "in good shape" and "affordable" to boot, and
the driving range and clubhouse restaurant are open to the public (but
not the three-hole practice course or indoor hitting stations).

San Antonio

Brackenridge Park

	-	-	-	-	$60

San Antonio | 2315 Ave. B | 210-226-5612 | www.alamocitygolftrail.com |
6243/5279; 70.3/71.1; 126/126

No other public course in Texas has as much history as this 1915 A.W.
Tillinghast design – it hosted the PGA Tour's Texas Open from 1922 to
1959 – and now 'the Brack' has the playing chops to match thanks to a
2008 restoration; nestled near Downtown San Antonio, it's a short

shot-makers course, with flat-bottomed bunkers and fairways hemmed in by pecans and oaks.

Canyon Springs

23 | 20 | 21 | 21 | $69

San Antonio | 24405 Wilderness Oak | 210-497-1770 | www.canyonspringsgc.com | 7077/5234; 74.9/70.4; 137/122

Admirers consider this "well-maintained" Thomas Walker design north of San Antonio to be a "great course for the money" (especially for county residents, who get a special rate), with "lots of trees and some very interesting holes", even though there are "many homes" along the fairways; "outstanding greens" and a "challenging" layout add to the "fun", as does a good clubhouse, although nitpickers note the "range and practice area could use a little work" and it's "crowded at times."

Hyatt Hill Country

21 | 24 | 22 | 19 | $145

San Antonio | 9800 Hyatt Resort Dr. | 210-520-4040 | 888-901-4653 | www.hyatt.com
Creeks/Oaks | 6867/4825; 73.3/68.2; 131/119
Lakes/Creeks | 6931/4939; 73.7/69.2; 132/118
Lakes/Oaks | 6940/4778; 73.7/67.8; 136/118

A "real gem in the Hill Country", this San Antonio track offers "pure Texas" golf in the form of a "scenic", "well-manicured" Arthur Hills design featuring some "tough but fair elevation changes" among its 27 holes; you're "assured to see some wildlife" during your round, and the "great facilities", "helpful staff" and "wonderful resort" amenities make it an ideal "place to vacation with the family."

☑ La Cantera, Palmer

26 | 26 | 26 | 22 | $140

San Antonio | 17865 Babcock Rd. | 210-558-2365 | 800-446-5387 | www.lacanteragolfclub.com | 6926/5066; 74.2/65.3; 142/116

Set in the "very scenic" Texas Hill Country, this "well-maintained" Arnold Palmer design is "fair but demanding", with "a few blind shots" and "dramatic changes in elevation on many holes" ("danger lurks on all sides"); it may not be as well-known as its sibling, but it "has character", leading some to argue it's "actually a nicer course" than the Resort; P.S. it's "on the expensive side" but comes complete with "a great hotel and facilities."

☑ La Cantera, Resort

26 | 27 | 25 | 22 | $140

San Antonio | 16641 La Cantera Pkwy. | 210-558-4986 | 800-446-5387 | www.lacanteragolfclub.com | 7021/4940; 72.5/67.1; 134/108

An "awesome" "roller-coaster ride" set at a "gorgeous resort" near San Antonio, this Weiskopf/Morrish design is the former home to the Valero Texas Open and offers "a little bit of everything", from an "interesting" 7th adjacent to the Six Flags amusement park to "dramatic views" from "tee boxes set on cliffs"; a "helpful staff" ups the ante, and regulars recommend warming up at the "nice practice facility", since the 665-yard opener "can be intimidating."

Quarry

23 | 20 | 20 | 21 | $109

San Antonio | 444 E. Basse Rd. | 210-824-4500 | 800-347-7759 | www.quarrygolf.com | 6128/4897; 69.3/69.2; 127/116

A "most unique" Keith Foster design that features two "totally different nines", this "gorgeous" San Antonio spread pairs a "treeless, links-style" front with a "spectacular back" "carved out of an old quarry"; "you'll think Satan's the greenskeeper" on the return, which can get "pretty steamy depending on the time of year", so "bring lots of water" to play a "really neat" layout that may have a "thermometer on the 18th" but is nevertheless "quite cool."

SilverHorn

| 21 | 17 | 19 | 21 | $99 |

San Antonio | 1100 W. Bitters Rd. | 210-545-5300 | www.silverhorngolfclub.com | 6922/5271; 73.4/72.0; 138/133

Although "right in the heart of San Antonio", "it doesn't feel like you're in the city" when traversing the tree-lined, "narrow fairways" on architect Randy Heckenkemper's "well-maintained" course; it's "right next to the airport", however, so "don't let the jet engines freak you out while putting on the slick greens"; P.S. it's "reasonably priced", with "super twilight fees", so "if you have three rounds in [the area], this should be in the rotation."

NEW TPC San Antonio, AT&T Canyons ⚲

| - | - | - | - | $199 |

San Antonio | 23808 Resort Pkwy. | 210-491-5800 | www.tpcsanantonio.com | 7106/4968; 74.1/70.4; 136/118

Wider and hillier than its Greg Norman–designed sibling, this joint effort from Pete Dye and pro Bruce Lietzke melds seamlessly into its surroundings, amid stands of mature oak and cedar trees as well as dramatic vistas of the adjacent Cibolo Canyons; as a course that favors skilled shot-makers, it's no surprise that Fred Couples mastered it to win the inaugural AT&T Championship in 2011.

NEW TPC San Antonio, AT&T Oaks ⚲

| - | - | - | - | $199 |

San Antonio | 23808 Resort Parkway | 210-491-5800 | www.tpcsanantonio.com | 7435/5514; 76.5/74.1; 148/132

Slender fairways, deep bunkers and abundant oaks define this 2010 Greg Norman/Sergio Garcia collaboration, the new home of the PGA Tour's Valero Texas Open, but perhaps most striking are the vexatious greens, contoured into individual sections, which makes chipping and putting an adventure; a stay at the adjacent JW Marriott San Antonio Hill Country Resort is required to play, but its six-acre River Bluff Water Experience and 26,000-sq.-ft. spa adds value to the package.

U.S. Virgin Islands

St. Croix

Carambola

∇ 23 | 19 | 21 | 22 | $95 |

Kingshill | 72 Estate River | 340-778-5638 | www.golfcarambola.com | 6865/5425; 74.3/71.7; 135/128

A 1966 classic that was built by Laurence Rockefeller and designed by Robert Trent Jones Sr., this "scenic course" on northwestern St. Croix is a "tough test of golf", with "lush surroundings" – spectacular tropical foliage, exotic birds and a rainforest jungle valley (but "no ocean views") – that may just distract you from "challenging" holes that include a deceptively difficult par-3 17th; as an added treat you can rent out one of the on-site luxury villas.

St. Thomas

Mahogany Run ⛳ | 21 | 18 | 20 | 17 | $165 |

St. Thomas | 1 Mahogany Run Rd. N. | 340-777-6250 | 800-253-7103 | www.mahoganyrungolf.com | 6008/4873; 70.5/70.9; 133/134

Some say this George and Tom Fazio design is "worth the price of admission" "just for the Devil's Triangle", a "diabolical" stretch of "extremely difficult", "strikingly beautiful" holes (the 13th–15th) that tiptoes "high above the ocean", offering "great views" along the St. Thomas coastline; it's an "interesting layout" that's suitable "for the intermediate golfer", but given that this is a one-course isle, "hopefully, you'll [be able to] avoid the cruise-ship" throngs.

Utah

Salt Lake City

Soldier Hollow, Gold | - | - | - | - | $29 |

Midway | 1370 W. Soldier Hollow Ln. | 435-654-7442 | www.stateparks.utah.gov | 7598/5658; 74.4/70.1; 131/119

Scheduled to host the 2012 U.S. Amateur Public Links Championship, this mountainside layout from Gene Bates brings home the gold as a "challenging" "links-style course" offering "nice elevation changes" along with "sand and water hazards" and "many blind shots", so "pick your tees wisely" and brace yourself for "some nasty fescue"; low greens fees make it a "good value all the time", but "shade is scarce", so "bring plenty of sunscreen."

Soldier Hollow, Silver | - | - | - | - | $29 |

Midway | 1370 W. Soldier Hollow Ln. | 435-654-7442 | www.stateparks.utah.gov | 7355/5532; 73.2/68.3; 131/111

Part of a state-owned facility nestled "on the side of a mountain", this Gene Bates effort is considered "easier than the Gold", "a fun course for all handicaps", with an unusual combination of par 3s, 4s and 5s (six each); "nice views" of Heber Valley and Mount Timpanogos, especially from the clubhouse restaurant with its floor-to-ceiling windows, add to the layout's "value for the money."

Thanksgiving Point ⛳ | ▽ 24 | 23 | 21 | 20 | $85 |

Lehi | 3300 W. Clubhouse Dr. | 801-768-7400 | www.thanksgivingpoint.com | 7716/6344; 76.2/69.7; 140/125

Stretching to over 7,700 yards, this "outstanding" Johnny Miller "monster" is "tough" "but worth playing for sure" thanks to a natural mountain desert landscape just south of Salt Lake City that enhances the golf experience with some of the most spectacular gardens in Utah; the "dramatic layout" has the designer's "typical buried-elephant greens" and is "usually very windy", so "long irons are a must", especially for the "demanding par 3s."

Valley View | - | - | - | - | $28 |

Layton | 2501 E. Gentile St. | 801-546-1630 | www.valleyviewutah.com | 7162/5689; 73.5/71.1; 132/125

A well-kept local secret, this mountainous course just north of Salt Lake City is a "demanding" layout, with 13 water holes, "multiple elevation changes" and "fast greens" that can make for some "difficult putting"; host of multiple Utah Amateur qualifying events, it's considered one of the state's "best values."

🆕 Victory Ranch Club   - | - | - | - | $150

Kamas | 7865 N. Victory Ranch Dr. | 435-785-5030 | 888-744-9479 | www.victoryranchclub.com | 7599/5422; 74.9/70.2; 133/123

Opened as a private club in 2009, this spectacular, high-altitude Rees Jones design outside of Park City is a mostly treeless mountain track that serves up panoramas of the Wasatch and Uinta Mountains, streams and the Jordanelle Reservoir; long, blond fescue grass borders most fairways and many greenside bunkers, but the main attractions are the par-5 16th, with its fairway ribboning straight up a ridge, and par-3 17th, which offers 360-degree views atop a steep rocky bluff called Flat Top.

Wasatch Mountain, Lakes   ▽ 24 | 14 | 20 | 23 | $29

Midway | 975 W. Golf Course Dr. | 435-654-0532 | www.stateparkgolf.utah.gov | 6942/5573; 72.0/71.5; 128/123

While "not incredibly challenging", "you won't believe the beauty" of this "fun little course" near Midway, an "old-style" state park track that offers "amazing views" of the Heber Valley; considered "fair for all handicaps" and "very walkable" compared to its Mountain sibling (which requires carts), it's particularly "nice during the week" when the crowds abate – although bargain-hunters hint "you can play everyday at these rates."

Wasatch Mountain, Mountain 🏑   ▽ 24 | 16 | 22 | 25 | $29

Midway | 975 W. Golf Course Dr. | 435-654-0532 | www.stateparkgolf.utah.gov | 6459/5009; 70.4/67.4; 125/119

Although the many "elevation changes and sidehill lies" make this mountain layout seem like it's "designed to mess with those who aren't used to the altitude", the track's "lovely surroundings" and "wildlife galore" ("watch out for moose") lead fans to conclude that it's "tough to find a better course with better views"; factor in "great service", and the reasonable "rates will leave you smiling and wondering why you'd play anywhere else."

St. George

Coral Canyon 🏑   27 | 22 | 22 | 23 | $105

Washington | 1925 N Canyon Greens Dr. | 435-688-1700 | www.coralcanyongolf.com | 7200/5052; 73.5/67.6; 142/118

"Desert golf doesn't get better" than this "sweet track", an "interesting" Keith Foster design that combines "green grass" and "red rocks" in the heart of southwest Utah's 'Color Country', so "bring your camera" and your straight ball to avoid the 55 bunkers and numerous washes; yes, it's "expensive compared to other locations", but it still offers a "much better value than Vegas", especially considering that it's "always in great shape."

Entrada at Snow Canyon 🏑 ⟳   26 | 24 | 23 | 23 | $145

St. George | 2511 Entrada Trail | 435-674-7500 | www.golfentrada.com | 7085/5249; 73.2/69.6; 128/116

"An unexpected delight" in the St. George area, this "amazing track" from Johnny Miller and Fred Bliss can be "very hard to get on" now that it's open only to club members and guests of the Inn at Entrada; if you do manage to get a tee time, however, you'll enjoy "great scenery" including sandstone cliffs, rolling dunes and "intimidating" "lava fields on the back nine" that require you to "like target golf."

Sand Hollow Resort, Championship ⛳

				$125
-	-	-	-	

Hurricane | 5625 W. Clubhouse Dr. | 435-656-4653 | www.sandhollowresort.com | 7315/5306; 73.7/68.6; 137/124

Take one glance at the jagged, red rock outcroppings and natural red sand bunkers that are part of this 2008 John Fought design, and you'll understand why locals call this region of Utah 'Color Country'; what stands out, however, is both the greenery – fairways and dance floors that were super-sized to accommodate the area's strong breezes – and the four-hole stretch (12–15) that skirts prehistoric-looking cliffs.

Vermont

Northern Vermont

Stowe Mountain Lodge ⛳

21	20	21	20	$205

Stowe | 7320 Mountain Rd. | 802-760-4700 | www.stowemountainlodge.com | 6411/4350; 72.1/62.9; 141/105

This 2007 Bob Cupp design is one of Vermont's newest layouts, a "great mountain course with beautiful views" that "must be played in October, with the foliage in full bloom" but is "fun to play" anytime of the year; whether you consider it "gimmicky" or "challenging but fair", the "steep holes" and "many blind shots" "make for a grueling round", so relax afterwards at the affiliated lodge, which also runs a semi-private country club just minutes away.

Sugarbush

22	20	20	20	$100

Warren | 1091 Golf Course Rd. | 802-583-6725 | 800-537-8427 | www.sugarbush.com | 6464/5231; 71.7/70.4; 128/119

One of two RTJ Sr. courses in Vermont, this "scenic" spread situated "right on a mountain with beautiful views" of the Mad River Valley is some "seriously hilly golf", so while it's not mandatory, you may want to "take a cart unless you're ready for a workout"; also, "bring a lot of balls" to deal with the "unforgiving woods" and don't forget to "check out" the "awesome resort."

Southern Vermont

Brattleboro Country Club

				$60
-	-	-	-	

Brattleboro | Rte. 30 & Upper Dummerston Rd. | 802-257-7380 | www.brattleborocountryclub.com | 6533/5051; 71.1/69.8; 126/114

Just 15 minutes from the MA border, this former nine-holer designed by Wayne Stiles was expanded in 2000 to include 10 fresh holes from native-son architect Steve Durkee; the blend of old and new has become increasingly seamless in the ensuing decade, and although there are minimal clubhouse amenities, the presence of an extensive practice range and decent bar/grill make it a place to stop during a trip up north.

	COURSE	FACIL.	SERVICE	VALUE	COST

Golf Club at Equinox
23 | 21 | 23 | 20 | $115

Manchester | 108 Union St. | 802-362-7870 | 800-362-4747 |
www.playequinox.com | 6423/5082; 70.8/64.3; 129/113

"Now under the Troon Golf aegis", this "grand old" Walter Travis design is nestled "in the heart of Manchester", a "picturesque town" that's "very scenic, especially in autumn", with "some vistas that Floridians can only see in their dreams"; it's a "fantastic" layout that's "always in great shape", and while there's "not a lot of water", "the bunkers and hilly terrain make for a challenging round" accompanied by "excellent facilities" and "a fabulous resort."

Green Mountain National
26 | 19 | 22 | 24 | $69

Killington | 476 Barrows Towne Rd. | 802-422-4653 | 888-483-4653 |
www.gmngc.com | 6589/4740; 72.1/68.9; 138/126

A "wonderful track surrounded by the Green Mountains", this Killington course sports "dramatic elevation changes" – it's "for mountain goats" – and "awesome views" on a "spectacular" Gene Bates design that's "not extremely long" but can be "unforgiving" thanks to the "tight fairways and tricky greens" ("lots of risk/reward"); the experience epitomizes "the true peacefulness of golf", so even if it is "target golf – oh, what beautiful targets."

Okemo Valley
25 | 22 | 22 | 23 | $83

Ludlow | 89 Fox Ln. | 802-228-1396 | www.okemo.com |
6434/5105; 71.1/70.1; 130/125

Vermont native Steve Durkee redid the old Fox Run track into this "gorgeous layout" sporting "spectacular views of the ski runs" on Okemo Mountain "across the road"; it's "not long", so "better golfers should play the back tees", although holes with "significant drop" and "interesting greens" ensure "you play the whole game"; P.S. there's "fantastic patio dining", so "go during the fall and enjoy the colorful surroundings."

Stratton Mountain
21 | 19 | 19 | 20 | $99

Stratton Mountain | Stratton Mountain Rd. | 802-297-2200 |
800-787-2886 | www.stratton.com
Forest/Lake | 6526/5153; 71.4/70.1; 130/120
Lake/Mountain | 6602/5410; 71.9/71.4; 125/123
Mountain/Forest | 6478/5163; 70.7/70.3; 126/120

Nestled in a "spectacular setting" at the base of Stratton Mountain, this "interesting course" has "three different nines", each offering "tight, challenging" "mountain golf with tons of blind shots" ("a bit frustrating") and water in play on 19 holes; "amazing views", a "great golf school" and a "wonderful staff" add to an "enjoyable" experience that some are "hesitant to tip off others about" – "but, hey, this is America!"

Woodstock Country Club
20 | 20 | 21 | 19 | $99

Woodstock | 14 The Green | 802-457-6674 | www.woodstockinn.com |
6052/5207; 69.7/65.7; 123/115

"Situated in the picturesque village of Woodstock", this "short but challenging" RTJ Sr. design (one of only two in Vermont) may be a "beautiful", "fairly flat course you can walk", but it's certainly "not easy": the "burbling" Kedron Brook forces players to "carry water 15 times over the 18 holes"; the experience can lead to "frustration but it's worth the effort" to test your skills in such a "lovely rustic setting."

	COURSE	FACIL.	SERVICE	VALUE	COST

Virginia

TOP COURSES IN STATE

28 Homestead, Cascades | *Roanoke*
   Golden Horseshoe, Gold | *Williamsburg*
26 Kingsmill, River | *Williamsburg*
   Royal New Kent | *Williamsburg*
   Golden Horseshoe, Green | *Williamsburg*

Charlottesville

Birdwood

| 21 | 17 | 21 | 21 | $62 |

Charlottesville | 410 Golf Course Dr. | 434-293-4653 |
www.boarsheadinn.com | 6907/5073; 74.4/69.4; 141/122

"You won't need your woods" at this Lindsay Ervin design, "one of the better university courses in the country", where "narrow fairways and doglegs beg use of the irons"; "popular with UVa students" (the college town of Charlottesville is "minutes away"), this "wonderful but difficult" layout features a "killer closing sequence", so even with "limited facilities", it delivers "good value."

⚡ Keswick Club ⌐

| 22 | 25 | 27 | 22 | $130 |

Keswick | 701 Club Dr. | 434-923-4363 | www.keswick.com |
6519/4732; 71.8/68.2; 136/118

An "elegant" course in the Blue Ridge Mountains that's "as picturesque as it is challenging", this Arnold Palmer redesign of a 1948 original blends classic and modern, with plenty of water and one of Virginia's longest par 4s, the 490-yard 9th; the "delightful round" is accompanied by "nice facilities", "superb service" (including caddies, with advance notice, in the summer) and "deluxe accommodations" at the Keswick Inn.

Wintergreen, Devil's Knob 🏌

| ▽ 24 | 19 | 22 | 23 | $89 |

Wintergreen | Rte. 664 | 434-325-8250 | 800-926-3723 |
www.wintergreenresort.com | 6712/4443; 72.2/66.7; 138/128

Thought to be Virginia's highest golf course, this "short, narrow" track in the Blue Ridge Mountains boasts cool summer temps and "dramatic elevation changes", with "challenging" holes that are "different from the norm", requiring "lots of clubbing up or down" and accuracy to survive drop-offs and slopes; what's more, the "beautiful" layout affords "great views over the Shenandoah Valley."

Wintergreen, Stoney Creek 🏌

| - | - | - | - | $107 |

Wintergreen | Rte. 664 | 434-325-8250 | 800-926-3723 |
www.wintergreenresort.com
Monocan/Shamokin | 7005/5500; 74.0/71.8; 132/127
Shamokin/Tuckahoe | 7158/5487; 74.2/72.4; 137/128
Tuckahoe/Monocan | 7081/5355; 73.8/71.6; 136/129

"A masterpiece that [demands] precision, power and finesse", this "well-maintained" Rees Jones 27-holer meanders through streams, forests and pristine wetlands in Virginia's "stunning Blue Ridge Mountains", so "you'll feel nice and alone" as you play; there's a lot of "challenge" and "diversity" among the three nines, and when you're not "concentrating on golf and nature", you can take advantage of the "good clubhouse, restaurant, pro shop and teaching staff."

	COURSE	FACIL.	SERVICE	VALUE	COST

DC Metro Area

Augustine

| 24 | 20 | 20 | 20 | $69 |

Stafford | 76 Monument Dr. | 540-720-7374 | www.augustinegolf.com | 6817/5415; 74.3/70.3; 142/124

Offering real "value in the DC area", this Rick Jacobson design delivers a "mixture of woods and open spaces", with five sets of tees that make it "enjoyable" but "challenging enough to keep the better golfers busy"; surveyors are split on course conditions, however, with some finding it "lush" and "well maintained" and others citing a "need for better upkeep" so it can be "a gem again."

Gauntlet ⌖

| 19 | 18 | 19 | 20 | $58 |

Fredericksburg | 18 Fairway Dr. | 540-752-0963 | www.golfgauntlet.com | 6857/4955; 73.4/69.6; 139/119

"P.B. Dye's diabolical hand is clearly evident" on this course located about an hour south of the DC metro area, where "small, challenging greens" and a "variety" of "interesting holes", including the daunting 17th and 18th, offer some "beautiful water plays" along with views of Curtis Lake; although many insist the "conditioning could be better" ("management has let it fall into disrepair"), it still remains an "entertaining" option for a golf outing.

Westfields

| 24 | 23 | 23 | 20 | $109 |

Clifton | 13940 Balmoral Greens Ave. | 703-631-3300 | www.westfieldsgolf.com | 6496/4597; 70.7/65.9; 130/114

"They charge top dollar, but they have a right to" at this "member-for-a-day experience" in northern Virginia, where the "enjoyable" Fred Couples creation is "carved through hardwoods with nary a house in sight" and the staff "hands out cold towels" (and warm ones on cool days) at the end of a round; "it's aged well" over more than a decade, and if some say it's "not spectacular", it happens to sit on some of "the lushest" land around.

Leesburg

Bull Run

| 18 | 16 | 18 | 18 | $90 |

Haymarket | 3520 James Madison Hwy. | 703-753-7777 | www.golfbullrun.com | 6961/6219; 73.6/68.5; 137/116

A "pleasant layout" located "out in the country" south of Leesburg, this Rick Jacobson design is "worth a look" thanks to "interesting holes" that offer "lots of room to spray the ball"; although a few feel it's "declined in recent years" and "needs work", it remains a "solid", "playable" option that also boasts one of the "DC area's least expensive daily fees."

Lansdowne Resort, Jones ⌖

| 24 | 25 | 21 | 19 | $145 |

Lansdowne | 44050 Woodridge Pkwy. | 703-729-4071 | 800-541-4801 | www.lansdowneresort.com | 7063/5165; 74.7/70.3; 145/128

For a "great getaway only minutes from Dulles International Airport", try this RTJ Jr. design, a "beautiful layout" complete with ancient rock walls, natural outcroppings and roaming wildlife ("watch out for the deer"); while a few "expected better conditions" from a semi-private course open only to members and resort guests, it does offer "wonderful practice facilities" as well as upscale accommodations that may entice you to stay "for a night or weekend."

Lansdowne Resort, Norman ⚬ ▽ | 26 | 26 | 24 | 19 | $145

Lansdowne | 44050 Woodridge Pkwy. | 703-729-4071 | 800-541-4801 | www.lansdowneresort.com | 7332/5371; 75.5/71.2; 145/130

"The two nines are a study in contrasts" at this "beautiful" Greg Norman design that pairs a "wide-open" front with a "narrow, tight and tricky" back, both of which have water on every hole courtesy of Goose Creek and the Potomac River; it also boasts fine practice facilities with a "clubhouse and locker room to match", but given its resort-guest-only status, you can expect it to be a "great value only when the company picks up the tab!"

Raspberry Falls | 24 | 22 | 21 | 21 | $105

Leesburg | 41601 Raspberry Dr. | 703-779-2555 | www.raspberryfalls.com | 7191/4854; 75.8/68.0; 141/115

Just an hour from DC, this Gary Player design is "top-flight in all respects", but you may want to "bring your passport, as the pot bunkers will remind you of Scotland" (some have sod walls so deep you "need a ladder to get out"); the raspberry farmland yields "great vistas", especially from the 3rd tee, and an "antebellum clubhouse", "beautiful practice facility" and golf academy help make this "fairly expensive" track "worth a splurge now and again."

Stonewall ⌘ | 26 | 23 | 22 | 19 | $119

Gainesville | 15601 Turtle Point Dr. | 703-753-5101 | www.stonewallgolfclub.com | 7002/4889; 74.2/67.9; 143/114

With the "prettiest vistas of any course near the Beltway", this DC-area "hidden gem" has "several great holes along Lake Manassas" that will entice you to "ignore the mega-mansions"; one of the "best public-access courses" around, it's "primo-priced" but "worth it" thanks to the "beautiful surroundings" and "immaculate" conditioning.

Virginia National | 21 | 16 | 20 | 23 | $49

Bluemont | 1400 Parker Ln. | 540-955-2966 | 888-283-4653 | www.virginianational.com | 6806/4981; 73.3/68.3; 137/116

Set on the site of a civil war battle and home to a 1799 manor house, this "remote" Shenandoah Valley course pairs a "flat front" featuring seven holes along the river with a "spectacular back" that "climbs and dips on the mountain", affording "stunning views during the long Indian summer"; although the "very modest clubhouse" has "no locker room facilities", the "friendly" staff helps make it a "good value."

Richmond

Mattaponi Springs ⌘ | - | - | - | - | $80

Ruther Glen | 22490 Penola Rd. | 804-633-7888 | www.mattaponisprings.com | 6937/4881; 73.9/69.1; 141/120

A mix of 18 distinctive holes complements the unique Virginia terrain at this "secluded retreat" whose "out-of-the-way" Ruther Glen location means "you'll feel like you own the course" as you play; it's a "real test, with some quirky holes", and given that it also boasts a "cool clubhouse" and a "great driving range" and practice area, it's considered well "worth the journey."

Roanoke

Draper Valley

| - | - | - | - | $50 |

Draper | 2800 Big Valley Dr. | 540-980-4653 | 866-980-4653 | www.drapervalleygolf.com | 7070/4683; 73.5/65.3; 127/113

You may have never heard of the architect Harold Louthen, a highway engineer, but his "wide-open" design in southwest Virginia is considered a "hidden gem", stretching over 7,000 yards across rolling terrain, with bentgrass greens and views of the Mid Mountains; walking is permitted after 2 PM, and low greens fees make it a "fun course to play."

❷ Homestead, Cascades

| 28 | 25 | 26 | 23 | $225 |

Hot Springs | 1766 Homestead Dr. | 540-839-7994 | www.thehomestead.com | 6679/4967; 73.0/70.3; 137/124

"Beautiful terrain" and "picturesque vistas" highlight this 1923 William Flynn design located 90 minutes north of Roanoke, voted Virginia's top-rated Course for its "classic mountain layout" full of "challenging holes" that "meander through trees" and around "clear, flowing streams", with "terrific", "subtle greens" and "lots of slope and elevation change"; what's more, it's part of a "fabulous resort" and spa offering "top-notch food, atmosphere" and service.

Homestead, Lower Cascades

| 25 | 24 | 26 | 22 | $125 |

Hot Springs | 1766 Homestead Dr. | 540-839-7995 | www.thehomestead.com | 6752/4710; 72.6/66.2; 134/110

"Just a small step down from the Cascades", this 1963 RTJ Sr. design is less expensive than its older sibling while still offering "pure golf the way it was meant to be" courtesy of a "challenging" layout that "plays in the valleys between mountains – a rare treat"; full of "old-world elegance", the entire resort is "a class act", with courses kept "in fabulous condition" and a staff that "knows how to take care of its customers"; P.S. "caddies are a must."

Homestead, Old

| 21 | 25 | 25 | 21 | $165 |

Hot Springs | 1766 Homestead Dr. | 540-839-7739 | www.thehomestead.com | 6227/4877; 69.0/67.7; 129/116

With the nation's oldest 1st tee in continuous use (dating back to 1892), this track offers a sense of history to go with "lots of quirky holes" – updated through the years by William Flynn, Donald Ross and Rees Jones – that promise "a challenge"; some admit they "play for the views, not the course" ("be sure to have your camera" for the 17th and 18th), but it's perfect for a "short", "relaxing round of golf."

Pete Dye River Course of Virginia Tech

| - | - | - | - | $80 |

Radford | 8400 River Course Dr. | 540-633-6732 | 888-738-3393 | www.petedyerivercourse.com | 7665/5142; 76.2/69.5; 138/120

"Great value and challenge" await the Hokies at this Virginia Tech layout that was reworked by Pete Dye in 2005 to include "maniacal mounds" on two nines that are separated by a 70-ft.-tall cliff; set "on the banks of the New River" "among the mountains" near Radford (i.e. "in the middle of nowhere"), it's a "beautiful course" that's somewhat marred by the view of "semi-clad collegians tubing on the river."

	COURSE	FACIL.	SERVICE	VALUE	COST

Primland Resort, Highland ⛳   — | — | — | — | $200

Meadows of Dan | 2200 Busted Rock Rd. | 276-222-3827 | 866-960-7746 | www.primland.com | 7053/5348; 74.6/72.3; 145/137

It's "hard to imagine a better combination of aesthetics, condition and difficulty" than at this course designed by British architect Donald Steel, who carved out a highland links layout amid the ridgetops and valleys of the Blue Ridge Mountains; the "greens are large enough to get lost on", and while it seems a bit "expensive", it boasts picturesque views overlooking a gorge and is part of a resort that also offers hunting, fishing and trail rides.

Virginia Beach

Bay Creek, Arnold Palmer ⛳   ∇ 29 | 26 | 27 | 25 | $115

Cape Charles | 1 Clubhouse Way | 757-331-8620 | 800-501-7141 | www.baycreekresort.com | 7250/5227; 75.3/71.3; 145/127

It may be "hard to get to" in historic Cape Charles, "but if you can take the time, you must" try this "terrific", Arnold Palmer–designed 7,250-yard championship course that's more player-friendly than its Nicklaus sibling and thus "wonderful for all levels"; it pampers with greens and fairways that "receive little play so are always in good shape", and the "knowledgeable staff" and "views of the Chesapeake" are added benefits.

Bay Creek, Jack Nicklaus ⛳   ∇ 27 | 23 | 26 | 25 | $115

Cape Charles | 1 Clubhouse Way | 757-331-8620 | 800-501-7141 | www.baycreekresort.com | 7417/5244; 76.3/71.9; 146/127

Set on a "terrific piece of land" in an "upscale community" along the Chesapeake Bay in southwest Virginia, this "beautiful" Jack Nicklaus design is both "challenging" and a "great value"; though some "don't like it as much as the [older] Palmer" sibling (who wants to "lose balls in high grass 10 yards from the green"?), it boasts the same "friendly" service and "well-maintained" conditions.

Williamsburg

☑ Golden Horseshoe, Gold   28 | 26 | 26 | 23 | $169

Williamsburg | 401 S. England St. | 757-220-7696 | www.goldenhorseshoegolf.com | 6817/5168; 73.8/65.5; 144/124

A "timeless" Robert Trent Jones Sr. design in Williamsburg, site of the 2007 NCAA Division 1 Men's Championship, this "tight, challenging" "oldie but goodie" is "a joy to play", with an "imaginative" routing "through pines and ponds" that features "some of the best par 3s over water anywhere"; plus a set of closing holes that "will test every golfer to the limit"; once you factor in "wonderful conditions", a "helpful staff" and "nice facilities", you have "one of the best layouts around."

Golden Horseshoe, Green   26 | 25 | 24 | 23 | $99

Williamsburg | 801 S. England St. | 757-220-7696 | www.goldenhorseshoegolf.com | 7120/5348; 74.8/66.6; 142/122

Perhaps "not as dramatic as the Gold course", this Rees Jones creation is considered "much more forgiving than its sister" (which was designed by the architect's father), with "perfectly manicured greens" and "lovely surroundings" making it "a pleasure for any level" (it hosted the 2006

Women's Public Links Championship); "excellent Southern hospitality" and carts are included in the price, although walking is allowed.

Kingsmill, Plantation 🏌️

23	26	25	21	$90

Williamsburg | 1010 Kingsmill Rd. | 757-253-3906 | 800-832-5665 | www.kingsmill.com | 6432/4880; 71.0/68.8; 128/125

A "perfect warm-up for the River", this short, "resort-style" layout is considered the "easiest of the Kingsmill courses" thanks to a "well-maintained", woman-friendly Arnold Palmer/Ed Seay design that's "always interesting", with "fairly challenging holes" that "wind through a residential area"; some suggest the "narrow fairways" are "lined by too many houses" (it feels "more like corn rows than a plantation"), but it nevertheless offers "some scenic" areas.

Kingsmill, River 🏌️

26	26	25	21	$149

Williamsburg | 1010 Kingsmill Rd. | 757-253-3906 | 800-832-5665 | www.kingsmill.com | 6831/4814; 73.1/68.4; 137/122

Considered "a must-play if you're in the Williamsburg area", this 1975 design from Pete Dye (who stopped by to renovate it in 2004) offers a "fantastic test throughout", with some claiming that "the first 15 holes are worth it just to get to the 16th–18th"; "incredible" James River views boost the "thrill" factor at this frequent LPGA Tour event host, while a "welcoming" staff adds to its status as a "superior venue."

Kingsmill, Woods 🏌️

23	23	24	23	$120

Williamsburg | 1010 Kingsmill Rd. | 757-253-3906 | 800-832-5665 | www.kingsmill.com | 6659/5148; 72.5/70.3; 139/122

Perhaps "the most interesting of the three courses at Kingsmill", this "Williamsburg-area must-play" is tucked away in a secluded, wooded corner of the resort, with a "great layout" designed by Curtis Strange and Tom Clark featuring a "signature double green" shared by the 12th and 15th; given that it also has the same "excellent facilities" as its siblings, including a golf academy, it's no wonder some surveyors dub it their "personal favorite."

Royal New Kent 🏌️

26	22	21	23	$99

Providence Forge | 10100 Kentland Rd. | 804-966-7023 | www.traditionalclubs.com | 7336/4971; 77.1/72.0; 153/130

"Even your A-game might not be enough" at this "idiosyncratic" course near Williamsburg that was "superbly designed" by Mike Strantz to be a "tough-as-nails" "time warp back to 1800s Scotland"; it might instead make you feel "like you're playing on Mars" given "long carries", "big bunkers" and "fast greens" that are "wilder than a roller coaster", but most agree the links-style layout is one of "the most innovative" – "and unforgettable" – options around.

Traditional Clubs at Kiskiack 🏌️

-	-	-	-	$99

Williamsburg | 8104 Club Dr. | 757-566-2200 | www.traditionalclubs.com | 6779/4915; 72.9/69.7; 137/119

Set on former Algonquin Native American land, this "fine course" is loaded with "varied challenges, from elevation changes to dramatic bunkering to water" (including a par-3 11th with agua on three sides) to what some consider "too many blind shots" – so "make sure you ask for hints from the pros before you play"; even though it's quite a test, it remains a "favorite choice" in the Williamsburg area.

| | COURSE | FACIL. | SERVICE | VALUE | COST |

Tradition at Stonehouse 🏠 | 25 | 21 | 22 | 22 | $99 |

Toano | 9700 Mill Pond Run | 757-566-1138 | 888-825-3436 |
www.traditionalclubs.com | 6963/5013; 75.0/69.1; 140/121
Weaving through the "fabulous rural surroundings" of central Virginia,
this "gem" is a "typical Mike Strantz" design: "big, brawny" and imaginative, with "many blind shots" and "some of the biggest greens you
will ever see", "in the most unusual places" (including two island
greens on the back nine); "good staffing" and a "nice clubhouse" help
make it "a must-play."

Washington

Bremerton

Gold Mountain, Cascade | - | - | - | - | $40 |

Bremerton | 7263 W. Belfair Valley Rd. | 360-415-5432 | www.goldmt.com |
6707/5306; 72.2/70.2; 125/119
Although "not as difficult" or "as highly regarded as the Olympic", the
older of the two Gold Mountain courses offers "a wider variety of
holes" while maintaining the same "well-kept greens and fairways",
making it "enjoyable for all levels" and "worth" the ferry ride from
Seattle; add a "great practice facility" and a "very nice clubhouse", and
you have "country-club golf and amenities at a budget price."

🅩 Gold Mountain, Olympic | 28 | 21 | 23 | 28 | $60 |

Bremerton | 7263 W. Belfair Valley Rd. | 360-415-5432 | www.goldmt.com |
7168/5220; 74.1/70.2; 135/122
"You're not likely to find a more beautiful setting" at such an "affordable" price, so enjoy "the sweeping mountain views" and rolling terrain, but "get your eye back on the ball" because this "true test" is
"tougher than its older sister"; a "must-play for anyone visiting the
Seattle area", it's a "premier public" that hosted the 2011 U.S. Jr.
Amateur Championship, explaining why it's "pretty, well run and a
pleasure to play" – in short, one of the "best values in the West."

McCormick Woods | ▽ 26 | 23 | 22 | 22 | $59 |

Port Orchard | 5155 McCormick Woods Dr. SW | 360-895-0130 |
800-323-0130 | www.mccormickwoodsgolf.com |
7040/5300; 74.3/71.6; 134/127
It may be "quite a long drive from Seattle", but "it's worth it to reach
this beautifully designed course" where no two holes border one another as it rambles through towering firs and cedar trees in an "awesome", secluded setting; although it's "difficult" enough to host top
state amateur events, it's still "fun to play" for all levels thanks to five
sets of tees, "good rates" and "well-kept" conditions.

Port Ludlow | ▽ 29 | 21 | 24 | 26 | $62 |

Port Ludlow | 751 Highland Dr. | 360-437-0272 | 888-793-1195 |
www.portludlowresort.com
Tide/Timber | 6861/5240; 73.9/71.5; 134/126
"Truly a hidden gem in the Pacific Northwest", this "old favorite"
"tucked away in the woods" on the Olympic Peninsula is "the prettiest
course" some swingers "have ever seen" thanks to two "challenging",
"beautiful" nines that are "well maintained" and offer "spectacular

views of the Puget Sound"; a "relaxing pace of play", "value" pricing and a layout that's "fair to all handicaps" are other reasons it's "worth a visit", especially "for couples."

Trophy Lake

| 25 | 23 | 22 | 25 | $85 |

Port Orchard | 3900 Lake Flora Rd. SW | 360-874-8337 | www.trophylakegolf.com | 7206/5342; 74.8/71.1; 138/127

"Hidden away" in Port Orchard, this "pearl is worth the trip" thanks to a "beautiful mountain" layout that's kept "in great shape", with "a nice variety of holes" featuring no homes on the fairways and "lots of water in play" – "folks fishing the ponds around the course makes for a unique golf experience"; what's more, you can play this "challenging but fair" John Fought design for a "reasonable rate", making it "another must-play in the Seattle area."

Olympia

NEW Salish Cliffs Golf Club, Salish Cliffs

| – | – | – | – | $89 |

Shelton | 91 W. State Rte. 108 | 360-462-3673 | www.salish-cliffs.com | 7269/5313; 75.4/70.5; 137/125

With sprawling, frilly-edged bunkers, 600-ft. elevation changes and 360-degree views of the Kamilche Valley, this Gene Bates design for the Squaxin Indian Tribe's Little Creek Casino Resort made a splashy debut in 2011; it starts with a 532-yard par 5 and ends with another gambler's par 5 of 537 yards – the perfect finish for a casino course – and you can refuel on the clubhouse's wraparound porch that over-looks the vast double green shared by the 9th and 18th holes.

Seattle

Druids Glen

| 22 | 19 | 18 | 21 | $42 |

Covington | 29925 207th Ave. SE | 253-638-1200 | www.druidsglengolf.com | 7146/5354; 75.1/66.3; 144/124

Head south of Seattle to enjoy a "fantastic view of Mt. Rainier" at this "nice" surprise where you'll "see deer and elk" but "very few houses" on a "beautiful" Keith Foster design that's also plenty "challenging", with "lots of water hazards" and over 60 sand traps; although it stretches to over 7,100 yards, "both high- and low-handicappers can enjoy it" thanks to a "fair course layout" featuring four sets of tees.

Golf Club at Newcastle, China Creek

| 21 | 26 | 23 | 16 | $80 |

Newcastle | 15500 Six Penny Ln. | 425-793-5566 | www.newcastlegolf.com | 6632/4782; 72.3/67.4; 129/115

For a view of "the Seattle skyline" that "goes on forever", head to this Bob Cupp/Fred Couples creation that may have "the occasional blind and oddly designed hole" but is still "a lot of fun"; it also boasts an "amazing clubhouse" with a "nice bar area" and outdoor patio, and while it's "expensive", "locals can get you a deal, so make friends in the area."

Golf Club at Newcastle, Coal Creek

| 22 | 25 | 24 | 15 | $125 |

Newcastle | 15500 Six Penny Ln. | 425-793-5566 | www.newcastlegolf.com | 7024/5153; 74.7/71.0; 142/123

"Sitting atop a hill" with "dramatic views of Downtown Seattle and the Olympic Mountains from nearly every tee box", this Bob Cupp/Fred

Couples collaboration features 300 feet of elevation change along with "many blind shots", "fierce winds" and "tall fescue that's nearly impossible to play out of"; although some suggest the "costly" greens fees are "a bit pricey for the overall experience", the "wonderful facilities and personnel" help to compensate.

Harbour Pointe

23 | 18 | 18 | 21 | $40

Mukilteo | 11817 Harbour Pointe Blvd. | 425-355-6060 | www.harbourpointegolf.com | 6878/4836; 73.3/69.1; 140/119

Soak in "spectacular vistas" of the Olympic Mountains at this Arthur Hills design that's a "local favorite" thanks to a "unique" layout featuring two very "different nines": the flatter, water-filled front combines with a "hilly, narrow" back to make the course "enjoyable, even if you play it every day"; located north of Seattle, it's an "all-around pleasurable experience" featuring a "view of the Puget Sound on the 11th that makes up for" the "houses lining the fairways."

Suncadia Inn, Prospector

- | - | - | - | $100

Cle Elum | 3320 Suncadia Trail | 509-649-6000 | 866-715-5050 | www.suncadia.com | 7112/5362; 73.4/70.3; 135/125

Routed through a "breathtaking Cascade Mountains setting", this Arnold Palmer design features "a lot of risk/reward holes" – the signature 10th goes downhill for 175 yards and affords panoramic views from its elevated tee; yes, "the resort's a little on the pricey side", but the "amazing" staff ensures you feel "no one is more important than you."

🆕 Suncadia Resort, Rope Rider

- | - | - | - | $100

Cle Elum | 3600 Suncadia Trail | 509-649-6400 | 866-904-6301 | www.suncadiaresort.com | 7271/6223

Named for the coal miners who worked the historic Roslyn mine nearby, the second public-access track at this residential community and resort 90 minutes east of Seattle is a walkable Peter Jacobsen/Jim Hardy creation accessible to all ages, with junior tees throughout, plus family-oriented three- and six-hole loops; still, you'll need your grown-up skills to conquer holes 7 through 9, which skirt Tipple Hill, a 120-ft.-high pile of now covered coal tailings.

White Horse

- | - | - | - | $55

Kingston | 22795 Three Lions Pl. NE | 360-297-4468 | www.whitehorsegolf.com | 7093/5673; 74.9/68.2; 144/125

Located on high ground between the Olympic and Cascade mountains, this "excellent layout" designed by Cynthia Dye McGarey (Pete Dye's niece) and updated in 2011 by John Harbottle is "just getting noticed" as a "scenic, challenging" option; construction of a new clubhouse is slated to begin sometime in 2012.

Spokane

Indian Canyon

▽ 28 | 21 | 25 | 27 | $27

Spokane | 4304 W. West Dr. | 509-747-5353 | www.spokaneparks.org | 6255/5336; 70.7/75.6; 126/136

Dating back to 1935, this municipal "must-play in Spokane" offers "lots of history" on a "classic woodland" layout that may be "seemingly easy" but offers "a unique challenge", "rewarding you for good shots and slamming you for bad ones" with its "tight fairways, lots of trees" and "hilly lies"; although the "quaint clubhouse" and "passable driving range" concern critics, the majority considers it one of the "best bangs for the buck" around.

Palouse Ridge Golf Club at Washington State University

– | **–** | **–** | **–** | **$100**

Pullman | 1260 NE Palouse Ridge Dr. | 509-335-4342 | www.palouseridge.com | 7308/5106; 75.9/69.4; 140/125

These days, the most popular classroom on the Washington State U. campus seems to be this 2008 track designed by John Harbottle, who created a sprawling layout that's routed over nearly treeless, tumbling terrain, with challenging greens and gigantic, whisker-edged bunkers; while students are schooled in course management and strategic shot placement, everyone else can warm to the mountain backdrops from across the Idaho and Oregon borders.

Tacoma

☒ Chambers Bay ♟

28 | **17** | **25** | **21** | **$109**

University Place | 6320 Grandview W. Dr. | 253-460-4653 | 877-295-4657 | www.chambersbaygolf.com | 7585/5253; 76.8/71.7; 142/130

"Worth a visit if you're in the Seattle area", this "emerging gem" is the top-rated Course in the state and will host the 2015 U.S. Open, although those who "love it" insist it's a "pure links" experience that's "worthy of a British Open" too; it "still needs to mature", but it has "unforgiving lies" that make it a "tough" "must-play"; P.S. the facilities are still being built, but there's "first-class service" and views of the Puget Sound.

Classic Golf Club

▽ **24** | **18** | **23** | **23** | **$38**

Spanaway | 4908 208th E. St. | 253-847-4440 | www.classicgolfclub.net | 6400/5656; 70.8/72.7; 130/126

"Prepare for a day of challenging golf" at this traditional William Overdorf design that features "big greens" and holes routed through "beautiful treelines"; it's the course where PGA Tour pro Ryan Moore honed his game growing up, and although there's "not much of a clubhouse", rest assured the layout is "spread out and peaceful", making it a "good value for a weekend out" while in the Tacoma area.

Washington National

25 | **18** | **20** | **20** | **$60**

Auburn | 14330 Husky Way SE | 253-333-5000 | www.washingtonnationalgolf.com | 7304/5117; 75.5/70.3; 143/120

"If you're looking for a combination of beauty and challenge", head to this relatively new "home of the Huskies" that's located "in the foothills of Mt. Rainier" and was a recent host of the NCAA Championships; "well-designed" by John Fought to feature "wide-open fairways", "undulating greens" and "tee options that truly change its difficulty", it also comes complete with a "fun pro shop" selling U. of Washington gear.

Vancouver Area

Semiahmoo Resort, Loomis Trail ⊘

– | **–** | **–** | **–** | **$90**

Blaine | 4342 Loomis Trail Rd. | 800-281-7002 | www.semiahmoo.com | 7137/5399; 75.4/71.7; 143/130

An extensive canal and lake system snakes through this Graham Cooke design, so you can expect "water, water everywhere" as you play a "beautiful, well-kept" course that's also one of the state's most "challenging" (it hosted the 2009 NCAA Division II Championship); located near the Canadian border, it has a separate clubhouse from its Semiahmoo sibling, with its own pro shop and lounge, but take note that it's open to the public on even days of the month only.

Semiahmoo Resort, Semiahmoo Course ⏱

| 24 | 22 | 23 | 21 | $90 |

Blaine | 8720 Semiahmoo Pkwy. | 800-231-4425 | www.semiahmoo.com | 7005/5288; 74.2/71.2; 140/124

The older of the two courses at the Semiahmoo Resort, this parkland "favorite" boasts a "wonderful location" on the northern Puget Sound, offering "one of the most enjoyable and quiet" experiences around; the traditional, tree-lined fairways are kept in "excellent condition", and while a few focus on the "fun layout", others "love" the entire package, so "stay at the resort and have a blast" (it's also open to the public on odd days of the month).

Walla Walla

🆕 Wine Valley Golf Club

| - | - | - | - | $85 |

Walla Walla | 176 Wine Valley Rd. | 877-333-9842 | www.winevalleygolfclub.com | 7360/5845; 75.5/68.3; 130/118

A rarity in southeastern Washington's wine country, architect Dan Hixson's full-bodied layout seven miles west of Walla Walla can be savored for its handsome, high-desert setting, gargantuan, jagged-edge bunkers and enormous, fast and skillfully contoured greens; compelling vistas of the Blue Mountains and swaying wheatgrass roughs also make it a back-to-nature destination worth seeking out.

Wenatchee

Desert Canyon 🏠

| 26 | 19 | 21 | 20 | $89 |

Orondo | 1201 Desert Canyon Blvd. | 509-784-1111 | 800-258-4173 | www.desertcanyon.com | 7285/5200; 75.3/70.2; 138/123

For "desert golf without going to Arizona", head to this Orondo-area "gem" where "the scenery is terrific" – with views of the surrounding foothills and the Columbia River – and you'll need to save your strength for the 6th hole, one of the nation's longest par 5s; some surveyors suggest this "former beauty has fallen on hard times", but a 2007 ownership change is "restoring its previous splendor" with upgrades to the course, restaurant and pro shop.

West Virginia

Davis

Canaan Valley Resort

| - | - | - | - | $56 |

Davis | Rte. 32 N. | 304-866-4121 | 800-622-4121 | www.canaanresort.com | 6856/5718; 72.9/72.5; 129/122

Proving that "West Virginia state parks have some of the finest golf" around, this 1968 Geoffrey Cornish design is set in a "beautiful" location in the Allegheny Mountains, with "wide fairways, receptive greens" and "lots of deer on the course"; given its 3,100-ft. elevation, you should "bring a jacket for those early morning rounds", and while it's over three hours from DC, staying at the adjacent resort ensures you won't need to drive far for your tee time.

Elkins

Raven at Snowshoe Mountain
– | – | – | – | $89

Snowshoe | 10 Snowshoe Dr. | 304-572-6500 | www.ravengolf.com | 6961/4295; 73.7/65.8; 141/116

Architect "Gary Player outdid himself on this remote piece of property" in Appalachia that offers a "true mountain experience" on a "beautiful" layout featuring "lots of elevation changes", "outstanding conditioning" and scenic views of the Alleghenies; the out-of-the-way facility, which doubles as a ski resort in winter, is an "adventure in nature."

Martinsburg

Cacapon Resort
– | – | – | – | $35

Berkeley Springs | 818 Cacapon Lodge Dr. | 304-258-1022 | www.cacaponresort.com | 6827/5647; 72.1/72.9; 134/128

Nestled over 2,000 feet above sea level in the foothills of Cacapon Mountain, this Robert Trent Jones Sr.-designed classic is one of West Virginia's highest courses, featuring "fun-to-play" holes that include a signature double green that's over 100 yards wide; part of a "great state park facility" offering hiking trails and a lake, it's an "excellent value", especially if you opt for one of the stay-and-play packages available at the on-site Cacapon Lodge.

Weston

Stonewall Resort, Palmer
▽ 26 | 24 | 25 | 23 | $99

Roanoke | 940 Resort Dr. | 304-269-8885 | 888-278-8150 | www.stonewallresort.com | 6227/5038; 70.0/69.6; 131/127

"A must-play anytime you're driving through West Virginia on I-79" (just two miles away), this mountain resort course is a "wonderfully shaped Arnold Palmer classic", with "scenic", "interesting holes" that require golfers to find "narrow fairways" off the tee and to "play from hillside lies to level ground"; although it's "hard to get to" near Stonewall Jackson Lake, "some of the best facilities" around, including a "great practice area", help make it worth the trip.

White Sulphur Springs

☑ Greenbrier, Greenbrier Course ⅍
25 | 28 | 28 | 22 | $285

White Sulphur Springs | 300 W. Main St. | 304-536-1110 | 800-453-4858 | www.greenbrier.com | 6675/5062; 73.1/70.3; 135/120

The "best of the three at the Greenbrier", this "classic gem" was renovated by Jack Nicklaus just prior to hosting the Ryder Cup in 1979, so "thank the golfing gods you're allowed to play" at this "heavenly" site; although the "tree-lined fairways will eat you alive", you'll still have a "relaxed experience" thanks to "conditions that match the beauty" plus the type of "attentive" and "exceptionally friendly" service you'd expect at White Sulphur Springs' "ideal golf resort."

	COURSE	FACIL.	SERVICE	VALUE	COST

☑ Greenbrier, Meadows 🏌 | 22 | 27 | 27 | 21 | $235

White Sulphur Springs | 300 W. Main St. | 304-536-1110 | 800-453-4858 |
www.greenbrier.com | 6660/4829; 72.3/68.0; 129/114

Although it's considered the "weakest of the three" at the Greenbrier,
even cynics admit this "challenging but fair" layout "has got tough
company"; still, while it's "not a favorite", it's "in good shape" after being updated by Bob Cupp in 1999 and is "lots of fun", particularly "for
anyone just starting to play a lot" – or for those who appreciate the
benefits of a classic "resort course" with panoramic mountain views.

☑ Greenbrier, Old White TPC 🏌 | 24 | 28 | 27 | 22 | $385

White Sulphur Springs | 300 W. Main St. | 304-536-1110 | 800-453-4858 |
www.greenbrier.com | 7274/5019; 75.7/69.4; 141/128

Part of a "wonderful resort" in the "scenic Allegheny Valley", this 1914
mountain "classic" (now a TPC course and home to the PGA's Greenbrier
Classic) "hearkens back to another era" and "the history is hard to ignore": the "old-style", "thinking man's course" has hosted such greats
as Ben Hogan, Sam Snead and Arnold Palmer (as well as several U.S.
presidents); it remains "in fine condition", although a couple of critics
claim they "loved it more before" it was restored to its original design.

Wisconsin

TOP COURSES IN STATE

Kohler

☑ Blackwolf Run, Meadow Valleys 🏌 | 25 | 28 | 27 | 23 | $185

Kohler | 1111 W. Riverside Dr. | 920-457-4446 | 800-618-5535 |
www.blackwolfrun.com | 7250/5065; 75.1/70.4; 145/118

Although "not as critically revered as the other courses at Kohler", this
"vastly underrated" option is perhaps the "most playable" of the resort destination's four Pete Dye designs, offering an "amazing experience" that's still "plenty hard" and filled with "beautiful scenery",
including "a great finishing hole over a river", and since it's part of the
same "first-class facility" as the River, you can expect "outstanding
service" and amenities; the 2012 U.S. Women's Open will be played
on holes from both Meadow Valleys and River.

☑ Blackwolf Run, River 🏌 ⏲ | 28 | 27 | 27 | 23 | $250

Kohler | 1111 W. Riverside Dr. | 920-457-4446 | 800-618-5535 |
www.blackwolfrun.com | 7404/5115; 76.2/70.3; 151/125

Considered the "more difficult of the two at Blackwolf Run" and
deemed by some even "better than Whistling Straits" (at least "a wonderful second"), this "shot-makers course" from Pete Dye "will humble and inspire you" with "dramatic risk/reward opportunities",
"treacherous greens" and championship tees that extend the tips to
over 7,400 yards; the "excellent facilities" include a "rustic" lodge-

style clubhouse, and it's all nestled in a "beautiful" "natural setting" in which the "river really does wind through almost every hole."

Bull at Pinehurst Farms
27 | 23 | 24 | 23 | $135

Sheboygan | 1 Long Dr. | 920-467-1500 | 800-584-3285 | www.golfthebull.com | 7354/5087; 76.6/70.4; 147/130

"One of the more aggressive courses in the area", this "outstanding" Jack Nicklaus design is a "must-play" that "makes great use of the natural terrain" in Sheboygan, with a "variety of holes" that offer "no room for errant shots"; given the "country-club conditions" and "great clubhouse and practice facility", the "price is right" – it's "cheaper than the Kohler courses" nearby.

☒ Whistling Straits, Irish 차
27 | 28 | 28 | 23 | $185

Sheboygan | N8501 County Rd. LS | 920-565-6050 | 800-618-5535 | www.americanclubresort.com | 7201/5109; 75.6/65.6; 146/121

Although it's "the little sister to the Straits", "one could easily like this course better" thanks to its "more forgiving" Pete Dye design, which doesn't front Lake Michigan but nevertheless offers a "lush, beautiful", rugged links experience that includes a "fantastic" "mix of lakes, valleys, elevation changes" and "countless bunkers of all shapes and sizes"; walking is recommended, with "professional caddies" there to ensure an "enjoyable day", and while it's "expensive", the "service and facilities are what they should be – superb."

☒ Whistling Straits, Straits 차 ⊘
29 | 29 | 28 | 23 | $360

Sheboygan | N8501 County Rd. LS | 920-565-6050 | 800-618-5535 | www.americanclubresort.com | 7790/5564; 77.2/66.4; 152/129

"Truly one of the finest in the country" and the top-rated Course in the state, this "brilliant" Pete Dye design – arguably "his best creation" – brings the links of "coastal Ireland" to "stunning" Lake Michigan; a "humbling play" that hosted the 2010 PGA Championship and is slated to host the 2020 Ryder Cup, it will also "take your breath away" with its "incredible lake views", "top-notch facilities" and "knowledgeable caddies" (required before twilight); P.S. it "carries a hefty price tag", but it's "worth every cent" for a "once-in-a-lifetime experience."

Lake Geneva

Geneva National, Gary Player ⌂
24 | 25 | 23 | 21 | $130

Lake Geneva | 1221 Geneva National Ave. S. | 262-245-7000 | www.genevanationalresort.com | 7018/4823; 74.3/68.4; 141/120

"Like its designer", this "terrific" track is "fair but challenging", delivering "some beautiful holes" with "large fairways and greens" on a layout that's "one of three very playable courses" on-site; overlooking Lake Como, it's particularly "scenic in the fall" – with "good off-season rates" to boot – and is part of an upscale facility that makes for a "first-class outing" (think "golf trip for the guys"), particularly if you take advantage of the stay-and-play packages.

Geneva National, Palmer ⌂
24 | 24 | 22 | 21 | $130

Lake Geneva | 1221 Geneva National Ave. S. | 262-245-7000 | www.genevanationalresort.com | 7171/4904; 74.7/69.4; 140/128

"No two holes are alike" on this Arnold Palmer design that's become "a Wisconsin favorite" thanks to a layout that "starts with a lake view tee-off" and then "winds into higher ground", finishing with "scenic holes on Lake Como", including a par-5 17th that's become one of Arnie's personal faves; you'll "need to play it more than once to do well", but it's "fair for all levels", "not too long" and "great for the price."

Geneva National, Trevino 🏌

| 21 | 24 | 22 | 20 | $130 |

Lake Geneva | 1221 Geneva National Ave. S. | 262-245-7000 | www.genevanationalresort.com | 7120/5193; 74.3/70.2; 136/124
While this Lee Trevino track is considered "a tad easier than the other two at Geneva National", it has "something for every swing" on a "mostly inland" layout that features some "great starting holes" followed by a few "dull ones on the back side"; still, it's "definitely better than average" when it comes to "both beauty and challenge", and it offers picturesque views of Lake Como from the ritzy Hunt Club restaurant.

Grand Geneva, Brute 🏌

| 25 | 24 | 24 | 22 | $155 |

Lake Geneva | 7036 Grand Geneva Way | 800-558-3417 | www.grandgeneva.com | 7085/5244; 73.8/70.0; 136/129
"As long as its name" suggests, this "challenging course" will require you to "bring extra balls" to tackle "lots of elevation changes" and "broad fairways" on which "everything, especially the traps and greens, is bigger than normal"; situated amid "beautiful" Lake Geneva surroundings, it's kept in "immaculate" condition and offers a "relaxed atmosphere" and upscale resort amenities, so "even if your game is off, you can't help but love it."

Grand Geneva, Highlands 🏌

| 23 | 24 | 23 | 22 | $130 |

Lake Geneva | 7036 Grand Geneva Way | 800-558-3417 | www.grandgeneva.com | 6659/5011; 71.5/68.3; 125/115
Part of a facility that "truly understands the meaning of a fine course", the younger sibling at Grand Geneva is "more fun to play than the Brute" even though its links-style "holes can be a challenge", "requiring accuracy" to deal with water hazards; you'll "get a feel for the Scottish Highlands" here ("the heather and prairie grasses are unbelievable"), and some suggest its numerous redos have "much improved the original" Jack Nicklaus/Pete Dye design.

Madison

Lawsonia, Links

| 25 | 17 | 20 | 24 | $90 |

Green Lake | 2615 S. Valley View Dr. | 920-294-3320 | www.lawsonia.com | 6764/5078; 72.8/65.2; 130/115
For "traditional links golf without going overseas", head to this "natural layout" that's "stood the test of time" (it was built in the "golden era of the 1930s"); featuring nearly 90 bunkers and "severely elevated greens" that will "make you play every shot you have", it's "one of the best and most affordable in the Midwest" and "worth the drive to Green Lake"; P.S. "combine it with Erin Hills" or a Kohler course since it's "about an hour away from both."

Lawsonia, Woodlands

| 25 | 16 | 20 | 24 | $90 |

Green Lake | 2615 S. Valley View Dr. | 920-294-3320 | www.lawsonia.com | 6618/5106; 72.7/65.2; 132/119
Set along Green Lake with steep elevation changes, this modern "treat" may be "one of the most beautiful courses in the state", so

"don't tell anyone"; "literally carved out of the woods" with "very little rough" ("it's either fairways or trees", so "bring a couple of extra sleeves if you hook or slice"), it's "totally different" than its links-style sibling, so if you're visiting this upscale resort, be sure to "play both."

Northern Bay, Castle Course   ▽ 25 | 18 | 19 | 21 | $90

Arkdale | 1844-A 20th Ave. | 608-339-2090 | 800-350-0049 | www.castleatthebay.com | 7223/5197; 74.4/69.7; 131/123

Situated on the northeast corner of Castle Rock Lake just above the Wisconsin Dells, this mix of 11 original holes and seven "very good replicas" of the world's most "famous" ones (including a mock-up of the island-green 17th at TPC Sawgrass) allows players to swing "fun, firm and fast"; it's part of a resort that offers on-site condo rentals, making it the type of place to bring family or friends on vacation.

Sentryworld   25 | 24 | 24 | 25 | $85

Stevens Point | 601 N. Michigan Ave. | 715-345-1600 | 866-479-6753 | www.sentryworld.com | 6951/5108; 73.9/70.9; 138/118

Although it's two hours north of Madison, this RTJ Jr. design "deserves to be played by enthusiasts" who enjoy a "good test, with lots of dog-legs and irregularly shaped greens with multiple tiers"; the "beautiful gardens" (most notably on the 'Flower Hole', which has an island green enveloped by over 55,000 annuals) make it "gorgeous in summer", but it's an "excellent value" at all times of the year.

Trappers Turn   ▽ 26 | 24 | 24 | 23 | $97

Wisconsin Dells | 2955 Wisconsin Dells Pkwy. | 608-253-7000 | 800-221-8876 | www.trappersturn.com
Arbor/Lake | 6958/5049; 73.5/69.4; 135/121
Canyon/Arbor | 6868/5004; 73.1/69.1; 135/120
Lake/Canyon | 6972/5021; 73.4/69.5; 136/122

"A true gem" set in the glacier-carved Wisconsin Dells countryside, this 27-hole course designed by two-time U.S. Open champ Andy North and architect Roger Packard offers views of Mystic Lake and the "enjoyable" opportunity to play your choice of three nines ("Lake/Canyon is excellent"); a regular stop for PGA events in Wisconsin, it now sports a recently renovated clubhouse that adds to its "very good value."

University Ridge   27 | 23 | 24 | 26 | $89

Verona | 9002 County Rd. PD | 608-845-7700 | 800-897-4343 | www.universityridge.com | 7259/5005; 74.9/68.9; 144/121

"Easily one of the top college courses in the U.S.", this U. of Wisconsin layout near Madison offers a "great deal for students" and Badgers team members, and "reasonable prices" for everybody else; it's a "challenging" but "fair" track that plays "like two different courses in one" – half tree-lined, half links-style – and the practice facility, which opened in 2008, makes it all the more "special."

Wild Rock   - | - | - | - | $95

Wisconsin Dells | 856 Canyon Rd. | 608-253-4653 | www.wildrockgolf.com | 7414/5132; 76.5/69.6; 141/124

A rugged Midwestern layout in the Wisconsin Dells, this Hurdzan/Fry design challenges your tee shots with roomy but rolling fairways edged with trees, sand and gravel mounds, affects your approaches with stone-dotted streams and disturbs your concentration with scenic

WISCONSIN

COURSE
FACIL.
SERVICE
VALUE
COST

vistas; Baraboo Bluffs is a highlight on the 6th, but perhaps the most dramatic hole is the 15th, a par 3 that plays over an old stone quarry.

Milwaukee

Bog, The
25 | 21 | 21 | 21 | $95

Saukville | 3121 County Hwy. I | 262-284-7075 | 800-484-3264 | www.golfthebog.com | 7221/5110; 75.3/65.4; 142/121

Located 25 miles north of Milwaukee, this 1995 Arnold Palmer design just "gets better as it gets older", offering "some of the best-rolling public-access greens in the state" on a "challenging" layout that's considered "solid" despite "three or four goofy holes"; "country-club conditions" and a large clubhouse and practice facility take the edge off "pricey" greens fees, as do preseason passes that are a "great deal."

Brown Deer Park
24 | 12 | 16 | 22 | $86

Milwaukee | 7625 N. Range Line Rd. | 414-352-8080 | www.milwaukeecountygolfcourses.com | 6759/5861; 72.9/73.8; 133/132

Whether you call it "a pleasant stroll in the park" or "a real test from the tips", this former host of the PGA Tour's U.S. Bank Championship "still holds its own" after more than 80 years, with a "solid, fair" layout that's "tree-lined the whole way"; a few feel it's "nothing spectacular" but it is "quite fun" (expect "rough up to your ankles") and a "great value" to boot, especially "for residents" of Milwaukee County.

Erin Hills ♔
27 | 25 | 25 | 23 | $200

Hartford | 7169 County Rd. O | 262-670-8600 | www.erinhills.com | 7824/5123; 77.9/69.3; 145/118

Just an hour's drive from Milwaukee, this "gem" is a "roller-coaster ride" over 652 acres of "natural", "rough-and-tumble" terrain that will "make you think on every shot"; while it may be "pricey", the combination of "outstanding" design, "delightful" service and an antique-style stone clubhouse that dishes up the "best Irish stew" (not to mention upstairs guestrooms) leads some to conclude that it'll "make history someday" – in 2017, at least, when it hosts the U.S. Open; post-Survey course renovations and an ownership change may not be reflected in the scores.

Fire Ridge
▽ 21 | 20 | 21 | 22 | $75

Grafton | 2241 County Hwy. W | 262-375-2252 | www.fireridgegc.com | 7064/5463; 74.5/72.3; 136/126

Tee it up like the pros at this former U.S. Bank Championship qualifying site that was once a country club but is now a "public course that plays like a private" one, with a signature 17th and elevated tee boxes that offer plentiful views; the variety of holes features 11 with water in play, and the facilities include a "great" bar/grill, so "plan to eat lunch!"

Naga-Waukee
▽ 22 | 12 | 16 | 22 | $55

Pewaukee | W307 N1897 Maple Ave. | 262-367-2153 | www.golfwaukeshacounty.com | 6830/5772; 72.0/72.2; 126/124

A "stout" "little local course" near Milwaukee, this layout is routed over 200 acres of wooded land, with "large greens [that] mean a lot of putts" and "great panoramic views on the back nine"; it's "always crowded" and thus "tough to get tee times", but rest assured that the course remains in "good condition for the amount of play."

Northern Wisconsin

Big Fish

| - | - | - | - | $59 |

Hayward | 14122 W. True North Ln. | 715-934-4770 | www.bigfishgolf.com | 7190/4938; 73.9/68.6; 135/116

Pete Dye delivers another "terrific layout" at this venue two hours north of the Twin Cities, where steep, strategic bunkering and tall fescue grasses characterize two distinctive nines: a "links front" with "lots of fun holes" and a back with rolling "hills and forests", including a sharply elevated 13th; together, they make for "interesting" play, and the full practice facility and grill/pub contribute to the "excellent value."

Northwood

| - | - | - | - | $45 |

Rhinelander | 3131 Golf Course Rd. | 715-282-6565 | www.northwoodgolfclub.com | 6724/5338; 73.1/71.3; 140/129

Don't be fooled by the modest length of this "great woodlands course", because "tight fairways" add a layer of challenge to a layout that's set on over 2,600 acres of rolling hills and dense forest in Wisconsin's far north (expect to see "deer and fox cross" your path); since it's "usually in good condition", this muni is considered a value "for the money."

Wyoming

Jackson

Jackson Hole Golf & Tennis ⊙

| 24 | 21 | 23 | 21 | $195 |

Jackson | 5000 Spring Gulch Rd. | 307-733-3111 | www.jhgtc.com | 7325/5375; 74.4/69.2; 133/123

With the Grand Tetons as "a spectacular backdrop", this "flat course in the mountains" near posh Jackson Hole offers "some of the best views in the world", but try to stay on task, as you can "hit it a mile in thin air" – and "that means the errant shot will also travel" that far; given its rustic location, you'll need the occasional "high fade over moose" that stray into the fairways; P.S. recent course renovations and a new clubhouse have "added a lot."

Wilson

Teton Pines 村 ⊙

∇ | 25 | 23 | 25 | 22 | $160 |

Wilson | 3450 Clubhouse Dr. | 307-733-1733 | 800-238-2223 | www.tetonpines.com | 7412/5474; 74.7/69.1; 131/124

Soak in the serenity of the Grand Teton National Forest at this Arnold Palmer/Ed Seay collaboration that's set on former ranch terrain just outside Jackson Hole; while mostly flat (try walking or taking a caddie), it boasts water on 14 holes, including a signature par-3 16th that's entirely over the drink, as well as dramatic mountain vistas and plenty of wildlife.

Private Courses

Access to play is limited to members and their guests.

Alotian Club
Roland | 101 Alotian Dr. | AR | 501-379-2568
Arkansas' answer to Augusta National is this graceful Tom Fazio creation that overlooks Lake Maumelle and which will host the prestigious Western Amateur in 2013.

Aronimink
Newtown Square | 3600 St. Davids Rd. | PA | 610-356-8000 | www.aronimink.org
Restored to its original Donald Ross design, this 1962 PGA Championship host features rugged par 4s with elevated greens.

Atlantic Golf Club
Bridgehampton | 1040 Scuttle Hole Rd. | NY | 631-537-1818 | www.atlanticgolf.org
Ocean breezes and native-grass mounding characterize Rees Jones' linksy spiritual cousin to England's Royal Birkdale.

Augusta National Golf Club
Augusta | 2604 Washington Rd. | GA | 706-667-6000 | www.masters.com
Home to the Masters Tournament, this hilly beauty at a men-only club is rich in trees, flowers, creeks and ponds.

Ballyneal Golf & Hunt Club
Holyoke | 1 Ballyneal Ln. | CO | 970-854-5900 | www.ballyneal.com
Hewn from the remote badlands of northeastern Colorado, this lay-of-the-land, walking-only 2006 Tom Doak creation features wildly undulating greens.

Baltimore Country Club, East
Timonium | 11500 Mays Chapel Rd. | MD | 410-561-3381 | www.bcc1898.com
A.W. Tillinghast crafted this host of the 1928 PGA Championship, 1932 U.S. Amateur, 1965 Walker Cup and 1988 U.S. Women's Open.

Baltusrol, Lower
Springfield | 201 Shunpike Rd. | NJ | 973-376-1900 | www.baltusrol.org
An hour from Manhattan, this club has hosted seven U.S. Opens, four on the Lower course, which closes with back-to-back par 5s.

Bel-Air Country Club
Los Angeles | 10768 Bellagio Rd. | CA | 310-472-9563 | www.bel-aircc.org
At this celebrity-studded enclave, golfers cross a barranca at the 10th via the famed 'Swinging Bridge.'

Bellerive Country Club
St. Louis | 12925 Ladue Rd. | MO | 314-434-4400 | www.bellerivecc.org
The 1965 U.S. Open, 1992 PGA Championship and 2004 U.S. Senior Open were played on RTJ Sr.'s elevated, fiercely trapped greens.

Calusa Pines Golf Club
Naples | 2000 Calusa Pines Dr. | FL | 239-348-2220 |
www.calusapinesgolfclub.com
Remarkable elevation changes for southwest Florida and innovative sand features are highlights of this 2001 Michael Hurdzan/Dana Fry design.

Camargo Club
Indian Hill | 8605 Shawnee Run Rd. | OH | www.camargoclub.com
Golden Age architect Seth Raynor crafted a wonderful variety of ravine-skirting par 3s and par 4s on this 1926 course.

Canterbury
Beachwood | 22000 S. Woodland Rd. | OH | 216-561-1000 |
www.canterburygc.org
Jack Nicklaus broke Bobby Jones' record for majors won when he took the 1973 PGA Championship on this 1922 woodlander.

Castle Pines
Castle Rock | 1000 Hummingbird Dr. | CO | 303-688-6000
At 7,559 yards, one of the PGA Tour's longest tracks is this 1982 Nicklaus design featuring sharp downhills framed in pines.

Cherry Hills Country Club
Cherry Hills Village | 4125 S. University Blvd. | CO | 303-350-5200 |
www.chcc.com
President Eisenhower's home away from home in the Rockies has hosted numerous championships, including the 1960 U.S. Open.

Chicago Golf Club
Wheaton | 25W253 Warrenville Rd. | IL | 630-665-2988
Considered American golf royalty, this 1892 classic was the first 18-holer in the country and has hosted U.S. Opens three times, in 1897, 1900 and 1911.

Colonial Country Club
Ft. Worth | 3735 Country Club Circle | TX | 817-927-4221 |
www.colonialfw.com
Ben Hogan won the PGA Tour's Colonial National Invitational five times here, providing the track its nickname, 'Hogan's Alley.'

Congressional Country Club, Blue
Bethesda | 8500 River Rd. | MD | 301-469-2032 | www.ccclub.org
This host of the 1964 and 1997 U.S. Opens was redone by Robert Trent Jones Sr. and son Rees in 1960 and 1989, respectively.

Country Club, The, Clyde/Squirrel
Brookline | 191 Clyde St. | MA | 617-566-0244 | www.tcclub.org
A Boston Brahmin enclave for more than 100 years, this tree-lined lay-out has hosted three U.S. Opens and the 1999 Ryder Cup.

Country Club of Fairfield
Fairfield | 936 Sasco Hill Rd. | CT | 203-254-2722 |
www.ccfairfield.com
Seth Raynor's 1914 breeze-fueled classic serves up a stout collection of par 4s plus handsome vistas of Long Island Sound.

Creek Club
Locust Valley | 1 Horse Hollow Rd. | NY | 516-671-1001
Wooded and links holes, an island green and lovely views of Long Island Sound are on offer at this short but exciting 1923 layout.

Crooked Stick
Carmel | 1964 Burning Tree Ln. | IN | 317-844-9938 | www.crookedstick.org
This Pete Dye design was the host of the 1991 PGA Championship, 1993 U.S. Women's Open and 2005 Solheim Cup.

Crystal Downs Country Club
Frankfort | 249 E. Crystal Downs Dr. | MI | 231-352-7979
Atop a bluff between Lake Michigan and Crystal Lake, Alister MacKenzie's windswept gem is thick with native rough.

Cypress Point Club
Pebble Beach | 3150 17-Mile Dr. | CA | 831-624-2223 | www.montereypeninsulagolf.com
Alister MacKenzie's seasider near Pebble Beach Resort hosted the PGA Tour's Bing Crosby National Pro-Am.

Desert Forest
Carefree | 37207 N. Mule Train Rd. | AZ | 480-488-4589 | www.desertforestgolfclub.com
Fairways and back-to-front sloping greens hemmed in by cacti demand accuracy on this desert beauty with mountain views.

Double Eagle Club
Galena | 6025 Cheshire Rd. | OH | 740-548-4017 | www.doubleeagleclub.net
This Weiskopf/Morrish track boasts dual fairways and conditioning so superb that the tee boxes could double as greens.

East Lake Golf Club
Atlanta | 2575 Alston Dr. SE | GA | 404-373-5722 | www.eastlakegolfclub.com
Bobby Jones' boyhood playground is reborn with a 1994 Rees Jones redesign and a caddie program for local underserved youth.

Estancia Club
Scottsdale | 27998 N. 99th Pl. | AZ | 480-473-4400 | www.estanciaclub.com
Tom Fazio set the tee boxes and greens on high desert outcroppings at this enclave that climbs Pinnacle Peak.

Eugene Country Club
Eugene | 255 Country Club Rd. | OR | 541-345-0181 | www.eugenecountryclub.com
In 1967, Robert Trent Jones Sr. reversed the tees and greens and enlarged the water hazards on this 1924 tree-laden track.

Firestone Country Club, South
Akron | 452 E. Warner Rd. | OH | 330-644-8441 | www.firestonecountryclub.com
RTJ Sr.'s redesign has hosted PGA Championships, the 2002 Senior PGA Championship and the World Series of Golf.

Fishers Island Club

Fishers Island | Fishers Island | NY | 631-788-7223 |
www.fishersislandclub.com
At a society retreat on Long Island Sound, this 1926 Seth Raynor links design is known for its Atlantic shore vistas.

Forest Highlands, Canyon

Flagstaff | 2425 William Palmer | AZ | 928-525-5200 | www.fhgc.com
Par 5s over 600 yards long are made more manageable by the 7,000-ft. altitude of this Weiskopf/Morrish design.

Friar's Head

Baiting Hollow | 3000 Sound Ave. | NY | 631-722-5200 |
www.friarshead.org
Tree-lined dunes, open meadows and blufftop views of CT and Long Island Sound spice the play on this Coore/Crenshaw design.

Garden City Golf Club

Garden City | 315 Stewart Ave. | NY | 516-746-8360
Host of the 1902 U.S. Open, this Long Island men-only institution plays like a British links, with tall fescue, bunkers and sea breezes.

Golf Club, The

New Albany | 4522 Kitzmiller Rd. | OH | 614-855-7326
Hidden at a men-only club, this early Pete Dye layout offers tall native rough, clever bunkers and outstanding par 5s.

Gozzer Ranch Golf & Lake Club

Coeur d'Alene | 5399 S. Gozzer Rd. | ID | 208-765-9034 |
www.gozzerranchclub.com
Rocky bluffs with 100-ft. spires, tattered-edge bunkers and dazzling vistas of Lake Coeur d'Alene are highlights of this 2007 Tom Fazio design.

Grandfather Golf & Country Club

Linville | 2120 Hwy. 105 S. | NC | 828-898-4531 |
www.grandfatherclubnc.org
In a high Blue Ridge valley next to the Linville River, this hilly design looks up through the pines at Grandfather Mountain.

Hazeltine National

Chaska | 1900 Hazeltine Blvd. | MN | 952-556-5401 |
www.hngc.com
Designed by RTJ Sr. and reworked by his son Rees, this farm/forest blend hosted the 1991 U.S. Open and 2002 PGA Championship.

Honors Course

Ooltewah | 9603 Lee Hwy. | TN | 423-238-9123 |
www.honorscourse.net
Tiger Woods' winning final-round 80 at the 1996 Men's NCAA Championship testifies to the difficulty of this Pete Dye design.

Interlachen Country Club

Edina | 6200 Interlachen Blvd. | MN | 952-929-1661 |
www.interlachencc.org
Bobby Jones skipped his second shot across the pond at the 9th to win the 1930 U.S. Open here in his Grand Slam year.

Inverness Club
Toledo | 4601 Dorr St. | OH | 419-578-9000 |
www.invernessclub.com
Donald Ross' centenarian remains a superb test; just ask Bob Tway,
who holed a sand shot here to win the 1986 PGA Championship.

Jupiter Hills Club, Hills
Tequesta | 11800 Hill Club Terrace SE | FL | 561-746-5228 |
www.jupiterhillsclub.org
Bob Hope and auto executive William Clay Ford were among the
founders of this track featuring 70 feet of elevation changes.

Kinloch
Manakin-Sabot | 100 Kinloch Ln. | VA | 804-784-8000 |
www.kinlochgolfclub.com
Near Richmond, this millennial design from Lester George and Vinny
Giles offers multiple avenues of play on nearly every hole.

Kittansett Club
Marion | 11 Point Rd. | MA | 508-748-0148 | www.kittansett.org
Windy Buzzards Bay is home to the 1953 Walker Cup Match host,
where the 3rd plays to an island green encircled by sand.

Laurel Valley
Ligonier | 175 Palmer Dr. | PA | 724-238-9555
On an old pheasant-hunting preserve sits this host of the 1965 PGA
Championship, 1975 Ryder Cup and 1989 U.S. Senior Open.

Long Cove Club
Hilton Head Island | 399 Long Cove Dr. | SC | 843-686-1070 |
www.longcoveclub.org
This 28-year-old Pete Dye design is laced with live oaks, palmettos
and waste bunkers on its amazing variety of holes.

Los Angeles Country Club, North
Los Angeles | 10101 Wilshire Blvd. | CA | 310-276-6104 |
www.thelacc.org
George Thomas' layout sits on pricey real estate at the meeting of
Santa Monica and Wilshire Boulevards near Beverly Hills.

Maidstone Club
East Hampton | 50 Old Beach Ln. | NY | 631-324-0510 |
www.maidstoneclub.org
The 19th-century links design at this tony Hamptons club is awash in
ocean breezes that make it play much longer than its yardage.

Medinah Country Club, No. 3
Medinah | 6N001 Medinah Rd. | IL | 630-773-1700 | www.medinahcc.org
Tiger Woods captured both the 1999 and 2006 PGA Championships
on this wooded brute with par 3s that play over Lake Kadijah.

Merion Golf Club, East
Ardmore | 450 Ardmore Ave. | PA | 610-642-5600 |
www.meriongolfclub.com
Bobby Jones clinched his Grand Slam in 1930 at this Main Line
Philadelphia classic's famed 'Babbling Brook' hole.

Milwaukee Country Club

River Hills | 8000 N. Range Line Rd. | WI | 414-362-5200 |
www.themilwaukeecountryclub.org
The host of the 1969 Walker Cup Match features a wooded back nine
that tumbles down to the Milwaukee River.

Monterey Peninsula Country Club, Shore

Pebble Beach | 3000 Club Rd. | CA | 831-373-1556 | www.mpccpb.org
Mike Strantz's 2004 redesign catapulted this oceanside test studded
with gnarled cypress trees to co-host status at the PGA Tour's AT&T
Pebble Beach event.

Muirfield Village

Dublin | 5750 Memorial Dr. | OH | 614-889-6700 |
www.thememorialtournament.com
Jack Nicklaus designed this track to host his own Memorial
Tournament, won by Tiger Woods in 1999, 2000 and 2001.

Myopia Hunt Club

South Hamilton | 435 Bay Rd. | MA | 978-468-4433 |
www.myopiahuntclub.org
The hilly host of four U.S. Opens in 1898–1908 provides a solid, old-
style test, thanks to bunkering and vexing putting surfaces.

Nanea Golf Club

Kailua-Kona | 72-2921 Kaupulehu Rd. | HI | 808-930-1300
David McLay Kidd etched a links-style, mountainside layout atop volcanic lava with elevated views of the Pacific from every hole.

Nantucket Golf Club

Siasconset | 250 Milestone Rd. | MA | 508-257-8520 |
www.nantucketgolfclub.com
Coastal gusts complicate this British links–style Rees Jones design, a
7,081-yard-long throwback to an earlier era.

National Golf Links of America

Southampton | 16 Sebonac Rd. | NY | 631-283-0410
This centenarian on Great Peconic Bay is by Charles Blair Macdonald,
who modeled creations after the British Isles' best.

Oak Hill Country Club, East

Rochester | 346 Kilbourn Rd. | NY | 585-586-1660 | www.oakhillcc.com
Host to three U.S. Opens and the 1995 Ryder Cup Match, Donald
Ross' 1920s design calls for long, accurate shot-making.

Oakland Hills Country Club, South

Bloomfield Hills | 3951 W. Maple Rd. | MI | 248-644-2500 |
www.oaklandhillscc.com
Ben Hogan called this track a 'monster', but he tamed its undulating
greens and many bunkers to win the 1951 U.S. Open.

Oakmont Country Club

Oakmont | 1233 Hulton Rd. | PA | 412-828-8000 |
www.oakmontcc.org
Host to its eighth U.S. Open in 2007, this centenarian has the most
bunkers and the largest, fastest greens in championship golf.

PRIVATE COURSES

Oak Tree National
Edmond | 1515 W. Oak Tree Dr. | OK | 405-348-2004 |
www.oaktreenational.com
Amid prairie gusts, Pete Dye dishes up undulations, moguls and superb variety for events like the 1988 PGA Championship.

Ocean Forest
Sea Island | 200 Ocean Rd. | GA | 912-638-5834
On an Atlantic island, Rees Jones' fairly flat mix of wooded holes and windy, open links hosted the 2001 Walker Cup Match.

Old Sandwich Golf Club
Plymouth | 41 Doublebrook Rd. | MA | 508-209-2200 |
www.osgolfclub.com
Bill Coore and Ben Crenshaw carved out this low-key, strategy-infused layout near Boston, where crowns and hollows amid pine-studded sandy terrain make for a superior short-game experience.

Olympia Fields Country Club, North
Olympia Fields | 2800 Country Club Dr. | IL | 708-748-0495 |
www.ofcc.info
The North course first hosted the U.S. Open in 1928 and just recently hosted it for a second time in 2003.

Olympic Club, The Lake
San Francisco | 599 Skyline Blvd. | CA | 415-404-4300 |
www.olyclub.com
You can see the Golden Gate Bridge from the 3rd tee of this pine-, cedar- and cypress-laced four-time U.S. Open site.

Peachtree Golf Club
Atlanta | 4600 Peachtree Rd. NE | GA | 404-233-4428
A onetime-only Bobby Jones/RTJ Sr. co-design, this hilly, forested Southerner boasts broad fairways and huge greens.

Pete Dye Golf Club
Bridgeport | 801 Aaron Smith Dr. | WV | 304-842-2801 |
www.petedye.com
Routed over a former strip coal mine, this undulating namesake forces healthy carries across Simpson Creek.

Pine Valley Golf Club
Pine Valley | E. Atlantic Ave. | NJ | 856-783-3000
This brutal but beautiful favorite dishes out multiple forced carries on holes hopscotching from one island of turf to the next.

Piping Rock Club
Locust Valley | 150 Piping Rock Rd. | NY | 516-676-2332 |
www.pipingrockclub.org
Near where Matinecock Indians smoked peace pipes, this 1911 design retooled in the '80s pays homage to Britain's best.

Plainfield Country Club
Edison | 1591 Woodland Ave. | NJ | 908-757-1800 | www.plainfieldcc.com
Host of the 1978 U.S. Amateur and 1987 U.S. Women's Open, this classic sports cross bunkers and contoured greens.

Prairie Dunes Country Club

Hutchinson | 4812 E. 30th Ave. | KS | 620-662-7301 | www.prairiedunes.com
Amid sandhills, yuca and plum thickets, this rolling, windswept layout
proved a formidable test at the 2002 U.S. Women's Open.

Quaker Ridge

Scarsdale | 146 Griffen Ave. | NY | 914-725-1100 | www.quakerridgegc.org
Hidden next to Winged Foot, this A.W. Tillinghast design boasts outstanding par 4s and was host to the 1997 Walker Cup Match.

Quarry at La Quinta

La Quinta | 1 Quarry Ln. | CA | 760-777-1100 | www.quarryinfo.com
Every hole offers scenic desert backdrops at this Palm Springs–area
Tom Fazio course that's draped across mountain slopes.

Ridgewood Country Club

Paramus | 96 W. Midland Ave. | NJ | 201-599-3900 | www.rcc1890.com
A.W. Tillinghast's 27-holer hosted the 1935 Ryder Cup, 1990 U.S.
Senior Open and 2001 Senior PGA Championship.

Riviera Country Club

Pacific Palisades | 1250 Capri Dr. | CA | 310-454-6591 | www.rccla.com
Host of the PGA Tour's Nissan Open, this eucalyptus-lined layout sits
in a canyon south of Sunset Boulevard.

Robert Trent Jones Golf Club

Gainesville | 1 Turtle Point Dr. | VA | 703-754-4050 | www.rtjgc.com
Named for the dean of U.S. golf architects, this former Presidents Cup
host is chock-full of water hazards and puzzle-piece bunkers.

Sahalee Country Club

Sammamish | 21200 Sahalee Country Club Dr. NE | WA |
425-868-8800 | www.sahalee.com
Meaning 'high, heavenly ground' in Chinook, this 1998 PGA
Championship site is bracketed by cedars, firs and hemlocks.

Salem Country Club

Peabody | 133 Forest St. | MA | 978-538-5400 |
www.salemcountryclub.org
Amid maples, oaks and pines, this Donald Ross design has hosted two
U.S. Women's Opens and the 2001 U.S. Senior Open.

Sand Hills

Mullen | 36410 Sand Hills Rd. | NE | 308-546-2237
This Bill Coore/Ben Crenshaw links, a noteworthy post–World War II
design, takes full advantage of its sandy, rolling terrain.

San Francisco Golf Club

San Francisco | 1310 Junipero Serra Blvd | CA | 415-469-4100
A.W. Tillinghast designed this beauty that features massive cypresses
and sensational bunkering, but nary a water hazard.

Scioto Country Club

Columbus | 2196 Riverside Dr. | OH | 614-486-4341 | www.sciotocc.com
Jack Nicklaus learned to play on this classic that's hosted the U.S.
Open, Ryder Cup, PGA Championship and U.S. Senior Open.

Sebonack Golf Club
Southampton | 405 Sebonac Rd. | NY | 631-287-4444 |
www.sebonack.com
Jack Nicklaus and Tom Doak meshed their design skills to create a
seaside gem that abuts the National Golf Links of America overlooking
the Great Peconic Bay.

Seminole
Juno Beach | 901 Seminole Blvd. | FL | 561-626-1331
At a posh retreat, this Donald Ross gem challenges with sea grape
bushes, palms, ocean breezes and nearly 200 bunkers.

Shinnecock Hills
Southampton | 200 Tuckahoe Rd. | NY | 631-283-1310
Wedged between the Atlantic Ocean and Great Peconic Bay, this links
was the site of the U.S. Open in 1986, 1995 and 2004.

Shoal Creek
Shoal Creek | 100 New Williamsburg Dr. | AL | 205-991-9000 |
www.shoalcreekclub.com
The 1984 and 1990 PGA Championships were played on this Nicklaus
course carved from dense forest.

Shoreacres
Lake Bluff | 1601 Shore Acres Rd. | IL | 847-234-1470 |
www.shoreacres1916.com
On Chicago's North Shore, this short but sweet 1921 Seth Raynor
masterpiece offers several exciting shots over steep ravines.

Somerset Hills Country Club
Bernardsville | 180 Mine Mount Rd. | NJ | 908-766-0043 |
www.somersetcc.org
Near the USGA headquarters sits this A.W. Tillinghast design featuring a well-bunkered front nine and a heavily wooded back.

Southern Hills Country Club
Tulsa | 2636 E. 61st St. | OK | 918-492-3351 | www.southernhillscc.com
Host of the 2001 U.S. Open and 2007 PGA Championship, this Perry
Maxwell parklander features Bermuda rough and prairie wind.

Stanwich Club
Greenwich | 888 North St. | CT | 203-869-0555 | www.stanwich.com
Fast greens, large bunkers, multiple water hazards and double-dogleg
par 5s make this 1962 design the state's toughest course.

Trump International Golf Club
West Palm Beach | 3505 Summit Blvd. | FL | 561-682-0700 |
www.trumpinternationalpalmbeaches.com
The host to the LPGA's ADT Championship features risk/reward holes
designed by Jim Fazio, with input from The Donald himself.

Trump National Golf Club, Briarcliff Manor
Briarcliff Manor | 339 Pine Rd. | NY | 914-944-0900 |
www.trumpnationalwestchester.com
A celebrity-laden membership enjoys this Jim Fazio/Donald Trump
design with a spectacular 'waterfall' par-3 13th.

Trump National Golf Club, Bedminster
Bedminster | 900 Lamington Rd. | NJ | 908-470-4400 |
www.trumpnationalbedminster.com
Hewn from John DeLorean's former estate in rolling horse country is
this sleek, gull-winged Tom Fazio beauty.

Valley Club of Montecito
Santa Barbara | 1901 E. Valley Rd. | CA | 805-969-2215
Amid sycamore and eucalyptus groves, this 1929 Alister MacKenzie
design offers stylish bunkering and superior par 3s.

Victoria National
Newburgh | 2000 Victoria National Blvd. | IN | 812-858-8230 |
www.victorianational.com
Tom Fazio transformed an old strip mine into this gorgeous layout featuring lush mounding and small ponds.

Wade Hampton Golf Club
Cashiers | Hwy. 107 S. | NC | 828-743-5465 | www.wadehamptongc.com
In the Smoky Mountains, Tom Fazio's 1987 design winds through a
valley heavy with pines and crisscrossed by clear streams.

Wannamoisett Country Club
Rumford | 96 Hoyt Ave. | RI | 401-434-1200 | www.wannamoisett.com
Donald Ross' rare par 69 is crammed into 104 acres yet still packs a
wallop with long, strong par 4s and speedy, undulating greens.

Whisper Rock, Lower
Scottsdale | 32000 N. Old Bridge Rd. | AZ | 480-575-8700
Lined in saguaro, prickly pear and ocotillo, Phil Mickelson's debut offers superb par 4s and risk/reward par 5s.

Winged Foot, East
Mamaroneck | 851 Fennimore Rd. | NY | 914-698-8400 | www.wfgc.info
West's shorter sister sports handsome par 3s and a tournament pedigree, including the inaugural U.S. Senior Open in 1980.

Winged Foot, West
Mamaroneck | 851 Fennimore Rd. | NY | 914-698-8400 | www.wfgc.info
A.W. Tillinghast designed this five-time U.S. Open test with pear-
shaped greens and deep bunkers on rolling parkland.

Yeamans Hall Club
Hanahan | 900 Yeamans Hall Rd. | SC | 843-744-5555 |
www.yeamanshallclub.com
In 1998, Tom Doak restored this layout to its 1925 glory with huge
square greens, yawning traps and aged oaks.

Urban Driving Ranges

Within a short ride from a major business district

Atlanta

Charlie Yates Golf Course
Atlanta | 10 Lakeside Village Dr. SE | 404-373-4655 |
www.charlieyatesgolfcourse.com

Steel Canyon Golf Club
Atlanta | 460 Morgan Falls Rd. | 770-390-0424 |
www.steelcanyongolfclub.com

Boston

CityGolf Boston
Boston | 38 Bromfield St. | 617-357-4653 | www.citygolfboston.com

Burbank

John Wells Golf Center
North Hollywood | 11501 Strathern St. | 818-767-1954 |
www.johnwellsgolfcenter.com

Chicago

Diversey Driving Range
Chicago | 141 W. Diversey Pkwy. | 312-742-7929 | www.cpdgolf.com

Dallas

Hank Haney Golf Ranch at Vista Ridge
Dallas | 2300 N. Stemmons Fwy. | 972-315-5300 | www.hankhaney.com

North Texas Golf Center
Dallas | 2101 Walnut Hill Ln. | 972-247-4653 | www.northtexasgolf.com

Denver

Kennedy Golf Course
Denver | 10500 E. Hampden Ave. | 720-865-0720 |
www.cityofdenvergolf.com

Overland Park Golf Course
Denver | 1801 S. Huron St. | 303-777-7331 | www.overlandgolfcourse.com

Houston

Clear Creek
Houston | 3902 Fellows Rd. | 713-738-8000 | www.clearcreekgolfclub.com

Las Vegas

Callaway Golf Center
Las Vegas | 6730 Las Vegas Blvd. S. | 702-896-4100 | 866-897-9500 |
www.callawaygolfcenter.com

Los Angeles

Griffith Park Golf Courses
Los Angeles | 4730 Crystal Springs Dr. | 323-663-2555 | www.laparks.org

Lakes at El Segundo
El Segundo | 400 S. Sepulveda Blvd. | 310-322-0202 | www.golfthelakes.com

Rancho Park Golf Course
Los Angeles | 10460 W. Pico Blvd. | 310-838-7373 | www.golf.lacity.org

New York City

Alley Pond Golf Center
Queens | 232-01 Northern Blvd. | 718-225-9187

Brooklyn Golf Center
Brooklyn | 3200 Flatbush Ave. | 718-253-6816 | www.brooklyngolfcenter.com

Chelsea Piers Golf Club
Manhattan | Pier 59 | 212-336-6400 | www.chelseapiers.com

Randall's Island Golf Center
Manhattan | 1 Randall's Island | 212-427-5689 |
www.randallsislandgolfcenter.com

Oahu

Coral Creek Driving Range
Ewa Beach | 91-1111 Geiger Rd. | 808-441-4653 | 888-868-3387 |
www.coralcreekgolfhawaii.com

Philadelphia

FDR Golf Club
Philadelphia | 1954 Pattison Ave. | 215-462-8997 | 866-785-2635 |
www.golfphilly.org

Karakung at Cobb's Creek
Philadelphia | 7400 Lansdowne Ave. | 215-877-8707 |
866-785-2635 | www.golfphilly.org

San Diego

JR South Bay Golf
San Diego | 540 Hollister St. | 619-575-7891

Stadium Golf Center
San Diego | 29-90 Murphy Canyon Rd. | 858-277-6667 |
www.stadiumgolfcenter.com

Seattle

Interbay Golf Center
Seattle | 2501 15th Ave. W. | 206-285-2200 | www.seattlegolf.com

Jefferson Park Golf Course
Seattle | 4101 Beacon Ave. S. | 206-762-4513 | www.seattlegolf.com

West Seattle Golf Course
Seattle | 4470 35th Ave. SW | 206-935-5187 | www.seattlegolf.com

Washington, DC

East Potomac Park Golf Course
Washington | 972 Ohio Dr. SW | 202-554-7660 | www.golfdc.com

INDEXES

Listings cover the best in each category, with names followed by nearest major city. Some indexes (e.g. Fine Food Too, Instruction) list clubs rather than individual courses.

ADDITIONS

Ballamor Golf Club | *Atlantic City, NJ*
Bandon Dunes, Old Macdonald |
    Coos Bay, OR
Cape Fear Nat'l | *Myrtle Beach Area, NC*
CommonGround | *Denver, CO*
Conestoga | *Las Vegas, NV*
Cougar Canyon | *Colorado Springs, CO*
Doral Resort, Jim McLean | *Miami, FL*
Dormie Club | *Raleigh-Durham, NC*
Escena | *Palm Springs, CA*
FarmLinks/Pursell Farms |
    Birmingham, AL
Firekeeper | *Topeka, KS*
French Lick, Pete Dye | *French Lick, IN*
Gray's Crossing | *Lake Tahoe, CA*
Harbor Shores | *Kalamazoo, MI*
Lonnie Poole/NC State Univ. |
    Raleigh-Durham, NC
Mirimichi | *Memphis, TN*
Old American Club | *Dallas, TX*
Prairie Club, Dunes | *Valentine, NE*
Prairie Club, Pines | *Valentine, NE*
Pronghorn Club, Nicklaus | *Bend, OR*
Quintero Golf, Founders | *Phoenix, AZ*
Ross Creek Landing | *Nashville, TN*
Salish Cliffs | *Olympia, WA*
Schaffer's Mill Club | *Lake Tahoe, CA*
Seneca Hickory Stick | *Finger Lakes, NY*
Sequoyah Nat'l | *Asheville, NC*
Southern Dunes Golf Club | *Phoenix, AZ*
Stone Canyon Golf Club |
    Kansas City, MO
Sugarloaf Mtn. | *Orlando, FL*
Suncadia Resort, Rope Rider |
    Seattle, WA
Superstition Mtn., Prospector |
    Phoenix, AZ
TPC San Antonio, AT&T Canyons |
    San Antonio, TX
TPC San Antonio, AT&T Oaks |
    San Antonio, TX
Victory Ranch | *Salt Lake City, UT*
Waldorf Astoria | *Orlando, FL*
Wine Valley | *Walla Walla, WA*

BUDGET

($50 and under)
Ala Wai | *Oahu, HI*
Aldeen | *Chicago, IL*

Alvamar Public | *Kansas City, KS*
Annbriar | *St. Louis Area, IL*
Apache Stronghold | *San Carlos, AZ*
Back Creek | *Wilmington, DE*
Baker Nat'l | *Minneapolis, MN*
Bear Trace | *Chattanooga, TN*
🔢 Bethpage, Blue | *Long Island, NY*
Bethpage, Green | *Long Island, NY*
Black Bear | *Orlando, FL*
Bloomingdale | *Tampa, FL*
Bluffs | *Vermillion, SD*
Breakfast Hill |
    Southern New Hampshire, NH
Bretwood, North |
    Southern New Hampshire, NH
Buffalo Dunes | *Garden City, KS*
Buffalo Run | *Denver, CO*
Bull/Boone's Trace | *Lexington, KY*
Cacapon Resort | *Martinsburg, WV*
Chenango Valley | *Finger Lakes, NY*
Cherokee Run | *Atlanta, GA*
Chestnut Ridge,
    Chestnut Ridge Course |
    Pittsburgh, PA
Classic Golf Club | *Tacoma, WA*
Cooks Creek | *Columbus, OH*
Copper Mill | *Baton Rouge, LA*
Diamond Woods | *Eugene, OR*
Draper Valley | *Roanoke, VA*
Druids Glen | *Seattle, WA*
Eagleglen | *Anchorage, AK*
El Diablo | *Ocala, FL*
Emerald Valley | *Eugene, OR*
Exeter | *Southern Rhode Island, RI*
Finkbine | *Iowa City, IA*
Forest Akers MSU, West | *Lansing, MI*
Gateway Nat'l | *St. Louis Area, IL*
Glenwood | *Hot Springs, AR*
Gold Mtn., Cascade | *Bremerton, WA*
Golf Club/Red Rock | *Rapid City, SD*
Granville | *Columbus, OH*
Harbour Pointe | *Seattle, WA*
Heritage Bluffs | *Chicago, IL*
Heron Lakes, Great Blue | *Portland, OR*
Indian Canyon | *Spokane, WA*
Indian Creek | *Omaha, NE*
Indian Peaks | *Boulder, CO*
Kearney Hill | *Lexington, KY*
Les Bolstad | *Minneapolis, MN*

Vote at zagat.com

BUNKERING

Marriott Shadow Ridge | *Palm Springs, CA*

Marriott's Wildfire, Faldo Championship | *Phoenix, AZ*

Murphy Creek | *Denver, CO*

Ojai Valley Inn | *Los Angeles, CA*

Palmetto Dunes, George Fazio | *Hilton Head, SC*

Palmetto Hall, Robert Cupp | *Hilton Head, SC*

PGA Golf Club, Dye | *Port St. Lucie, FL*

PGA West, Stadium | *Palm Springs, CA*

Pilgrim's Run | *Grand Rapids, MI*

🄏 Purgatory | *Indianapolis, IN*

🄏 Raven/Three Peaks | *Vail, CO*

Rawls/TX Tech | *Lubbock, TX*

🄏 Red Sky, Norman | *Vail, CO*

Red Tail | *Worcester, MA*

Reunion Resort, Tom Watson | *Orlando, FL*

Rustic Canyon | *Los Angeles, CA*

Saddle Creek | *Stockton, CA*

NEW Salish Cliffs | *Olympia, WA*

Sand Barrens | *Cape May, NJ*

🄏 Sea Island, Seaside | *Low Country, GA*

Shadow Creek | *Las Vegas, NV*

Shore Gate | *Atlantic City, NJ*

Southern Dunes | *Orlando, FL*

Talking Stick, North | *Scottsdale, AZ*

Tanglewood Park, Championship | *Winston-Salem, NC*

NEW TPC San Antonio, AT&T Oaks | *San Antonio, TX*

🄏 TPC Sawgrass, PLAYERS Stadium | *Jacksonville, FL*

TPC Tampa Bay | *Tampa, FL*

Trump Nat'l | *Los Angeles, CA*

Walt Disney World, Magnolia | *Orlando, FL*

🄏 Whistling Straits, Irish | *Kohler, WI*

NEW Wine Valley | *Walla Walla, WA*

🄏 World Woods, Pine Barrens | *Tampa, FL*

CELEBRITY DESIGNS

ARNOLD PALMER
(Design and Signature)

Angel Park, Mountain | *Las Vegas, NV*

Angel Park, Palm | *Las Vegas, NV*

🄏 Aviara | *San Diego, CA*

Barton Creek, Palmer Lakeside | *Austin, TX*

Bay Creek, Arnold Palmer | *Virginia Beach, VA*

Bluffs | *Baton Rouge, LA*

Bog | *Milwaukee, WI*

Bridges/Hollywood Casino | *Gulfport, MS*

Carolina Club | *Pinehurst, NC*

Cherokee Run | *Atlanta, GA*

Classic Club | *Palm Springs, CA*

Craft Farms, Cotton Creek | *Mobile, AL*

Geneva Nat'l, Palmer | *Lake Geneva, WI*

Gillette Ridge | *Hartford, CT*

🄏 Grand View Lodge, Deacon's | *Brainerd, MN*

Half Moon Bay, Old Course | *San Francisco Bay Area, CA*

Hawaii Prince | *Oahu, HI*

🄏 Kapalua, Bay | *Maui, HI*

🄏 Keswick Club | *Charlottesville, VA*

Kingsmill, Plantation | *Williamsburg, VA*

🄏 La Cantera, Palmer | *San Antonio, TX*

Legacy/Lakewood Rch. | *Sarasota, FL*

Marriott's Wildfire, Palmer Signature | *Phoenix, AZ*

Myrtle Beach Nat'l, King's North | *Myrtle Beach, SC*

Myrtle Beach Nat'l, South Creek | *Myrtle Beach, SC*

Oasis, Palmer | *Las Vegas, NV*

Orange Lake, Legends | *Orlando, FL*

Osage Nat'l | *Lake of the Ozarks, MO*

PGA Nat'l, Palmer | *Palm Beach, FL*

Reunion Resort, Arnold Palmer | *Orlando, FL*

Running Y Rch. | *Klamath Falls, OR*

Saddlebrook | *Tampa, FL*

Semiahmoo Resort, Semiahmoo Course | *Vancouver Area, WA*

Shanty Creek, The Legend | *Traverse City, MI*

SilverRock Resort, Arnold Palmer Classic | *Palm Springs, CA*

Spencer T. Olin | *St. Louis Area, IL*

Starr Pass | *Tucson, AZ*

Stonewall Resort, Palmer |
Weston, WV

Suncadia Inn, Prospector | *Seattle, WA*

Teton Pines | *Wilson, WY*

Tournament Club/IA | *Des Moines, IA*

Turtle Bay, Arnold Palmer |
Oahu, HI

World Golf Vill., King & Bear |
Jacksonville, FL

ARTHUR HILLS

☒ Bay Harbor | *Petoskey, MI*

Black Gold | *Orange County, CA*

Boyne Highlands, Arthur Hills |
Petoskey, MI

Camelback, Padre | *Scottsdale, AZ*

Chaska Town | *Minneapolis, MN*

CrossCreek | *San Diego, CA*

Dunes West | *Charleston, SC*

El Conquistador Resort |
Las Croabas, PR

Forest Akers MSU, West |
Lansing, MI

☒ Half Moon Bay, Ocean |
San Francisco Bay Area, CA

Harbour Pointe | *Seattle, WA*

Hyatt Hill Country | *San Antonio, TX*

Journey/Pechanga | *San Diego, CA*

Legacy | *Las Vegas, NV*

Legacy Ridge | *Denver, CO*

Links/Lighthouse Sound |
Ocean City, MD

☒ Longaberger | *Columbus, OH*

LPGA Int'l, Legends | *Daytona Beach, FL*

Maryland Nat'l | *Frederick, MD*

Maumee Bay | *Toledo, OH*

Newport Nat'l, Orchard |
Southern Rhode Island, RI

Normandy Shores | *Miami, FL*

Palmetto Dunes, Arthur Hills |
Hilton Head, SC

Palmetto Hall, Arthur Hills |
Hilton Head, SC

Pevely Farms | *St. Louis, MO*

Red Hawk | *Bay City, MI*

Red Hawk Run | *Toledo, OH*

Shaker Run | *Cincinnati, OH*

Shepherd's Hollow | *Detroit, MI*

Stonewall Orchard | *Chicago, IL*

Walking Stick | *Colorado Springs, CO*

Waverly Woods | *Baltimore, MD*

Wolfdancer | *Austin, TX*

BEN CRENSHAW/BILL COORE

☒ Bandon Dunes, Bandon Trails |
Coos Bay, OR

Barton Creek, Crenshaw Cliffside |
Austin, TX

Cuscowilla | *Lake Oconee, GA*

NEW Dormie Club |
Raleigh-Durham, NC

☒ Kapalua, Plantation | *Maui, HI*

Talking Stick, North | *Scottsdale, AZ*

Talking Stick, South | *Scottsdale, AZ*

☒ We-Ko-Pa, Saguaro | *Scottsdale, AZ*

DONALD ROSS

Balsams, Panorama |
Northern New Hampshire, NH

Biltmore | *Miami, FL*

☒ Broadmoor, East |
Colorado Springs, CO

☒ Broadmoor, West |
Colorado Springs, CO

French Lick, Donald Ross |
French Lick, IN

Granville | *Columbus, OH*

Grove Pk. Inn | *Asheville, NC*

Linville | *Asheville, NC*

Mid Pines Inn | *Pinehurst, NC*

Mount Washington |
Northern New Hampshire, NH

Omni Bedford Springs, The
Old Course | *Bedford, PA*

Pinehurst, No. 1 | *Pinehurst, NC*

Pinehurst, No. 2 | *Pinehurst, NC*

Pinehurst, No. 3 | *Pinehurst, NC*

Pine Needles Lodge | *Pinehurst, NC*

Sagamore | *Adirondacks, NY*

Seaview Resort, Bay |
Atlantic City, NJ

Shennecossett | *New London, CT*

Triggs Memorial |
Northern Rhode Island, RI

Wachusett | *Worcester, MA*

JACK NICKLAUS

(Design and Signature)

Achasta | *Atlanta, GA*

Bay Creek, Jack Nicklaus |
Virginia Beach, VA

Bayside | *Rehoboth Beach, DE*

Bear's Best Atlanta | *Atlanta, GA*

Bear's Best LV | *Las Vegas, NV*

Bear Trace | *Chattanooga, TN*

Breckenridge | *Vail, CO*

☑ Broadmoor, Mountain |
  Colorado Springs, CO
Bull at Pinehurst Farms | *Kohler, WI*
☑ Challenge/Manele | *Lanai, HI*
Cordillera, Summit | *Vail, CO*
Cougar Canyon |
  Colorado Springs, CO
Coyote Springs | *Las Vegas, NV*
Daufuskie Island, Melrose |
  Hilton Head, SC
Diablo Grande, Legends West |
  Sacramento, CA
Escena | *Palm Springs, CA*
Golden Bear/Indigo Run |
  Hilton Head, SC
Grand Biloxi, Grand Bear |
  Gulfport, MS
Grand Cypress | *Orlando, FL*
Grand Cypress, New | *Orlando, FL*
Grand Traverse, The Bear |
  Traverse City, MI
Hammock Beach Resort, Ocean |
  Daytona Beach, FL
NEW Harbor Shores | *Kalamazoo, MI*
☑ Hualalai | *Big Island, HI*
Kauai Lagoons,
  Kiele Mauka/Kiele Moana | *Kauai, HI*
Kiawah Island, Turtle Point |
  Charleston, SC
La Paloma | *Tucson, AZ*
Legacy | *Pinehurst, NC*
Long Bay | *Myrtle Beach, SC*
Mansion Ridge | *NYC Metro, NY*
May River/Palmetto Bluff |
  Hilton Head, SC
North Palm Beach Club,
  Jack Nicklaus Signature |
  Palm Beach, FL
Old Corkscrew | *Ft. Myers, FL*
Old Greenwood | *Lake Tahoe, CA*
Old Works | *Butte, MT*
Pawleys Plantation | *Pawleys Island, SC*
☑ Pinehills, Nicklaus | *Boston, MA*
Pronghorn Club, Nicklaus | *Bend, OR*
Reunion Resort, Jack Nicklaus |
  Orlando, FL
Reynolds Plantation, Great Waters |
  Lake Oconee, GA
Ritz-Carlton, Dove Mtn. | *Tucson, AZ*
Rocky Gap Lodge |
  Cumberland, MD
Ross Creek Landing | *Nashville, TN*
Stonewolf | *St. Louis Area, IL*

Superstition Mtn. | *Phoenix, AZ*
World Golf Vill., King & Bear |
  Jacksonville, FL

PETE DYE
Amelia Island, Oak Marsh |
  Jacksonville, FL
Amelia Island, Ocean Links |
  Jacksonville, FL
ASU Karsten | *Phoenix, AZ*
Avalon Lakes | *Cleveland, OH*
Barefoot, Dye | *Myrtle Beach, SC*
Big Fish | *Northern Wisconsin, WI*
Big Island | *Big Island, HI*
☑ Blackwolf Run, Meadow Valleys |
  Kohler, WI
☑ Blackwolf Run, River | *Kohler, WI*
Brickyard Crossing | *Indianapolis, IN*
☑ Bulle Rock | *Baltimore, MD*
Carmel Valley Rch. |
  Monterey Peninsula, CA
Eagle Eye | *Lansing, MI*
Fort | *Indianapolis, IN*
Fowler's Mill | *Cleveland, OH*
NEW French Lick, Pete Dye |
  French Lick, IN
Grand Geneva, Highlands |
  Lake Geneva, WI
Kearney Hill | *Lexington, KY*
☑ Kiawah Island, Ocean |
  Charleston, SC
Kingsmill, River | *Williamsburg, VA*
La Quinta, Dunes | *Palm Springs, CA*
La Quinta, Mountain | *Palm Springs, CA*
Las Vegas Paiute, Snow Mountain |
  Las Vegas, NV
Las Vegas Paiute, Sun Mountain |
  Las Vegas, NV
Las Vegas Paiute, Wolf | *Las Vegas, NV*
Lost Canyons, Shadow | *Los Angeles, CA*
Lost Canyons, Sky | *Los Angeles, CA*
☑ Nemacolin Woodlands,
  Mystic Rock | *Pittsburgh, PA*
Pete Dye/VA Tech | *Roanoke, VA*
PGA Golf Club, Dye |
  Port St. Lucie, FL
PGA West, Stadium | *Palm
  Springs, CA*
Pound Ridge | *NYC Metro, NY*
Riverdale, Dunes | *Denver, CO*
Royal Hawaiian | *Oahu, HI*
Ruffled Feathers | *Chicago, IL*
Rum Pointe | *Ocean City, MD*

Ⓩ Sea Pines, Harbour Town | *Hilton Head, SC*

Sea Pines, Heron Point | *Hilton Head, SC*

TPC Louisiana | *New Orleans, LA*

🆕 TPC San Antonio, AT&T Canyons | *San Antonio, TX*

Ⓩ TPC Sawgrass, Dye's Valley | *Jacksonville, FL*

Ⓩ TPC Sawgrass, PLAYERS Stadium | *Jacksonville, FL*

Westin Mission Hills, Pete Dye | *Palm Springs, CA*

Ⓩ Whistling Straits, Irish | *Kohler, WI*

Ⓩ Whistling Straits, Straits | *Kohler, WI*

Wintonbury Hills | *Hartford, CT*

REES JONES

Black Lake | *Gaylord, MI*

Blackstone Nat'l | *Worcester, MA*

Breakers, Rees Jones | *Palm Beach, FL*

Bryan Park, Champions | *Greensboro, NC*

Ⓩ Cascata | *Las Vegas, NV*

Charleston Nat'l | *Charleston, SC*

Country Club/Hilton Head | *Hilton Head, SC*

Currituck | *Outer Banks, NC*

Dacotah Ridge | *Minneapolis, MN*

Falcon's Fire | *Orlando, FL*

Golden Horseshoe, Green | *Williamsburg, VA*

Lake of Isles, North | *New London, CT*

Legend Trail | *Scottsdale, AZ*

LPGA Int'l, Champions | *Daytona Beach, FL*

Marriott's Griffin Gate | *Lexington, KY*

Otter Creek | *Indianapolis, IN*

Oyster Reef | *Hilton Head, SC*

Ⓩ Pinehills, Jones | *Boston, MA*

Pinehurst, No. 7 | *Pinehurst, NC*

Poppy Ridge | *San Francisco Bay Area, CA*

Ⓩ Redstone, Tournament | *Houston, TX*

Reynolds Plantation, Oconee | *Lake Oconee, GA*

Rio Secco | *Las Vegas, NV*

Riverside Casino/Golf, Blue Top Ridge | *Iowa City, IA*

Sandestin, Burnt Pine | *Panhandle, FL*

Sandpines | *Central Coast, OR*

Ⓩ Sea Island, Plantation | *Low Country, GA*

Sea Trail, Rees Jones | *Myrtle Beach Area, NC*

Talamore | *Pinehurst, NC*

🆕 Victory Ranch | *Salt Lake City, UT*

🆕 Waldorf Astoria | *Orlando, FL*

Wintergreen | *Charlottesville, VA*

ROBERT TRENT JONES JR.

Arizona Nat'l | *Tucson, AZ*

Arrowhead | *Denver, CO*

Beaver Creek | *Vail, CO*

Celebration | *Orlando, FL*

Ⓩ Chambers Bay | *Tacoma, WA*

Ⓩ CordeValle | *San Francisco Bay Area, CA*

Deer Creek | *Kansas City, KS*

Desert Dunes | *Palm Springs, CA*

Dove Valley Rch. | *Phoenix, AZ*

Eagleglen | *Anchorage, AK*

Edinburgh USA | *Minneapolis, MN*

Heron Lakes, Great Blue | *Portland, OR*

Jackson Hole Golf | *Jackson, WY*

Keystone Rch., Ranch | *Vail, CO*

Kiahuna | *Kauai, HI*

Lansdowne Resort, Jones | *Leesburg, VA*

Las Sendas | *Phoenix, AZ*

Links/Bodega Harbour | *Santa Rosa, CA*

Long Island Nat'l | *Long Island, NY*

Makena, North | *Maui, HI*

Monarch Beach | *Orange County, CA*

Orchards | *Detroit, MI*

Ⓩ Poipu Bay | *Kauai, HI*

Ⓩ Poppy Hills | *Monterey Peninsula, CA*

Prairie Landing | *Chicago, IL*

Prairie View | *Indianapolis, IN*

Ⓩ Princeville/Prince | *Kauai, HI*

Rancho San Marcos | *Santa Barbara, CA*

Rock Barn, Robert Trent Jones, Jr. | *Charlotte, NC*

Sandestin, Raven | *Panhandle, FL*

Seneca Hickory Stick | *Finger Lakes, NY*

Sentryworld | *Madison, WI*

🆕 Sequoyah Nat'l | *Asheville, NC*

Ⓩ Spanish Bay | *Monterey Peninsula, CA*

Sugarloaf | *Central Maine, ME*

Sunday River | *Central Maine, ME*
Sunriver, Woodlands | *Bend, OR*
Sun Valley, Trail Creek | *Sun Valley, ID*
Tamarack, Osprey Meadows |
  Boise, ID
ThunderHawk | *Chicago, IL*
Tiffany Greens | *Kansas City, MO*
🄕 Turning Stone, Kaluhyat |
  Finger Lakes, NY
Univ. Ridge | *Madison, WI*
Waikoloa Bch., Beach | *Big Island, HI*
Waikoloa Vill. | *Big Island, HI*
Wailea Club, Emerald | *Maui, HI*
Wailea Club, Gold | *Maui, HI*

ROBERT TRENT JONES SR.
Boyne Highlands, Heather |
  Petoskey, MI
Bristol Harbour | *Finger Lakes, NY*
🄕 Broadmoor, East |
  Colorado Springs, CO
🄕 Broadmoor, West |
  Colorado Springs, CO
Cacapon Resort | *Martinsburg, WV*
🄕 Cambrian Ridge | *Montgomery, AL*
🄕 Capitol Hill, Judge | *Montgomery, AL*
🄕 Capitol Hill, Legislator |
  Montgomery, AL
🄕 Capitol Hill, Senator |
  Montgomery, AL
Carambola | *St. Croix, USVI*
Celebration | *Orlando, FL*
Crumpin-Fox | *Berkshires, MA*
Dorado Bch., East | *Dorado, PR*
Duke Univ. Golf | *Raleigh-Durham, NC*
Dunes Golf | *Myrtle Beach, SC*
🄕 Golden Horseshoe, Gold |
  Williamsburg, VA
Golf Club/Rancho California |
  San Diego, CA
🄕 Grand Nat'l, Lake | *Auburn, AL*
🄕 Grand Nat'l, Links | *Auburn, AL*
Hampton Cove, Highlands |
  Huntsville, AL
Hampton Cove, River | *Huntsville, AL*
Homestead, Lower Cascades |
  Roanoke, VA
Hominy Hill | *Freehold, NJ*
Horseshoe Bay, Apple Rock |
  Austin, TX
Horseshoe Bay, Ram Rock | *Austin, TX*
Horseshoe Bay, Slick Rock | *Austin, TX*
Kaanapali, Royal Kaanapali | *Maui, HI*

Lely, Flamingo Island | *Naples, FL*
Lodge/Four Seasons, Cove |
  Lake of the Ozarks, MO
Lyman Orchards, Robert Trent Jones |
  Hartford, CT
Mauna Kea, Hapuna | *Big Island, HI*
Mauna Kea | *Big Island, HI*
🄕 Montauk Downs | *Long Island, NY*
Otter Creek | *Indianapolis, IN*
Oxmoor Valley, Ridge |
  Birmingham, AL
Oxmoor Valley, Valley | *Birmingham, AL*
Palmetto Dunes, Robert Trent Jones |
  Hilton Head, SC
Portsmouth Club |
  Southern New Hampshire, NH
Seven Oaks | *Finger Lakes, NY*
Silver Lakes | *Birmingham, AL*
🄕 Spyglass Hill |
  Monterey Peninsula, CA
Sugarbush | *Northern Vermont, VT*
Tanglewood Park, Championship |
  Winston-Salem, NC
Tanglewood Park, Reynolds |
  Winston-Salem, NC
Treetops,
  Robert Trent Jones Masterpiece |
  Gaylord, MI
Wigwam, Gold | *Phoenix, AZ*
Woodstock Club | *Southern Vermont, VT*

TOM FAZIO
Amelia Island, Long Point |
  Jacksonville, FL
Barefoot, Fazio | *Myrtle Beach, SC*
Barton Creek, Fazio Canyons |
  Austin, TX
Barton Creek, Fazio Foothills |
  Austin, TX
Beau Rivage, Fallen Oak | *Gulfport, MS*
Belterra | *Cincinnati Area, IN*
🄕 Branson Creek | *Springfield, MO*
Butterfield Trail | *El Paso, TX*
🄕 Camp Creek | *Panhandle, FL*
Cordillera, Valley | *Vail, CO*
🄕 Dancing Rabbit, Azaleas |
  Jackson, MS
Dancing Rabbit, Oaks | *Jackson, MS*
Frog/Georgian | *Atlanta, GA*
Glen Club | *Chicago, IL*
Grand Club | *San Diego, CA*
🄕 Grayhawk, Raptor |
  Scottsdale, AZ

Karsten Creek | *Stillwater, OK*
Kiawah Island, Osprey Point |
   Charleston, SC
Mahogany Run | *St. Thomas, USVI*
Missouri Bluffs | *St. Louis, MO*
Oak Creek | *Orange County, CA*
Oyster Bay Town Golf | *Long Island, NY*
🄯 Pelican Hill, Ocean North |
   Orange County, CA
🄯 Pelican Hill, Ocean South |
   Orange County, CA
PGA Golf Club, Ryder |
   Port St. Lucie, FL
PGA Golf Club, Wanamaker |
   Port St. Lucie, FL
PGA Nat'l, Champion | *Palm Beach, FL*
PGA Nat'l, Haig | *Palm Beach, FL*
PGA Nat'l, Squire | *Palm Beach, FL*
Pinehurst, No. 4 | *Pinehurst, NC*
Pinehurst, No. 6 | *Pinehurst, NC*
Pinehurst, No. 8 | *Pinehurst, NC*
Porters Neck | *Myrtle Beach Area, NC*
Primm Valley, Lakes | *Las Vegas, NV*
🄯 Red Sky, Fazio | *Vail, CO*
Reynolds Plantation | *Lake Oconee, GA*
Ritz-Carlton Members Club |
   Sarasota, FL
Sawmill Creek | *Cleveland, OH*
🄯 Sea Island, Seaside | *Low Country, GA*
Shadow Creek | *Las Vegas, NV*
TPC Myrtle Beach |
   Myrtle Beach, SC
Treetops, Tom Fazio Premier |
   Gaylord, MI
🄯 Turning Stone, Atunyote |
   Finger Lakes, NY
UNC Finley | *Chapel Hill, NC*
Ventana Canyon, Canyon | *Tucson, AZ*
Ventana Canyon, Mountain |
   Tucson, AZ
Walt Disney World, Osprey Ridge |
   Orlando, FL
Westin Stonebriar, Fazio | *Dallas, TX*
Wild Dunes, Harbor | *Charleston, SC*
Wild Dunes, Links | *Charleston, SC*
🄯 World Woods, Pine Barrens |
   Tampa, FL
World Woods, Rolling Oaks |
   Tampa, FL
Wyndham Rio Mar, Ocean |
   Rio Grande, PR
Wynn | *Las Vegas, NV*

CONDITIONING

🄯 Arnold Palmer/Bay Hill | *Orlando, FL*
🄯 Aviara | *San Diego, CA*
🄯 Bandon Dunes, Bandon Dunes
   Course | *Coos Bay, OR*
🄯 Bandon Dunes, Pacific Dunes |
   Coos Bay, OR
Barton Creek, Fazio Foothills |
   Austin, TX
Baywood Greens | *Rehoboth Beach, DE*
🄯 Belgrade Lakes | *Central Maine, ME*
🄯 Bethpage, Black | *Long Island, NY*
🄯 Blackwolf Run, River | *Kohler, WI*
🄯 Boulders, North | *Phoenix, AZ*
🄯 Boulders, South | *Phoenix, AZ*
🄯 Broadmoor, East |
   Colorado Springs, CO
🄯 Broadmoor, West |
   Colorado Springs, CO
🄯 Bulle Rock | *Baltimore, MD*
🄯 Caledonia Golf/Fish |
   Pawleys Island, SC
🄯 Cascata | *Las Vegas, NV*
Coeur d'Alene | *Coeur d'Alene, ID*
🄯 CordeValle |
   San Francisco Bay Area, CA
Desert Willow, Firecliff |
   Palm Springs, CA
🄯 Forest Dunes | *Gaylord, MI*
Frog/Georgian | *Atlanta, GA*
🄯 Gold Canyon, Dinosaur Mountain |
   Phoenix, AZ
🄯 Golden Horseshoe, Gold |
   Williamsburg, VA
🄯 Greenbrier, Old White TPC |
   White Sulphur Springs, WV
🄯 Homestead, Cascades |
   Roanoke, VA
Karsten Creek | *Stillwater, OK*
🄯 Kiawah Island, Ocean |
   Charleston, SC
Lake of Isles, North | *New London, CT*
Lansdowne Resort, Norman |
   Leesburg, VA
Las Vegas Paiute, Snow Mountain |
   Las Vegas, NV
Las Vegas Paiute, Sun Mountain |
   Las Vegas, NV
🄯 Longaberger | *Columbus, OH*
Maderas | *San Diego, CA*
Mauna Kea | *Big Island, HI*
Mauna Lani, North | *Big Island, HI*
Mauna Lani, South | *Big Island, HI*

☑ Nemacolin Woodlands, Mystic Rock | *Pittsburgh, PA*
Old Corkscrew | *Ft. Myers, FL*
Old Greenwood | *Lake Tahoe, CA*
Old Kinderhook | *Lake of the Ozarks, MO*
Orchards | *Detroit, MI*
Orchard Valley | *Chicago, IL*
☑ Pelican Hill, Ocean North | *Orange County, CA*
☑ Pelican Hill, Ocean South | *Orange County, CA*
PGA West, Jack Nicklaus Tournament | *Palm Springs, CA*
PGA West, Stadium | *Palm Springs, CA*
☑ Pinehills, Jones | *Boston, MA*
Pinehurst, No. 2 | *Pinehurst, NC*
Pinehurst, No. 4 | *Pinehurst, NC*
Pinehurst, No. 8 | *Pinehurst, NC*
Pine Needles Lodge | *Pinehurst, NC*
☑ Poppy Hills | *Monterey Peninsula, CA*
Pound Ridge | *NYC Metro, NY*
Primland Resort, Highland | *Roanoke, VA*
Primm Valley, Lakes | *Las Vegas, NV*
Pronghorn Club, Nicklaus | *Bend, OR*
Pumpkin Ridge, Ghost Creek | *Portland, OR*
☑ Red Sky, Fazio | *Vail, CO*
Reynolds Plantation, Great Waters | *Lake Oconee, GA*
Ridge/Castle Pines N. | *Denver, CO*
Ritz-Carlton Members Club | *Sarasota, FL*
Ritz-Carlton Orlando | *Orlando, FL*
Rock Hill | *Long Island, NY*
Sagamore | *Adirondacks, NY*
☑ Sea Island, Plantation | *Low Country, GA*
☑ Sea Island, Seaside | *Low Country, GA*
Semiahmoo Resort, Loomis Trail | *Vancouver Area, WA*
Shadow Creek | *Las Vegas, NV*
☑ Spyglass Hill | *Monterey Peninsula, CA*
Stonewall Golf Club | *Leesburg, VA*
Sunriver, Crosswater | *Bend, OR*
Superstition Mtn. | *Phoenix, AZ*
☑ Taconic | *Berkshires, MA*
ThunderHawk | *Chicago, IL*
☑ Tiburón, Black | *Naples, FL*
TPC Las Vegas | *Las Vegas, NV*
TPC Myrtle Beach | *Myrtle Beach, SC*

☑ TPC Sawgrass, PLAYERS Stadium | *Jacksonville, FL*
☑ Troon North, Monument | *Scottsdale, AZ*
Troon North, Pinnacle | *Scottsdale, AZ*
Trump Nat'l | *Los Angeles, CA*
☑ Turning Stone, Kaluhyat | *Finger Lakes, NY*
Wailea Club, Gold | *Maui, HI*
NEW Waldorf Astoria | *Orlando, FL*
Walt Disney World, Osprey Ridge | *Orlando, FL*
☑ We-Ko-Pa, Cholla | *Scottsdale, AZ*
☑ Whistling Straits, Straits | *Kohler, WI*
Whitehawk Rch. | *Lake Tahoe, CA*
Wintonbury Hills | *Hartford, CT*
☑ Wolf Creek | *Las Vegas, NV*
World Golf Vill., Slammer & Squire | *Jacksonville, FL*
Wynn | *Las Vegas, NV*

EASIEST

(Courses with the lowest slope ratings from the back tees)
Ala Wai | *Oahu, HI*
Barton Creek, Crenshaw Cliffside | *Austin, TX*
Berkshire Valley | *NYC Metro, NJ*
Coeur d'Alene | *Coeur d'Alene, ID*
Grand Cypress, New | *Orlando, FL*
Les Bolstad | *Minneapolis, MN*
Los Verdes | *Los Angeles, CA*
☑ Pacific Grove | *Monterey Peninsula, CA*
Peninsula Golf | *Mobile, AL*
Pinehurst, No. 1 | *Pinehurst, NC*
Pinehurst, No. 3 | *Pinehurst, NC*
Richmond Club | *Southern Rhode Island, RI*

ENVIRONMENTALLY FRIENDLY

(As certified by Audubon International)
Aldeen | *Chicago, IL*
Amana Colonies | *Cedar Rapids, IA*
Amelia Island | *Jacksonville, FL*
Augustine Golf Club | *DC Metro Area, VA*
Baker Nat'l | *Minneapolis, MN*
Barona Creek | *San Diego, CA*
Barton Creek | *Austin, TX*

Tamarack | Boise, ID
Teton Pines | Wilson, WY
ThunderHawk | Chicago, IL
Tiburón | Naples, FL
TPC Deere Run | Moline, IL
TPC Myrtle Beach | Myrtle Beach, SC
TPC Sawgrass | Jacksonville, FL
TPC Scottsdale | Scottsdale, AZ
TPC Tampa Bay | Tampa, FL
Troon North | Scottsdale, AZ
Tukwet Canyon | San Bernardino, CA
Turning Stone | Finger Lakes, NY
Walt Disney World | Orlando, FL
Westfields Golf Club |
    DC Metro Area, VA
Wintonbury Hills | Hartford, CT

EXCEPTIONAL CLUBHOUSES

Arcadia Bluffs | Traverse City, MI
Arnold Palmer/Bay Hill | Orlando, FL
Barefoot | Myrtle Beach, SC
Blackwolf Run | Kohler, WI
Boca Raton Resort | Palm Beach, FL
Breakers | Palm Beach, FL
Broadmoor | Colorado Springs, CO
Caledonia Golf/Fish | Pawleys Island, SC
Camelback | Scottsdale, AZ
Cascata | Las Vegas, NV
ChampionsGate | Orlando, FL
CordeValle | San Francisco Bay Area, CA
Desert Willow | Palm Springs, CA
Doral | Miami, FL
Elk Ridge | Gaylord, MI
Escena | Palm Springs, CA
Fox Hopyard | East Haddam, CT
Glen Club | Chicago, IL
Golf Club/Newcastle | Seattle, WA
Grand Cypress | Orlando, FL
Grayhawk | Scottsdale, AZ
Great River | New Haven, CT
Greystone | Baltimore, MD
Harvester | Des Moines, IA
Heritage Club | Pawleys Island, SC
Heron Bay | Ft. Lauderdale, FL
Keswick Club | Charlottesville, VA
Kiawah Island | Charleston, SC
Kierland | Scottsdale, AZ
Kingsmill | Williamsburg, VA
La Costa | San Diego, CA
La Quinta | Palm Springs, CA
Las Vegas Paiute | Las Vegas, NV
Legends Club | Minneapolis, MN

Lost Canyons | Los Angeles, CA
Maderas | San Diego, CA
Olde Stonewall | Pittsburgh, PA
Pebble Beach | Monterey Peninsula, CA
Pelican Hill | Orange County, CA
PGA Nat'l | Palm Beach, FL
Phoenician | Scottsdale, AZ
Poppy Hills | Monterey Peninsula, CA
Pronghorn Club | Bend, OR
Ranch | Springfield, MA
Red Sky | Vail, CO
Reynolds Plantation | Lake Oconee, GA
Sea Island | Low Country, GA
Seaview Resort | Atlantic City, NJ
Semiahmoo Resort |
    Vancouver Area, WA
Shadow Creek | Las Vegas, NV
Spanish Bay | Monterey Peninsula, CA
Superstition Mtn. | Phoenix, AZ
Tiburón | Naples, FL
TPC Sawgrass | Jacksonville, FL
TPC Scottsdale | Scottsdale, AZ
Troon North | Scottsdale, AZ
Trump Nat'l | Los Angeles, CA
Turning Stone | Finger Lakes, NY
Walt Disney World | Orlando, FL
We-Ko-Pa | Scottsdale, AZ
World Golf Vill. | Jacksonville, FL

EXPENSE ACCOUNT

($250 and over)
🗹 Arnold Palmer/Bay Hill |
    Orlando, FL
Bali Hai | Las Vegas, NV
🗹 Bandon Dunes,
    Bandon Dunes Course |
    Coos Bay, OR
🗹 Bandon Dunes, Bandon Trails |
    Coos Bay, OR
🗹 Bandon Dunes, Pacific Dunes |
    Coos Bay, OR
NEW Bandon Dunes, Old
    Macdonald | Coos Bay, OR
🗹 Blackwolf Run, River | Kohler, WI
🗹 Cascata | Las Vegas, NV
Coeur d'Alene | Coeur d'Alene, ID
🗹 CordeValle |
    San Francisco Bay Area, CA
🗹 Doral, TPC Blue Monster |
    Miami, FL
NEW Doral Resort, Jim McLean |
    Miami, FL
Grand Cypress | Orlando, FL

Grand Club | San Diego, CA

🄩 Greenbrier, Greenbrier Course |
    White Sulphur Springs, WV

🄩 Greenbrier, Old White TPC |
    White Sulphur Springs, WV

🄩 Hualalai | Big Island, HI

🄩 Kapalua, Plantation | Maui, HI

Karsten Creek | Stillwater, OK

🄩 Kiawah Island, Ocean |
    Charleston, SC

Mauna Kea | Big Island, HI

May River/Palmetto Bluff |
    Hilton Head, SC

🄩 Pebble Beach |
    Monterey Peninsula, CA

🄩 Pelican Hill, Ocean North |
    Orange County, CA

🄩 Pelican Hill, Ocean South |
    Orange County, CA

PGA Nat'l, Champion | Palm Beach, FL

PGA Nat'l, Haig | Palm Beach, FL

PGA Nat'l, Palmer | Palm Beach, FL

PGA Nat'l, Squire | Palm Beach, FL

Pinehurst, No. 2 | Pinehurst, NC

🄩 Red Sky, Fazio | Vail, CO

🄩 Red Sky, Norman | Vail, CO

Reynolds Plantation, Great Waters |
    Lake Oconee, GA

Rio Secco | Las Vegas, NV

🄩 Sea Island, Seaside | Low Country, GA

🄩 Sea Pines, Harbour Town |
    Hilton Head, SC

Shadow Creek | Las Vegas, NV

🄩 Spanish Bay | Monterey Peninsula, CA

🄩 Spyglass Hill |
    Monterey Peninsula, CA

🄩 TPC Sawgrass, PLAYERS Stadium |
    Jacksonville, FL

TPC Scottsdale, Stadium |
    Scottsdale, AZ

🄩 Troon North, Monument |
    Scottsdale, AZ

Troon North, Pinnacle | Scottsdale, AZ

Trump Nat'l | Los Angeles, CA

Turnberry Isle Resort, Soffer |
    Miami, FL

🄩 Whistling Straits, Straits |
    Kohler, WI

Wynn | Las Vegas, NV

FINE FOOD TOO

Arizona Biltmore | Phoenix, AZ

Arroyo Trabuco | Orange County, CA

Aviara | San Diego, CA

Bali Hai | Las Vegas, NV

Balsams | Northern New Hampshire, NH

Bandon Dunes | Coos Bay, OR

Barnsley Gdns. | Atlanta, GA

Biltmore | Miami, FL

Blackwolf Run | Kohler, WI

Boca Raton Resort | Palm Beach, FL

Boulders | Phoenix, AZ

Breakers | Palm Beach, FL

Broadmoor | Colorado Springs, CO

Caledonia Golf/Fish | Pawleys Island, SC

Camelback | Scottsdale, AZ

Carmel Valley Rch. |
    Monterey Peninsula, CA

Cascata | Las Vegas, NV

Château Élan | Atlanta, GA

Classic Club | Palm Springs, CA

CordeValle | San Francisco Bay Area, CA

Cordillera | Vail, CO

Eagle Ridge | Freehold, NJ

Forest Dunes | Gaylord, MI

Four Seasons/Las Colinas | Dallas, TX

Fox Hopyard | East Haddam, CT

Geneva Nat'l | Lake Geneva, WI

Grand Cypress | Orlando, FL

Grayhawk | Scottsdale, AZ

Great River | New Haven, CT

Greenbrier | White Sulphur Springs, WV

Harvester | Des Moines, IA

Homestead | Roanoke, VA

Kapalua | Maui, HI

Keswick Club | Charlottesville, VA

Keystone Rch. | Vail, CO

Kiawah Island | Charleston, SC

La Costa | San Diego, CA

Lansdowne Resort | Leesburg, VA

La Quinta | Palm Springs, CA

Legends Club | Minneapolis, MN

Lely | Naples, FL

Links/Lighthouse Sound |
    Ocean City, MD

Linville | Asheville, NC

Lodg/ Four Seasons |
    Lake of the Ozarks, MO

Lookout Mountain | Phoenix, AZ

Marriott Desert Springs |
    Palm Springs, CA

Mauna Lani | Big Island, HI

May River/Palmetto Bluff |
    Hilton Head, SC

Mid Pines Inn | Pinehurst, NC

Nemacolin Woodlands | *Pittsburgh, PA*

Ocotillo | *Phoenix, AZ*

Ojai Valley Inn | *Los Angeles, CA*

Omni Bedford Springs | *Bedford, PA*

Pebble Beach | *Monterey Peninsula, CA*

Pelican Hill | *Orange County, CA*

PGA Nat'l | *Palm Beach, FL*

Phoenician | *Scottsdale, AZ*

Poipu Bay | *Kauai, HI*

Princeville/Prince | *Kauai, HI*

Quail Lodge | *Monterey Peninsula, CA*

Ranch | *Springfield, MA*

Rancho Bernardo | *San Diego, CA*

Raven/Snowshoe Mtn. | *Elkins, WV*

Raven/Verrado | *Phoenix, AZ*

Reserve Vineyards | *Portland, OR*

Reynolds Plantation | *Lake Oconee, GA*

Ridge/Castle Pines N. | *Denver, CO*

Ritz-Carlton Members Club | *Sarasota, FL*

Sagamore | *Adirondacks, NY*

Salishan | *Central Coast, OR*

Samoset | *Southern Maine, ME*

Saratoga Nat'l | *Albany, NY*

Sea Island | *Low Country, GA*

Seaview Resort | *Atlantic City, NJ*

Shadow Creek | *Las Vegas, NV*

Spanish Bay | *Monterey Peninsula, CA*

Strawberry Farms | *Orange County, CA*

SunRidge Canyon | *Scottsdale, AZ*

Sunriver | *Bend, OR*

Temecula Creek | *San Diego, CA*

Tiburón | *Naples, FL*

Torrey Pines | *San Diego, CA*

TPC Sawgrass | *Jacksonville, FL*

TPC Scottsdale | *Scottsdale, AZ*

Treetops | *Gaylord, MI*

Troon North | *Scottsdale, AZ*

Trump Nat'l | *Los Angeles, CA*

Turnberry Isle Resort | *Miami, FL*

Twin Warriors | *Albuquerque, NM*

Ventana Canyon | *Tucson, AZ*

NEW Waldorf Astoria | *Orlando, FL*

Walt Disney World | *Orlando, FL*

Wente Vineyards | *San Francisco Bay Area, CA*

Whirlwind | *Phoenix, AZ*

Whistling Straits | *Kohler, WI*

Wigwam | *Phoenix, AZ*

World Golf Vill. | *Jacksonville, FL*

FINISHING HOLES

Arizona Nat'l | *Tucson, AZ*

☑ Arnold Palmer/Bay Hill | *Orlando, FL*

☑ Bulle Rock | *Baltimore, MD*

Butterfield Trail | *El Paso, TX*

☑ Capitol Hill, Judge | *Montgomery, AL*

Daufuskie Island, Melrose | *Hilton Head, SC*

☑ Doral, TPC Blue Monster | *Miami, FL*

Eagle Mtn. | *Scottsdale, AZ*

NEW French Lick, Pete Dye | *French Lick, IN*

☑ Grand Nat'l, Links | *Auburn, AL*

☑ Grayhawk, Raptor | *Scottsdale, AZ*

Half Moon Bay, Old Course | *San Francisco Bay Area, CA*

Industry Hills, Eisenhower | *Los Angeles, CA*

☑ Kapalua, Plantation | *Maui, HI*

Leatherstocking | *Albany, NY*

Mid Pines Inn | *Pinehurst, NC*

Old Corkscrew | *Ft. Myers, FL*

Omni Tucson Nat'l, Catalina | *Tucson, AZ*

☑ Pebble Beach | *Monterey Peninsula, CA*

☑ Pelican Hill, Ocean South | *Orange County, CA*

Pete Dye/VA Tech | *Roanoke, VA*

PGA West, Stadium | *Palm Springs, CA*

☑ Sea Pines, Harbour Town | *Hilton Head, SC*

☑ St. Ives Resort, Tullymore | *Grand Rapids, MI*

Superstition Mtn., Prospector | *Phoenix, AZ*

ThunderHawk | *Chicago, IL*

☑ Torrey Pines, South | *San Diego, CA*

☑ TPC Sawgrass, PLAYERS Stadium | *Jacksonville, FL*

TPC Scottsdale, Stadium | *Scottsdale, AZ*

Trump Nat'l | *Los Angeles, CA*

Turnberry Isle Resort, Soffer | *Miami, FL*

Ventana Canyon, Canyon | *Tucson, AZ*

Wynn | *Las Vegas, NV*

INSTRUCTION

Amelia Island | *Jacksonville, FL*

Arnold Palmer/Bay Hill | *Orlando, FL*

ASU Karsten | *Phoenix, AZ*
Aviara | *San Diego, CA*
Boca Raton Resort | *Palm Beach, FL*
Boulders | *Phoenix, AZ*
Breakers | *Palm Beach, FL*
Broadmoor | *Colorado Springs, CO*
Camelback | *Scottsdale, AZ*
ChampionsGate | *Orlando, FL*
Cordillera | *Vail, CO*
Crystal Springs | *NYC Metro, NJ*
Desert Willow | *Palm Springs, CA*
Doral | *Miami, FL*
Grand Cypress | *Orlando, FL*
Grand Traverse | *Traverse City, MI*
Grayhawk | *Scottsdale, AZ*
Innisbrook | *Tampa, FL*
Kiawah Island | *Charleston, SC*
Kierland | *Scottsdale, AZ*
La Costa | *San Diego, CA*
LPGA Int'l | *Daytona Beach, FL*
Marriott Shadow Ridge |
    Palm Springs, CA
Mid Pines Inn | *Pinehurst, NC*
Orange County Nat'l | *Orlando, FL*
Orange Lake | *Orlando, FL*
Pala Mesa | *San Diego, CA*
Pebble Beach | *Monterey Peninsula, CA*
Pelican Hill | *Orange County, CA*
PGA Golf Club | *Port St. Lucie, FL*
PGA Nat'l | *Palm Beach, FL*
PGA West | *Palm Springs, CA*
Pine Needles Lodge | *Pinehurst, NC*
Poppy Hills | *Monterey Peninsula, CA*
Pronghorn Club | *Bend, OR*
Pumpkin Ridge | *Portland, OR*
Quail Lodge | *Monterey Peninsula, CA*
Rancho Bernardo | *San Diego, CA*
Reunion Resort | *Orlando, FL*
Reynolds Plantation | *Lake Oconee, GA*
Rio Secco | *Las Vegas, NV*
Saddlebrook | *Tampa, FL*
Seaview Resort | *Atlantic City, NJ*
Smithtown Landing |
    Long Island, NY
Spyglass Hill | *Monterey Peninsula, CA*
Sunriver | *Bend, OR*
Talking Stick | *Scottsdale, AZ*
Tiburón | *Naples, FL*
TPC Las Vegas | *Las Vegas, NV*
TPC Sawgrass | *Jacksonville, FL*
TPC Scottsdale | *Scottsdale, AZ*
Treetops | *Gaylord, MI*
Troon North | *Scottsdale, AZ*

Turtle Bay | *Oahu, HI*
World Golf Vill. | *Jacksonville, FL*

JUNIOR-FRIENDLY

Alvamar Public | *Kansas City, KS*
Annbriar | *St. Louis Area, IL*
Arrowhead | *Myrtle Beach, SC*
Arroyo Trabuco | *Orange County, CA*
ASU Karsten | *Phoenix, AZ*
Barton Creek, Crenshaw Cliffside |
    Austin, TX
Bay Creek, Arnold Palmer |
    Virginia Beach, VA
Baywood Greens | *Rehoboth Beach, DE*
Big Mountain | *Kalispell, MT*
Blackmoor | *Myrtle Beach, SC*
Z Boulders, North | *Phoenix, AZ*
Z Boulders, South | *Phoenix, AZ*
Boyne Highlands, Moor | *Petoskey, MI*
Butterfield Trail | *El Paso, TX*
Z Caledonia Golf/Fish |
    Pawleys Island, SC
Callaway Gdns., Lake View |
    Columbus, GA
Callippe Preserve |
    San Francisco Bay Area, CA
Cantigny | *Chicago, IL*
Cape May Nat'l | *Cape May, NJ*
Carmel Valley Rch. |
    Monterey Peninsula, CA
Celebration | *Orlando, FL*
Cinnabar Hills |
    San Francisco Bay Area, CA
Cobblestone | *Atlanta, GA*
Colbert Hills | *Topeka, KS*
NEW CommonGround | *Denver, CO*
Crumpin-Fox | *Berkshires, MA*
Dacotah Ridge | *Minneapolis, MN*
Eagle Vail | *Vail, CO*
Golden Bear/Indigo Run |
    Hilton Head, SC
Gray Plantation | *Lake Charles, LA*
Grossinger, Big G | *Catskills, NY*
Harbor Pines | *Atlantic City, NJ*
Z Harding Park |
    San Francisco Bay Area, CA
Hawaii Prince | *Oahu, HI*
Hog Neck | *Easton, MD*
Howell Park | *Freehold, NJ*
Hyatt Hill Country | *San Antonio, TX*
Indian Peaks | *Boulder, CO*
Kebo Valley | *Central Maine, ME*
Kiahuna | *Kauai, HI*

Kiva Dunes | *Mobile, AL*
Kona Club, Mountain | *Big Island, HI*
Kona Club, Ocean | *Big Island, HI*
Lederach | *Philadelphia, PA*
Legacy Ridge | *Denver, CO*
Longbow | *Phoenix, AZ*
Memorial Park | *Houston, TX*
Mirimichi | *Memphis, TN*
Murphy Creek | *Denver, CO*
Myrtle Beach Nat'l, South Creek |
   Myrtle Beach, SC
Oyster Bay Town Golf | *Long Island, NY*
Z Pacific Grove |
   Monterey Peninsula, CA
Palmetto Dunes, Robert Trent Jones |
   Hilton Head, SC
Penn Nat'l, Founders | *Gettysburg, PA*
PGA Golf Club, Ryder |
   Port St. Lucie, FL
Pinehurst, No. 1 | *Pinehurst, NC*
Pinehurst, No. 3 | *Pinehurst, NC*
Z Poipu Bay | *Kauai, HI*
Ross Creek Landing | *Nashville, TN*
Sandestin, Baytowne | *Panhandle, FL*
Smithtown Landing | *Long Island, NY*
SouthWood | *Panhandle, FL*
Spencer T. Olin | *St. Louis Area, IL*
Sterling Farms | *Stamford, CT*
NEW Suncadia Resort, Rope Rider |
   Seattle, WA
Tan-Tar-A, The Oaks |
   Lake of the Ozarks, MO
Tennessean | *Nashville, TN*
TPC Scottsdale, Champions |
   Scottsdale, AZ
Valley View | *Salt Lake City, UT*

LINKS-STYLE

Amelia Island, Ocean Links |
   Jacksonville, FL
Z Arcadia Bluffs | *Traverse City, MI*
Z Bandon Dunes,
   Bandon Dunes Course |
   Coos Bay, OR
Z Bandon Dunes, Pacific Dunes |
   Coos Bay, OR
NEW Bandon Dunes, Old
   Macdonald | *Coos Bay, OR*
Z Bay Harbor | *Petoskey, MI*
Bear Trap Dunes | *Rehoboth Beach, DE*
Currituck | *Outer Banks, NC*
Grand Cypress, New | *Orlando, FL*

Z Half Moon Bay, Ocean |
   San Francisco Bay Area, CA
Harbor Links | *Long Island, NY*
Harborside Int'l, Port | *Chicago, IL*
Harborside Int'l, Starboard |
   Chicago, IL
Hawktree | *Bismarck, ND*
Z Kapalua, Plantation | *Maui, HI*
Z Kiawah Island, Ocean |
   Charleston, SC
Lake Placid Club, Links |
   Adirondacks, NY
Lakewood Shores, Gailes |
   Bay City, MI
Links/Bodega Harbour |
   Santa Rosa, CA
Links/Hiawatha Landing |
   Finger Lakes, NY
Links/Lighthouse Sound |
   Ocean City, MD
Links/Union Vale | *Hudson Valley, NY*
Long Island Nat'l | *Long Island, NY*
McCullough's Emerald |
   Atlantic City, NJ
Miacomet | *Nantucket, MA*
Nags Head | *Outer Banks, NC*
Z Pacific Grove |
   Monterey Peninsula, CA
Royal Links | *Las Vegas, NV*
Royal New Kent | *Williamsburg, VA*
Rustic Canyon | *Los Angeles, CA*
Salishan | *Central Coast, OR*
Samoset | *Southern Maine, ME*
Z Sea Island, Seaside |
   Low Country, GA
Z Spanish Bay |
   Monterey Peninsula, CA
Twisted Dune | *Atlantic City, NJ*
Vineyard Golf/Renault |
   Atlantic City, NJ
Wailua Course | *Kauai, HI*
Z Whistling Straits, Irish |
   Kohler, WI
Z Whistling Straits, Straits |
   Kohler, WI
Wild Dunes, Links | *Charleston, SC*

19TH HOLES

Arnold Palmer/Bay Hill | *Orlando, FL*
Aviara | *San Diego, CA*
NEW Bandon Dunes | *Coos Bay, OR*
Biltmore | *Miami, FL*
Boca Raton Resort | *Palm Beach, FL*

OPENING HOLES

Raven/Snowshoe Mtn. | *Elkins, WV*
🔁 Red Sky, Norman | *Vail, CO*
Ritz-Carlton Members Club |
   Sarasota, FL
Sagamore | *Adirondacks, NY*
Sandestin, Burnt Pine | *Panhandle, FL*
Seven Oaks | *Finger Lakes, NY*
🔁 Spanish Bay |
   Monterey Peninsula, CA
🔁 Spyglass Hill |
   Monterey Peninsula, CA
Sun Valley, Trail Creek | *Sun Valley, ID*
Talamore | *Pinehurst, NC*
Tot Hill Farm | *Greensboro, NC*
Trump Nat'l | *Los Angeles, CA*
Victoria Hills | *Daytona Beach, FL*
🔁 We-Ko-Pa, Cholla | *Scottsdale, AZ*
Wente Vineyards |
   San Francisco Bay Area, CA
Whitehawk Rch. | *Lake Tahoe, CA*
🔁 World Woods, Pine Barrens |
   Tampa, FL

OUTSTANDING LODGINGS

Aviara | *San Diego, CA*
NEW Bandon Dunes | *Coos Bay, OR*
Barnsley Gdns. | *Atlanta, GA*
Bay Harbor | *Petoskey, MI*
Blackwolf Run | *Kohler, WI*
Boulders | *Phoenix, AZ*
Breakers | *Palm Beach, FL*
Broadmoor | *Colorado Springs, CO*
Carmel Valley Rch. |
   Monterey Peninsula, CA
Challenge/Manele | *Lanai, HI*
Cordillera | *Vail, CO*
Experience/Koele | *Lanai, HI*
Four Seasons/Las Colinas | *Dallas, TX*
Golden Horseshoe |
   Williamsburg, VA
Grand Cypress | *Orlando, FL*
Greenbrier | *White Sulphur Springs, WV*
Half Moon Bay |
   San Francisco Bay Area, CA
Homestead | *Roanoke, VA*
Hualalai | *Big Island, HI*
Kiawah Island | *Charleston, SC*
La Cantera | *San Antonio, TX*
La Costa | *San Diego, CA*
La Quinta | *Palm Springs, CA*
Monarch Beach | *Orange County, CA*
Nemacolin Woodlands | *Pittsburgh, PA*

Ojai Valley Inn | *Los Angeles, CA*
Pebble Beach | *Monterey Peninsula, CA*
Phoenician | *Scottsdale, AZ*
Poipu Bay | *Kauai, HI*
Princeville/Prince | *Kauai, HI*
Red Sky | *Vail, CO*
Reynolds Plantation | *Lake Oconee, GA*
Ritz-Carlton Members Club |
   Sarasota, FL
Ritz-Carlton Orlando | *Orlando, FL*
Sea Island | *Low Country, GA*
Semiahmoo Resort |
   Vancouver Area, WA
Shadow Creek | *Las Vegas, NV*
Spanish Bay | *Monterey Peninsula, CA*
Tiburón | *Naples, FL*
Torrey Pines | *San Diego, CA*
TPC Scottsdale | *Scottsdale, AZ*
Troon North | *Scottsdale, AZ*
Twin Warriors | *Albuquerque, NM*
Wailea Club | *Maui, HI*
NEW Waldorf Astoria | *Orlando, FL*
Walt Disney World | *Orlando, FL*
Whistling Straits | *Kohler, WI*
Wynn | *Las Vegas, NV*

PAR-3 HOLES

Amelia Island, Long Point |
   Jacksonville, FL
Amelia Island, Ocean Links |
   Jacksonville, FL
🔁 Arcadia Bluffs | *Traverse City, MI*
🔁 Arnold Palmer/Bay Hill |
   Orlando, FL
Arrowhead | *Denver, CO*
Carambola | *St. Croix, USVI*
🔁 Cascata | *Las Vegas, NV*
🔁 Challenge/Manele | *Lanai, HI*
🔁 Chambers Bay | *Tacoma, WA*
🔁 Circling Raven | *Coeur d'Alene, ID*
Coeur d'Alene | *Coeur d'Alene, ID*
Cougar Canyon | *Colorado Springs, CO*
Fox Hopyard | *East Haddam, CT*
Giants Ridge, Quarry | *Duluth, MN*
🔁 Golden Horseshoe, Gold |
   Williamsburg, VA
🔁 Grand Nat'l, Lake | *Auburn, AL*
🔁 Grand Nat'l, Links | *Auburn, AL*
Grayhawk, Talon | *Scottsdale, AZ*
Harvester | *Des Moines, IA*
Island's End | *Long Island, NY*
🔁 Kapalua, Bay | *Maui, HI*
Lake of Isles, North | *New London, CT*

La Quinta, Mountain | *Palm Springs, CA*

Lodge/Four Seasons, Cove |
Lake of the Ozarks, MO

Mauna Kea | *Big Island, HI*

Mauna Lani, South | *Big Island, HI*

Mirimichi | *Memphis, TN*

Myrtle Beach Nat'l, King's North |
Myrtle Beach, SC

Oak Quarry | *San Bernardino, CA*

Omni Bedford Springs,
The Old Course | *Bedford, PA*

Oyster Reef | *Hilton Head, SC*

Pawleys Plantation | *Pawleys Island, SC*

🖬 Pebble Beach |
Monterey Peninsula, CA

🖬 Pelican Hill, Ocean South |
Orange County, CA

PGA Nat'l, Champion | *Palm Beach, FL*

PGA West, Stadium | *Palm Springs, CA*

Phoenician | *Scottsdale, AZ*

Ponte Vedra Bch., Ocean |
Jacksonville, FL

Pound Ridge | *NYC Metro, NY*

Primland Resort, Highland |
Roanoke, VA

🖬 Princeville/Prince | *Kauai, HI*

Quintero Golf, Founders | *Phoenix, AZ*

Redlands Mesa | *Grand Junction, CO*

🖬 Sea Pines, Harbour Town |
Hilton Head, SC

Sedona Golf | *Sedona, AZ*

🖬 Spanish Bay |
Monterey Peninsula, CA

🖬 Spyglass Hill |
Monterey Peninsula, CA

Stowe Mtn. | *Northern Vermont, VT*

Sunday River | *Central Maine, ME*

SunRidge Canyon | *Scottsdale, AZ*

Tot Hill Farm | *Greensboro, NC*

🖬 TPC Sawgrass, PLAYERS Stadium |
Jacksonville, FL

Ventana Canyon, Mountain |
Tucson, AZ

Wynn | *Las Vegas, NV*

PAR-4 HOLES

Apache Stronghold | *San Carlos, AZ*

🖬 Arnold Palmer/Bay Hill | *Orlando, FL*

NEW Bandon Dunes, Old Macdonald |
Coos Bay, OR

Barona Creek | *San Diego, CA*

🖬 Bethpage, Black | *Long Island, NY*

Bull at Pinehurst Farms | *Kohler, WI*

🖬 Capitol Hill, Judge |
Montgomery, AL

🖬 Chambers Bay | *Tacoma, WA*

Desert Willow, Firecliff |
Palm Springs, CA

NEW Dormie Club |
Raleigh-Durham, NC

Erin Hills | *Milwaukee, WI*

🖬 Forest Dunes | *Gaylord, MI*

NEW French Lick, Pete Dye |
French Lick, IN

Giants Ridge, Quarry | *Duluth, MN*

🖬 Gold Canyon, Dinosaur Mountain |
Phoenix, AZ

🖬 Grand Nat'l, Links | *Auburn, AL*

Hammock Beach Resort, Ocean |
Daytona Beach, FL

🖬 Harding Park |
San Francisco Bay Area, CA

Harvester | *Des Moines, IA*

Innisbrook, Copperhead | *Tampa, FL*

🖬 Kiawah Island, Ocean |
Charleston, SC

La Purisima | *Santa Barbara, CA*

Madden's/Gull Lake, Classic |
Brainerd, MN

Mansion Ridge | *NYC Metro, NY*

🖬 Montauk Downs | *Long Island, NY*

Murphy Creek | *Denver, CO*

Old Silo | *Lexington, KY*

Palmetto Dunes, Arthur Hills |
Hilton Head, SC

🖬 Pasatiempo | *Santa Cruz, CA*

🖬 Pebble Beach |
Monterey Peninsula, CA

PGA Nat'l, Champion | *Palm Beach, FL*

PGA West, Jack Nicklaus Tournament |
Palm Springs, CA

PGA West, Stadium | *Palm Springs, CA*

Pound Ridge | *NYC Metro, NY*

Primland Resort, Highland |
Roanoke, VA

🖬 Purgatory | *Indianapolis, IN*

Rawls/TX Tech | *Lubbock, TX*

Red Tail | *Worcester, MA*

Ridge/Castle Pines N. | *Denver, CO*

Ross Creek Landing | *Nashville, TN*

Sagamore | *Adirondacks, NY*

🖬 Spanish Bay |
Monterey Peninsula, CA

🖬 Spyglass Hill |
Monterey Peninsula, CA

ThunderHawk | *Chicago, IL*

☑ Torrey Pines, South | *San Diego, CA*

TPC Las Vegas | *Las Vegas, NV*

☑ TPC Sawgrass, PLAYERS Stadium | *Jacksonville, FL*

TPC Scottsdale, Stadium | *Scottsdale, AZ*

☑ Troon North, Monument | *Scottsdale, AZ*

Troon North, Pinnacle | *Scottsdale, AZ*

Trump Nat'l | *Los Angeles, CA*

☑ We-Ko-Pa, Cholla | *Scottsdale, AZ*

☑ We-Ko-Pa, Saguaro | *Scottsdale, AZ*

Wente Vineyards | *San Francisco Bay Area, CA*

Wintonbury Hills | *Hartford, CT*

☑ World Woods, Pine Barrens | *Tampa, FL*

PAR-5 HOLES

Arizona Nat'l | *Tucson, AZ*

Bay Creek, Arnold Palmer | *Virginia Beach, VA*

☑ Boulders, South | *Phoenix, AZ*

Bull at Pinehurst Farms | *Kohler, WI*

☑ Bulle Rock | *Baltimore, MD*

☑ Capitol Hill, Judge | *Montgomery, AL*

Dorado Bch., East | *Dorado, PR*

Dunes Golf | *Myrtle Beach, SC*

Edgewood Tahoe | *Reno, NV*

Fossil Trace | *Denver, CO*

Gauntlet Golf Club | *DC Metro Area, VA*

Geneva Nat'l, Palmer | *Lake Geneva, WI*

Giants Ridge, Quarry | *Duluth, MN*

Grand Cypress | *Orlando, FL*

Great River | *New Haven, CT*

Harvester | *Des Moines, IA*

Hershey, West | *Harrisburg, PA*

Innisbrook, Copperhead | *Tampa, FL*

☑ Kiawah Island, Ocean | *Charleston, SC*

La Paloma | *Tucson, AZ*

Omni Bedford Springs, The Old Course | *Bedford, PA*

☑ Pebble Beach | *Monterey Peninsula, CA*

☑ Pelican Hill, Ocean North | *Orange County, CA*

PGA West, Stadium | *Palm Springs, CA*

☑ Poppy Hills | *Monterey Peninsula, CA*

Pound Ridge | *NYC Metro, NY*

NEW Prairie Club, Dunes | *Valentine, NE*

Raven/Snowshoe Mtn. | *Elkins, WV*

Rawls/TX Tech | *Lubbock, TX*

Riverside Casino/Golf, Blue Top Ridge | *Iowa City, IA*

Shore Gate | *Atlantic City, NJ*

☑ Spanish Bay | *Monterey Peninsula, CA*

☑ Spyglass Hill | *Monterey Peninsula, CA*

☑ St. Ives Resort, Tullymore | *Grand Rapids, MI*

ThunderHawk | *Chicago, IL*

☑ Tiburón, Black | *Naples, FL*

Tobacco Road | *Pinehurst, NC*

☑ TPC Sawgrass, PLAYERS Stadium | *Jacksonville, FL*

☑ Troon North, Monument | *Scottsdale, AZ*

Ventana Canyon, Mountain | *Tucson, AZ*

World Golf Vill., King & Bear | *Jacksonville, FL*

☑ World Woods, Pine Barrens | *Tampa, FL*

PRACTICE FACILITIES

Arnold Palmer/Bay Hill | *Orlando, FL*

ASU Karsten | *Phoenix, AZ*

Bandon Dunes | *Coos Bay, OR*

Blackwolf Run | *Kohler, WI*

Centennial | *NYC Metro, NY*

ChampionsGate | *Orlando, FL*

Circling Raven | *Coeur d'Alene, ID*

Duke Univ. Golf | *Raleigh-Durham, NC*

Four Seasons/Las Colinas | *Dallas, TX*

Gaylord Springs | *Nashville, TN*

Golden Horseshoe | *Williamsburg, VA*

Golf Club/Newcastle | *Seattle, WA*

Grand Cypress | *Orlando, FL*

Grande Dunes | *Myrtle Beach, SC*

Grayhawk | *Scottsdale, AZ*

Great River | *New Haven, CT*

Greenbrier | *White Sulphur Springs, WV*

Harborside Int'l | *Chicago, IL*

Hawk Hollow | *Lansing, MI*

Homestead | *Roanoke, VA*

Hyatt Hill Country | *San Antonio, TX*

Jimmie Austin UOK | *Oklahoma City, OK*

Kapalua | *Maui, HI*

Karsten Creek | *Stillwater, OK*

Kiawah Island | *Charleston, SC*

Kingsmill | *Williamsburg, VA*

La Cantera | *San Antonio, TX*

Legends | *Myrtle Beach, SC*

Pebble Beach | *Monterey Peninsula, CA*
Phoenician | *Scottsdale, AZ*
Pine Needles Lodge | *Pinehurst, NC*
Piper Glen | *Springfield, IL*
Princeville/Prince | *Kauai, HI*
Raven/Three Peaks | *Vail, CO*
Reynolds Plantation | *Lake Oconee, GA*
Ritz-Carlton Orlando | *Orlando, FL*
Samoset | *Southern Maine, ME*
Sand Barrens | *Cape May, NJ*
Sea Island | *Low Country, GA*
Sea Pines | *Hilton Head, SC*
Seaview Resort | *Atlantic City, NJ*
Sedona Golf | *Sedona, AZ*
Shennecossett | *New London, CT*
Shepherd's Crook | *Chicago, IL*
Spanish Bay | *Monterey Peninsula, CA*
Starr Pass | *Tucson, AZ*
Sunriver | *Bend, OR*
Sun Valley | *Sun Valley, ID*
Tot Hill Farm | *Greensboro, NC*
TPC Myrtle Beach | *Myrtle Beach, SC*
TPC Sawgrass | *Jacksonville, FL*
TPC Tampa Bay | *Tampa, FL*
Triggs Memorial |
   Northern Rhode Island, RI
Troon North | *Scottsdale, AZ*
Trump Nat'l | *Los Angeles, CA*
Vineyard Golf/Renault |
   Atlantic City, NJ
Wailea Club | *Maui, HI*
NEW Waldorf Astoria | *Orlando, FL*
We-Ko-Pa | *Scottsdale, AZ*
Wente Vineyards |
   San Francisco Bay Area, CA
Whirlwind | *Phoenix, AZ*
Whistling Straits | *Kohler, WI*
Wigwam | *Phoenix, AZ*
Wild Dunes | *Charleston, SC*
World Golf Vill. | *Jacksonville, FL*
Wynn | *Las Vegas, NV*

PRO-EVENT HOSTS

☑ Arnold Palmer/Bay Hill |
   Orlando, FL
Atlantic City Club | *Atlantic City, NJ*
Augusta Pines | *Houston, TX*
☑ Bethpage, Black | *Long Island, NY*
☑ Blackwolf Run, Meadow Valleys |
   Kohler, WI
☑ Blackwolf Run, River | *Kohler, WI*
☑ Broadmoor, East |
   Colorado Springs, CO

Brown Deer Pk. | *Milwaukee, WI*
☑ Bulle Rock | *Baltimore, MD*
Classic Club | *Palm Springs, CA*
Club/Savannah Harbor |
   Savannah, GA
Cog Hill, No. 4 (Dubsdread) |
   Chicago, IL
☑ Doral, TPC Blue Monster |
   Miami, FL
Eagle Ridge | *Freehold, NJ*
☑ Four Seasons/Las Colinas, TPC |
   Dallas, TX
NEW French Lick, Pete Dye |
   French Lick, IN
Glen Club | *Chicago, IL*
☑ Grayhawk, Raptor | *Scottsdale, AZ*
NEW Harbor Shores | *Kalamazoo, MI*
☑ Harding Park |
   San Francisco Bay Area, CA
☑ Hualalai | *Big Island, HI*
Indian Wells, Celebrity |
   Palm Springs, CA
Innisbrook, Copperhead | *Tampa, FL*
Kaanapali, Royal Kaanapali |
   Maui, HI
☑ Kapalua, Bay | *Maui, HI*
☑ Kapalua, Plantation | *Maui, HI*
☑ Keswick Club | *Charlottesville, VA*
☑ Kiawah Island, Ocean |
   Charleston, SC
Kinderlou Forest | *Valdosta, GA*
Kingsmill, River | *Williamsburg, VA*
Ko Olina | *Oahu, HI*
☑ La Cantera, Resort | *San Antonio, TX*
☑ Pebble Beach |
   Monterey Peninsula, CA
PGA Nat'l, Champion | *Palm Beach, FL*
Pinehurst, No. 2 | *Pinehurst, NC*
☑ Poppy Hills | *Monterey Peninsula, CA*
Pumpkin Ridge, Ghost Creek |
   Portland, OR
☑ Redstone, Tournament |
   Houston, TX
Reynolds Plantation, Great Waters |
   Lake Oconee, GA
Reynolds Plantation, Oconee |
   Lake Oconee, GA
Ritz-Carlton, Dove Mtn. |
   Tucson, AZ
Rock Barn, Robert Trent Jones, Jr. |
   Charlotte, NC
☑ Ross Bridge | *Birmingham, AL*
Sandestin, Raven | *Panhandle, FL*

PRO SHOPS

Pinehurst | *Pinehurst, NC*
Poppy Hills | *Monterey Peninsula, CA*
Princeville/Prince | *Kauai, HI*
Ranch | *Springfield, MA*
Rancho Bernardo | *San Diego, CA*
Red Sky | *Vail, CO*
Redstone | *Houston, TX*
Reunion Resort | *Orlando, FL*
Revere | *Las Vegas, NV*
Reynolds Plantation | *Lake Oconee, GA*
Ridge/Castle Pines N. | *Denver, CO*
Ritz-Carlton Members Club |
    Sarasota, FL
Ritz-Carlton Orlando | *Orlando, FL*
Sandia | *Albuquerque, NM*
Scotland Run | *Camden, NJ*
Sea Island | *Low Country, GA*
Sea Pines | *Hilton Head, SC*
Sedona Golf | *Sedona, AZ*
Spanish Bay | *Monterey Peninsula, CA*
Spyglass Hill | *Monterey Peninsula, CA*
Starr Pass | *Tucson, AZ*
St. Ives Resort, St. Ives |
    Grand Rapids, MI
SunRidge Canyon | *Scottsdale, AZ*
Sunriver | *Bend, OR*
Talking Stick | *Scottsdale, AZ*
Tiburón | *Naples, FL*
Tiffany Greens | *Kansas City, MO*
Torrey Pines | *San Diego, CA*
TPC Deere Run | *Moline, IL*
TPC Las Vegas | *Las Vegas, NV*
TPC Louisiana | *New Orleans, LA*
TPC Myrtle Beach | *Myrtle Beach, SC*
TPC Sawgrass | *Jacksonville, FL*
TPC Scottsdale | *Scottsdale, AZ*
TPC Tampa Bay | *Tampa, FL*
Troon North | *Scottsdale, AZ*
Trump Nat'l | *Los Angeles, CA*
Univ. Ridge | *Madison, WI*
Wailea Club | *Maui, HI*
Walt Disney World | *Orlando, FL*
We-Ko-Pa | *Scottsdale, AZ*
Whirlwind | *Phoenix, AZ*
Whistling Straits | *Kohler, WI*
Wild Wing | *Myrtle Beach, SC*
Windmill Lakes | *Akron, OH*
World Golf Vill. | *Jacksonville, FL*

PUTTING COURSES

Angel Park | *Las Vegas, NV*
Arizona Biltmore | *Phoenix, AZ*
Desert Canyon | *Wenatchee, WA*

Golf Club/Newcastle | *Seattle, WA*
Hawk Hollow | *Lansing, MI*
Horseshoe Bay | *Austin, TX*
Marriott Desert Springs |
    Palm Springs, CA
Orange County Nat'l | *Orlando, FL*
Quail Lodge | *Monterey Peninsula, CA*
Running Y Rch. | *Klamath Falls, OR*
Sunriver | *Bend, OR*
Sun Valley | *Sun Valley, ID*
Turtle Creek | *Philadelphia, PA*
Waikoloa Bch. | *Big Island, HI*
World Golf Vill. | *Jacksonville, FL*

QUICK PACE OF PLAY

Atlantic City Club | *Atlantic City, NJ*
Balsams, Panorama |
    Northern New Hampshire, NH
Black Mesa | *Albuquerque, NM*
◪ Boulders, North | *Phoenix, AZ*
◪ Boulders, South | *Phoenix, AZ*
◪ Broadmoor, East |
    Colorado Springs, CO
◪ Broadmoor, West |
    Colorado Springs, CO
Bull Run Golf Club | *Leesburg, VA*
◪ Camp Creek | *Panhandle, FL*
◪ Cascata | *Las Vegas, NV*
◪ Circling Raven | *Coeur d'Alene, ID*
◪ CordeValle |
    San Francisco Bay Area, CA
Diablo Grande, Legends West |
    Sacramento, CA
Diablo Grande, Ranch |
    Sacramento, CA
NEW Dormie Club |
    Raleigh-Durham, NC
◪ Forest Dunes | *Gaylord, MI*
Golf Club/La Quinta | *Palm Springs, CA*
Grand Club | *San Diego, CA*
Great River | *New Haven, CT*
Harbor Club | *Lake Oconee, GA*
Hershey, East | *Harrisburg, PA*
Links/Union Vale | *Hudson Valley, NY*
Little Mountain | *Cleveland, OH*
Los Caballeros | *Phoenix, AZ*
Mauna Lani, South | *Big Island, HI*
McCullough's Emerald |
    Atlantic City, NJ
Orange County Nat'l, Panther Lake |
    Orlando, FL
PGA Golf Club, Ryder | *Port St. Lucie, FL*
Quail Lodge | *Monterey Peninsula, CA*

🅩 Red Sky, Fazio | *Vail, CO*

Ritz-Carlton Members Club |
  Sarasota, FL

Ritz-Carlton Orlando | *Orlando, FL*

Robinson Rch., Mountain |
  Los Angeles, CA

SilverHorn | *San Antonio, TX*

Sonnenalp | *Vail, CO*

Tiffany Greens | *Kansas City, MO*

TPC Las Vegas | *Las Vegas, NV*

🆕 Waldorf Astoria | *Orlando, FL*

🅩 World Woods, Pine Barrens |
  Tampa, FL

World Woods, Rolling Oaks |
  Tampa, FL

Worthington Manor | *Frederick, MD*

REPLICAS

Bear's Best Atlanta | *Atlanta, GA*

Bear's Best LV | *Las Vegas, NV*

Boyne Highlands,
  Donald Ross Memorial |
  Petoskey, MI

McCullough's Emerald | *Atlantic City, NJ*

Northern Bay, Castle Course |
  Madison, WI

🆕 Old American Club | *Dallas, TX*

Royal Links | *Las Vegas, NV*

Tour 18 Dallas | *Dallas, TX*

Tour 18 Houston | *Houston, TX*

🅩 Tribute | *Dallas, TX*

SCENIC

Amelia Island, Ocean Links |
  Jacksonville, FL

🅩 Arcadia Bluffs | *Traverse City, MI*

Arrowhead | *Denver, CO*

🅩 Aviara | *San Diego, CA*

Balsams, Panorama |
  Northern New Hampshire, NH

🅩 Bandon Dunes,
  Bandon Dunes Course |
  Coos Bay, OR

🅩 Bandon Dunes, Bandon Trails |
  Coos Bay, OR

🅩 Bandon Dunes, Pacific Dunes |
  Coos Bay, OR

🆕 Bandon Dunes, Old Macdonald |
  Coos Bay, OR

🅩 Bay Harbor | *Petoskey, MI*

Baywood Greens | *Rehoboth Beach, DE*

Beau Rivage, Fallen Oak | *Gulfport, MS*

🅩 Blackwolf Run, River | *Kohler, WI*

🅩 Boulders, South | *Phoenix, AZ*

🅩 Broadmoor, East |
  Colorado Springs, CO

🅩 Caledonia Golf/Fish |
  Pawleys Island, SC

Carambola | *St. Croix, USVI*

🅩 Cascata | *Las Vegas, NV*

🅩 Challenge/Manele | *Lanai, HI*

🅩 Chambers Bay | *Tacoma, WA*

🅩 Circling Raven | *Coeur d'Alene, ID*

Coeur d'Alene | *Coeur d'Alene, ID*

🆕 Conestoga | *Las Vegas, NV*

Cordillera, Summit | *Vail, CO*

Crandon | *Miami, FL*

Crumpin-Fox | *Berkshires, MA*

🅩 Dancing Rabbit, Azaleas |
  Jackson, MS

Daufuskie Island, Melrose |
  Hilton Head, SC

Desert Willow, Firecliff |
  Palm Springs, CA

Dorado Bch., East | *Dorado, PR*

Edgewood Tahoe | *Reno, NV*

🅩 Experience/Koele | *Lanai, HI*

Farm Neck | *Martha's Vineyard, MA*

Fossil Trace | *Denver, CO*

Giants Ridge, Quarry | *Duluth, MN*

🅩 Gold Canyon, Dinosaur Mountain |
  Phoenix, AZ

Golf Club/Equinox |
  Southern Vermont, VT

Grove Pk. Inn | *Asheville, NC*

🅩 Half Moon Bay, Ocean |
  San Francisco Bay Area, CA

Hammock Beach Resort, Ocean |
  Daytona Beach, FL

Hershey, West | *Harrisburg, PA*

🅩 Homestead, Cascades | *Roanoke, VA*

Indian Wells, Celebrity |
  Palm Springs, CA

Indian Wells, Players |
  Palm Springs, CA

🅩 Kapalua, Plantation | *Maui, HI*

Kauai Lagoons,
  Kiele Mauka/Kiele Moana |
  Kauai, HI

🅩 Kiawah Island, Ocean |
  Charleston, SC

Kingsmill, River | *Williamsburg, VA*

Kiva Dunes | *Mobile, AL*

Ko'olau | *Oahu, HI*

Lake of Isles, North | *New London, CT*

La Paloma | *Tucson, AZ*

La Quinta, Mountain | *Palm Springs, CA*
Leatherstocking | *Albany, NY*
Links/Bodega Harbour | *Santa Rosa, CA*
Links/Lighthouse Sound |
  Ocean City, MD
Linville | *Asheville, NC*
Mahogany Run | *St. Thomas, USVI*
Makena, North | *Maui, HI*
Mauna Kea | *Big Island, HI*
Mauna Lani, South | *Big Island, HI*
May River/Palmetto Bluff |
  Hilton Head, SC
Monarch Beach | *Orange County, CA*
Z Montauk Downs | *Long Island, NY*
Z Nemacolin Woodlands,
  Mystic Rock | *Pittsburgh, PA*
Z Paa-Ko Ridge | *Albuquerque, NM*
Z Pacific Grove |
  Monterey Peninsula, CA
Z Pebble Beach |
  Monterey Peninsula, CA
Z Pelican Hill, Ocean North |
  Orange County, CA
Z Pelican Hill, Ocean South |
  Orange County, CA
Phoenician | *Scottsdale, AZ*
Z Poipu Bay | *Kauai, HI*
Pound Ridge | *NYC Metro, NY*
Primland Resort, Highland |
  Roanoke, VA
Z Princeville/Prince | *Kauai, HI*
Pronghorn Club, Nicklaus | *Bend, OR*
Puakea | *Kauai, HI*
Quintero Golf, Founders | *Phoenix, AZ*
Raven/Snowshoe Mtn. | *Elkins, WV*
Redlands Mesa | *Grand Junction, CO*
Z Red Sky, Fazio | *Vail, CO*
Z Red Sky, Norman | *Vail, CO*
Reynolds Plantation, Great Waters |
  Lake Oconee, GA
Reynolds Plantation, Oconee |
  Lake Oconee, GA
Sagamore | *Adirondacks, NY*
NEW Salish Cliffs | *Olympia, WA*
Samoset | *Southern Maine, ME*
Sandpiper | *Santa Barbara, CA*
Z Sea Island, Seaside | *Low Country, GA*
Z Sea Pines, Harbour Town |
  Hilton Head, SC
Sedona Golf | *Sedona, AZ*
NEW Sequoyah Nat'l | *Asheville, NC*
Shadow Creek | *Las Vegas, NV*

Z Spanish Bay |
  Monterey Peninsula, CA
Z Spyglass Hill |
  Monterey Peninsula, CA
Stowe Mtn. | *Northern Vermont, VT*
Sugarloaf | *Central Maine, ME*
Sunday River | *Central Maine, ME*
Sunriver, Crosswater | *Bend, OR*
Superstition Mtn., Prospector |
  Phoenix, AZ
Z Taconic | *Berkshires, MA*
Tidewater | *Myrtle Beach, SC*
Z Torrey Pines, North | *San Diego, CA*
Z Torrey Pines, South | *San Diego, CA*
Z TPC Sawgrass, PLAYERS Stadium |
  Jacksonville, FL
Treetops, Robert Trent Jones
  Masterpiece | *Gaylord, MI*
Trump Nat'l | *Los Angeles, CA*
Ventana Canyon, Mountain |
  Tucson, AZ
NEW Victory Ranch | *Salt Lake City, UT*
Wailea Club, Emerald | *Maui, HI*
Z We-Ko-Pa, Cholla |
  Scottsdale, AZ
Z We-Ko-Pa, Saguaro |
  Scottsdale, AZ
Z Whistling Straits, Straits |
  Kohler, WI
Z Wolf Creek | *Las Vegas, NV*
Wynn | *Las Vegas, NV*

STORIED

Arizona Biltmore, Adobe |
  Phoenix, AZ
Z Arnold Palmer/Bay Hill |
  Orlando, FL
Atlantic City Club | *Atlantic City, NJ*
Z Bethpage, Black | *Long Island, NY*
Biltmore | *Miami, FL*
Boca Raton Resort, Resort Course |
  Palm Beach, FL
Breakers, Ocean | *Palm Beach, FL*
Brickyard Crossing | *Indianapolis, IN*
Z Broadmoor, East |
  Colorado Springs, CO
Z Broadmoor, West |
  Colorado Springs, CO
Z Chambers Bay | *Tacoma, WA*
Cog Hill, No. 4 (Dubsdread) |
  Chicago, IL
Z Doral, TPC Blue Monster |
  Miami, FL

Hammock Beach Resort, Ocean | *Daytona Beach, FL*
Karsten Creek | *Stillwater, OK*
Ko'olau | *Oahu, HI*
Lake Presidential | *DC Metro Area, MD*
Lakota Canyon Rch. | *Grand Junction, CO*
La Paloma | *Tucson, AZ*
Las Vegas Paiute, Wolf | *Las Vegas, NV*
Lost Canyons, Shadow | *Los Angeles, CA*
Lost Canyons, Sky | *Los Angeles, CA*
LPGA Int'l, Legends | *Daytona Beach, FL*
Z Nemacolin Woodlands, Mystic Rock | *Pittsburgh, PA*
Old Corkscrew | *Ft. Myers, FL*
Olde Stonewall | *Pittsburgh, PA*
Palmetto Hall, Robert Cupp | *Hilton Head, SC*
PGA Golf Club, Dye | *Port St. Lucie, FL*
PGA Nat'l, Champion | *Palm Beach, FL*
PGA West, Stadium | *Palm Springs, CA*
Pinehurst, No. 7 | *Pinehurst, NC*
Pronghorn Club, Nicklaus | *Bend, OR*
Quintero Golf, Founders | *Phoenix, AZ*
Reserve/Thunder Hill | *Cleveland, OH*
Reunion Resort, Jack Nicklaus | *Orlando, FL*
Revere, Concord | *Las Vegas, NV*
Rio Secco | *Las Vegas, NV*
Ritz-Carlton, Dove Mtn. | *Tucson, AZ*
Robinson Rch., Valley | *Los Angeles, CA*
Royal New Kent | *Williamsburg, VA*
Rush Creek | *Minneapolis, MN*
Saratoga Nat'l | *Albany, NY*
Shattuck | *Southern New Hampshire, NH*
Shepherd's Hollow | *Detroit, MI*
Silver Lakes | *Birmingham, AL*
Z Spyglass Hill | *Monterey Peninsula, CA*
Z St. Ives Resort, Tullymore | *Grand Rapids, MI*
Stonewall Orchard | *Chicago, IL*
Sunriver, Crosswater | *Bend, OR*
Sycamore Ridge | *Kansas City, KS*
Z Tiburón, Black | *Naples, FL*
Tobacco Road | *Pinehurst, NC*
NEW TPC San Antonio, AT&T Oaks | *San Antonio, TX*
Z TPC Sawgrass, PLAYERS Stadium | *Jacksonville, FL*
Z Troon North, Monument | *Scottsdale, AZ*
Troon North, Pinnacle | *Scottsdale, AZ*
Turnberry Isle Resort, Miller | *Miami, FL*
Turnberry Isle Resort, Soffer | *Miami, FL*
Z Turning Stone, Kaluhyat | *Finger Lakes, NY*
Z Whistling Straits, Straits | *Kohler, WI*
Wilds, Wilds, The | *Minneapolis, MN*
Z Willingers | *Minneapolis, MN*
Z Wolf Creek | *Las Vegas, NV*

UNIVERSITY

Arizona Nat'l | *Tucson, AZ*
ASU Karsten | *Phoenix, AZ*
Birdwood | *Charlottesville, VA*
Duke Univ. Golf | *Raleigh-Durham, NC*
Forest Akers MSU | *Lansing, MI*
Jimmie Austin UOK | *Oklahoma City, OK*
Karsten Creek | *Stillwater, OK*
Les Bolstad | *Minneapolis, MN*
Lonnie Poole/NC State Univ. | *Raleigh-Durham, NC*
Palouse Ridge/Washington State | *Spokane, WA*
Pete Dye/VA Tech | *Roanoke, VA*
Rawls/TX Tech | *Lubbock, TX*
Seven Oaks | *Finger Lakes, NY*
Taconic | *Berkshires, MA*
UNC Finley | *Chapel Hill, NC*
UNM Championship | *Albuquerque, NM*
Univ. Ridge | *Madison, WI*
Washington Nat'l | *Tacoma, WA*

WALKING ONLY

Z Bandon Dunes, Bandon Dunes Course | *Coos Bay, OR*
Z Bandon Dunes, Bandon Trails | *Coos Bay, OR*
Z Bandon Dunes, Pacific Dunes | *Coos Bay, OR*
NEW Bandon Dunes, Old Macdonald | *Coos Bay, OR*
Z Bethpage, Black | *Long Island, NY*
Z Chambers Bay | *Tacoma, WA*

Rancho Bernardo | *San Diego, CA*
Reunion Resort, Arnold Palmer |
Orlando, FL
Reynolds Plantation, Oconee |
Lake Oconee, GA
Ritz-Carlton Orlando | *Orlando, FL*
River Marsh | *Easton, MD*
Ross Creek Landing | *Nashville, TN*
Sagamore | *Adirondacks, NY*
Samoset | *Southern Maine, ME*
Z Sea Island, Seaside | *Low Country, GA*
Sea Trail, Dan Maples |
Myrtle Beach Area, NC
Seaview Resort, Bay |
Atlantic City, NJ
Sedona Golf | *Sedona, AZ*
SouthWood | *Panhandle, FL*

Z Spanish Bay |
Monterey Peninsula, CA
NEW Suncadia Resort, Rope Rider |
Seattle, WA
Sunriver, Meadows | *Bend, OR*
Tan-Tar-A, The Oaks |
Lake of the Ozarks, MO
Temecula Creek | *San Diego, CA*
Treetops, Rick Smith Signature |
Gaylord, MI
Turnberry Isle Resort, Miller |
Miami, FL
Wachesaw Plantation E. |
Myrtle Beach, SC
Wailea Club, Emerald | *Maui, HI*
Walking Stick | *Colorado Springs, CO*
Westin Mission Hills, Gary Player |
Palm Springs, CA

ALPHABETICAL
PAGE INDEX

Private courses are listed beginning on page TK.

ALPHA INDEX

ALPHA INDEX

ALPHA INDEX

ALPHA INDEX

ALPHA INDEX

ALPHA INDEX

ALPHA INDEX

ALPHA INDEX